NUMERICAL METHODS
OF REACTOR ANALYSIS

NUCLEAR SCIENCE AND TECHNOLOGY

A Series of Monographs and Textbooks

CONSULTING EDITOR

V. L. PARSEGIAN

School of Engineering
Rensselaer Polytechnic Institute
Troy, New York

1. John F. Flagg (Ed.)
   CHEMICAL PROCESSING OF REACTOR FUELS, 1961

2. M. L. Yeater (Ed.)
   NEUTRON PHYSICS, 1962

3. Melville Clark, Jr., and Kent F. Hansen
   NUMERICAL METHODS OF REACTOR ANALYSIS, 1964

Other volumes in preparation

NUMERICAL METHODS
OF REACTOR ANALYSIS

MELVILLE CLARK, JR.

Melville Clark Associates
Cochituate, Massachusetts

KENT F. HANSEN

Department of Nuclear Engineering
Massachusetts Institute of Technology
Cambridge, Massachusetts

1964

ACADEMIC PRESS • NEW YORK AND LONDON

ACADEMIC PRESS INC.
111 Fifth Avenue, New York, New York 10003

United Kingdom Edition published by
ACADEMIC PRESS INC. (LONDON) LTD.
Berkeley Square House, London W.1

LIBRARY OF CONGRESS CATALOG CARD NUMBER: 64-20318

PRINTED IN THE UNITED STATES OF AMERICA

PREFACE

This volume is an introduction to topics of numerical analysis frequently used in the nuclear reactor field. Numerical methods are very much more powerful than analytical ones in finding solutions to the specific, exceedingly complex problems which arise as a result of the complicated dependence of nuclear cross sections upon energy and the very intricate geometries so often found in nuclear reactors. These difficulties confronting the nuclear engineer are aggravated by the demand for safety of a very high order and the need for accuracy. Therefore numerical methods employed in the design and analysis of nuclear reactors require the use of computers for their solution. In addition, most nuclear reactor problems involve many dimensions. For this reason and because of their great flexibility, digital computers have been used almost exclusively in the nuclear reactor field, except for problems involving control. Consequently, training in the use of computers and the numerical methods pertinent to the reactor field is required of every serious nuclear engineer. With these thoughts in mind, we have written a text to introduce students to the methods by which machine calculations are performed on practical problems in the reactor field, with emphasis on those methods specific to the field.

A number of special numerical methods for the treatment of neutron and gamma-ray transport problems have evolved. These were taught for three years as part of courses that also included analytical methods. It was realized that the material in numerical analysis could be taught to those with far less preparation in mathematics by the addition of certain introductory material and that, further, the need and interest in training in numerical methods was much broader than that in analytical methods. Accordingly, the methods special to reactor analysis are presented in the last three chapters of this book. The preparatory subjects appear in the first three chapters; these are very useful to the nuclear engineer in their own right.

It has been our experience in some five years of teaching the material as presently organized that it can be assimilated in one term in some forty or so lectures by students at the graduate level who have had a basic course in differential equations and an introductory course in reactor physics. Thus, first and second year graduate students can use this book. We have found that most students digest new subjects properly only by working problems. Accordingly,

v

a number may be found at the end of each chapter; frequently these serve to extend the text.

We have provided only the rudiments of matrix algebra, difference equations, and the methods of solving these equations. We have found that this material will suffice for the needs of most nuclear engineers. Indeed, problems in heat transfer and stress analysis can be treated in almost all cases by the simple methods and the information contained in the first three chapters. For those who wish to explore further, a number of excellent, more comprehensive references and monographs exist relating to this material. These are listed at the end of each chapter together with a few comments to guide the interested reader. Since this book is specifically directed to reactor analysis and since the references to many of the methods special to the field are scattered and in some cases difficult for the student to read, we have put more emphasis on the discussions of these methods. These include the multigroup, the spherical harmonics, the S_N, the moments or Spencer-Fano, and the Monte Carlo methods as they apply to numerical analysis. Some students will have had most of the material of the first chapter, which relates to matrices. They may skip this chapter except for a few special topics in Sections 1.12, 1.13, and 1.14.

The use of digital computers is taught in part by the text. The remaining information on the use of digital computers and when to use them can be taught only in a laboratory course. We regard it essential that the prospective student have some exposure to the running of a simple problem on a computer. In this way only can he gain an appreciation for the capabilities and limitations of digital computers and of the problems in using them. Accordingly, we expose the students taking the course based on the text to an additional 13 hours of lectures on computers and programming. The students practice programming and run a sample problem on a large digital computer. By this method they develop a feeling for the problems of the professional programmer and an ability to discuss mutual problems meaningfully with him. They develop an appreciation for some of the error locating and correcting techniques, methods of checking a program, and the time required in various operations and phases thereof. In addition, they acquire a feeling for the interaction of the various numerical methods with the computer and motivation for the use of these methods.

Material on the aspects of particular computers is not included in this book for several reasons. First, the details of machines and of the utility and systems programs differ greatly from one installation to another. It would not be practical to try to present all this information in one book. Second, there is little of a general nature in such material that can by itself be regarded as of an educational nature. Third, such material is quite elementary, is provided by the makers of the machines, and may have already been acquired by the student in some other connection. The construction of a theoretical, paper computer for the purposes of this book would only confuse the student who must be exposed to the details of his own installation in any event to gain the appreciation sought.

We have tried to keep the general tone of this book readable and easy to understand. We have attempted to motivate the student in regard to the different methods and have tried to select the simplest examples and explanations known to us. There are certainly more abstract, general, and rigorous ways of presenting much of the information discussed, and these would be of interest to the specialist. They may be found in the literature to which references are given. We have avoided the discussion of the thousands of codes used in the field because of the lack of general principles of educational value that the student can master, remember, and use later on in his professional life. The details of any particular code are best learned at the time of use. In the later chapters on specific methods for transport problems, we merely indicate the computational steps beyond the formulation of the method, since the principles of iteration and the like have already been discussed in Chapter 3.

Many persons have contributed to the development of this text. The financial support and encouragement of the Department of Nuclear Engineering of the Massachusetts Institute of Technology is most gratefully acknowledged. Professor Paul Daitch of the Rensselaer Polytechnic Institute reviewed the manuscript and made many helpful suggestions and comments. We most gratefully acknowledge our past students and especially our teaching assistants for their help as critics and as subjects on whom this material has been tested. Earlier versions of this manuscript were typed by Mrs. Ruth Kugelman and Mrs. Sally Oeler. Later versions, including the final draft, were prepared by Miss Angelina Carbone. To Miss Carbone the authors offer their greatest thanks for her painstaking efforts of typing, editing, and correction. Finally we offer our thanks to our colleagues for their advice and encouragement.

Cambridge, Massachusetts
June, 1964

MELVILLE CLARK, JR.
KENT F. HANSEN

CONTENTS

1

LINEAR EQUATIONS
AND MATRIX ALGEBRA

Many physical problems are described by sets of simultaneous algebraic equations. Further, more difficult physical problems lead to approximations involving sets of these equations. For instance, the numerical approximation for the multigroup diffusion method results in rather simple algebraic equations.

The frequency with which sets of simultaneous algebraic equations arise motivates the introduction of a matrix notation. This notation provides a compact and convenient statement of physical and mathematical relationships, and lends itself readily to theoretical investigations and deductions. Furthermore, matrix notation leads to useful interpretation of simultaneous equations and greater understanding, which in turn induces improved methods of solution.

In this chapter we shall introduce this simplified formulation of linear algebra. We first define matrices and operations with matrices and then discuss properties of special matrices. Following the introduction of a geometric interpretation of matrix equations, we shall derive many matrix relations applied later in the text. Special attention is directed to relations of use in nuclear engineering.

1.1 Linear Equations and Matrix Notation

A simple set of linear equations in three variables might be given as

$$3x + 2y + \ z = 1 \,,$$
$$x - 2y + 4z = 2 \,, \qquad (1.1.1)$$
$$-x - \ y + 2z = -1 \,.$$

1

The solution of Eqs. (1.1.1) may be found by substitution, determinants, or other means. For the moment, we postpone a discussion of solving the equations. In problems with more than three variables, the notation of Eqs. (1.1.1) is inconvenient, and we adopt a more general subscript notation. Equations (1.1.1) are written in the form

$$a_{11}x_1 + a_{12}x_2 + a_{13}x_3 = y_1 ,$$
$$a_{21}x_1 + a_{22}x_2 + a_{23}x_3 = y_2 , \qquad (1.1.2)$$
$$a_{31}x_1 + a_{32}x_2 + a_{33}x_3 = y_3 .$$

The quantities x_1, x_2, x_3 are the variables or unknowns. The elements on the right-hand side, y_1, y_2, y_3, are assumed known, as are the coefficients a_{ij}. The notation of Eqs. (1.1.2) is conveniently extended to problems of many unknowns. Each equation of (1.1.2) is represented by one line or row of the set of equations. The first equation can be written in the compact form

$$\sum_{j=1}^{3} a_{1j}x_j = y_1 . \qquad (1.1.3)$$

Note the summation is over the index identifying the column of the set of equations. In a similar manner, the entire set of equations may be written

$$\sum_{j=1}^{3} a_{ij}x_j = y_i \qquad (i = 1, 2, 3) . \qquad (1.1.4)$$

For n equations in n unknowns, the set of equations may be written

$$\sum_{j=1}^{n} a_{ij}x_j = y_i \qquad (i = 1, 2, ..., n) . \qquad (1.1.5)$$

The notation may be simplified even further by defining several arrays of elements. We define the one-column arrays

$$\mathbf{x} = \begin{bmatrix} x_1 \\ x_2 \\ \vdots \\ x_n \end{bmatrix} , \qquad \mathbf{y} = \begin{bmatrix} y_1 \\ y_2 \\ \vdots \\ y_n \end{bmatrix} , \qquad (1.1.6)$$

as column matrices. Similarly, we define the one row array

$$[a_{i1}, a_{i2}, ..., a_{in}]$$

as a row matrix. The ith equation of the set (1.1.5) may then be written

$$[a_{i1}, a_{i2}, \ldots, a_{in}] \begin{bmatrix} x_1 \\ x_2 \\ \vdots \\ x_n \end{bmatrix} = \sum_{j=1}^{n} a_{ij}x_j = y_i \, . \tag{1.1.7}$$

The definition (1.1.7) implies that the element in the jth column of the row matrix multiplies the element in the jth row of the column matrix. We define the entire array of coefficients as the square matrix

$$\begin{bmatrix} a_{11} & a_{12} & \cdots & a_{1n} \\ a_{21} & a_{22} & \cdots & a_{2n} \\ \vdots & \vdots & & \vdots \\ a_{n1} & a_{n2} & \cdots & a_{nn} \end{bmatrix} \, .$$

The entire set of equations may then be written

$$\begin{bmatrix} a_{11} & a_{12} & \cdots & a_{1n} \\ a_{21} & a_{22} & \cdots & a_{2n} \\ \vdots & \vdots & & \vdots \\ a_{n1} & a_{n2} & \cdots & a_{nn} \end{bmatrix} \begin{bmatrix} x_1 \\ x_2 \\ \vdots \\ x_n \end{bmatrix} = \begin{bmatrix} y_1 \\ y_2 \\ \vdots \\ y_n \end{bmatrix} \, . \tag{1.1.8}$$

The ith equation of the set is found by multiplying the elements of the ith row of the square matrix into the column matrix of x_j's.

The notation may be further simplified by denoting the one column matrices as single quantities, such as

$$\mathbf{x} = \begin{bmatrix} x_1 \\ x_2 \\ \vdots \\ x_n \end{bmatrix} \equiv [x_j] \, , \qquad \mathbf{y} = \begin{bmatrix} y_1 \\ y_2 \\ \vdots \\ y_n \end{bmatrix} \equiv [y_j] \, . \tag{1.1.9}$$

Similarly, we denote the square array as

$$\begin{bmatrix} a_{11} & a_{12} & \cdots & a_{1n} \\ a_{21} & a_{22} & \cdots & a_{2n} \\ \vdots & \vdots & & \vdots \\ a_{n1} & a_{n2} & \cdots & a_{nn} \end{bmatrix} = \mathbf{A} \equiv [a_{ij}] \, . \tag{1.1.10}$$

The set of equations (1.1.8) become

$$\sum_{j=1}^{n} a_{ij}x_j = [y_i] ,\qquad(1.1.11)$$

or, equivalently

$$\mathbf{Ax} = \mathbf{y} .\qquad(1.1.12)$$

The form of equation (1.1.12) suggests that the quantity $\mathbf{A}$ multiplies the quantity $\mathbf{x}$. We shall call this multiplication of a column matrix by a square matrix. Obviously the multiplication is defined only when the number of columns of $\mathbf{A}$ equals the number of rows of $\mathbf{x}$. It is easily seen that the definition of multiplication may be extended to the case where the matrix $\mathbf{A}$ is rectangular rather than square, provided only that the number of columns of $\mathbf{A}$ equals the number of rows of $\mathbf{x}$. A matrix of m rows and n columns is referred to as an m by n matrix.

1.2   Matrix Operations

Matrices may be manipulated in a manner similar to numbers. The rules for manipulation are derivable from previous results. We define two matrices as equal if corresponding elements are equal. The rule for the addition of matrices can be derived by noting that

$$\sum_{j} a_{ij}x_j + \sum_{j} b_{ij}x_j = \sum_{j} (a_{ij} + b_{ij})x_j ,\qquad(1.2.1)$$

and hence

$$[a_{ij}] + [b_{ij}] = [a_{ij} + b_{ij}] .\qquad(1.2.2)$$

Thus addition of matrices is performed by adding corresponding elements. The definition applies only when $\mathbf{A}$ and $\mathbf{B}$ have the same number of rows and columns. Addition of matrices is commutative and associative.

$$\mathbf{A} + \mathbf{B} = \mathbf{B} + \mathbf{A},\qquad(1.2.3)$$

$$\mathbf{A} + (\mathbf{B} + \mathbf{C}) = (\mathbf{A} + \mathbf{B}) + \mathbf{C}.\qquad(1.2.4)$$

The rule for multiplication of two matrices may be derived by considering two sets of simultaneous equations. Consider the sets of equations

$$\mathbf{Ax} = \mathbf{y} ,\qquad(1.2.5)$$

and

$$\mathbf{By} = \mathbf{z} ,\qquad(1.2.6)$$

where the products are assumed to exist. The ith equation of (1.2.5) is

$$y_i = \sum_j a_{ij} x_j , \qquad (1.2.7)$$

whereas the kth equation of (1.2.6) is

$$z_k = \sum_i b_{ki} y_i . \qquad (1.2.8)$$

Thus,

$$z_k = \sum_i b_{ki} \sum_j a_{ij} x_j = \sum_j \left(\sum_i b_{ki} a_{ij} \right) x_j . \qquad (1.2.9)$$

In matrix notation we have

$$\mathbf{z} = \mathbf{By}, \qquad (1.2.10)$$

$$\mathbf{y} = \mathbf{Ax}, \qquad (1.2.11)$$

$$\mathbf{z} = \mathbf{BAx}. \qquad (1.2.12)$$

Consequently,

$$[(\mathbf{BA})_{kj}] = \left[\sum_i b_{ki} a_{ij} \right]. \qquad (1.2.13)$$

The summation in Eq. (1.2.13) is to extend over the columns of $\mathbf{B}$ and the rows of $\mathbf{A}$. Therefore, matrix multiplication is defined only when the number of columns of the first matrix equals the number of rows of the second matrix. The product matrix will have as many rows as $\mathbf{B}$ and as many columns as $\mathbf{A}$.

It is easily seen that matrix multiplication is associative and distributive

$$\mathbf{A(BC)} = \mathbf{(AB)C}, \qquad (1.2.14)$$

$$\mathbf{A(B + C)} = \mathbf{AB} + \mathbf{AC}. \qquad (1.2.15)$$

It is easily shown that matrix multiplication is not commutative; that is,

$$\mathbf{AB} \neq \mathbf{BA} \qquad (1.2.16)$$

in general. Note that if $\mathbf{A}$ and $\mathbf{B}$ are not square, the products cannot be equal. Even for square matrices, the matrices do not commute in general. For the special case when $\mathbf{AB} = \mathbf{BA}$, we say the matrices are commutative.

Occasionally it is convenient to partition a matrix into smaller matrices or submatrices. Thus, if

$$\mathbf{A} = \begin{bmatrix} a_{11} & a_{12} & a_{13} \\ a_{21} & a_{22} & a_{23} \\ a_{31} & a_{32} & a_{33} \end{bmatrix}, \tag{1.2.17}$$

then a partition of $\mathbf{A}$ might be

$$\mathbf{A} = \left[\begin{array}{cc|c} a_{11} & a_{12} & a_{13} \\ a_{21} & a_{22} & a_{23} \\ \hline a_{31} & a_{32} & a_{33} \end{array} \right] = \begin{bmatrix} \mathbf{A}_{11} & \mathbf{A}_{12} \\ \mathbf{A}_{21} & \mathbf{A}_{22} \end{bmatrix} \tag{1.2.18}$$

where the submatrices $\mathbf{A}_{11}$, $\mathbf{A}_{12}$, $\mathbf{A}_{21}$, $\mathbf{A}_{22}$ are

$$\mathbf{A}_{11} = \begin{bmatrix} a_{11} & a_{12} \\ a_{21} & a_{22} \end{bmatrix},$$

$$\mathbf{A}_{12} = \begin{bmatrix} a_{13} \\ a_{23} \end{bmatrix},$$

$$\mathbf{A}_{21} = [a_{31}, a_{32}],$$

$$\mathbf{A}_{22} = [a_{33}].$$

The matrix $\mathbf{A}$ is called a supermatrix. Although we shall not use more than the two levels of matrices illustrated here, it is apparent that any number of levels could be used. The usual rules of matrix algebra apply at all levels.

1.3 Determinants

A determinant may be associated with any square matrix. Whereas a matrix is an ordered collection of numbers, a determinant represents a quantity having just one value. The determinant of a square matrix is the sum of the $n!$ terms, all formed differently, each of which is constructed of n factors, one and only one factor being chosen from each row and column. No two factors may come from either the same row or the same column. The sign of each term is determined by drawing straigth lines connecting each factor with every other factor in the given term. If the number of these lines from all factors sloping upward to the right is odd, the sign of the term is negative, and if the number of these lines is even, the sign of the term is positive. The determinant is represented as follows:

$$|\mathbf{A}| = |[a_{ij}]| = \begin{vmatrix} a_{11} & a_{12} & \cdots & a_{1n} \\ a_{21} & a_{22} & \cdots & a_{2n} \\ \vdots & \vdots & & \vdots \\ a_{n1} & a_{n2} & \cdots & a_{nn} \end{vmatrix} \qquad (1.3.1)$$

As an example, note that

$$\begin{vmatrix} a_{11} & a_{12} & a_{13} \\ a_{21} & a_{22} & a_{23} \\ a_{31} & a_{32} & a_{33} \end{vmatrix} = \begin{aligned} & (a_{11}a_{22}a_{33}) - (a_{11}a_{23}a_{32}) \\ & + (a_{12}a_{23}a_{31}) - (a_{12}a_{21}a_{33}) \\ & + (a_{13}a_{21}a_{32}) - (a_{13}a_{22}a_{31}). \end{aligned}$$

The determinant formed from an n by n array of numbers is said to be of order n.

There are a number of useful theorems that facilitate the evaluation of a determinant:

1. If all elements of a row or column are zero, the determinant is zero.

2. If all elements of a row or column are multiplied by the same factor, the determinant is multiplied by that factor.

3. The interchange of two rows or two columns changes the sign of the determinant but otherwise leaves its value unaltered.

4. Interchanging the rows and columns of a determinant does not change the value of a determinant.

5. If each element of a row of a determinant is the sum of two terms, then the value of the determinant equals the sum of the values of two determinants, one formed by omission of the first term of each binomial and the other formed by omission of the second term in each binomial.

6. The value of a determinant is not altered by adding to the elements of any row a multiple times the corresponding elements of any other row. Likewise, for columns.

The proof of these theorems is left to the problems.

The Laplace development of a determinant will enable us to find the rule for solving an array of linear equations. The minor M_{ij} of an element a_{ij} is the determinant of the matrix formed by deleting the ith row and the jth column of the original determinant. The cofactor C_{ij} of a_{ij} is then defined by

$$C_{ij} = (-)^{i+j} M_{ij}. \qquad (1.3.2)$$

The Laplace development of a determinant is then given by

$$|\mathbf{A}| = \sum_{j=1}^{n} a_{ij}C_{ij}, \qquad (1.3.3a)$$

or

$$|\mathbf{A}| = \sum_{i=1}^{n} a_{ij}C_{ij}. \qquad (1.3.3b)$$

In words, the determinant is equal to the sum of the products of the elements in any row or column by their corresponding cofactors. The validity of this theorem follows immediately from the definition of the determinant since $a_{ij} C_{ij}$ is just the sum over all terms containing the element a_{ij}.

The sum of the products of the elements in any row by the cofactors of corresponding elements in another row is zero:

$$\sum_{j=1}^{n} a_{ij}C_{kj} = 0 \qquad (i \neq k). \qquad (1.3.4a)$$

Similarly for columns

$$\sum_{i=1}^{n} a_{ij}C_{ik} = 0 \qquad (k \neq j). \qquad (1.3.4b)$$

The proof follows from the observation that the sum (1.3.4) is merely the determinant itself with one of its original rows replaced by another of its original rows. Such a determinant is zero since by Theorem 6 above relating to the evaluation of determinants, we could reduce one of the identical rows to zero by subtracting the other from it. Then by Theorem 1 above, the determinant would be zero. A similar development for columns applies.

The unknown x_k in a set of n linear equations in n unknowns is easily found by multiplying the equations (1.1.5) by C_{ik}, by summing over i from 1 to n, and by use of the relation (1.3.4b) above.

$$|\mathbf{A}|x_k = \sum_{i=1}^{n} C_{ik}y_i. \qquad (1.3.5)$$

This result is known as Cramer's rule. A solution exists only if

$$|\mathbf{A}| \neq 0. \qquad (1.3.6)$$

Matrices satisfying this last condition are called nonsingular; matrices whose determinants are zero are called singular. We note that the solution exists and is unique if the number of unknowns equals the number of equations and if the determinant of the matrix formed from the coefficients is nonsingular.

The product of two determinants $|\mathbf{A}|$ and $|\mathbf{B}|$ is equal to the determinant $|\mathbf{AB}|$ of the product. This fact is proved in a straightforward manner. By Theorem 5 for the evaluation of determinants, the determinant of the product can be expanded in n^n determinants of the form

$$\begin{bmatrix} a_{1k_1}b_{k_11} & a_{1k_2}b_{k_22} & \cdots & a_{1k_n}b_{k_nn} \\ a_{2k_1}b_{k_11} & a_{2k_2}b_{k_22} & \cdots & a_{2k_n}b_{k_nn} \\ \vdots & \vdots & & \vdots \\ a_{nk_1}b_{k_11} & a_{nk_2}b_{k_22} & \cdots & a_{nk_n}b_{k_nn} \end{bmatrix} \tag{1.3.7}$$

where the $k_1, k_2, \ldots, k_n$ stands for any n values of the subscript j. Only the determinants in which the values of all j are different contribute to the sum in the expansion of the determinant of the product by Theorems 1, 2, and 6 above. (If any two columns are multiples of each other, the determinant is zero.) Therefore, the sum of n^n terms in the expansion of the determinant of the product consists of only $n!$ terms each of the form

$$(b_{k_11}b_{k_22} \cdots b_{k_nn}) \begin{bmatrix} a_{1k_1} & a_{1k_2} & \cdots & a_{1k_n} \\ a_{2k_1} & a_{2k_2} & \cdots & a_{2k_n} \\ \vdots & \vdots & & \vdots \\ a_{nk_1} & a_{nk_2} & \cdots & a_{nk_n} \end{bmatrix} \tag{1.3.8}$$

in which all k_j are different. An interchange of the columns of the determinant shown reduces it to the exact form of $|\mathbf{A}|$. We have thus $n!$ terms, all different, in the expansion of $|\mathbf{AB}|$ made above, each comprising $|\mathbf{A}|$ times one term of $|\mathbf{B}|$ together with the correct sign. Thus

$$|\mathbf{AB}| = |\mathbf{A}| \cdot |\mathbf{B}|, \tag{1.3.9}$$

as was to be proved.

1.4 Solution of Simultaneous Equations

We now consider a systematic procedure for solving sets of equations and determine conditions under which solutions do exist. The procedure to be outlined is called the Gauss reduction. Consider a set of m equations in n unknowns

$$\sum_{j=1}^{n} a_{ij}x_j = y_i \qquad (i = 1, 2, \ldots, m), \tag{1.4.1}$$

or

$$a_{11}x_1 + a_{12}x_2 + \ldots + a_{1n}x_n = y_1 \,,$$
$$a_{21}x_1 + a_{22}x_2 + \ldots + a_{2n}x_n = y_2 \,,$$
$$\vdots \tag{1.4.2}$$
$$a_{m1}x_1 + a_{m2}x_2 + \ldots + a_{mn}x_n = y_m \,.$$

We assume the coefficient $a_{11} \neq 0$, otherwise renumber the equations so that we have an $a_{11} \neq 0$. We may eliminate the variable x_1 from the other $m - 1$ equations. To this end divide the first equation by a_{11} to obtain

$$x_1 + \frac{a_{12}}{a_{11}} x_2 + \ldots + \frac{a_{1n}}{a_{11}} x_n = \frac{y_1}{a_{11}} \,, \tag{1.4.3a}$$

or

$$x_1 + a'_{12}x_2 + \ldots + a'_{1n}x_n = y'_1 \,. \tag{1.4.3b}$$

We multiply Eq. (1.4.3b) successively by $a_{21}, a_{31}, \ldots, a_{m1}$ and subtract the resultant equations from the second, third, etc. equations of (1.4.2). The result is a set of equations of the form

$$x_1 + a'_{12}x_2 + \quad \ldots \quad + a'_{1n}x_n = y'_1 \,,$$
$$a'_{22}x_2 + a'_{23}x_3 + \ldots + a'_{2n}x_n = y'_2 \,,$$
$$\vdots \tag{1.4.4}$$
$$a'_{m2}x_2 + a'_{m3}x_3 + \ldots + a'_{mn}x_n = y'_m \,.$$

We now divide the second equation of (1.4.4) by a'_{22} and eliminate x_2 from the remaining $m-2$ equations as before. We continue in this manner to eliminate the unknowns x_i. If $m = n$, the set of equations takes the form

$$x_1 + a'_{12}x_2 + \quad \ldots \quad + a'_{1n}x_n \quad = y'_1 \,,$$
$$x_2 + a''_{23}x_3 + \ldots + a''_{2n}x_n \quad = y''_2 \,,$$
$$\vdots \tag{1.4.5}$$
$$x_{n-1} + a''_{n-1,n}x_n = y''_{n-1} \,,$$
$$a''_{nn}x_n \quad = y''_n \,.$$

If $a''_{nn} \neq 0$, then by back substitution we may evaluate the x_i. If $a''_{nn} = 0$ and $y''_n = 0$, then x_n is indeterminate, and we do not obtain a unique solution. It is easily shown $a''_{nn} = 0$ only if $|\mathbf{A}| = 0$. If $a''_{nn} = 0$ and $y''_n \neq 0$, then no solution to the equations exists.

The results may be generalized for $m \neq n$. If $m > n$ the reduction process will lead to a set of equations of the form

$$x_1 + a'_{12}x_2 + \quad \ldots \quad + a'_{1n}x_n = y'_1 ,$$

$$x_2 + a''_{23}x_3 + \ldots + a''_{2n}x_n = y''_2 ,$$

$$\vdots$$

$$x_n = y''_n ,$$

$$0 = y''_{n+1} ,$$

$$\vdots$$

$$0 = y''_m . \tag{1.4.6}$$

If the $y''_{n+1}, y''_{n+2}, \ldots, y''_m$ are all zero, then we again have a unique solution; the last m-n equations are merely linear combinations of the first n equations. On the other hand, if any y''_p $(n < p \leqslant m)$ are not zero, then the equations are inconsistent and no solution exists. In like manner, for $m < n$ the reduction leads to

$$x_1 + a'_{12}x_2 + \quad \ldots \quad + a'_{1n}x_n = y'_1 ,$$

$$x_2 + a''_{23}x_3 + \quad \ldots \quad + a''_{2n}x_n = y''_2 ,$$

$$\vdots \tag{1.4.7}$$

$$x_m + a''_{m+1}x_{m+1} \ldots + a''_{mn}x_n = y''_m .$$

In this case the variables $x_{m+1}, x_{m+2}, \ldots, x_n$ may be assigned arbitrarily and the remaining x_i determined in terms of the arbitrary variables. Obviously there is not a unique solution in this case.

The above results may be expressed in a compact theorem. To this end we introduce the concept of the rank of a matrix and define the coefficient and augmented matrices associated with a set of linear equations. Consider the set of equations (1.4.1). The coefficient matrix associated with this set of equations is

$$\begin{bmatrix} a_{11} & a_{12} & \ldots & a_{1n} \\ a_{21} & a_{22} & \ldots & a_{2n} \\ \vdots & \vdots & & \vdots \\ a_{m1} & a_{m2} & \ldots & a_{mn} \end{bmatrix} . \tag{1.4.8}$$

The augmented matrix is defined as the m by $n + 1$ matrix formed by appending the column matrix $[y_i]$ to the coefficient matrix. Thus, the augmented matrix associated with Eq. (1.4.1) is

$$\begin{bmatrix} a_{11} & a_{12} & \cdots & a_{1n} & y_1 \\ a_{21} & a_{22} & \cdots & a_{2n} & y_2 \\ \vdots & \vdots & & \vdots & \vdots \\ a_{m1} & a_{m2} & \cdots & a_{mn} & y_m \end{bmatrix}. \tag{1.4.9}$$

The rank of a matrix is defined to be the order of the largest nonvanishing determinant contained in the matrix. Obviously, the rank of the coefficient matrix can never exceed the rank of the augmented matrix.

The rank of a matrix is unaltered by multiplying all the elements of a row by a constant or by adding a row times a constant to another row of the matrix. The result follows from Theorems 2 and 6 relating to the evaluation of determinants.

The simple theorem relating to the solution of a system of linear equations may now be stated as follows: a solution to a system of linear equations exists if and only if the ranks of the coefficient and augmented matrices are equal. The proof of the theorem follows from the Gauss reduction. The ranks of the coefficient matrices of the array of Eqs. (1.4.2) and (1.4.6) are equal by Theorems 2 and 6. Likewise, the ranks of the augmented matrices are equal. Accordingly, consider Eq. (1.4.6); the coefficient matrix is of rank n. If any $y_p \neq 0$, $n < p \leqslant m$, then the augmented matrix is of rank greater than n. But under these circumstances, no solution exists and hence the theorem follows.

From the previous work, it is also clear that if the common rank, r, of the augmented and coefficient matrices is less than the number, n, of unknowns, then $n-r$ of the unknowns may have their values assigned arbitrarily. In this case, the remaining variables are uniquely determined as linear functions of the $n-r$ unknowns whose values have been arbitrarily chosen.

A special case occurs if all the inhomogeneous terms y_i are zero. In this case the coefficient and augmented matrices are always of the same rank, and hence a solution always exists. However, this result is evident, since in this case we have the trivial solution $x_i = 0$. A nontrivial solution will exist only if the rank of the coefficient matrix is less than the number of unknowns, otherwise only the trivial solution exists.

1.5   Special Matrices and Their Properties

There are many special matrices that are of frequent interest. We shall assume throughout the chapter that all of the matrices have real elements. There are generalizations of the results to matrices with complex elements, but the generalizations are not of interest for this work. The zero matrix **0** is a square matrix, each of whose elements is zero. The product of the zero matrix and any other matrix is a zero matrix. Note that if the product of two matrices is zero, we cannot conclude one of the matrices is zero, however. Consider the simple example

$$\begin{bmatrix} 1 & -1 \\ -1 & 1 \end{bmatrix}\begin{bmatrix} 1 & 1 \\ 1 & 1 \end{bmatrix} = \begin{bmatrix} 0 & 0 \\ 0 & 0 \end{bmatrix}. \tag{1.5.1}$$

The unit matrix **I** is a square matrix, each of whose nondiagonal elements is zero, and each of whose diagonal elements is unity:

$$\mathbf{I} = [\delta_{ij}], \tag{1.5.2}$$

where δ_{ij} is the Kronecker delta function

$$\delta_{ij} = \begin{cases} 0, & i \neq j, \\ 1, & i = j. \end{cases} \tag{1.5.3}$$

The product of the unit matrix with any other matrix **A** of the same order is merely **A**. Further, the unit matrix commutes with any other matrix.

A diagonal matrix is a matrix each of whose nondiagonal elements is zero.

$$\mathbf{D} = [d_i \delta_{ij}]. \tag{1.5.4}$$

Two diagonal matrices commute, but a diagonal matrix does not commute with other matrices in general. A scalar matrix is a diagonal matrix all of whose diagonal elements are equal. A scalar matrix commutes with any other matrix.

The transpose of a matrix **A**, denoted $\mathbf{A}^T$, is formed from **A** by interchanging rows and columns of **A**. Therefore

$$\mathbf{A}^T = [a_{ij}^T] = [a_{ji}]. \tag{1.5.5}$$

The transpose of a product of matrices satisfies the relation

$$(\mathbf{AB})^T = \mathbf{B}^T\mathbf{A}^T, \tag{1.5.6}$$

a result readily proved. Note that

$$(\mathbf{AB})^T = \left[\sum_k a_{ik}b_{kj}\right]^T = \left[\sum_k a_{jk}b_{ki}\right] = \mathbf{B}^T\mathbf{A}^T. \tag{1.5.7}$$

If $\mathbf{A}^T = \mathbf{A}$, then the matrix is said to be symmetric. If $\mathbf{A}^T = -\mathbf{A}$, then the matrix is said to be antisymmetric.

The adjoint[1] of a matrix is defined only for square matrices. We define the adjoint of **A**, written adj **A**, as the matrix formed by replacing each element of **A** by the cofactor of its transpose:

$$\text{adj } \mathbf{A} = [\text{adj } a_{ij}] = [C_{ji}] , \tag{1.5.8}$$

where C_{ij} is the cofactor of the ijth element of **A**. It is easily proved that

$$\text{adj}(\mathbf{AB}) = (\text{adj } \mathbf{B})(\text{adj } \mathbf{A}). \tag{1.5.9}$$

The inverse of a matrix **A**, written $\mathbf{A}^{-1}$, is a matrix such that

$$\mathbf{AA}^{-1} = \mathbf{I}. \tag{1.5.10}$$

Note that

$$\mathbf{A}^{-1}\mathbf{A} = \mathbf{I}. \tag{1.5.11}$$

Since

$$|\mathbf{A}||\mathbf{A}^{-1}| = |\mathbf{AA}^{-1}| = |\mathbf{I}| = 1, \tag{1.5.12}$$

the inverse of a matrix exists only for nonsingular square matrices. Let a_{jk}^{-1} be the jkth element of the inverse matrix $\mathbf{A}^{-1}$. Then

$$\left[\sum_j a_{ij} a_{jk}^{-1} \right] = \mathbf{I}. \tag{1.5.13}$$

To find the elements of $\mathbf{A}^{-1}$, we recall the Laplace expansion theorem (1.3.3), which can be written

$$\sum_j a_{ij} \frac{C_{kj}}{|\mathbf{A}|} = \mathbf{I}. \tag{1.5.14}$$

Hence, if

$$a_{jk}^{-1} = \frac{C_{kj}}{|\mathbf{A}|} = \frac{\text{adj } a_{jk}}{|\mathbf{A}|} , \tag{1.5.15}$$

$$\mathbf{A}^{-1} = \frac{\text{adj}[a_{jk}]}{|\mathbf{A}|} , \tag{1.5.16}$$

Eq. (1.5.13) will be satisfied. The uniqueness of $\mathbf{A}^{-1}$ is proved by supposing that there were a second inverse, say **B**. In this case,

$$\mathbf{A}(\mathbf{A}^{-1} - \mathbf{B}) = \mathbf{I} - \mathbf{I} = 0.$$

---

[1] In this book we have no need to define the Hermitian adjoint, often called merely the adjoint, of a matrix. The Hermitian adjoint and the adjoint are not related.

Now, multiply on the left by either inverse to learn that

$$\mathbf{B} = \mathbf{A}^{-1}$$

and the two inverses are identical. It is easily shown that

$$(\mathbf{AB})^{-1} = \mathbf{B}^{-1}\mathbf{A}^{-1}. \tag{1.5.17}$$

The inverse matrix is essentially that which has been calculated in Cramer's rule (1.3.5). If

$$\mathbf{Ax} = \mathbf{y}, \tag{1.5.18}$$

then

$$\mathbf{x} = \mathbf{A}^{-1}\mathbf{y}. \tag{1.5.19}$$

If, for a real matrix $\mathbf{A}$

$$\mathbf{A}^T = \mathbf{A}^{-1}, \tag{1.5.20}$$

then the matrix $\mathbf{A}$ is called orthogonal. Note that

$$|\mathbf{A}^T| = |\mathbf{A}|, \tag{1.5.21}$$

and

$$|\mathbf{A}^{-1}| = |\mathbf{A}|^{-1}, \tag{1.5.22}$$

and consequently the determinant of an orthogonal matrix is ± 1.

1.6 Vector Interpretation

Matrix equations may be given a very convenient and useful interpretation in terms of vectors and operations among these vectors. Vectors may be interpreted as special cases of matrices of such importance that a special abbreviated notation is used. As we shall see, operations on these vectors may then be given a geometric interpretation. We recall that a vector[2] in three dimensions may be written

$$\mathbf{t} = t_1\mathbf{i} + t_2\mathbf{j} + t_3\mathbf{k}, \tag{1.6.1}$$

where $\mathbf{i}$, $\mathbf{j}$, and $\mathbf{k}$ are unit vectors along three mutually perpendicular coordinate axes, and t_1, t_2 and t_3 are the components of $\mathbf{t}$ along the various axes. If we define the row matrix $\mathbf{E}$ as

$$\mathbf{E} = (\mathbf{i}, \mathbf{j}, \mathbf{k}), \tag{1.6.2}$$

[2] We define a vector here as an ordered collection of n entities, called components, in an n-dimensional space, without implying any particular transformation properties. [A vector is also often defined to be a quantity whose components transform as the coordinates. We do not use this definition in this book].

then Eq. (1.6.1) can be written

$$\mathbf{t} = \mathbf{E} \begin{bmatrix} t_1 \\ t_2 \\ t_3 \end{bmatrix}. \tag{1.6.3}$$

It is usually convenient to assume the underlying coordinate system $\mathbf{E}$ is fixed throughout the discussion and to denote the vector $\mathbf{t}$ as a column matrix

$$\mathbf{t} = \begin{bmatrix} t_1 \\ t_2 \\ t_3 \end{bmatrix}. \tag{1.6.4}$$

We shall adopt this shorthand notation and shall further assume the coordinate system $\mathbf{E}$ is constructed of mutually orthogonal axes.[3]
The scalar product of two vectors, $\mathbf{t}$ and $\mathbf{u}$, in vector analysis is

$$(\mathbf{t}, \mathbf{u}) = t_1 u_1 + t_2 u_2 + t_3 u_3. \tag{1.6.5}$$

In matrix notation the scalar product is

$$(\mathbf{t}, \mathbf{u}) = \mathbf{u}^T \mathbf{t} = \mathbf{t}^T \mathbf{u}, \tag{1.6.6}$$

where the transpose of a column matrix is a row matrix. Frequently we shall refer to a column matrix as a column vector.

Matrix equations may also be given a useful vector interpretation. The equation

$$\mathbf{y} = \mathbf{Ax} \tag{1.6.7}$$

is interpreted as a relation between two vectors $\mathbf{y}$ and $\mathbf{x}$. In particular, the matrix $\mathbf{A}$ acts as a transformation which transforms the vector $\mathbf{x}$ into another vector $\mathbf{y}$. An alternative viewpoint is to consider $\mathbf{x}$ and $\mathbf{y}$ as the same vector expressed in two different coordinate systems. The matrix $\mathbf{A}$ then specifies the relation between the components of the vector in the two different coordinate systems. A geometric portrayal of the two different interpretations is given in Figs. 1.6.1 and 1.6.2.

Either interpretation of the equation is found to be useful. For our later purposes, the first viewpoint will be more frequently employed. The concepts of the vector interpretation of matrices may be extended

---

[3] If the coordinate system is not an orthogonal system, the results to be obtained subsequently must be generalized. See Section 1.12.

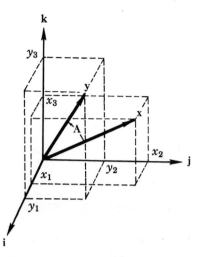

FIG. 1.6.1.   Geometric view of the matrix equation $\mathbf{Ax} = \mathbf{y}$ considered as a transformation of a vector.

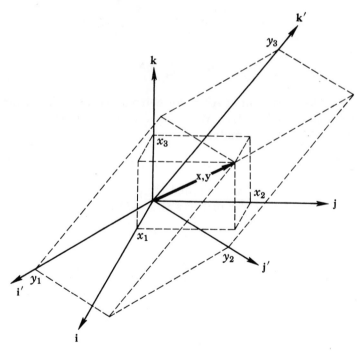

FIG. 1.6.2.   Geometric view of the matrix equation $\mathbf{Ax} = \mathbf{y}$ considered as a transformation of the coordinate system.

to n-dimensional spaces in a straightforward manner. The column matrix

$$
\mathbf{x} = \begin{bmatrix} x_1 \\ x_2 \\ \vdots \\ x_n \end{bmatrix} \tag{1.6.8}
$$

is interpreted as a vector in n space where x_i are components of $\mathbf{x}$ along the ith coordinate axis.

1.7   Matrix Functions and Similarity Transformations

We can now define under certain conditions a function $f(\mathbf{A})$ of a nonsingular matrix $\mathbf{A}$, since both positive and negative integral powers of this matrix are available. If $f(x)$ may be expanded in a Laurent series so that

$$
f(x) = \sum_{i=-\infty}^{\infty} b_i x^i, \tag{1.7.1}
$$

then

$$
f(\mathbf{A}) = \sum_{i=-\infty}^{\infty} b_i \mathbf{A}^i, \tag{1.7.2}
$$

where b_i is the coefficient of $\mathbf{A}^i$, b_i not being a matrix. If $\mathbf{A}$ is symmetric, then $f(\mathbf{A})$ will be symmetric. We observe that two functions f and g of the same matrix $\mathbf{A}$ commute:

$$
f(\mathbf{A})g(\mathbf{A}) = g(\mathbf{A})f(\mathbf{A}). \tag{1.7.3}
$$

Two matrices $\mathbf{A}$ and $\mathbf{B}$ are called equivalent if and only if they are related by two nonsingular matrices $\mathbf{R}$ and $\mathbf{Q}$ as follows:

$$
\mathbf{RAQ} = \mathbf{B}. \tag{1.7.4}
$$

The factor $\mathbf{R}$ merely causes each new row of $\mathbf{B}$ to be a linear combination of the original rows of $\mathbf{A}$, and the factor $\mathbf{Q}$ merely linearly combines the old columns of $\mathbf{A}$ into new columns of $\mathbf{B}$, as follows from the definition of a product. The matrix operators $\mathbf{R}$ may also exchange rows; the matrix $\mathbf{Q}$ may exchange columns. Since these operations leave the rank of a matrix unchanged, $\mathbf{A}$ and $\mathbf{B}$ have the same rank.

The matrices $\mathbf{R}$ and $\mathbf{Q}$ that linearly combine the rows or columns of. $\mathbf{A}$ in a particular way are easily constructed by linearly combining the rows or columns, respectively, of the unit matrix in the same way. The first and second rows, for example, are interchanged by the nonsingular operator

$$\begin{bmatrix} 0 & 1 & 0 & 0 & \dots \\ 1 & 0 & 0 & 0 & \dots \\ 0 & 0 & 1 & 0 & \dots \\ 0 & 0 & 0 & 1 & \dots \\ \vdots & \vdots & \vdots & \vdots & \dots \end{bmatrix}.$$

Again, a multiple C of the second row of $\mathbf{A}$ is added to the first row of $\mathbf{A}$ by the operator

$$\begin{bmatrix} 1 & C & 0 & 0 & \dots \\ 0 & 1 & 0 & 0 & \dots \\ 0 & 0 & 1 & 0 & \dots \\ \vdots & \vdots & \vdots & \vdots & \dots \end{bmatrix}.$$

The matrix is nonsingular. Since exchanging the rows or columns of a matrix and since linearly combining the rows or columns of a matrix do not alter the value of any minor, the matrices $\mathbf{R}$ and $\mathbf{Q}$ are clearly nonsingular since the unit matrix is.

If $\mathbf{R} = \mathbf{Q}^{-1}$, the transformation is called a similarity transformation:

$$\mathbf{B} = \mathbf{Q}^{-1}\mathbf{A}\mathbf{Q}. \tag{1.7.5}$$

If, on the other hand, $\mathbf{R} = \mathbf{Q}^T$, the transformation is called a congruence transformation:

$$\mathbf{B} = \mathbf{Q}^T\mathbf{A}\mathbf{Q}. \tag{1.7.6}$$

If $\mathbf{R} = \mathbf{Q}^{-1} = \mathbf{Q}^T$, so that $\mathbf{Q}$ is orthogonal, the transformation is called an orthogonal transformation.

All matrix relations are equally valid if all matrices occurring in these relations are subjected to the same similarity transformation. If $\mathbf{AB} = \mathbf{C}$

$$\mathbf{Q}^{-1}\mathbf{C}\mathbf{Q} = (\mathbf{Q}^{-1}\mathbf{A}\mathbf{Q})(\mathbf{Q}^{-1}\mathbf{B}\mathbf{Q}), \tag{1.7.7}$$

and if $\mathbf{A} + \mathbf{B} = \mathbf{C}$,

$$\mathbf{Q}^{-1}\mathbf{C}\mathbf{Q} = \mathbf{Q}^{-1}\mathbf{A}\mathbf{Q} + \mathbf{Q}^{-1}\mathbf{B}\mathbf{Q}. \tag{1.7.8}$$

Again, suppose we had two vectors $\mathbf{x}_0$ and $\mathbf{y}_0$ related by

$$\mathbf{y}_0 = \mathbf{A}\mathbf{x}_0. \tag{1.7.9}$$

If we introduce new vectors, $\mathbf{x}$ and $\mathbf{y}$, defined by

$$\mathbf{x}_0 = \mathbf{Q}\mathbf{x}, \; \mathbf{y}_0 = \mathbf{Q}\mathbf{y}, \tag{1.7.10}$$

where $\mathbf{Q}$ is nonsingular, then

$$\mathbf{y} = \mathbf{Q}^{-1}\mathbf{A}\mathbf{Q}\mathbf{x} = \mathbf{B}\mathbf{x}, \tag{1.7.11}$$

whence we see that the two new vectors, $\mathbf{x}$ and $\mathbf{y}$, are related to each other exactly like the old ones, $\mathbf{x}_0$ and $\mathbf{y}_0$, providing the new and old operators are related by

$$\mathbf{B} = \mathbf{Q}^{-1}\mathbf{A}\mathbf{Q}. \tag{1.7.12}$$

If $\mathbf{Q}$ be a real orthogonal matrix, then $\mathbf{Q}$ satisfies the definition (1.5.20), and the scalar product of two vectors $\mathbf{x}_0$ and $\mathbf{y}_0$ is given by

$$\mathbf{y}_0^T\mathbf{x}_0 = \mathbf{y}^T\mathbf{Q}^T\mathbf{Q}\mathbf{x} = \mathbf{y}^T\mathbf{x} \tag{1.7.13}$$

from which we see that the length of a vector is unaltered (i.e., if we let $\mathbf{y}_0 = \mathbf{x}_0$, then the present result shows that the length of $\mathbf{x}$ equals the length of $\mathbf{x}_0$), and the angle between two original vectors is also unchanged by an orthogonal transformation. Thus, unit vectors which are originally orthogonal will remain orthogonal unit vectors, hence the name orthogonal transformation.

A particularly useful orthogonal transformation is the permutation transformation. A permutation matrix is any matrix for which there is one and only one nonzero element in each row and column of the matrix, and the nonzero element is unity. Thus, the unit matrix is a permutation matrix. If we denote a permutation matrix as $\mathbf{P}$, then a permutation transformation is a similarity (orthogonal) transformation of the form

$$\mathbf{P}\mathbf{A}\mathbf{P}^T = \mathbf{P}\mathbf{A}\mathbf{P}^{-1}.$$

A permutation matrix merely interchanges certain rows and columns of a matrix.

The trace of a matrix is the sum of the diagonal elements:

$$\mathrm{Tr}\,\mathbf{A} = \sum_i a_{ii}. \tag{1.7.14}$$

The trace of the product of two matrices is independent of the order of the factors

$$\mathrm{Tr}(\mathbf{A}\mathbf{B}) = \sum_{i=1}^{n}\sum_{j=1}^{n} a_{ij}b_{ji} = \mathrm{Tr}(\mathbf{B}\mathbf{A}). \tag{1.7.15}$$

The trace of a matrix is unaltered by a similarity transformation:

$$\text{Tr}(\mathbf{Q}^{-1}\mathbf{A}\mathbf{Q}) = \sum_{i,j,k=1}^{n} (\mathbf{Q}^{-1})_{ij}a_{jk}(\mathbf{Q})_{ki} = \sum_{j=1}^{n} a_{jj} = \text{Tr } \mathbf{A}. \qquad (1.7.16)$$

1.8   Linear Independence of Vectors and Orthogonalization of Vectors

An array $\mathbf{x}_i$, $1 \leqslant i \leqslant n$, of vectors is said to be linearly dependent when

$$\sum_{i=1}^{n} b_i \mathbf{x}_i = 0, \qquad (1.8.1)$$

where not all b_i are zero. When no set of b_i exists in which at least one b_i differs from zero for which equation (1.8.1) is true, the array of vectors is said to be linearly independent. We can easily generate a linearly independent array of vectors from a linearly dependent array by discarding all zero vectors (which are not very interesting anyway), by examining each of the remaining vectors one by one, and by keeping only those which are linearly independent of all the vectors already selected. The remaining vectors are then linearly related to those selected, since otherwise they would have been selected.

A test for linear independence is readily constructed by observing that the equation (1.8.1) may be regarded as an array of n linear homogeneous equations in which the components x_{ji} of the vectors $\mathbf{x}_i$ are the coefficients of the unknowns b_i:

$$\sum_{i=1}^{n} b_i x_{ji} = 0 \qquad (j = 1, ..., n). \qquad (1.8.2)$$

Indeed, one can associate the jith element x_{ji} of a matrix with the jth component of the ith vector, in which case each vector forms one column of a matrix, or with the ith component of the jth vector, in which case each vector forms one row of a matrix. The vectors will then be linearly dependent if and only if nontrivial solutions b_i of the array of linear homogeneous equations (1.8.2) exist. By Section 1.4, we have seen that the necessary and sufficient condition for the existence of nontrivial solutions of such equations is that the determinant $|x_{ji}|$ of x_{ji} vanish. Consequently, an array of vectors is linearly dependent if and only if the determinant formed from their components vanishes. The square of this determinant is called the Gram determinant of the vector array.

If and only if the Gram determinant vanishes, the array of vectors is linearly dependent. The present test requires only that the components of each vector along the others be known.

$$\begin{vmatrix} \mathbf{x}_1^2 & (\mathbf{x}_1 , \mathbf{x}_2) & (\mathbf{x}_1 , \mathbf{x}_3) & \cdots & (\mathbf{x}_1 , \mathbf{x}_n) \\ (\mathbf{x}_2 , \mathbf{x}_1) & \mathbf{x}_2^2 & (\mathbf{x}_2 , \mathbf{x}_3) & \cdots & (\mathbf{x}_2 , \mathbf{x}_n) \\ (\mathbf{x}_3 , \mathbf{x}_1) & (\mathbf{x}_3 , \mathbf{x}_2) & \mathbf{x}_3^2 & \cdots & (\mathbf{x}_3 , \mathbf{x}_n) \\ \vdots & \vdots & \vdots & & \vdots \\ (\mathbf{x}_n , \mathbf{x}_1) & (\mathbf{x}_n , \mathbf{x}_2) & (\mathbf{x}_n , \mathbf{x}_3) & \cdots & \mathbf{x}_n^2 \end{vmatrix} = 0.$$

The condition

$$\begin{vmatrix} x_{11} & x_{12} & x_{13} & \cdots & x_{1n} \\ x_{21} & x_{22} & x_{23} & \cdots & x_{2n} \\ x_{31} & x_{32} & x_{33} & \cdots & x_{3n} \\ \vdots & \vdots & \vdots & & \vdots \\ x_{n1} & x_{n2} & x_{n3} & \cdots & x_{nn} \end{vmatrix} = 0$$

requires that the components along some arbitrary coordinate system be known.

There cannot be more than n linearly independent vectors each of which is of dimension n. If then a space has n dimensions, any vector $\mathbf{u}$ can be expanded in terms of any set of n linearly independent vectors.

$$\mathbf{u} = \sum_{i=1}^{n} b_i \mathbf{x}_i \tag{1.8.3}$$

where the b_i can be found by Cramer's rule if the equation (1.8.3) be written out in component form. A set of n linearly independent vectors in a space of n dimensions and in terms of which other vectors are expanded is called a basis. An incomplete set of r vectors is said to be of rank r for evident reasons and to be of defect $n - r$. A basis is usually chosen to be orthogonal and normal.

Should the basis not be orthogonal, it may be made orthogonal quite easily by the Schmidt procedure, which essentially consists in subtracting the projection of any particular vector on any previously orthogonalized vectors from that particular vector in forming a new vector. Consider the set of vectors $\mathbf{x}_i$ which are not orthogonal. The first vector of the orthogonal set, say the $\mathbf{t}_i$ set, is defined by

$$\mathbf{t}_1 = \mathbf{x}_1 , \tag{1.8.4}$$

and the second by

$$t_2 = x_2 - \frac{(x_2, t_1)t_1}{(t_1, t_1)}. \tag{1.8.5}$$

The vector t_2 is orthogonal to t_1 because any component of x_2 that lies along t_1 has been subtracted from x_2. The third orthogonal vector t_3 is then given by

$$t_3 = x_3 - \frac{(x_3, t_1)}{(t_1, t_1)} t_1 - \frac{(x_3, t_2)}{(t_2, t_2)} t_2. \tag{1.8.6}$$

The remaining vectors of the set t_i are computed in like manner. If there are as many vectors t_i as dimensions of the space, then these vectors form an orthogonal, linearly independent set which span the space, i.e., are such that any arbitrary vector can be expressed in terms of them.

The method of orthogonalization cannot fail. Suppose it were to fail. Then some vector t_r would be zero. Thus, x_r would be some linear combination of $x_1, x_2, \ldots, x_{r-1}$ contrary to the hypothesis that the original basis was linearly independent. Therefore, all t_r must differ from zero. The new vectors may now be normalized by dividing them by their own length.

1.9   Eigenvalues and Eigenvectors

The transformation applied to a vector by a matrix may conceivably merely lead to a multiple of the original vector.

$$Ax = \lambda x. \tag{1.9.1}$$

Such a vector x is called an eigenvector and the multiple λ is called an eigenvalue. These two concepts are of transcendent importance in theoretical work. There may be a number of eigenvectors and eigenvalues associated with a particular operator.

We see that the eigenvector-eigenvalue equation (1.9.1) actually represents a series of linear, homogeneous equations. In order that there be a nontrivial solution in Section 1.3, we have seen it is necessary and sufficient that

$$|A - \lambda I| = 0. \tag{1.9.2}$$

This equation determines the possible eigenvalues and is called the characteristic equation. In a space of n dimensions, it is a polynomial equation of order n, which will therefore have n roots. The roots will occur in complex conjugate pairs; some of the roots may have the same value. The number that do is called the multiplicity of the root. If the n roots are distinct, then there are n associated eigenvectors. For repeated roots, there may be less than n eigenvectors.

A similarity transformation does not change the eigenvalues, since the characteristic equation is unaltered.

$$| \mathbf{Q}^{-1}\mathbf{A}\mathbf{Q} - \gamma \mathbf{I} | = | \mathbf{Q}^{-1}(\mathbf{A} - \gamma \mathbf{I})\mathbf{Q} |$$
$$= | \mathbf{Q}^{-1} | | \mathbf{A} - \gamma \mathbf{I} | | \mathbf{Q} | = | \mathbf{A} - \gamma \mathbf{I} | = 0. \tag{1.9.3}$$

Therefore, $\gamma_i = \lambda_i$ if roots of the two polynomials be properly ordered.

Since Eq. (1.9.1) is homogeneous, only the directions of the eigenvectors are determined. The eigenvectors may be multiplied by any arbitrary constant and still be eigenvectors. It is usually convenient to scale the eigenvectors so that they have unit length.

The eigenvalues of a real symmetric matrix are real. To prove the result, let $\mathbf{x}_i$ be such that

$$\mathbf{A}\mathbf{x}_i = \lambda_i \mathbf{x}_i . \tag{1.9.4}$$

Since the characteristic equation is a polynomial with real coefficients, there is also a root $\bar{\lambda}_i$, which is the complex conjugate of λ_i. The corresponding eigenvector $\bar{\mathbf{x}}_i$ will have components which are complex conjugate to those of $\mathbf{x}_i$. Therefore, we also have

$$\mathbf{A}\bar{\mathbf{x}}_i = \bar{\lambda}_i \bar{\mathbf{x}}_i . \tag{1.9.5}$$

We multiply Eq. (1.9.4) by $\bar{\mathbf{x}}_i^T$, Eq. (1.9.5) by $\mathbf{x}_i^T$, subtract and obtain

$$\bar{\mathbf{x}}_i^T \mathbf{A}\mathbf{x}_i - \mathbf{x}_i^T \mathbf{A}\bar{\mathbf{x}}_i = (\lambda_i - \bar{\lambda}_i)\bar{\mathbf{x}}_i^T \mathbf{x}_i . \tag{1.9.6}$$

But

$$\mathbf{x}_i^T \mathbf{A}\bar{\mathbf{x}}_i = \bar{\mathbf{x}}_i^T \mathbf{A}^T \mathbf{x}_i = \bar{\mathbf{x}}_i^T \mathbf{A}\mathbf{x}_i , \tag{1.9.7}$$

the last result since $\mathbf{A}$ is symmetric. Equation (1.9.6) becomes

$$(\lambda_i - \bar{\lambda}_i)\bar{\mathbf{x}}_i^T \mathbf{x}_i = 0. \tag{1.9.8}$$

The quantity

$$\bar{\mathbf{x}}_i^T \mathbf{x}_i = (\bar{\mathbf{x}}_i , \mathbf{x}_i) \tag{1.9.9}$$

is the generalization of the length of a vector for complex components. Since the elements are complex conjugate, the length is a positive real number. Equation (1.9.8) can be true only if

$$\lambda_i = \bar{\lambda}_i , \tag{1.9.10}$$

which proves the theorem.

The eigenvectors associated with eigenvalues of different value of a real symmetric matrix are orthogonal. To prove this, let λ_1, $\mathbf{x}_1$ and λ_2, $\mathbf{x}_2$ be such that

$$\mathbf{A}\mathbf{x}_1 = \lambda_1 \mathbf{x}_1, \tag{1.9.11}$$

$$\mathbf{A}\mathbf{x}_2 = \lambda_2 \mathbf{x}_2. \tag{1.9.12}$$

with $\lambda_1 \neq \lambda_2$. We again multiply by $\mathbf{x}_2^T$ and $\mathbf{x}_1^T$ respectively and subtract. We have

$$(\mathbf{x}_2^T \mathbf{A} \mathbf{x}_1 - \mathbf{x}_1^T \mathbf{A} \mathbf{x}_2) = (\lambda_1 - \lambda_2) \mathbf{x}_2^T \mathbf{x}_1 = 0. \tag{1.9.13}$$

Since $\lambda_1 \neq \lambda_2$, we must have

$$\mathbf{x}_1^T \mathbf{x}_2 = \mathbf{x}_2^T \mathbf{x}_1 = 0. \tag{1.9.14}$$

If the eigenvalues of a real symmetric matrix are all distinct, then for each eigenvalue there is an eigenvector which is orthogonal to all of the other eigenvectors. If there are n vectors in all, then these n vectors are complete: that is, the vectors span the n-dimensional space and may therefore be used as a basis. The orthogonal basis of eigenvectors is a particularly useful coordinate system for a given problem. As an example, suppose we desire to study the effect of a transformation $\mathbf{A}$ on an arbitrary vector $\mathbf{x}$. If the eigenvectors of $\mathbf{A}$ are the complete orthonormal set $\mathbf{e}_i$, then we may expand $\mathbf{x}$ in the form

$$\mathbf{x} = \sum_i a_i \mathbf{e}_i \tag{1.9.15}$$

where the a_i are expansion coefficients given by

$$a_i = \mathbf{x}^T \mathbf{e}_i. \tag{1.9.16}$$

We then have

$$\mathbf{A}\mathbf{x} = \mathbf{A}\left(\sum_i a_i \mathbf{e}_i\right) = \sum_i a_i \mathbf{A} \mathbf{e}_i = \sum_i a_i \lambda_i \mathbf{e}_i. \tag{1.9.17}$$

Hence the operation of multiplying by $\mathbf{A}$ merely multiplies the various components of $\mathbf{x}$ by the corresponding eigenvalues. In our later work we shall make frequent use of this result.

In the event that not all the eigenvalues of a real symmetric matrix are distinct, it is still possible to construct a set of complete orthogonal eigenvectors. For any repeated root of multiplicity k, there are k associated eigenvectors, which may be made orthogonal.[4]

---

[4] The proof of these remarks is simple but detailed. See Reference 1, pp. 59–61.

A real symmetric matrix $\mathbf{A}$ may be transformed into a particularly simple form by a similarity transformation. Let the components of the eigenvectors be written as column matrices, thus

$$\mathbf{e}_i = \begin{bmatrix} e_{i1} \\ e_{i2} \\ \vdots \\ e_{in} \end{bmatrix}. \tag{1.9.18}$$

Let the matrix $\mathbf{M}$ be defined as

$$\mathbf{M} = [\mathbf{e}_1, \mathbf{e}_2, \dots, \mathbf{e}_n] = \begin{bmatrix} e_{11} & e_{21} & \cdots & e_{n1} \\ e_{12} & e_{22} & \cdots & e_{n2} \\ \vdots & \vdots & & \vdots \\ e_{1n} & e_{2n} & \cdots & e_{nn} \end{bmatrix}. \tag{1.9.19}$$

The eigenvectors are orthogonal, and we assume they are normalized. The matrix $\mathbf{M}$ is called the normalized modal matrix. The product $\mathbf{AM}$ is then

$$\mathbf{AM} = \begin{bmatrix} \lambda_1 e_{11} & \lambda_2 e_{21} & \cdots & \lambda_n e_{n1} \\ \lambda_1 e_{12} & \lambda_2 e_{22} & \cdots & \lambda_n e_{n2} \\ \vdots & \vdots & & \vdots \\ \lambda_1 e_{1n} & \lambda_2 e_{2n} & \cdots & \lambda_n e_{nn} \end{bmatrix} = \mathbf{MD}, \tag{1.9.20}$$

where

$$\mathbf{D} = \begin{bmatrix} \lambda_1 & 0 & \cdots & 0 \\ 0 & \lambda_2 & \cdots & 0 \\ \vdots & \vdots & & \vdots \\ 0 & 0 & \cdots & \lambda_n \end{bmatrix}. \tag{1.9.21}$$

Thus, we have

$$\mathbf{M}^{-1}\mathbf{AM} = \mathbf{D}. \tag{1.9.22}$$

The inversion of $\mathbf{M}$ is always possible since $\mathbf{M}$ cannot vanish by the orthogonality and consequent independence of the $\mathbf{e}_i$.

The result shows that a real symmetric matrix is similar to a diagonal matrix. The process of so transforming a matrix is called diagonalization.

It is interesting to note that the similarity transformation used above is also an orthogonal transformation. To see this, we form the product

$$\mathbf{M}^T\mathbf{M} = \begin{bmatrix} e_{11} & e_{12} & \cdots & e_{1n} \\ e_{21} & e_{22} & \cdots & e_{2n} \\ \vdots & \vdots & & \vdots \\ e_{n1} & e_{n2} & \cdots & e_{nn} \end{bmatrix} \begin{bmatrix} e_{11} & e_{21} & \cdots & e_{n1} \\ e_{12} & e_{22} & \cdots & e_{n2} \\ \vdots & \vdots & & \vdots \\ e_{1n} & e_{2n} & \cdots & e_{nn} \end{bmatrix}. \qquad (1.9.23)$$

Since the vectors $\mathbf{e}_i$ are orthogonal and normalized, we have

$$\mathbf{M}^T\mathbf{M} = \mathbf{I}, \qquad (1.9.24)$$

and hence

$$\mathbf{M}^T = \mathbf{M}^{-1}. \qquad (1.9.25)$$

The normalized modal matrix is an orthogonal matrix.

1.10 Nonsymmetric Matrices

The results of the previous section do not apply in full generality to a nonsymmetric matrix. We again consider only matrices with real elements.

We show first that, if the characteristic roots of a square n by n nonsymmetric matrix $\mathbf{A}$ are distinct, then there are n linearly independent eigenvectors associated with the matrix. Let the eigenvalues be denoted λ_i and the eigenvectors as $\mathbf{e}_i$. We have

$$\mathbf{A}\mathbf{e}_i = \lambda_i\mathbf{e}_i \qquad (1.10.1)$$

for $i = 1, 2, ..., n$. If the eigenvectors are linearly dependent, then at least one of the eigenvectors, say $\mathbf{e}_n$, is a linear combination of the remaining $n - 1$. Then

$$\mathbf{e}_n = \sum_{i=1}^{n-1} a_i\mathbf{e}_i . \qquad (1.10.2)$$

Not all of the a_i are zero. Applying the operator $\mathbf{A}$ to both sides of Eq. (1.10.2), we have

$$\mathbf{A}\mathbf{e}_n = \lambda_n\mathbf{e}_n = \sum_{i=1}^{n-1} a_i\mathbf{A}\mathbf{e}_i = \sum_{i=1}^{n-1} a_i\lambda_i\mathbf{e}_i . \qquad (1.10.3)$$

We use the expansion (1.10.2) in (1.10.3) to find

$$\sum_{i=1}^{n-1} a_i e_i \lambda_n = \sum_{i=1}^{n-1} a_i \lambda_i e_i , \qquad (1.10.4)$$

or

$$\sum_{i=1}^{n-1} a_i e_i (\lambda_n - \lambda_i) = 0. \qquad (1.10.5)$$

Thus if the λ_i are all distinct, and since not all the a_i are zero, Eq. (1.10.5) cannot be true. Consequently, the assumption (1.10.2) is invalid.

Even though the eigenvectors are linearly independent, we cannot assume they are orthogonal. In fact they cannot be. Of course, the eigenvectors may be normalized. A nonsymmetric matrix with distinct eigenvalues may be diagonalized by using the modal matrix constructed from the eigenvectors of the matrix. However, since the eigenvectors are not generally orthogonal, the diagonalization is accomplished by a similarity transformation which is not an orthogonal transformation in general.

If the eigenvalues of a nonsymmetric matrix are not all distinct, it may not be possible to find a complete set of eigenvectors, but, nevertheless, it is always possible to find a complete set of some other vectors, called principal vectors, which permit some simplification of the original matrix (see Reference 6, pp. 32–36). Let the matrix $\mathbf{A}$ have n roots, λ_i , where some of the roots are repeated. Let λ_1 be repeated k times. We can always find one eigenvector $\mathbf{e}_1$ such that

$$\mathbf{A}\mathbf{e}_1 = \lambda_1 \mathbf{e}_1 . \qquad (1.10.6)$$

We assume this is the only eigenvector associated with λ_1 . We now seek a vector $\mathbf{t}_1$ satisfying

$$(\mathbf{A} - \lambda_1 \mathbf{I})\mathbf{t}_1 = \mathbf{e}_1 . \qquad (1.10.7)$$

Any solution of Eq. (1.10.7) may be chosen orthogonal to $\mathbf{e}_1$ (see Problem 17). Let us assume we have found the vector $\mathbf{t}_1$. We then seek another vector $\mathbf{t}_2$ from the relation

$$(\mathbf{A} - \lambda_1 \mathbf{I})\mathbf{t}_2 = \mathbf{t}_1 . \qquad (1.10.8)$$

This implies that $\mathbf{t}_2$ must be orthogonal to $\mathbf{t}_1$ and furthermore, from Eq. (1.10.7) we have

$$(\mathbf{A} - \lambda_1 \mathbf{I})^2 \mathbf{t}_2 = \mathbf{e}_1 . \qquad (1.10.9)$$

Consequently, $\mathbf{t}_2$ may also be chosen orthogonal to $\mathbf{e}_1$. We continue generating vectors in sequence of the form

$$(\mathbf{A} - \lambda_1\mathbf{I})\mathbf{t}_p = \mathbf{t}_{p-1}. \tag{1.10.10}$$

Each new vector $\mathbf{t}_p$ will be orthogonal to $\mathbf{t}_{p-1}$, $\mathbf{t}_{p-2}$, ... , $\mathbf{e}_1$. It can be shown that we can only find $k - 1$ vectors $\mathbf{t}_p$ in this manner (see below).

Let us assume for the moment that λ_1 is the only repeated root of $\mathbf{A}$. Thus, for the $n - k$ remaining distinct roots λ_i, we have $n - k$ linearly independent eigenvectors $\mathbf{e}_i$. We assert that the set of vectors $\mathbf{e}_1$, $\mathbf{t}_1$, $\mathbf{t}_2$, ... , $\mathbf{t}_{k-1}$, $\mathbf{e}_{k+1}$, $\mathbf{e}_{k+2}$, ... , $\mathbf{e}_n$ are linearly independent. This follows from the fact that if any of the $\mathbf{t}_j$ were linear combinations of the $\mathbf{e}_i$, $i \neq 1$, then we would have

$$\mathbf{t}_j = \sum_{i=k+1}^{n} a_i\mathbf{e}_i. \tag{1.10.11}$$

But from the definition of $\mathbf{t}_j$, we also have

$$\mathbf{e}_1 = (\mathbf{A} - \lambda_1\mathbf{I})^j\mathbf{t}_j = \sum_{i=k+1}^{n} a_i(\mathbf{A} - \lambda_1\mathbf{I})^j\mathbf{e}_i, \tag{1.10.12}$$

which implies $\mathbf{e}_1$ is a linear combination of the $\mathbf{e}_i$. Therefore, the $\mathbf{t}_j$ are linearly independent of the $\mathbf{e}_i$, $i \neq 1$. Since the set $\mathbf{e}_1$, $\mathbf{t}_1$, $\mathbf{t}_2$, ... , $\mathbf{t}_{k-1}$ are orthogonal, they are linearly independent of each other. Thus, the sets $\mathbf{e}_i$, $\mathbf{t}_j$ are linearly independent of each other and constitute a basis. Since we have $n - k + 1$ eigenvectors, we see that we cannot find more than $k - 1$ independent principal vectors, hence the statement in the preceding paragraph.

The particular advantage of the set of vectors so chosen can be seen by constructing the modal matrix. We again define $\mathbf{M}$ as

$$\mathbf{M} = \begin{bmatrix} e_{11} & t_{11} & t_{21} & \cdots & e_{n1} \\ e_{12} & t_{12} & t_{22} & \cdots & e_{n2} \\ \vdots & \vdots & \vdots & & \vdots \\ e_{1n} & t_{1n} & t_{2n} & \cdots & e_{nn} \end{bmatrix}. \tag{1.10.13}$$

We operate on $\mathbf{M}$ by the matrix $\mathbf{A}$. The first column of the product is merely $\lambda_1\mathbf{e}_1$. Similarly, all the eigenvectors are reproduced times their corresponding eigenvalue. Now consider the second column of the product. This is merely

$$\mathbf{At}_1 \equiv \mathbf{e}_1 + \lambda_1 \mathbf{t}_1 . \tag{1.10.14}$$

For the third column, we have

$$\mathbf{At}_2 \equiv \mathbf{t}_1 + \lambda_1 \mathbf{t}_2 \tag{1.10.15}$$

and so forth, for the $k - 1$ principal vectors. The matrix formed from the product $\mathbf{AM}$ is then seen to be of the form

$$\mathbf{AM} = \begin{bmatrix} \lambda_1 e_{11} & e_{11} + \lambda_1 t_{11} & t_{11} + \lambda_1 t_{21} & \cdots & \lambda_n e_{n1} \\ \lambda_1 e_{12} & e_{12} + \lambda_1 t_{12} & t_{12} + \lambda_1 t_{22} & \cdots & \lambda_n e_{n2} \\ \vdots & \vdots & \vdots & & \vdots \\ \lambda_1 e_{1n} & e_{1n} + \lambda_1 t_{1n} & t_{1n} + \lambda_1 t_{2n} & \cdots & \lambda_n e_{nn} \end{bmatrix} . \tag{1.10.16}$$

This product may be factored in the form

$$\mathbf{AM} = \begin{bmatrix} e_{11} & t_{11} & \cdots & e_{n1} \\ e_{12} & t_{12} & \cdots & e_{n2} \\ \vdots & \vdots & & \vdots \\ & & & \\ e_{1n} & t_{1n} & \cdots & e_{nn} \end{bmatrix} \begin{bmatrix} \lambda_1 & 1 & 0 & \cdots & 0 \\ 0 & \lambda_1 & 1 & & \vdots \\ \vdots & & \ddots & & \\ 0 & \cdots & & \lambda_1 & \\ & & & & \lambda_{k+1} & & \\ & & \mathbf{0} & & & \ddots \\ & & & & & & \lambda_n \end{bmatrix} \tag{1.10.17}$$

where the submatrix in λ_1 is k by k. The product is of the form $\mathbf{MJ}$, where

$$\mathbf{J} = \begin{bmatrix} \lambda_1 & 1 & 0 & 0 & \cdots & 0 & 0 & | & 0 & 0 & \cdots & 0 \\ 0 & \lambda_1 & 1 & 0 & \cdots & 0 & 0 & | & 0 & 0 & \cdots & 0 \\ 0 & 0 & \lambda_1 & 1 & \cdots & 0 & 0 & | & 0 & 0 & \cdots & 0 \\ \vdots & \vdots & \vdots & \vdots & & \vdots & \vdots & | & \vdots & \vdots & & \vdots \\ 0 & 0 & 0 & 0 & \cdots & \lambda_1 & 1 & | & 0 & 0 & \cdots & 0 \\ 0 & 0 & 0 & 0 & \cdots & 0 & \lambda_1 & | & 0 & 0 & \cdots & 0 \\ \hline 0 & 0 & 0 & 0 & \cdots & 0 & 0 & \lambda_{k+1} & 0 & \cdots & 0 \\ 0 & 0 & 0 & 0 & \cdots & 0 & 0 & 0 & \lambda_{k+2} & \cdots & 0 \\ \vdots & \vdots & \vdots & \vdots & & \vdots & \vdots & \vdots & \vdots & & \vdots \\ 0 & 0 & 0 & 0 & \cdots & 0 & 0 & 0 & 0 & \cdots & \lambda_n \end{bmatrix} . \tag{1.10.18}$$

The similarity transformation

$$\mathbf{M^{-1}AM = J} \tag{1.10.19}$$

yields a nearly diagonal matrix $\mathbf{J}$, which is called the Jordan canonical form. Note that the matrix has the form of a diagonal matrix for the eigenvectors, while the submatrix for the repeated root contains the eigenvalue λ_1 along the diagonal and the element unity along the upper subdiagonal.

In the case of a repeated root with more than one eigenvector, the submatrix has a form similar to that below.

$$\mathbf{J}_{11} = \begin{bmatrix} \lambda_1 & 1 & 0 & \cdots & 0 & 0 \\ 0 & \lambda_1 & 1 & \cdots & 0 & 0 \\ 0 & 0 & \lambda_1 & \cdots & 0 & 0 \\ \vdots & \vdots & \vdots & & \vdots & \vdots \\ 0 & 0 & 0 & \cdots & \lambda_1 & 1 \\ 0 & 0 & 0 & \cdots & 0 & \lambda_1 \end{bmatrix}. \tag{1.10.20}$$

For more than one repeated root, the Jordan canonical form (also called normal form) is

$$\mathbf{J} = \begin{bmatrix} \mathbf{J}_{11} & 0 & \cdots & 0 \\ 0 & \mathbf{J}_{22} & \cdots & 0 \\ \vdots & \vdots & & \vdots \\ 0 & 0 & \cdots & \mathbf{J}_{pp} \end{bmatrix}, \tag{1.10.21}$$

where each of the $\mathbf{J}_{ii}$ is a submatrix in canonical form (for repeated roots) or diagonal (for distinct roots).

It is important to realize that any real matrix may be reduced to the canonical form as above. If there is a complete set of eigenvectors, the canonical form is diagonal. Otherwise, some of the submatrices contain off-diagonal elements. We shall find this result leads to considerable simplification of the analysis of later problems.

If the eigenvalues of a matrix are all greater than zero, the matrix is said to be positive definite. Conversely, a matrix all of whose eigenvalues are less than zero is said to be negative definite.

1.11 Geometric Interpretation

The eigenvalue problem can be given a very useful and illustrative setting in terms of the geometry of quadratic surfaces. We first consider the equation of a quadratic surface in n-dimensional space

$$\frac{x_1^2}{d_1} + \frac{x_2^2}{d_2} + \dots + \frac{x_n^2}{d_n} = 1. \tag{1.11.1}$$

We note that the equation can be written in matrix form as

$$\mathbf{x}^T \mathbf{D} \mathbf{x} = 1, \tag{1.11.2}$$

where

$$\mathbf{x} = \begin{bmatrix} x_1 \\ x_2 \\ \vdots \\ x_n \end{bmatrix} \tag{1.11.3}$$

and

$$\mathbf{D} = \begin{bmatrix} 1/d_1 & 0 & \dots & 0 \\ 0 & 1/d_2 & \dots & 0 \\ \vdots & \vdots & & \vdots \\ 0 & 0 & \dots & 1/d_n \end{bmatrix}. \tag{1.11.4}$$

This result suggests that there is some intimate relation between the quadratic equation (1.11.1) and the diagonalization of matrices. To see this relation, consider a real symmetric matrix $\mathbf{A}$ and the quadratic form $\mathbf{x}^T \mathbf{A} \mathbf{x}$. The quadratic form can be written

$$\begin{aligned} \mathbf{x}^T \mathbf{A} \mathbf{x} = a_{11} x_1^2 \;\; &+ a_{12} x_1 x_2 + \dots a_{1n} x_1 x_n \\ &+ a_{21} x_2 x_1 + a_{22} x_2^2 \;\; + \dots a_{2n} x_2 x_n \\ &\;\;\vdots \qquad\quad \vdots \qquad\quad \vdots \\ &+ a_{n1} x_n x_1 + a_{n2} x_n x_2 + \dots a_{nn} x_n^2 \;. \end{aligned} \tag{1.11.5}$$

If we set $\mathbf{x}^T \mathbf{A} \mathbf{x} = 1$, then the equation represents a general second-order surface. The normal, $\mathbf{N}$, to the surface

$$f(x_1, x_2, \dots, x_n) = 1 \tag{1.11.6}$$

is given by[5]

$$
\mathbf{N} = \begin{bmatrix}
\dfrac{\partial f}{\partial x_1} \\[2mm]
\dfrac{\partial f}{\partial x_2} \\[2mm]
\vdots \\[2mm]
\dfrac{\partial f}{\partial x_n}
\end{bmatrix}. \tag{1.11.7}
$$

The normal to the surface $\mathbf{x}^T\mathbf{A}\mathbf{x}$ is thus

$$
\mathbf{N} = 2\mathbf{A}\mathbf{x}, \tag{1.11.8}
$$

which follows from the symmetry of $\mathbf{A}$.

The principal axes of a quadratic surface are defined as the directions at which the normal vector is parallel to the radius vector. Thus, a principal $\mathbf{x}$ axis is a direction such that

$$
\beta\mathbf{x} = \mathbf{N}, \tag{1.11.9}
$$

where β is some constant. Consequently, the principal axes satisfy the equation

$$
\mathbf{A}\mathbf{x} = \lambda\mathbf{x}. \tag{1.11.10}
$$

The principal axes are particularly useful since the equation of the quadratic surface expressed in terms of the principal axes contains only a sum of squares. The eigenvectors of the matrix $\mathbf{A}$ are seen to be just the principal axes of the quadratic surface. If we transform the matrix $\mathbf{A}$ by the modal matrix, say $\mathbf{M}$, then we find

$$
\mathbf{A}' = \mathbf{M}^{-1}\mathbf{A}\mathbf{M} = \Lambda, \tag{1.11.11}
$$

---

[5] This relation may be proved by noting that Eq. (1.11.6) implies that

$$
\sum_{i=1}^{n} \frac{\partial f}{\partial x_i} \frac{dx_i}{dt} = 0,
$$

where the x_i are assumed to be functions of some parameter t. Since the tangent to the surface is proportional to the vector $[dx_i/dt]$, the normal must be proportional to the vector $[\partial f/\partial x_i]$.

and the quadratic form

$$\mathbf{x}^T \mathbf{A} \mathbf{x} = \mathbf{x}'^T \Lambda \mathbf{x}' = 1, \tag{1.11.12}$$

which is just the form of Eq. (1.11.2). Notice that the expanded equation is

$$\mathbf{x}^T \mathbf{A} \mathbf{x} = \lambda_1 x_1'^2 + \lambda_2 x_2'^2 + \dots + \lambda_n x_n'^2 = 1. \tag{1.11.13}$$

The eigenvalues are equal to the reciprocal of the square of the length of the principal axes.

The occurrence of repeated roots can be interpreted in this geometric view. If two roots are equal, then the quadratic surface has rotational symmetry about the axes orthogonal to the eigenvectors of the repeated root. A zero root implies the quadratic surface lies in a space orthogonal to the given direction.

1.12   Biorthogonal Vectors

For a real symmetric matrix, we have shown that the eigenvectors form a set of mutually orthogonal vectors. The eigenvectors are a convenient basis for the space of the problem. In the case of a nonsymmetric matrix, the eigenvectors may not be mutually orthogonal however. It is convenient, in this case, to generate a second set of vectors which are not orthogonal amongst themselves, but are orthogonal with respect to the original set of vectors. Such relationships are known as biorthogonality relationships.

The importance of such relationships can be seen from the following simple example. Consider a vector $\mathbf{x}$ in two-dimensional space, as shown in Fig. 1.12.1.

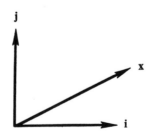

FIG. 1.12.1.   Vector $\mathbf{x}$ in the orthogonal coordinate system $\mathbf{i}$, $\mathbf{j}$.

We write $\mathbf{x}$ as the matrix

$$\mathbf{x} = \begin{bmatrix} x_1 \\ x_2 \end{bmatrix}. \tag{1.12.1}$$

The square of the length of $\mathbf{x}$ is

$$\mathbf{x}^T\mathbf{x} = x_1^2 + x_2^2. \tag{1.12.2}$$

Now consider the same vector in a nonorthogonal coordinate system of base vectors, $\mathbf{u}_1$, $\mathbf{u}_2$, as shown in Fig. 1.12.2 as an example.

FIG. 1.12.2. Vector $\mathbf{x}$ in the nonorthogonal coordinate system $\mathbf{u}_1$, $\mathbf{u}_2$.

We shall assume $\mathbf{u}_1$ and $\mathbf{u}_2$ are related to $\mathbf{i}$, $\mathbf{j}$ as

$$\mathbf{u}_1 = \mathbf{i}, \tag{1.12.3}$$

$$\mathbf{u}_2 = (-1/\sqrt{2})\mathbf{i} + (1/\sqrt{2})\mathbf{j}. \tag{1.12.4}$$

The vector $\mathbf{x}$ may be written as

$$\mathbf{x} = \begin{bmatrix} x_1' \\ x_2' \end{bmatrix}, \tag{1.12.5}$$

when the components of $\mathbf{x}$ are referred to the $\mathbf{u}_1$, $\mathbf{u}_2$ basis. To find the components x_1', x_2', we take projections of $\mathbf{x}$ parallel to the $\mathbf{u}_1$, $\mathbf{u}_2$ axes. We have

$$x_1' = x_1 + x_2, \tag{1.12.6}$$

$$x_2' = \sqrt{2}\, x_2. \tag{1.12.7}$$

If we consider the length squared of $\mathbf{x}$ in this coordinate system as

$$\mathbf{x}^T\mathbf{x} = (x_1')^2 + (x_2')^2 = x_1^2 + 2x_1x_2 + x_2^2 + 2x_2^2, \tag{1.12.8}$$

the result obviously does not agree with the earlier results. The difficulty is that the length is not given by $\mathbf{x}^T\mathbf{x}$ when the components are expressed in nonorthogonal coordinates. In order to find a simple expression for the length of a vector, it is necessary to introduce another coordinate system which is said to be biorthogonal to the $\mathbf{u}_1$, $\mathbf{u}_2$ system. Thus, we desire a system, say $\mathbf{w}_1$, $\mathbf{w}_2$, with the property

$$\mathbf{w}_m^T\mathbf{u}_n = \delta_{mn}. \tag{1.12.9}$$

Obviously the system

$$\mathbf{w}_1 = \begin{bmatrix} 1 \\ 1 \end{bmatrix}, \tag{1.12.10}$$

$$\mathbf{w}_2 = \begin{bmatrix} 0 \\ \sqrt{2} \end{bmatrix}, \tag{1.12.11}$$

is the desired one, where the components of $\mathbf{w}_1$, $\mathbf{w}_2$ are expressed in the $\mathbf{i}$, $\mathbf{j}$ system. Notice that the biorthogonality condition (1.12.9) is also a statement relating the normalization of both sets of vectors. Although the lengths of $\mathbf{u}_1$, $\mathbf{u}_2$ are unity, the lengths of $\mathbf{w}_1$, $\mathbf{w}_2$ are both $\sqrt{2}$. The vector $\mathbf{x}$ in the $\mathbf{w}$ system is shown in Fig. 1.12.3.

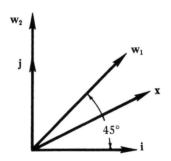

FIG. 1.12.3.   Vector $\mathbf{x}$ in the nonorthogonal coordinate system $\mathbf{w}_1$, $\mathbf{w}_2$.

The vector $\mathbf{x}$ may be written

$$\mathbf{x} = \begin{bmatrix} x_1'' \\ x_2'' \end{bmatrix}, \tag{1.12.12}$$

when the components are referred to the $\mathbf{w}_1$, $\mathbf{w}_2$ system. The components are found to be

$$x_1'' = \sqrt{2}x_1(1/\sqrt{2}) = x_1, \tag{1.12.13}$$

$$x_2'' = (-x_1 + x_2)(1/\sqrt{2}) = -\frac{x_1}{\sqrt{2}} + \frac{x_2}{\sqrt{2}}. \tag{1.12.14}$$

The component of a vector $\mathbf{x}$ along some basis vector, such as $\mathbf{w}_1$ or $\mathbf{w}_2$, is the length of the vector $\mathbf{x}$ when projected on that basis vector. The length is the number of units of the basis vector contained in the component of the projection of the vector $\mathbf{x}$. Consequently, since the basis vector, $\mathbf{w}_1$ or $\mathbf{w}_2$, is not of the same length as the original basis vectors, $\mathbf{i}$ or $\mathbf{j}$, each component x_1'' and x_2'' must be rescaled according to the ratio of the lengths of the final and original basis vectors. In the present example, the rescaling happens to be identical for each term or component. The length squared

$$(x_1'')^2 + (x_2'')^2 = x_1^2 + \frac{x_1^2}{2} + \frac{x_2^2}{2} - x_1 x_2 , \qquad (1.12.15a)$$

is again incorrect. However, the product

$$(x_1', x_1'') + (x_2', x_2'') = x_1^2 + x_1 x_2 - x_1 x_2 + x_2^2 \qquad (1.12.15b)$$

is correct. The correct length is computed when we use the components expressed in a nonorthogonal system and the coordinate system biorthogonal thereto.

An algebraic proof of this geometric result is derived by expressing coordinate axes in matrix equations (see Eq. (1.6.2) et seq.). Thus, if[6]

$$\mathbf{x} = [\mathbf{i}, \mathbf{j}] \begin{bmatrix} x_1 \\ x_2 \end{bmatrix}, \qquad (1.12.16)$$

then

$$\mathbf{x}^T \mathbf{x} = [x_1 , x_2] \begin{bmatrix} \mathbf{i} \\ \mathbf{j} \end{bmatrix} [\mathbf{i}, \mathbf{j}] \begin{bmatrix} x_1 \\ x_2 \end{bmatrix} = [x_1 , x_2] \begin{bmatrix} x_1 \\ x_2 \end{bmatrix}, \qquad (1.12.17)$$

since $\mathbf{i}, \mathbf{j}$ are orthogonal. For the $\mathbf{u}_1 , \mathbf{u}_2$ system, we have

$$\mathbf{x} = [\mathbf{u}_1 , \mathbf{u}_2] \begin{bmatrix} x_1' \\ x_2' \end{bmatrix}, \qquad (1.12.18)$$

while for the $\mathbf{w}_1 , \mathbf{w}_2$ system we have

$$\mathbf{x} = [\mathbf{w}_1 , \mathbf{w}_2] \begin{bmatrix} x_1'' \\ x_2'' \end{bmatrix} \qquad (1.12.19)$$

and hence

$$\mathbf{x}^T \mathbf{x} = [x_1'', x_2''] \begin{bmatrix} \mathbf{w}_1 \\ \mathbf{w}_2 \end{bmatrix} [\mathbf{u}_1 , \mathbf{u}_2] \begin{bmatrix} x_1' \\ x_2' \end{bmatrix} = [x_1'', x_2''] \begin{bmatrix} x_1' \\ x_2' \end{bmatrix}, \qquad (1.12.20)$$

[6] Note here $\mathbf{i}$ and $\mathbf{j}$ are regarded as submatrices of the matrix $[\mathbf{i}, \mathbf{j}]$.

since $\mathbf{w}_1$, $\mathbf{w}_2$ and $\mathbf{u}_1$, $\mathbf{u}_2$ are biorthogonal. Note further that

$$\mathbf{x}^T\mathbf{x} = [x_1, x_2] \begin{bmatrix} \mathbf{i} \\ \mathbf{j} \end{bmatrix} [\mathbf{u}_1, \mathbf{u}_2] \begin{bmatrix} x_1' \\ x_2' \end{bmatrix} \qquad (1.12.21)$$

$$= [x_1, x_2] \begin{bmatrix} (\mathbf{i}, \mathbf{u}_1) & (\mathbf{i}, \mathbf{u}_2) \\ (\mathbf{j}, \mathbf{u}_1) & (\mathbf{j}, \mathbf{u}_2) \end{bmatrix} \begin{bmatrix} x_1' \\ x_2' \end{bmatrix} \neq x_1 x_1' + x_2 x_2'. \qquad (1.12.22)$$

The square matrix in Eq. (1.12.22) is known as the metric tensor. One invariably prefers to use orthogonal systems, or at worst biorthogonal systems, since then the metric is thus unity.

The procedure for constructing a dual system to a set of nonorthogonal eigenvectors is relatively simple. Let the matrix $\mathbf{A}$ be nonsymmetric but with distinct roots. Denote the eigenvalues as λ_i and the corresponding eigenvectors as $\mathbf{e}_i$. The eigenvalues satisfy the determinant

$$|\mathbf{A} - \lambda\mathbf{I}| = 0. \qquad (1.12.23)$$

We now consider the transpose matrix $\mathbf{A}^T$. The eigenvalues of $\mathbf{A}^T$ are obviously the same λ's as above, since interchanging rows and columns does not change the value of the determinant. Let the eigenvectors of the transpose matrix be denoted as $\mathbf{u}_j$. We then have

$$\mathbf{A}\mathbf{e}_i = \lambda_i\mathbf{e}_i, \qquad (1.12.24)$$

$$\mathbf{A}^T\mathbf{u}_j = \lambda_j\mathbf{u}_j, \qquad (i \neq j). \qquad (1.12.25)$$

We now multiply the first equation by $\mathbf{u}_j^T$, the second by $\mathbf{e}_i^T$ and subtract. We have

$$\mathbf{u}_j^T\mathbf{A}\mathbf{e}_i - \mathbf{e}_i^T\mathbf{A}^T\mathbf{u}_j = 0 = (\lambda_i - \lambda_j)\mathbf{u}_j^T\mathbf{e}_i. \qquad (1.12.26)$$

Since the eigenvalues are not equal, the eigenvectors must be orthogonal. Thus the original set of eigenvectors and the transposed set (sometimes called the adjoint eigenvectors) form a biorthogonal system.

This result may immediately be interpreted in terms of quadratic forms. A vector $\mathbf{x}$ has a representation in a coordinate system, say $\mathbf{u}_i$, as

$$\mathbf{x} = x_1\mathbf{u}_1 + x_2\mathbf{u}_2 + \dots + x_n\mathbf{u}_n. \qquad (1.12.27)$$

The vector may also be represented in the dual coordinate system, say $\mathbf{w}_i$, as

$$\mathbf{x} = x_1'\mathbf{w}_1 + x_2'\mathbf{w}_2 + \dots + x_n'\mathbf{w}_n. \qquad (1.12.28)$$

A general quadratic surface in these coordinates would be represented as

$$(\mathbf{x})^T \mathbf{A} \mathbf{x} = f(x_i', x_i) = \text{constant}. \qquad (1.12.29)$$

The expanded form of Eq. (1.12.29) is known as a bilinear form rather than a quadratic form. The normal to the surface is again given by

$$\mathbf{N} = \frac{\partial f}{\partial x_i'}, \qquad (1.12.30)$$

and hence the principal axes $\mathbf{x}$ are given by

$$\mathbf{A}\mathbf{x} = \lambda \mathbf{x}. \qquad (1.12.31)$$

The dual problem is then

$$\mathbf{x}^T \mathbf{A}^T \mathbf{x} = f(x_i', x_i) = \text{constant}, \qquad (1.12.32)$$

with principal axes $\mathbf{x}$ given by

$$\mathbf{A}^T \mathbf{x} = \lambda \mathbf{x}, \qquad (!.12.33)$$

since the eigenvalues of the transpose matrix $\mathbf{A}^T$ equal the eigenvalues of the matrix $\mathbf{A}$. The eigenvectors of the matrix operator are the principal axes of the associated quadratic form. The principal axes of the surface are skewed in general. Nevertheless, if the eigenvectors are complete, the surface can be transformed to the form

$$\lambda_1 x_1^2 + \lambda_2 x_2^2 + \ldots + \lambda_n x_2^2 = \text{constant} \qquad (1.12.34)$$

and

$$\lambda_1 (x_1')^2 + \lambda_2 (x_2')^2 + \ldots + \lambda_n (x_n')^2 = \text{constant}. \qquad (1.12.35)$$

In this case if a root is repeated, we may not be able to assume rotational symmetry. Instead the two eigenvectors may collapse into only one vector, since there is no orthogonality relationship between eigenvectors of a given skewed system.

1.13 Nonnegative Matrices

Of particular usefulness in the numerical solution of differential equations is the theory of nonnegative matrices. In this section we define several matrix properties and relate these properties to nonnegative matrices.

Frequently one is interested in estimating the largest eigenvalue of a matrix without actually solving the secular equation. A useful theorem is the Gerschgorin theorem which states that the largest eigenvalue is equal to or less than the maximum value of the sum of the magnitudes of the elements in any row. That is, if $\mathbf{A} = [a_{ij}]$

$$|\lambda_{max}| \leqslant \max_i \sum_j |a_{ij}|. \tag{1.13.1}$$

The proof of this theorem is simple. Let λ be any eigenvalue of $\mathbf{A}$ and $\mathbf{e}$ the corresponding eigenvector. We then have

$$\lambda e_i = \sum_j a_{ij} e_j, \tag{1.13.2}$$

which is true for all i. Now choose the element of $\mathbf{e}$ of largest amplitude, say e_k. Then we have

$$|\lambda| \leqslant \sum_j |a_{kj}| \left| \frac{e_j}{e_k} \right| \leqslant \sum_j |a_{kj}|. \tag{1.13.3}$$

Consequently, the largest eigenvalue is bounded by Eq. (1.13.1).

Frequently the largest eigenvalue is called the spectral radius of a matrix, since all eigenvalues lie within or on a circle of radius λ_{max} in the complex plane. We shall denote the spectral radius of $\mathbf{A}$ as $r(\mathbf{A})$. Gerschgorin's theorem is then

$$r(\mathbf{A}) \leqslant \max_i \sum_j |a_{ij}|. \tag{1.13.4}$$

Any matrix $\mathbf{A}$ is said to be reducible if there exists a permutation transformation $\mathbf{P}$, i.e., if the rows and columns can be permuted similarly, such that

$$\mathbf{PAP}^T = \begin{bmatrix} \mathbf{A}_{11} & \mathbf{A}_{12} \\ \mathbf{0} & \mathbf{A}_{22} \end{bmatrix} \tag{1.13.5}$$

where the submatrices $\mathbf{A}_{11}$, $\mathbf{A}_{22}$ are square, but not necessarily of the same order. If no permutation transformation exists such that (1.13.5) is true, then $\mathbf{A}$ is called irreducible. The property of irreducibility implies a connectedness in the problem as seen by the following example. Consider a vector $\mathbf{x}$ and a reducible matrix $\mathbf{A}$. The product $\mathbf{Ax}$ can be written

$$\begin{bmatrix} \mathbf{A}_{11} & \mathbf{A}_{12} \\ \mathbf{0} & \mathbf{A}_{22} \end{bmatrix} \begin{bmatrix} \mathbf{x}_1 \\ \mathbf{x}_2 \end{bmatrix} = \begin{bmatrix} \mathbf{A}_{11}\mathbf{x}_1 + \mathbf{A}_{12}\mathbf{x}_2 \\ \mathbf{A}_{22}\mathbf{x}_2 \end{bmatrix}. \tag{1.13.6}$$

The result indicates that the transformation of the components of $\mathbf{x}_2$ is independent of the components of $\mathbf{x}_1$. The solution of the equation

$$\mathbf{Ax} = \mathbf{y} \tag{1.13.7}$$

can be accomplished as two separate problems

$$\mathbf{A}_{11}\mathbf{x}_1 + \mathbf{A}_{12}\mathbf{x}_2 = \mathbf{y}_1 , \tag{1.13.8a}$$

$$\mathbf{A}_{22}\mathbf{x}_2 = \mathbf{y}_2 . \tag{1.13.8b}$$

The values of $\mathbf{x}_2$ are independent of $\mathbf{x}_1$. Physically this implies that some portion of the solution is independent of certain other values of the solution. Such a case arises in multigroup approximations where the fast flux in the core is "disconnected" from the thermal flux in the reflector. On the other hand, if the matrix $\mathbf{A}$ is irreducible, then the components of the solution of Eq. (1.13.7) are related to and dependent upon one another.

A nonnegative matrix $\mathbf{A}$ is a matrix such that

$$\mathbf{A} = [a_{ij}], \tag{1.13.9}$$

and

$$a_{ij} \geqslant 0, \quad \text{all } i, j. \tag{1.13.10}$$

We denote a nonnegative matrix $\mathbf{A}$ as $\mathbf{A} \geqslant \mathbf{0}$. Similarly, if

$$a_{ij} > 0, \quad \text{all } i, j, \tag{1.13.11}$$

then $\mathbf{A}$ is called a positive matrix denoted $\mathbf{A} > \mathbf{0}$. A very useful theorem regarding nonnegative matrices is the following. If $\mathbf{A}$ is nonnegative, then $\mathbf{A}$ has a nonnegative real eigenvalue, and the corresponding eigenvector has nonnegative components, not all zero. The proof of the theorem is involved (see Reference 7, pp. 66–68), and we offer a heuristic justification instead. Since $\mathbf{A}$ is nonnegative, the quadratic form associated with $\mathbf{A}$ represents an ellipsoid and must have a principal axis somewhere in the first quadrant. Since $\mathbf{A}$ is nonnegative, any vector with nonnegative components is transformed by $\mathbf{A}$ into a nonnegative vector, hence the eigenvalue is nonnegative.

A sharpened form of the above theorem is the following[7]: if $\mathbf{A}$ is a nonnegative irreducible matrix, then $\mathbf{A}$ has a positive real eigenvalue, and the corresponding eigenvector has positive components. To prove

---

[7] From Reference 8. Some further results in this section are also from Reference 8, Chapter II.

this we note first that $\mathbf{A}$ has an eigenvector $\mathbf{x} \geqslant \mathbf{0}$, $\mathbf{x} \neq \mathbf{0}$ by the previous theorem. If the corresponding eigenvalue is zero, then we have

$$\mathbf{Ax} = \lambda\mathbf{x} = \mathbf{0}. \tag{1.13.12}$$

Since $\mathbf{x} \neq \mathbf{0}$, then $\mathbf{A}$ must have at least one column identically zero, which implies $\mathbf{A}$ is reducible, contrary to hypothesis. Therefore, $\lambda \neq 0$. Conversely, if the eigenvector has some zero components, then we have, after a permutation of rows of $\mathbf{x}$ and corresponding rows and columns of $\mathbf{A}$,

$$\mathbf{x} = \begin{bmatrix} \mathbf{x}_1 \\ \mathbf{0} \end{bmatrix} \tag{1.13.13}$$

and

$$\mathbf{Ax} = \begin{bmatrix} \mathbf{A}_{11} & \mathbf{A}_{12} \\ \mathbf{A}_{21} & \mathbf{A}_{22} \end{bmatrix} \begin{bmatrix} \mathbf{x}_1 \\ \mathbf{0} \end{bmatrix} = \begin{bmatrix} \mathbf{A}_{11}\mathbf{x}_1 \\ \mathbf{A}_{21}\mathbf{x}_1 \end{bmatrix} = \lambda \begin{bmatrix} \mathbf{x}_1 \\ \mathbf{0} \end{bmatrix}. \tag{1.13.14}$$

But then $\mathbf{A}_{21} = \mathbf{0}$ and again $\mathbf{A}$ is reducible contrary to the hypothesis. Therefore, $\mathbf{x} > \mathbf{0}$.

The above result is contained in a classical theorem by Perron and Frobenius which can be stated: If $\mathbf{A}$ is a nonnegative irreducible matrix, then $\mathbf{A}$ has a positive simple real eigenvalue λ_0 equal to the spectral radius of $\mathbf{A}$. The corresponding eigenvector has all positive components.

To prove that λ_0 equals the spectral radius of $\mathbf{A}$, we consider the matrix $\mathbf{B}$ with $\mathbf{0} \leqslant \mathbf{B}$, and $0 \leqslant b_{ij} \leqslant a_{ij}$, all i, j. Thus every element of $\mathbf{B}$ is nonnegative and equal to or less than the corresponding element of $\mathbf{A}$. We denote the relationship as $\mathbf{0} \leqslant \mathbf{B} \leqslant \mathbf{A}$. We have

$$\mathbf{Ax} = \lambda_0\mathbf{x}, \tag{1.13.15}$$

where $\mathbf{x}$ has positive components. Similarly,

$$\mathbf{A}^T\mathbf{y} = \lambda_0\mathbf{y}, \tag{1.13.16}$$

where $\mathbf{y}$ has positive components. Now let

$$\mathbf{Bz} = \gamma\mathbf{z}, \tag{1.13.17}$$

where γ is any eigenvalue of $\mathbf{B}$. We now show $\gamma < \lambda_0$ for $\mathbf{B} < \mathbf{A}$ and $\gamma = \lambda_0$ for $\mathbf{B} = \mathbf{A}$, which proves λ_0 equals the spectral radius. From Eq. (1.13.17) we have

$$\gamma z_i = \sum_j b_{ij} z_j, \tag{1.13.18}$$

and

$$|\gamma| |z_i| \leqslant \sum_j b_{ij} |z_j| \leqslant \sum_j a_{ij} |z_j|, \qquad (1.13.19)$$

since all elements of $\mathbf{A}$, $\mathbf{B}$ are nonnegative. We multiply Eq. (1.13.19) by y_i and sum on i to obtain

$$|\gamma| \sum_i y_i |z_i| \leqslant \sum_i \sum_j a_{ij} y_i |z_j| = \lambda_0 \sum_j y_i |z_j|, \qquad (1.13.20)$$

hence

$$|\gamma| \leqslant \lambda_0. \qquad (1.13.21)$$

If $\gamma = \lambda_0$, then the equality holds in Eq. (1.13.19) and requires that

$$\gamma |z_i| = \sum_j b_{ij} |z_j| = \sum_j a_{ij} |z_j|, \qquad (1.13.22)$$

and then $\mathbf{B} = \mathbf{A}$.

To prove that λ_0 is a simple root, we need only show that the determinant

$$|\mathbf{A} - \lambda\mathbf{I}| = P(\lambda) \qquad (1.13.23)$$

has a zero of multiplicity one when $\lambda = \lambda_0$. If any polynomial $P(\lambda)$ has a repeated root at λ_0

$$\frac{dP(\lambda)}{d\lambda}\bigg|_{\lambda_0} = 0. \qquad (1.13.24)$$

From Eq. (1.13.23) we readily see that the derivative of the secular polynomial can be written

$$\frac{dP(\lambda)}{d\lambda} = -\sum_{i=1}^{n} |\mathbf{M}_{ii} - \lambda\mathbf{I}|, \qquad (1.13.25)$$

where M_{ii} is the ith principal minor of $\mathbf{A}$. From previous results we know $0 \leqslant \mathbf{M}_{ii} \leqslant \mathbf{A}$ and hence

$$-|\mathbf{M}_{ii} - \lambda_0\mathbf{I}| > 0 \qquad \text{(all } i). \qquad (1.13.26)$$

We then have

$$\frac{dP(\lambda_0)}{d\lambda} > 0 \qquad (1.13.27)$$

and hence λ_0 is a simple root.

Thus we have shown that λ_0 equals the spectral radius of $\mathbf{A}$ and further, if any element of $\mathbf{A}$ increases, then the spectral radius increases. Having established the Perron-Frobenius theorem for nonnegative irreducible matrices, we may immediately sharpen the earlier theorem regarding nonnegative matrices in general. In particular, if $\mathbf{A}$ is a nonnegative reducible matrix, then $\mathbf{A}$ has a nonnegative real eigenvalue which equals the spectral radius of $\mathbf{A}$, and as before the corresponding eigenvector has nonnegative components. To prove that the nonnegative eigenvalue is the spectral radius, we merely write $\mathbf{A}$ in reduced form

$$\mathbf{A} = \begin{bmatrix} \mathbf{A}_{11} & \mathbf{A}_{12} \\ 0 & \mathbf{A}_{22} \end{bmatrix} \tag{1.13.28}$$

and examine the matrices $\mathbf{A}_{11}$, $\mathbf{A}_{22}$. If they are also reducible, we continue the reduction until all diagonal submatrices are irreducible or null. If the $\mathbf{A}_{ii} = 0$, then *all* the eigenvalues are zero. If any $\mathbf{A}_{ii} \neq 0$ then the largest eigenvalue of the nonzero $\mathbf{A}_{ii}$ determines the spectral radius. Also, for two matrices $\mathbf{A}, \mathbf{B}$ such that $0 \leqslant \mathbf{B} \leqslant \mathbf{A}$, it follows from above that

$$r(\mathbf{B}) \leqslant r(\mathbf{A}).$$

We shall have occasion to use these results in Chapters III and IV when we discuss the technique for solving simultaneous equations.

1.14 Special Forms and Matrix Factorization

We now consider a few special matrices of interest in our later work. Consider first the square matrix

$$\mathbf{A} = \begin{bmatrix} a_{11} & a_{12} & \cdots & a_{1n} \\ a_{21} & a_{22} & \cdots & a_{2n} \\ \vdots & \vdots & & \vdots \\ a_{n1} & a_{n2} & \cdots & a_{nn} \end{bmatrix}. \tag{1.14.1}$$

The matrix $\mathbf{A}$ may be factored into the form

$$\mathbf{A} = \mathbf{L} + \mathbf{D} + \mathbf{U} \tag{1.14.2}$$

with

$$\mathbf{L} = \begin{bmatrix} 0 & 0 & \cdots & \cdots & 0 \\ a_{21} & 0 & \cdots & \cdots & 0 \\ \vdots & \vdots & & \vdots & \vdots \\ a_{n1} & a_{n2} & \cdots & a_{n,n-1} & 0 \end{bmatrix}. \tag{1.14.3a}$$

$$\mathbf{D} = \begin{bmatrix} a_{11} & 0 & \cdots & 0 \\ 0 & a_{22} & \cdots & 0 \\ \vdots & \vdots & & \vdots \\ 0 & & \cdots & a_{nn} \end{bmatrix} \qquad (1.14.3b)$$

$$\mathbf{U} = \begin{bmatrix} 0 & a_{12} & a_{13} & \cdots & a_{1n} \\ 0 & 0 & a_{23} & \cdots & a_{2n} \\ \vdots & \vdots & \vdots & & \vdots \\ & & & & a_{n-1,n} \\ & & & & 0 \end{bmatrix} \qquad (1.14.3c)$$

The matrix $\mathbf{L}$ contains elements only beneath the principal diagonal and is called strictly lower triangular. Similarly, $\mathbf{U}$, which has elements only above the main diagonal, is called strictly upper triangular. $\mathbf{D}$ is obviously diagonal. A matrix of the form $\mathbf{L} + \mathbf{D}$ is then called lower triangular, whereas a matrix of the form $\mathbf{U} + \mathbf{D}$ is called upper triangular. Notice that if $\mathbf{B}$ is defined as

$$\mathbf{B} = \mathbf{L} + \mathbf{D}, \qquad (1.14.4)$$

then $|\mathbf{B}| = |\mathbf{D}|$. If $|\mathbf{D}| \neq 0$, then $\mathbf{B}^{-1}$ exists and is of the form

$$\mathbf{B}^{-1} = \mathbf{L}' + \mathbf{D}'.$$

That is, if $\mathbf{B}$ lower triangular and if $\mathbf{B}^{-1}$ exists, then $\mathbf{B}^{-1}$ is also lower triangular. Similarly, if $\mathbf{C}$ upper triangular, and if $\mathbf{C}^{-1}$ exists, then $\mathbf{C}^{-1}$ is also upper triangular. We apply the terms upper triangular, diagonal, and lower triangular only to matrices whose elements are simple elements, and not submatrices.

Frequently one encounters a matrix of the form

$$\mathbf{A} = \begin{bmatrix} a_{11} & a_{12} & 0 & 0 & \cdots & 0 & 0 \\ a_{21} & a_{22} & a_{23} & 0 & \cdots & 0 & 0 \\ 0 & a_{32} & a_{33} & a_{34} & \cdots & 0 & 0 \\ 0 & 0 & a_{43} & a_{44} & \cdots & 0 & 0 \\ \vdots & \vdots & \vdots & \vdots & & \vdots & \vdots \\ 0 & 0 & 0 & 0 & \cdots & a_{n-1,n-1} & a_{n-1,n} \\ 0 & 0 & 0 & 0 & \cdots & a_{n,n-1} & a_{n,n} \end{bmatrix}. \qquad (1.14.5)$$

Such a matrix has elements only along the main diagonal and the two nearest adjacent diagonals. A matrix of this form is called a tridiagonal matrix. We shall encounter such matrices in approximating second derivatives of functions.

A generalization of the tridiagonal matrix is a matrix of the form

$$\mathbf{A} = \begin{bmatrix} \mathbf{A}_{11} & \mathbf{A}_{12} & 0 & \cdots & 0 & 0 \\ \mathbf{A}_{21} & \mathbf{A}_{22} & \mathbf{A}_{23} & \cdots & 0 & 0 \\ 0 & \mathbf{A}_{32} & \mathbf{A}_{33} & \cdots & 0 & 0 \\ \vdots & \vdots & \vdots & & \vdots & \vdots \\ 0 & 0 & 0 & \cdots & \mathbf{A}_{n-1,n-1} & \mathbf{A}_{n-1,n} \\ 0 & 0 & 0 & \cdots & \mathbf{A}_{n,n-1} & \mathbf{A}_{nn} \end{bmatrix}, \quad (1.14.6)$$

where the elements $\mathbf{A}_{ij}$ are themselves submatrices. If the submatrices $\mathbf{A}_{ii}$ are tridiagonal and if the submatrices $\mathbf{A}_{i,i\pm1}$ are diagonal, then the matrix $\mathbf{A}$ is called block tridiagonal. Such matrices occur in approximating the Laplacian operator in two dimensions.

The inversion of tridiagonal matrices may be readily accomplished by taking advantage of the large number of zero elements contained in the matrix. Consider the matrix equation

$$\mathbf{A}\mathbf{x} = \mathbf{y}, \quad (1.14.7)$$

where $\mathbf{A}$ is assumed tridiagonal. We factor $\mathbf{A}$ in the form

$$\mathbf{A} = \mathbf{C}\mathbf{B} \quad (1.14.8)$$

with

$$\mathbf{C} = \begin{bmatrix} 1 & 0 & \cdots & 0 & 0 \\ c_{21} & 1 & \cdots & 0 & 0 \\ 0 & c_{32} & \cdots & 0 & 0 \\ \vdots & \vdots & & \vdots & \vdots \\ 0 & 0 & \cdots & 1 & 0 \\ 0 & 0 & \cdots & c_{n,n-1} & 1 \end{bmatrix} \quad (1.14.9a)$$

and

$$\mathbf{B} = \begin{bmatrix} b_{11} & b_{12} & 0 & \cdots & 0 \\ 0 & b_{22} & b_{23} & \cdots & 0 \\ 0 & 0 & b_{33} & \cdots & 0 \\ \vdots & \vdots & \vdots & & \vdots \\ 0 & 0 & 0 & \cdots & b_{n-1,n} \\ 0 & 0 & 0 & \cdots & b_{nn} \end{bmatrix}. \quad (1.14.9b)$$

In order for the factorization to be true, we must require

$$b_{11} = a_{11},$$
$$b_{12} = a_{12},$$

(1.14.10a, b)

$$c_{21}b_{11} = a_{21},$$
$$c_{21}b_{12} + b_{22} = a_{22},$$
$$b_{23} = a_{23},$$

(1.14.11a, b, c)

$$c_{p,p-1}b_{p-1,p-1} = a_{p,p-1},$$
$$c_{p,p-1}b_{p-1,p} + b_{pp} = a_{pp},$$
$$b_{p,p+1} = a_{p,p+1},$$

(1.14.12a, b, c)

$$c_{n,n-1}b_{n-1,n-1} = a_{n,n-1},$$
$$c_{n,n-1}b_{n-1,n} + b_{n,n} = a_{n,n}.$$

(1.14.13a, b)

The above equations may be solved in the order b_{11}, b_{12}, c_{21}, b_{22}, b_{23}, ... , $c_{p,p-1}$, b_{pp}, $b_{p,p+1}$, ... , $c_{n,n-1}$, b_{nn}. In order for the solution to exist, we must require $|\mathbf{A}| \neq 0$. We now write Eq. (1.14.7) in the form

$$\mathbf{CBx} = \mathbf{y}.$$

(1.14.14)

We define a vector $\mathbf{z}$ such that

$$\mathbf{y} = \mathbf{Cz}.$$

(1.14.15)

This definition leads to the requirement

$$z_1 = y_1,$$
$$c_{21}z_1 + z_2 = y_2,$$
$$\vdots$$
$$c_{p,p-1}z_{p-1} + z_p = y_p,$$
$$\vdots$$
$$c_{n,n-1}z_{n-1} + z_n = y_n.$$

(1.14.16)

Equations (1.14.16) can readily be solved for $\mathbf{z}$. The entire set of equations now becomes

$$\mathbf{Bx} = \mathbf{z}.$$

(1.14.17)

The solution is then given by

$$b_{11}x_1 + b_{12}x_2 = z_1 ,$$

$$b_{22}x_2 + b_{23}x_3 = z_2 ,$$

$$\vdots$$

$$b_{pp}x_p + b_{p,p+1}x_{p+1} = z_p , \qquad (1.14.18)$$

$$\vdots$$

$$b_{nn}x_n = z_n ,$$

from which the x_i are readily found by starting from z_n and working in sequence back to z_1 .

Let us consider the number of operations[8] involved in this scheme (called matrix factorization) and compare this number with that involved in the Gauss reduction method. To generate the matrices **B** and **C**, we refer to equations (1.14.10, 11, 12, 13). The elements b_{11} , b_{12} are obtained without algebraic operations. To obtain c_{21} requires 1 operation (division), b_{22} requires 2 operations (multiplication and sub-traction). Therefore, 3 operations are needed per set of equations. For N unknowns, a total of $3N-3 \approx 3N$ operations are necessary.

To find the vector **z**, a total of $2N$ operations are necessary; likewise, for finding **x**, $3N$ operations are required. A total of $8N$ steps are needed to solve the original set of equations.

We now consider solving the same set of equations by the straight-forward reduction method. To reduce the first equation of (1.14.7) to the form

$$x_1 + a'_{12}x_2 = y'_1 \qquad (1.14.19)$$

requires 2 operations. To eliminate x_1 from the second equation requires 4 operations. There are, therefore, $6N$ steps to reduce the equations to the upper triangular form. An additional $2N$ steps are needed in the back substitution to solve. Consequently, a total of $9N$ steps are needed. Thus, the factorization and Gauss reduction method involve the same number of operations; indeed, the former is a special case of the latter (see Problem 9). We shall encounter the technique again in Chapter III.

---

[8] For computing purposes, the important operations are addition and multi-plication. For most computing devices, these operations take longer than control operations of various types.

A generalization of the method is applicable to block tridiagonal matrices but requires inversion of the submatrices occuring in Eq. (1.14.6).

References

There are innumerable books devoted to matrix algebra or having chapters concerning matrices. For a very readable discussion, references *1* and *2* are particularly recommended. References dealing with numerical methods for handling matrices (obtaining inverses, finding the eigenvalues and eigenvectors, etc.) include *3*, *4*, *5*, and *6*. A very rigorous discussion of matrices, including discussion of the Perron-Frobenius theorem and related topics, is found in *7*. An excellent distillation of the important matrix properties useful in the numerical solution of boundary-value problems is reference *8*.

1. Hildebrand, F. B., "Methods of Applied Mathematics." Prentice-Hall, New York, 1952.
2. Courant, R., and Hilbert, D., "Methods of Mathematical Physics," Vol. I. Wiley (Interscience), New York, 1953.
3. Faddeeva, V. N., "Computational Methods of Linear Algebra" (translation by C. D. Benster). Dover, New York, 1959.
4. Lanczos, C., "Applied Analysis." Prentice-Hall, Englewood Cliffs, New Jersey, 1956.
5. Bodewig, E., "Matrix Calculus." Wiley (Interscience), New York, 1956.
6. Householder, A. S., "Principles of Numerical Analysis." McGraw-Hill, New York, 1953.
7. Gantmacher, F. R., "The Theory of Matrices" (translation by K. A. Hirsch), Vols. I and II. Chelsea, New York, 1959.
8. Varga, R. S., "Matrix Iterative Analysis." Prentice-Hall, Englewood Cliffs, New Jersey, 1962.

Problems

1. Prove the associative law of matrix multiplication, that is

$$(\mathbf{AB})\mathbf{C} = \mathbf{A}(\mathbf{BC}).$$

2. Write out the following matrix products:

(a) $\quad [x_1, x_2, \ldots, x_n] \begin{bmatrix} y_1 \\ y_2 \\ \vdots \\ y_n \end{bmatrix}$

(b) $\quad \begin{bmatrix} x_1 \\ x_2 \\ \vdots \\ x_n \end{bmatrix} [y_1, y_2, \ldots, y_n]$

3. Prove Theorems 2 and 5 relating to determinants [p. 7].

4. Show that the variable x_i of a set of n homogeneous equations of rank $n - 1$ is proportional to any one of the cofactors of its coefficients in the coefficient matrix.

5. Prove that for any matrix $\mathbf{A}$ that $\mathbf{A}\mathbf{A}^T$ is a square symmetric matrix.

6. Prove that for square matrices $\mathbf{A}$ and $\mathbf{B}$ of order n that
$$\text{adj}(\mathbf{A}\,\mathbf{B}) = (\text{adj }\mathbf{B})(\text{adj }\mathbf{A}).$$

7. Find the transpose and inverse of the matrix
$$\begin{bmatrix} 1/2 & 1/\sqrt{2} & -1/2 \\ 1/\sqrt{2} & 0 & 1/\sqrt{2} \\ 1/2 & -1/\sqrt{2} & -1/2 \end{bmatrix}.$$

8. Derive the matrix describing the rotation of a vector, in a plane perpendicular to the z axis, about the z axis through the angle φ. Derive the matrix describing the rotation of a vector through the angle φ about the z axis and followed by a rotation through the angle θ in a plane containing the vector and the z axis.

9. Consider the solution of the equations $\mathbf{At} = \mathbf{u}$, or
$$\begin{bmatrix} a_{11} & a_{12} & a_{13} \\ a_{21} & a_{22} & a_{23} \\ a_{31} & a_{32} & a_{33} \end{bmatrix} \begin{bmatrix} t_1 \\ t_2 \\ t_3 \end{bmatrix} = \begin{bmatrix} u_1 \\ u_2 \\ u_3 \end{bmatrix}$$
by Gauss reduction. The reduced set of equations can be written $\mathbf{A't} = \mathbf{u'}$, or
$$\begin{bmatrix} 1 & a'_{12} & a'_{13} \\ 0 & 1 & a'_{23} \\ 0 & 0 & 1 \end{bmatrix} \begin{bmatrix} t_1 \\ t_2 \\ t_3 \end{bmatrix} = \begin{bmatrix} u'_1 \\ u'_2 \\ u'_3 \end{bmatrix}.$$
Derive the sequence of matrix operations which when applied successively to $\mathbf{A}$ yield $\mathbf{A'}$, that is, find the transformations $\mathbf{F}_i$ such that
$$\mathbf{F}_i \dots \mathbf{F}_2\mathbf{F}_1\mathbf{At} = \mathbf{A't}.$$

10. Modify the Gauss reduction in problem 9 to eliminate all unknowns from the ith row except a_{ii}, that is derive the reduced matrix in the form
$$\mathbf{A'} = \begin{bmatrix} 1 & 0 & 0 \\ 0 & 1 & 0 \\ 0 & 0 & 1 \end{bmatrix}.$$
This modification is sometimes called the Gauss-Jordan reduction.

11. If a set of linearly independent vectors $\mathbf{u}_n$ are orthogonalized by the Schmidt process to yield an orthogonal set $\mathbf{t}_n$, then the sets are related by a transformation in the form
$$\mathbf{t}_n = \mathbf{Tu}_n.$$
Derive an expression for the matrix $\mathbf{T}$.

12. Show that, if an array of vectors is linearly dependent, the array formed by transforming each vector similarly is also linearly dependent.

13. Find the eigenvalues and eigenvectors of the matrix

$$A = \begin{bmatrix} 3 & 0 & 1 \\ 0 & 2 & 0 \\ 1 & 0 & 3 \end{bmatrix}.$$

Diagonalize the above matrix. Express the vector x (below) in terms of the eigenvectors of A.

$$x = \begin{bmatrix} 1 \\ 1 \\ 1 \end{bmatrix}.$$

14. Use the results of the above problem to evaluate $A^7 x$ where A and x are given in problem 13.

15. If A is a real symmetric matrix, show that solutions of the inhomogeneous equation

$$At - \lambda t = u$$

can be written in the form

$$t = \sum_n \frac{\alpha_n}{\lambda_n - \lambda} e_n,$$

where λ_n, e_n are the eigenvalues and eigenvectors of A. (Assume $\lambda \neq \lambda_n$, all n). What are the coefficients α_n?

16. Show that the above problem has no solution if λ equals an eigenvalue of A unless u is orthogonal to the eigenvector corresponding to the eigenvalue λ.

17. Prove the solution t_1 of Eq. (1.10.7) may be chosen orthogonal to the vector e_1.

18. Show that if two matrices A and B commute, then A and B possess the same eigenvectors, and conversely.

19. Find the eigenvalues and eigenvectors of the following matrix operators

$$[a] \quad \begin{bmatrix} 1 & 0 & 0 \\ 0 & 1 & 0 \\ 0 & 0 & 1 \end{bmatrix}$$

$$[b] \quad \begin{bmatrix} 1 & 1 & 1 \\ 0 & 1 & 0 \\ 0 & 0 & 1 \end{bmatrix}$$

$$[c] \quad \begin{bmatrix} 1 & 1 & 1 \\ 0 & 1 & 1 \\ 0 & 0 & 1 \end{bmatrix}.$$

20. Show that the inverse of a nonsingular matrix A can be written

$$A^{-1} = M\Lambda^{-1}V^T,$$

where the matrices M and V are constructed from the eigenvectors of A and A^T, respectively, and where Λ is a diagonal matrix whose elements are the eigenvalues of A.

21. Show that the number of operations needed to solve a set of N simultaneous equations in N unknowns by Gaussian reduction is proportional to N^3 in general.

22. Solve the matrix differential equation

$$\frac{d\mathbf{u}(t)}{dt} = \mathbf{A}\mathbf{u}(t)$$

where

$$\mathbf{A} = \begin{bmatrix} 4 & 2 \\ -1 & 1 \end{bmatrix}$$

and $\mathbf{u}[0] = \mathbf{i} + \mathbf{j}$, i.e.,

$$\mathbf{u}(0) = \begin{bmatrix} 1 \\ 1 \end{bmatrix}.$$

Use matrix methods and express the solution in closed form.

II

DIFFERENCE EQUATIONS

In this chapter we shall review the elementary properties of finite difference equations. These equations can be readily solved by the use of high-speed digital computers. This type of equation arises in practice usually as an approximation to a differential equation whose solution cannot easily be found analytically. The prominence of differential equations in science and engineering leads to concentrating our numerical studies on the difference equation.

We shall be concerned primarily with techniques suited to digital computers, even though they certainly are not a panacea for all problems. Frequently the exact solution of a problem requires an infinite number of steps. Although a machine can perform an extremely large number of operations, this number is finite. For this reason, the numerical calculation must be terminated at some stage. Usually the termination of a calculation introduces an error, called the truncation error.

Other types of errors arise in the use of computers. A digital computer carries only a finite number of digits, and any number requiring more digits will be represented only approximately. The error introduced by carrying a limited number of digits is called the round-off error.

A large portion of the numerical analysts' effort is involved in estimating the errors of all types present in a given numerical procedure. In many cases reliable estimates of the error are unobtainable. Experiments or other measures are then necessary to test the accuracy of the approximation. Whenever practical we shall discuss errors; however, our main concern will be with the formulation of methods of solution.

2.1 A Simple Example

As an introduction to numerical techniques, we consider the problem of finding the area A under a curve as shown in Fig. 2.1.1. We assume the curve $y(x)$ is specified as the solution of the following first order differential equation.

$$\frac{dy}{dx} = f(x), \qquad (2.1.1)$$

where $f(x)$ and $y(a)$ are known. The analytic solution to this problem is simply

$$A = \int_a^b dx \left[\int f(x') \, dx' \right] + c(b - a), \qquad (2.1.2)$$

where the constant c is determined from the condition at $x = a$.

The elementary definition of a derivative, viz.,

$$\frac{dy}{dx} = \lim_{\Delta x \to 0} \frac{y(x + \Delta x) - y(x)}{\Delta x}, \qquad (2.1.3)$$

leads to a suitable numerical procedure. The limit is approximated by the so-called first divided difference:

$$\frac{y(x + \Delta x) - y(x)}{\Delta x} \approx f(x). \qquad (2.1.4)$$

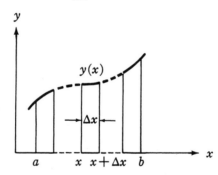

FIG. 2.1.1.   An arbitrary curve the area under which is to be calculated.

This approximation corresponds to replacing the actual curve between x and $x + \Delta x$ by the secant line. Let us divide the entire interval from a to b into J equal subintervals of width Δx. The abscissas are numbered from 0 to J starting at $x = a$. For the jth abscissa,

$$x_j = a + j\Delta x, \qquad j = 0, 1, ..., J. \qquad (2.1.5)$$

The corresponding ordinates are

$$y(x_j) \equiv y_j = y(a + j\Delta x). \qquad (2.1.6)$$

By Eqs. (2.1.4) and (2.1.6), we find[1] that

$$y_{j+1} = y_j + f(x_j)\, \Delta x, \tag{2.1.7}$$

and

$$y_j = y_0 + \sum_{k=0}^{j-1} f(x_k)\, \Delta x, \qquad j = 1, 2, ..., J. \tag{2.1.8}$$

To find the approximate area under the curve, we must estimate the behavior of $y(x)$ at values of x intermediate between the x_j . For simplicity we approximate $y(x)$ by a series of rectangles

$$y(x) = y_j, \qquad x_j \leqslant x < x_{j+1}. \tag{2.1.9}$$

The total area under $y(x)$ in the interval $a \leqslant x \leqslant b$ is then

$$A = \left\{ y_0 + \sum_{k=2}^{J} \left[y_0 + \sum_{j=0}^{k-2} f(x_j)\, \Delta x \right] \right\} \Delta x, \tag{2.1.10}$$

$$A = y_0(b - a) + \sum_{k=2}^{J} \sum_{j=0}^{k-2} f(x_j)(\Delta x)^2, \tag{2.1.11}$$

an approximate solution whose form is similar to the exact solution (2.1.2).

The present example is typical: divided differences replace derivatives, finite sums replace integrals. The independent variable is divided into a finite number of values.

2.2 Difference and Summation Operators

In order to develop approximations to differential and integral equations, it is convenient to define various difference and summation operators. In this section we shall introduce several operators of use and derive a number of relationships between the operators. Further, we shall show certain properties of the operators which are analogous to properties of differential and integral operators.

Let $h = \Delta x$, the spacing between abscissas. The first forward difference Δ is defined by

$$\Delta y(x) = y(x + h) - y(x), \tag{2.2.1}$$

[1] Henceforth the equals sign is used in relations such as (2.1.7), even though the divided difference is only an approximation.

the first backward difference ∇ by

$$\nabla y(x) = y(x) - y(x - h), \tag{2.2.2}$$

and the central difference operator δ by

$$\delta y(x) = y(x + h/2) - y(x - h/2). \tag{2.2.3}$$

The first forward difference operator was used in the previous section. Repeated application of the operators leads to the expression

$$\Delta^n y(x) = \sum_{k=0}^{n} (-)^k \frac{n!}{k!(n-k)!} y[x + (n-k)h], \tag{2.2.4}$$

$$\nabla^n y(x) = \sum_{k=0}^{n} (-)^k \frac{n!}{k!(n-k)!} y(x - kh), \tag{2.2.5}$$

and

$$\delta^{2n} y(x) = \sum_{k=0}^{2n} (-)^k \frac{(2n)!}{k!(2n-k)!} y[x + (n-k)h], \tag{2.2.6}$$

as may be seen by induction. It has been assumed that the spacing h is constant.

These difference operators have many properties in common with the differentiation operator, as can be seen from Table 2.2.1. The relations in the table are easily verified.

TABLE 2.2.1

PROPERTIES OF THE FORWARD DIFFERENCE OPERATOR

$$\Delta c = 0 \quad (c = \text{constant})$$
$$\Delta c f(x) = c \Delta f(x)$$
$$\Delta[f(x) + g(x)] = \Delta f(x) + \Delta g(x)$$
$$\Delta[f(x)g(x)] = f(x)\Delta g(x) + g(x + h)\Delta f(x)$$
$$\Delta \left[\frac{f(x)}{g(x)} \right] = \frac{g(x)\Delta f(x) - f(x)\Delta g(x)}{g(x + h)g(x)}$$
$$\Delta^m[\Delta^n f(x)] = \Delta^{m+n} f(x)$$

The shift operator E is defined by

$$E y(x) = y(x + h), \tag{2.2.7}$$

and the inverse shift operator E^{-1} by

$$E^{-1}y(x) = y(x - h).$$

(2.2.8)

The indefinite summation operator Σ (sometimes denoted $\varDelta^{-1}$) is defined as follows: if

$$z(x) = \varDelta y(x),$$

(2.2.9)

then

$$\sum z(x) = y(x).$$

(2.2.10)

The addition of an arbitrary constant is omitted for our purposes.

The various operators have many relations among themselves. For examples,

$$\frac{y(x+h) - y(x)}{\varDelta = E - 1,} = y(x+h) - 1 \Rightarrow y(x) = 1$$

(2.2.11)

$$\nabla = 1 - E^{-1},$$

(2.2.12)

$$\delta^2 = \varDelta \nabla,$$

(2.2.13)

$$\sum \varDelta = 1.$$

(2.2.14)

Table 2.2.2 lists various summation formulas.

TABLE 2.2.2

SUMMATION FORMULAS

$$\sum cf(x) = c \sum f(x)$$
$$\sum [f(x) + g(x)] = \sum f(x) + \sum g(x)$$
$$\sum [f(x) \varDelta g(x)] = f(x)g(x) - \sum g(x + h) \varDelta f(x)$$
$$\sum [f(x + h) \varDelta g(x)] = f(x)g(x) - \sum g(x) \varDelta f(x)$$

The factorial series are defined by

$$x^{(n)} = x[x - h][x - 2h] \dots [x - (n - 1)h],$$

(2.2.15)

$$x^{)n(} = x[x + h][x + 2h] \dots [x + (n - 1)h].$$

(2.2.16)

Let the arguments be denoted by subscripts, viz.,

$$x_j = x + jh,$$

(2.2.17)

$$x_{-j} = x - jh,$$

(2.2.18)

so that

$$x^{(n)} = x_0 x_{-1} \cdots x_{-n+1},$$
(2.2.19)

$$x^{)n(} = x_0 x_1 \cdots x_{n-1}.$$
(2.2.20)

Note that

$$x^{(1)} = x_0,$$
(2.2.21)

and define

$$x^{(0)} = 1.$$
(2.2.22)

Application of the operator Δ to $x^{(n)}$ shows that

$$\frac{\Delta x^{(n)}}{h} = n x^{(n-1)},$$
(2.2.23)

which is analogous to the usual rule for differentiation. A rule analogous to the usual one for integration is found by applying the operator Σ to Eq. (2.2.23).

$$\sum x^{(n)} = \frac{x^{(n+1)}}{(n+1)h}.$$
(2.2.24)

A series of numbers summed between definite limits is called a definite sum. Let $z(x)$ be such that

$$z(x) = \Delta y(x).$$

We observe that

$$\sum_{j=j_1}^{j_2} z(x_j) = y(x_j) \Big|_{j_1}^{j_2+1}.$$
(2.2.25)

The sum formula (2.2.25) is very useful in summing the terms of a series in n^j. For example, consider the sum of the first n terms of the series in n^3. Since $n^{(j)}$ is a polynomial of degree j in n, any polynomial of degree j can be expressed in terms of the factorial series up to and including degree j. In the example

$$n^{(1)} = n,$$
$$n^{(2)} = n(n-1) = n^2 - n,$$
$$n^{(3)} = n(n-1)(n-2) = n^3 - 3n^2 + 2n,$$
(2.2.26)

so that

$$n^3 = n^{(3)} + 3n^{(2)} + n^{(1)}.$$
(2.2.27)

Therefore,

$$\sum_1^N n^3 = \left[\frac{n^{(4)}}{4} + n^{(3)} + \frac{n^{(2)}}{2} \right]_1^{N+1} \tag{2.2.28}$$

$$= \frac{(N+1)^{(4)}}{4} + (N+1)^{(3)} + \frac{(N+1)^{(2)}}{2} \tag{2.2.29}$$

$$= \frac{N^2(N+1)^2}{4}. \tag{2.2.30}$$

2.3 Formation of Difference Equations and Truncation Error

The construction of a difference equation from a differential equation is not a unique process. Many different difference approximations are possible for a given differential equation. The selection of a particular difference relation is usually determined by the nature of the truncation error associated with the approximation.

As an introductory example, let us develop expressions for the second derivative in terms of the forward, backward, and central difference operators. A uniform spacing h is postulated.

We assume the function $y(x)$ may be expanded in a Taylor series in the closed interval $x - 2h \leqslant x \leqslant x + 2h$. We have

$$y(x \pm h) = y(x) \pm hy'(x) + \frac{h^2 y''(x)}{2!} + \cdots + \frac{(\pm)^n h^n y^{(n)}(x)}{n!} + \cdots, \tag{2.3.1}$$

$$y(x \pm 2h) = y(x) \pm (2h)y'(x) + \frac{(2h)^2}{2!} y''(x) + \cdots + \frac{(\pm)^n (2h)^n y^{(n)}(x)}{n!} + \cdots, \tag{2.3.2}$$

where a prime denotes differentiation. We have then

$$\frac{y(x+2h) - 2y(x+h) + y(x)}{h^2} \equiv y''(x) + hy'''(x) + O(h^2) + \cdots, \tag{2.3.3}$$

or

$$\frac{\Delta^2 y(x)}{h^2} = \frac{d^2 y(x)}{dx^2} + O(h), \tag{2.3.4}$$

where the notation $O(h)$ means the first term neglected is of order h. Similarly we have

$$\frac{\nabla^2 y(x)}{h^2} = \frac{d^2 y(x)}{dx^2} + O(h). \tag{2.3.5}$$

However,

$$\frac{\delta^2 y(x)}{h^2} = \frac{d^2 y(x)}{dx^2} + O(h^2). \tag{2.3.6}$$

The forward and backward differences are accurate to order h; the central difference, to order h^2, a result that is intuitively and geometrically obvious. The second forward difference approximates the second derivative by taking the difference in slope of the secant lines de and cd in Fig. 2.3.1. The backward difference uses the secants ab and bc, whereas the central difference uses the lines bc and cd. Since the latter pair are centered with respect to the point of interest, we should expect the central difference to be more accurate, as indeed it is.

To consider higher order approximations and other derivatives, we return to the Taylor series. We then have

$$y(x + h) = y(x) + h \frac{d}{dx} y(x) + \frac{h^2}{2!} \left(\frac{d}{dx}\right)^2 y(x) + \cdots + \frac{h^n}{n!} \left(\frac{d}{dx}\right)^n y(x) + \cdots, \tag{2.3.7}$$

or

$$Ey(x) = \left[1 + h \frac{d}{dx} + \frac{\left(h \frac{d}{dx}\right)^2}{2!} + \cdots + \frac{\left(h \frac{d}{dx}\right)^n}{n!} + \cdots \right] y(x). \tag{2.3.8}$$

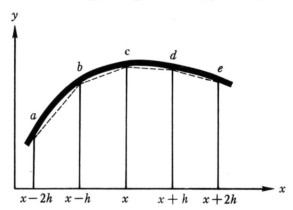

FIG. 2.3.1.   Approximation of a curve by secant lines.

The series in brackets is the expansion for the exponential and hence we have (formally)

$$E = \exp\left(h \frac{d}{dx}\right). \tag{2.3.9}$$

Treating Eq. (2.3.9) as an identity, we may derive expressions for any order derivative in terms of the various difference operators. For example,

$$\frac{dy(x)}{dx} = \left(\frac{1}{h} \ln E\right) y(x) = \frac{1}{h} \ln (\Delta + 1)y(x). \tag{2.3.10}$$

Using the logarithmic expansion, we have

$$\frac{dy(x)}{dx} = \frac{1}{h} \left[\Delta - \frac{\Delta^2}{2} + \frac{\Delta^3}{3} \cdots\right] y(x). \tag{2.3.11}$$

For higher order derivatives, we have

$$\frac{d^n y(x)}{dx^n} = \frac{1}{h^n} [\ln (\Delta + 1)]^n y(x), \tag{2.3.12}$$

$$= \frac{1}{h^n} \left[\Delta^n - \frac{n}{2} \Delta^{n+1} + \frac{n(3n + 5)}{24} \Delta^{n+2} + \cdots\right] y(x). \tag{2.3.13}$$

In terms of the backward difference operator, we have

$$\frac{dy(x)}{dx} = -\frac{1}{h} \ln (1 - \nabla)y(x), \tag{2.3.14}$$

or

$$\frac{dy(x)}{dx} = \frac{1}{h} \left[\nabla + \frac{\nabla^2}{2} + \frac{\nabla^3}{3} + \cdots\right] y(x). \tag{2.3.15}$$

The higher derivatives are

$$\frac{d^n y(x)}{dx^n} = \frac{1}{h^n} \left[\nabla^n + \frac{n}{2} \nabla^{n+1} + \frac{n(3n + 5)}{24} \nabla^{n+2} + \cdots\right] y(x). \tag{2.3.16}$$

For the central difference operator, one is usually interested in even powers of the operator. By performing the necessary expansions (see problem 4), we find

$$\frac{d^2 y(x)}{dx^2} = \frac{1}{h^2} \left[\delta^2 - \frac{1}{12} \delta^4 + \frac{1}{90} \delta^6 + \cdots\right] y(x), \tag{2.3.17}$$

and

$$\frac{d^{2n} y(x)}{dx^{2n}} = \frac{1}{h^{2n}} \left[\delta^{2n} - \frac{n}{12} \delta^{2n+2} + \cdots\right] y(x). \tag{2.3.18}$$

For any differential operator, we may use the expansions (2.3.13), (2.3.16), or (2.3.18) to develop a difference relation. To determine the order of the truncation error, we must express the various differences in terms of the function and its derivatives, again using the Taylor series. From (2.3.9) we find

$$\Delta = \exp h \frac{d}{dx} - 1 \tag{2.3.19}$$

$$= h \frac{d}{dx} + \frac{\left(h \frac{d}{dx}\right)^2}{2!} + \dots + \frac{\left(h \frac{d}{dx}\right)^n}{n!} + \dots . \tag{2.3.20}$$

Powers of the difference operator are then

$$\Delta^n = \left(h \frac{d}{dx}\right)^n + \frac{n}{2} \left(h \frac{d}{dx}\right)^{n+1} + \frac{n(3n+1)}{24} \left(h \frac{d}{dx}\right)^{n+2} + \dots . \tag{2.3.21}$$

Similarly,

$$(-\nabla)^n = \left(-h \frac{d}{dx}\right)^n + \frac{n}{2} \left(-h \frac{d}{dx}\right)^{n+1} + \frac{n(3n+1)}{24} \left(-h \frac{d}{dx}\right)^{n+2} + \dots \tag{2.3.22}$$

and

$$\delta^{2n} = \left(h \frac{d}{dx}\right)^{2n} + \frac{n}{12} \left(h \frac{d}{dx}\right)^{2n+2} + \frac{n}{360} \left(h \frac{d}{dx}\right)^{2n+4} + \dots . \tag{2.3.23}$$

Using a high order approximation reduces the truncation error associated with the substitution. As an example, consider approximating the first derivative of a function with the expression

$$\frac{dy}{dx} = \frac{1}{h} \left[\Delta - \frac{1}{2} \Delta^2 + \frac{\Delta^3}{3}\right] y. \tag{2.3.24}$$

From (2.3.21) we have

$$\frac{1}{h} \left[\Delta - \frac{\Delta^2}{2} + \frac{\Delta^3}{3}\right] = \frac{d}{dx} + \frac{h^3}{4} \frac{d^4}{dx^4} . \tag{2.3.25}$$

Consequently the approximation has a truncation error of order h^3 whereas the simple expression

$$\frac{d}{dx} = \frac{\Delta}{h} \tag{2.3.26}$$

has a truncation error of order h.

It should be noted that the simple form (2.3.26) is merely a two-point formula, viz.,

$$\frac{y(x+h)-y(x)}{h} \approx \frac{dy}{dx},$$

(2.3.27)

whereas (2.3.24) is a four-point formula

$$\frac{2y(x+3h)-9y(x+2h)+18y(x+h)-11y(x)}{6h} \approx \frac{dy}{dx}.$$

(2.3.28)

The more complicated expression (2.3.28) requires more effort in computation and furthermore is a third order difference relation. In the next section we shall discuss the properties of solutions of difference equations and indicate additional difficulties encountered with using high order approximations.

Thus far we have only considered approximating rather elementary differential expressions. In later chapters we shall introduce a method of constructing appropriate difference equations for more involved equations which arise in the multigroup diffusion theory and transport theory.

2.4 Analytic Solution of Difference Equations

In order to analyze the truncation error in replacing differential equations with difference equations, we now consider the analytic solution of difference equations. Generally speaking, the methods of solution parallel the techniques used in the differential calculus. Furthermore, the solutions of an inhomogeneous difference equation can be found by specializing the corresponding solutions of the homogeneous equation.

Except for a few simple forms of a difference equation, it is impossible to obtain a solution in closed form. Recourse is then made to a series evaluation with an attendent question of convergence. Once a problem has achieved such a degree of complexity, it is usually more satisfactory to consider numerical solutions. In the next chapter we shall take up methods of numerically solving finite difference equations.

The order of a difference equation is the number of intervals separating the largest and smallest arguments of the dependent variable. The order is not necessarily the highest power of a difference operator. For example,

$$\Delta^2 y(x) - \nabla y(x) = y(x+2h) - 2y(x+h) + y(x-h) = 0 \quad (2.4.1)$$

and

$$y(x + 3h) - 2xy(x + h) + y(x - h) = 3x \qquad (2.4.2)$$

are equations of third and fourth order respectively.

A linear difference equation is one in which no products of the dependent variable with itself or any of its differences appear. Thus Eq. (2.4.1) and (2.4.2) are linear, whereas

$$x^2y(x)\, \Delta^2y(x) + \nabla^2y^2(x) = 0 \qquad (2.4.3)$$

is nonlinear.

A difference equation is homogeneous if all non-zero terms involve the dependent variable; otherwise it is inhomogeneous. Equation (2.4.1) and (2.4.3) are homogeneous, but Eq. (2.4.2) is inhomogeneous. Furthermore, a difference equation may have coefficients which are constant or functions of the independent variable. If the coefficients are constant, we speak of a difference equation with constant coefficients, otherwise we speak of an equation with variable coefficients.

2.4.1   THE FIRST ORDER DIFFERENCE EQUATION

A first order difference equation may be simply written as

$$y_{j+1} - y_j = hf_j \qquad (2.4.4)$$

for which the solution is

$$y_j = y_0 + h \sum_{k=0}^{j-1} f_k . \qquad (2.4.5)$$

The solution is given by the homogeneous solution y_0 plus the particular solution, due to the inhomogeneous term f_j . A slightly more complicated first order equation would be

$$\Delta y_j = y_{j+1} - y_j = a_j y_j . \qquad (2.4.6)$$

The solution is obviously

$$y_j = y_0 \prod_{k=0}^{j-1} (1 + a_k), \qquad (2.4.7)$$

$$= y_0 \exp\left[\sum_{k=0}^{j-1} \ln (1 + a_k) \right] . \qquad (2.4.8)$$

The second form of the solution corresponds to the analytic solution of the differential analog to (2.4.6).

As might be inferred from the above examples, all difference equations can be treated as recurrence relations. The approach is generally not too useful for more difficult equations, however; consequently we seek other more powerful techniques.

2.4.2 HOMOGENEOUS DIFFERENCE EQUATIONS WITH CONSTANT COEFFICIENTS

Homogeneous equations with constant coefficients can be treated by methods precisely the same as those used in differential equations. The general form of the difference equations would be

$$\sum_{i=0}^{n} a_i y_{k+n-i} = 0. \tag{2.4.9}$$

We use the trial solution

$$y_k = \beta^k = e^{mk}. \tag{2.4.10}$$

Inserting (2.4.10) in (2.4.9), we find nontrivial solutions exist if β is a root of the polynomial

$$\sum_{i=0}^{n} (a_i)\beta^{n-i} = 0. \tag{2.4.11}$$

Thus, if β_j are the roots of (2.4.11)

$$y_k = \sum_{j=1}^{n} b_j \beta_j^k = \sum_{j=1}^{n} b_j \exp\left[k \ln \beta_j\right]. \tag{2.4.12}$$

The n coefficients b_j are determined by suitable boundary conditions. Several examples will illustrate the procedure. The solution of

$$y_{k+2} - 4y_{k+1} + 2y_k = 0, \tag{2.4.13}$$

or

$$\Delta^2 y_k - 2\Delta y_k - y_k = 0, \tag{2.4.14}$$

is found by letting y_k be given the first form of (2.4.10). Thus we have

$$\beta^2 - 4\beta + 2 = 0, \tag{2.4.15}$$

i.e.,

$$\beta = 2 \pm \sqrt{2}. \tag{2.4.16}$$

The solution is then

$$y_k = b_1(2 + \sqrt{2})^k + b_2(2 - \sqrt{2})^k. \tag{2.4.17}$$

As a second example, we note that

$$y_{k+2} - 6y_{k+1} + 11y_k - 6y_{k-1} = 0 \qquad (2.4.18)$$

has nontrivial solutions determined by the equation

$$\beta^3 - 6\beta^2 + 11\beta - 6 = 0. \qquad (2.4.19)$$

Thus, the solution is

$$y_k = c_1 + c_2 2^k + c_3 3^k. \qquad (2.4.20)$$

As with differential equations, if one or more roots of the polynomial Eq. (2.4.11) are repeated, then a special form of the solution results. Suppose a root, say β_0, is repeated s times, the other roots being simple. Let the difference operator be represented by Θ, i.e., let

$$\Theta y_k = \sum_{i=0}^{n} a_i y_{k+n-i} = 0, \qquad (2.4.21)$$

where k is the independent variable. Then,

$$\Theta \beta^k = \beta^k (\beta - \beta_0)^s (\beta - \beta_1) \dots (\beta - \beta_{n-s}) = 0, \qquad (2.4.22)$$

where β_i are the various roots of Eq. (2.4.21). Further, we note that

$$\frac{\partial^m}{\partial \beta^m} [\Theta \beta^k] = \Theta \left[\frac{\partial^m \beta^k}{\partial \beta^m} \right] = \Theta \left[\frac{k!}{(k-m)!} \beta^{k-m} \right]. \qquad (2.4.23)$$

But according to Eq. (2.4.22)

$$\frac{\partial^m}{\partial \beta^m} [\Theta \beta^k] = 0 \qquad (2.4.24)$$

at $\beta = \beta_0$ if $m \leqslant s - 1$. Hence, $[k!/(k-m)!] \beta_0^{k-m}$, i.e., $[k!/(k-m)!] \beta_0^k$, must be a solution of (2.4.21). In general, therefore,

$$y_k = \beta_0^k \sum_{i=0}^{s-1} b_i k^i \qquad (2.4.25)$$

must be a solution of (2.4.11). The totality of solutions consists of the roots β_1, β_2, ... , β_{n-s} plus the s independent solutions in (2.4.25). An example illustrates the matter. We desire to solve

$$y_{k+2} - 4y_{k+1} + 4y_k = 0. \qquad (2.4.26)$$

The solutions are

$$\beta_1 = 2, \beta_2 = 2.$$

The complete solution is then

$$y_k = c_1 2^k + c_2 k 2^k. \tag{2.4.27}$$

Several special forms of solutions for second order equations are worth noting. If the equation is

$$y_{k+2} - b y_{k+1} + y_k = 0, \tag{2.4.28}$$

then the substitution of $y_k = e^{mk}$ yields

$$e^{m(k+1)}(e^m - b + e^{-m}) = 0. \tag{2.4.29}$$

If $b > 2$, a more convenient way of writing Eq. (2.4.29) is

$$2 \cosh m = b \tag{2.4.30}$$

or

$$m = \cosh^{-1}(b/2) = \pm\alpha. \tag{2.4.31}$$

The solution is then

$$y_k = c_1 e^{\alpha k} + c_2 e^{-\alpha k}, \tag{2.4.32}$$

which can also be written

$$y_k = c_3 \cosh \alpha k + c_4 \sinh \alpha k. \tag{2.4.33}$$

Another special form may be derived for the equation

$$y_{k+2} - b y_{k+1} + a y_k = 0 \tag{2.4.34}$$

for $b^2 < 4a$. In this case, the roots are complex conjugate, and a solution is of the form

$$y_k = \rho^k[c_1 e^{\iota\theta k} + c_2 e^{-\iota\theta k}], \tag{2.4.35}$$

where $\iota = \sqrt{-1}$, ρ is the magnitude of the roots β_i of Eq. (2.4.21), and θ is the arctan of the ratio of imaginary part to real part of the roots. Alternatively

$$y_k = \rho^k[c_3 \sin \theta k + c_4 \cos \theta k]. \tag{2.4.36}$$

2.4.3   INHOMOGENEOUS DIFFERENCE EQUATIONS

The solution $y(j)$ of an inhomogeneous difference equation consists of a solution to the homogeneous equation, say $y_H(j)$, plus a particular solution, say $y_P(j)$, of the inhomogeneous part. In certain cases, the particular solution may be found by the method of undetermined coefficients. We shall not discuss this method because it is identical to the method of undetermined coefficients used with differential equations.

A more general procedure is the method of variation of parameters, which applies to difference equations with constant or variable coefficients. Let the difference equation be of the form

$$\Theta y(j) = \sum_{k=0}^{n} p_k(j)y(j + k) = S(j), \tag{2.4.37}$$

where $p_n(j) = 1$, $p_0(j) \neq 0$, and all other $p_k(j)$ are arbitrary. We assume we have n linearly independent solutions for the homogeneous form of Eq. (2.4.37). Denote the homogeneous solution

$$y_H(j) = \sum_{i=1}^{n} c_i y_i(j). \tag{2.4.38}$$

We assume a particular solution of the form

$$y_P(j) = \sum_{i=1}^{n} a_i(j)y_i(j). \tag{2.4.39}$$

In order to find the $a_i(j)$ we need n simultaneous equations relating the $a_i(j)$. To accomplish this end, we consider Eq. (2.4.39) at the point $j + 1$; we have

$$y_P(j + 1) = \sum_{i=1}^{n} a_i(j + 1)y_i(j + 1) = \sum_{i=1}^{n} a_i(j)y_i(j + 1) + \sum_{i=1}^{n} \Delta a_i(j)y_i(j + 1), \tag{2.4.40}$$

since

$$a_i(j + 1) = a_i(j) + \Delta a_i(j). \tag{2.4.41}$$

In order that the form of the solution be similar to Eq. (2.4.39), we try the condition

$$\sum_{i=1}^{n} \Delta a_i(j)y_i(j + 1) = 0 \tag{2.4.42}$$

to see where it leads. Continuing in this manner, we generate a series of solutions of the form

$$y_P(j + m) = \sum_{i=1}^{n} a_i(j)y_i(j + m), \tag{2.4.43}$$

and assumed conditions

$$\sum_{i=1}^{n} \Delta a_i(j) y_i(j + m) = 0, \qquad 1 \leqslant m \leqslant n - 1. \qquad (2.4.44)$$

At the last point we then find

$$y_P(j + n) = \sum_{i=1}^{n} a_i(j) y_i(j + n) + \sum_{i=1}^{n} \Delta a_i(j) y_i(j + n). \qquad (2.4.45)$$

We now insert Eqs. (2.4.39), (2.4.40), etc., and Eq. (2.4.45) in the original difference equation (2.4.37). We use the assumption that terms such as (2.4.44), vanish, and further, we use the fact that the $y_i(j)$ satisfy the homogeneous equation. The result of the algebra leads to the condition

$$\sum_{i=1}^{n} \Delta a_i(j) y_i(j + n) = S(j). \qquad (2.4.46)$$

The set of assumptions [Eqs. (2.4.44) and (2.4.46)] represent a set of simultaneous equations

$$y_1(j + 1)\Delta a_1 + y_2(j + 1)\Delta a_2 + \ldots + y_n(j + 1)\Delta a_n = 0,$$
$$y_1(j + 2)\Delta a_1 + y_2(j + 2)\Delta a_2 + \ldots + y_n(j + 2)\Delta a_n = 0,$$
$$\vdots \qquad (2.4.47)$$
$$y_1(j + n)\Delta a_1 + y_2(j + n)\Delta a_2 + \ldots + y_n(j + n)\Delta a_n = S(j).$$

The set of Eqs. (2.4.47) always has a unique solution since the determinant of the coefficients, $y_i(j + m)$, cannot vanish since the y_i are linearly independent by hypothesis. Once the Δa_i are found, the a_i are found by summation. Note that if $S(j) = 0$, then the only solution of Eq. (2.4.47) is the trivial solution as indeed it must be.

The procedure is illustrated by the equation

$$\delta^2 y(j) = y(j + 1) - 2y(j) + y(j - 1) = j. \qquad (2.4.48)$$

The homogeneous solution is

$$y_H(j) = c_1 + c_2 j. \qquad (2.4.49)$$

Hence we have

$$y_1(j) = 1$$
$$y_2(j) = j. \qquad (2.4.50)$$

The particular solution is then

$$y_P(j) = a_1(j) + a_2(j)j, \tag{2.4.51}$$

which leads to the equation

$$\Delta a_1(j) + j\Delta a_2(j) = 0,$$
$$\Delta a_1(j) + (j+1)\Delta a_2(j) = j. \tag{2.4.52}$$

We find that

$$\Delta a_1(j) = -j^2, \qquad \Delta a_2(j) = j \tag{2.4.53}$$

from which we find

$$a_1(j) = a_1(0) - \sum_{i=0}^{j-1} i^2 = -\frac{(j-1)}{6} j(2j-1), \tag{2.4.54}$$

the constant $a_1(0)$ being taken as zero, since it may be included in the homogeneous solution anyway. Likewise,

$$a_2(j) = \sum_{i=0}^{j-1} i = \frac{j(j-1)}{2}. \tag{2.4.55}$$

The complete solution is then

$$y(j) = c_1 + c_2 j + \frac{j^3}{6}.$$

As the second example we consider the most general first order equation

$$\Delta y(j) = c(j)y(j) + b(j). \tag{2.4.56}$$

The homogeneous solution by Eq. (2.4.7) is

$$y_H(j) = y_0 \prod_{i=0}^{j-1} [1 + c(i)], \tag{2.4.57}$$

where y_0 is a constant of integration. The particular solution is taken to be

$$y_P(j) = a(j) \prod_{i=0}^{j-1} [1 + c(i)]y_0. \tag{2.4.58}$$

The usual condition yields

$$y_0 \prod_{i=0}^{j} [1 + c(i)]\Delta a(j) = b(j)$$

or

$$a(j) = \frac{1}{y_0} \sum_{k=0}^{j-1} b(k) \prod_{i=0}^{k} [1 + c(i)]^{-1}, \tag{2.4.59}$$

the constant of "integration" being incorporated in the homogeneous solution. The complete solution is thus

$$y(j) = y_0 \prod_{n=0}^{j-1} [1 + c(n)] + \prod_{n=0}^{j-1} [1 + c(n)] \sum_{k=0}^{j-1} b(k) \prod_{i=0}^{k} [1 + c(i)]^{-1}. \tag{2.4.60}$$

Although the method of variation of parameters is quite general, its ability is limited to those problems for which the homogeneous solution can be found. Unfortunately the number of problems for which analytic forms of the homogeneous solution can be found is limited. Indeed, there is no general technique for solving difference equations with variable coefficients, save for rather special cases. For intractable problems approximate methods are necessary. The bulk of the remainder of the text is specifically devoted to methods of finding approximate solutions to difference equations.

2.5 Partial Difference Equations

Partial difference equations arise from problems involving two or more independent variables. Such equations are solved by methods similar to those used in solving partial differential equations. The method of separation of variables will be used in this section. We shall consider two simple problems: an initial value problem and a boundary value problem.

For the first example consider the heat flow equation

$$\frac{\partial T(x, t)}{\partial t} = \frac{\partial^2 T(x, t)}{\partial x^2}, \tag{2.5.1}$$

where T is the temperature. One possible difference approximation to Eq. (2.5.1) is

$$\frac{\Delta T}{h_t} = \frac{\delta^2 T}{h_x^2} \tag{2.5.2}$$

with h_t as the time increment and h_x the spatial increment, both assumed constant. The solution is desired in the semi-infinite strip $0 \leqslant x \leqslant a$,

$0 \leqslant t \leqslant \infty$, as in Fig. 2.5.1. The difference equation is applied at the mesh points (k, l), that is, we desire $T(k, l) = T_{k,l}$. We shall assume the boundary conditions in the form

$$T_{0,l} = T_{K,l} = 0, \quad \text{all } l, \tag{2.5.3a}$$

and initial conditions of the form

$$T_{k,0} = f_k, \quad 0 \leqslant k \leqslant K. \tag{2.5.3b}$$

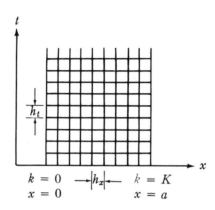

FIG. 2.5.1.   Mesh for the solution of the time dependent heat-flow problem.

As in the treatment of differential equations, we assume the function T separable in the form

$$T_{k,l} = R_k S_l, \tag{2.5.4}$$

where R_k is a function of k only, and S_l a function of l only. Substituting the trial solution in the original equation, we find

$$\frac{\Delta S_l}{h_t S_l} = \frac{\delta^2 R_k}{h_x^2 R_k} = -\alpha^2, \tag{2.5.5}$$

where α^2 is an advisedly chosen separation constant and independent of k and l. The resulting ordinary equations in S and R may be solved by the methods of the previous section. We find

$$R_k = a_n \sin \frac{n\pi k}{K}, \quad n = 1, 2, \dots K - 1, \tag{2.5.6}$$

$$S_l = S_0 \exp\left[l \ln\left(1 - \alpha^2 h_t\right)\right], \tag{2.5.7}$$

where S_0 is an integration constant and

$$\alpha^2 = \frac{2}{h_x^2}\left[1 - \cos\frac{n\pi}{K}\right]. \tag{2.5.8}$$

The complete solution is

$$T_{k,l} = \sum_{n=1}^{K-1} a_n \sin\frac{n\pi k}{K}\exp\left[l\ln(1 - \alpha^2 h_t)\right], \tag{2.5.9}$$

where the constant S_0 has been absorbed in the a_n. The coefficients a_n are computed from the initial condition at $l = 0$. To this end, we use the relation (see problem 11),

$$\sum_{k=0}^{K-1}\sin\frac{k\pi n}{K}\sin\frac{k\pi m}{K} = \frac{K}{2}(1 - \delta_{n0})\delta_{mn}. \tag{2.5.10}$$

Multiplying (2.5.9) by $\sin(m\pi k/K)$ and summing over k from 0 to $K - 1$, we have, at $l = 0$,

$$a_m = \frac{2}{K}\sum_{k=1}^{K-1} f_k \sin\frac{m\pi k}{K}, \tag{2.5.11}$$

which completes the solution.

In connection with the evaluation of coefficients, the following relations are useful:

$$\sum_{k=0}^{K-1}\cos\frac{k\pi n}{K}\cos\frac{k\pi m}{K} = \begin{cases} \dfrac{K}{2}(\delta_{n0} + 1), & m = n, \\ 0, & m \neq n,\ m - n\ \text{even}, \\ 1, & m \neq n,\ m - n\ \text{odd}, \end{cases} \tag{2.5.12}$$

$$\sum_{k=0}^{K-1}\sin\frac{k\pi n}{K}\cos\frac{k\pi m}{K} = \begin{cases} 0, & m = n, \\ 0, & m \neq n,\ m - n\ \text{even}, \\ \cot\dfrac{\pi(n - m)}{2K} + \cot\dfrac{\pi(n + m)}{2K}, & m \neq n,\ m - n\ \text{odd}. \end{cases} \tag{2.5.13}$$

$$\sum_{k=1}^{K}\cos\frac{2\pi kn}{K}\cos\frac{2\pi km}{K} = \frac{K}{2}\delta_{nm}(1 + \delta_{n0}), \tag{2.5.14}$$

$$\sum_{k=0}^{K}\sin\frac{2\pi km}{K}\sin\frac{2\pi kn}{K} = \frac{K}{2}\delta_{nm}(1 - \delta_{n0}), \tag{2.5.15}$$

$$\sum_{k=0}^{K}\cos\frac{2\pi kn}{K}\sin\frac{2\pi km}{K} = 0. \tag{2.5.16}$$

As an example of a boundary value problem, we consider the Laplace difference equation

$$\frac{\delta^2 \psi_{kj}}{h_x^2} + \frac{\delta^2 \psi_{kj}}{h_y^2} = 0 \tag{2.5.17}$$

in the interval $0 \leqslant x \leqslant a$, $0 \leqslant y \leqslant b$. We take a uniform spacing $h_x = a/K$ and $h_y = b/J$. The boundary conditions are

$$\psi_{0j} = \psi_{Kj} = 0,$$
$$\psi_{kJ} = 0,$$
$$\psi_{k0} = g_k . \tag{2.5.18}$$

The mesh for this problem is shown in Fig. 2.5.2. The dependent variable may be separated into two functions, say R_k and S_j. We assume then,

$$\psi_{kj} = R_k S_j . \tag{2.5.19}$$

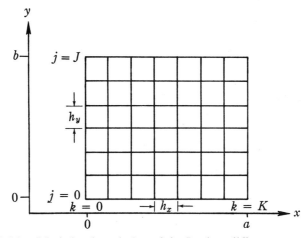

FIG. 2.5.2.   Mesh for the solution of the Laplace difference equation.

Substituting into (2.5.17), we have

$$\frac{R_{k+1} - 2R_k + R_{k-1}}{R_k h_x^2} = - \frac{S_{j+1} - 2S_j + S_{j-1}}{S_j h_y^2} = -\alpha^2. \tag{2.5.20}$$

From the boundary conditions, we solve the above equations to find

$$R_k = \sin \frac{n\pi k}{K}, \qquad n = 1, 2, ..., K - 1, \tag{2.5.21}$$
$$S_j = a_n \sinh \beta_n (J - j), \tag{2.5.22}$$

where

$$\alpha_n^2 = \frac{2}{h_x^2}\left(1 - \cos\frac{n\pi}{K}\right),$$

(2.5.23)

and

$$\beta_n = \cosh^{-1}\left(1 + \frac{\alpha_n^2 h_y^2}{2}\right).$$

(2.5.24)

The complete solution is

$$\psi_{kj} = \sum_{n=1}^{K-1} a_n \sinh \beta_n(J - j)\sin\frac{\pi nk}{K},$$

(2.5.25)

where

$$a_n = \frac{2}{K \sinh \beta_n J}\sum_{k=1}^{K-1} g_k \sin\frac{\pi nk}{K}.$$

(2.5.26)

The resemblance to the analytic solution to Laplace's equation is noted.

2.6 Convergence of Difference Solutions

The convergence of the solutions of difference equations to the solutions of the corresponding differential equation will be examined in this section for several simple cases. The differential equation is the limit of zero mesh spacing for the difference equation. The subject has been studied extensively, and the present state of the theory goes well beyond our present purposes. We shall be content here with illustrating a particular method of studying convergence. The results will be indicative of the hazards implicit in difference approximation to differential equations.

For a simple problem, consider the ordinary differential equation

$$\frac{dy}{dx} = -\alpha y.$$

(2.6.1)

The solution is

$$y = y_0 e^{-\alpha x}.$$

(2.6.2)

If we approximate the derivative by a forward difference, we have

$$y_{j+1} - y_j = -\alpha h y_j.$$

(2.6.3)

The solution is merely

$$y_j = y_0 \exp\left[j \ln\left(1 - \alpha h\right)\right].$$

(2.6.4)

We expand the logarithm in the form

$$\ln (1 - \alpha h) = -\alpha h - \frac{(\alpha h)^2}{2} - \frac{(\alpha h)^3}{3}. \qquad (2.6.5)$$

If we neglect terms beyond h^2, we have

$$y_j = y_0 \exp \left[-j\alpha h - \frac{j(\alpha h)^2}{2} \right]. \qquad (2.6.6)$$

We identify jh as x_j and then find

$$y_j = y_0 \exp \left[-\alpha x_j \left(1 + \frac{\alpha h}{2} \right) \right]. \qquad (2.6.7)$$

The error is thus of the form

$$\exp \left[-\alpha x_j \frac{(\alpha h)}{2} \right], \qquad (2.6.8)$$

i.e., proportional to h. The smaller we take h, the smaller the error. The result is consistent with the discussion of Section 2.3 where we noted that the first forward difference approximates the derivative to order h. Note that as h approaches 0, the difference solution converges to the differential solution.

We might be tempted to use a more accurate difference approximation to reduce the truncation error. For instance, the approximation

$$\frac{dy}{dx} = \frac{y_{j+1} - y_{j-1}}{2h} + O(h^2) \qquad (2.6.9)$$

is of higher order in the truncation error. Approximating the first derivative with the difference expression in Eq. (2.6.9), we have

$$y_{j+1} - y_{j-1} = -2h\alpha y_j. \qquad (2.6.10)$$

The solutions are of the form

$$y_j = c_1(\sqrt{1 + \alpha^2 h^2} - \alpha h)^j + c_2(-\sqrt{1 + \alpha^2 h^2} - \alpha h)^j. \qquad (2.6.11)$$

Using the binomial expansion for the radicals, we have

$$\sqrt{1 + \alpha^2 h^2} = 1 + \tfrac{1}{2}\alpha^2 h^2 - \tfrac{1}{8}\alpha^4 h^4 + \dots . \qquad (2.6.12)$$

If terms beyond h^4 are neglected, the first term becomes

$$y_1(j) = \left(1 - \alpha h + \frac{\alpha^2 h^2}{2} - \frac{1}{8}\alpha^4 h^4\right)^j, \tag{2.6.13}$$

$$= \exp j\left[-\alpha h + \frac{\alpha^3 h^3}{6}\right], \tag{2.6.14}$$

where we have truncated the logarithmic expansion to obtain (2.6.14). Note that the function y_1 indeed approximates the analytic solution to order h^2 and is more accurate than Eq. (2.6.7) for the same h. However, reference to the second term of Eq. (2.6.11) shows that the second independent solution is of the form

$$y_2(j) = (-)^j(\sqrt{1 + \alpha^2 h^2} + \alpha h)^j. \tag{2.6.15}$$

For all $h > 0$ this function is ever increasing in magnitude and oscillatory in sign. Hence, this second form of the solution would completely dominate the decaying exponential of the first term, and an entirely erroneous solution would result. It might be argued that the coefficient $c_2 = 0$, and hence this difficulty does not arise. However, for numerical computations any round-off might introduce the second independent solution and continued calculation would result in a complete degeneration of the problem.

The basic difficulty with the higher order approximation is the introduction of additional independent solutions. In many cases various procedures may be adopted to control the behavior of such extraneous solutions, and we shall consider such problems in later chapters. For now we merely note one of the difficulties encountered in attempting to find high order accuracy in our solution.

As a more detailed study of convergence, we consider the boundary value problem of Section 2.5. The solution (2.5.25) contained the term $\sin(\pi n k/K)$. In the limit we have

$$\lim_{h_x \to 0} \sin \frac{\pi n k}{K} = \lim_{h_x \to 0} \sin \frac{n\pi k h_x}{a} = \sin \frac{n\pi x}{a}, \tag{2.6.16}$$

which is the analytic result for this factor. For the separation constants, we have

$$\lim_{h_x \to 0} \alpha_n^2 = \lim_{h_x \to 0} \left[\left(\frac{n\pi}{a}\right)^2 - \frac{1}{12}\left(\frac{n\pi}{a}\right)^4 h_x^2\right], \tag{2.6.17}$$

$$= \left(\frac{n\pi}{a}\right)^2, \tag{2.6.18}$$

which is the analytic result. Further,

$$\lim_{h_y \to 0} \cosh \beta_n = \lim_{h_y \to 0} \left[1 + \frac{\beta_n^2}{2!} \right], \tag{2.6.19}$$

so that

$$\lim_{h_y \to 0} \beta_n = \lim_{h_y \to 0} \alpha_n h_y = \lim_{h_y \to 0} \frac{n\pi}{a} h_y . \tag{2.6.20}$$

Therefore,

$$\lim_{h_y \to 0} \sinh \beta_n(J - j) = \sinh \frac{n\pi}{a} (b - y), \tag{2.6.21}$$

which is the correct result. In other words, the difference solution does indeed converge to the differential solution. The truncation error in the solution appears in the separation constants and is of the form

$$\alpha_n^2 \big|_{\text{difference}} = \alpha_n^2 \big|_{\text{differential}} \left[1 - \frac{1}{12} \left(\frac{n\pi}{a} \right)^2 h_x^2 \right], \tag{2.6.22}$$

$$\beta_n^2 \big|_{\text{difference}} = \beta_n^2 \big|_{\text{differential}} \left[1 - \frac{1}{12} \left(\frac{n\pi}{a} \right)^2 h_y^2 \right]. \tag{2.6.23}$$

The truncation error is proportional to the square of the mesh spacing since central differences were used.

For the final study we consider the exponential term in the heat-flow example of the previous section. From Eq. (2.5.9) we have

$$\lim_{h_t \to 0} l \ln (1 - \alpha_n^2 h_t) = \lim_{h_t \to 0} l \ln \left[1 - \frac{2h_t}{h_x^2} \left(1 - \cos \frac{n\pi}{K} \right) \right]. \tag{2.6.24}$$

Upon expanding the logarithm in the left-hand side of (2.6.24), we have

$$\lim_{h_t \to 0} l \left(-\alpha_n^2 h_t - \frac{(\alpha_n h_t)^2}{2} \right). \tag{2.6.25}$$

If we take $t = lh_t$, then the first term becomes

$$e^{-\alpha_n^2 t} = e^{-(n\pi/a)^2 t}, \tag{2.6.26}$$

which is the analytic solution. From this we might conclude the solution converges. However, examination of the right-hand side of (2.6.24) shows that for large n ($n \leqslant K - 1$ by Eq. (2.5.6)), the term

$$1 - \cos \frac{n\pi}{K} \approx + 2. \tag{2.6.27}$$

The right-hand side becomes

$$\lim_{h_t \to 0} l \ln \left[1 - \frac{4h_t}{h_x^2} \right]. \qquad (2.6.28)$$

If h_x and h_t are related such that $h_t/h_x^2 > \frac{1}{2}$, then the argument in (2.6.28) is of magnitude greater than unity. The logarithm is positive (plus a phase factor) and hence the solution will diverge, thereby entirely failing to represent the desired solution. In order to guarantee the convergence of the approximation, we must require

$$\frac{h_t}{h_x^2} < \frac{1}{2} \qquad (2.6.29)$$

even as h_t, $h_x \to 0$.

Requirements such as (2.6.29) are very frequent in numerical studies, and we shall encounter such relations often in our later analysis.

2.7 Matrix Form of Difference Equations

In our later work we shall frequently use a compact matrix notation for the simultaneous equations resulting from difference approximation to differential equations. To illustrate the construction of the matrix form of the equation, we now consider the two examples of partial difference equations given in Section 2.5.

We approximate the heat-flow equation by the simple difference relation

$$T_{k,l+1} - T_{k,l} = \frac{h_t}{h_x^2} [T_{k+1,l} - 2T_{k,l} + T_{k-1,l}]. \qquad (2.7.1)$$

We assume the boundary conditions as before, Eqs. (2.5.3a,b). Equation (2.7.1) can be factored in the form

$$T_{k,l+1} = \frac{h_t}{h_x^2} [T_{k+1,l} - \alpha T_{k,l} + T_{k-1,l}] \qquad (2.7.2)$$

with $\alpha = 2 - h_x^2/h_t$.

The various equations for a given l are then

$$\frac{h_t}{h_x^2} (-\alpha T_{1,l} + T_{2,l}) = T_{1,l+1}, \qquad (2.7.3a)$$

$$\frac{h_t}{h_x^2} (T_{1,l} - \alpha T_{2,l} + T_{3,l}) = T_{2,l+1}, \qquad (2.7.3b)$$

$$\vdots$$

$$\frac{h_t}{h_x^2} (T_{K-2,l} - \alpha T_{K-1,l}) = T_{K-1,l+1}. \qquad (2.7.3c)$$

The above set of simultaneous equations can evidently be written

$$
\frac{h_t}{h_x^2}
\begin{bmatrix}
-\alpha & 1 & 0 & \cdots & 0 & 0 \\
1 & -\alpha & 1 & \cdots & 0 & 0 \\
\vdots & \vdots & \vdots & & \vdots & \vdots \\
0 & 0 & 0 & \cdots & -\alpha & 1 \\
0 & 0 & 0 & \cdots & 1 & -\alpha
\end{bmatrix}
\begin{bmatrix}
T_{1l} \\
T_{2l} \\
\vdots \\
\\
T_{K-1,l}
\end{bmatrix}
=
\begin{bmatrix}
T_{1,l+1} \\
T_{2,l+1} \\
\vdots \\
\\
T_{K-1,l+1}
\end{bmatrix}.
$$

$$(2.7.4)$$

If we denote the matrix in (2.7.4) as $\mathbf{A}$, and define the vector $\boldsymbol{\psi}_l$ as

$$
\boldsymbol{\psi}_l =
\begin{bmatrix}
T_{1l} \\
T_{2l} \\
\vdots \\
\\
T_{K-1,l}
\end{bmatrix},
$$

$$(2.7.5)$$

then the entire set of equations can be written

$$
\frac{h_t}{h_x^2} \mathbf{A} \boldsymbol{\psi}_l = \boldsymbol{\psi}_{l+1}.
$$

$$(2.7.6)$$

If we denote the starting vector as $\boldsymbol{\psi}_0$, then Eq. (2.7.6) can also be written

$$
[(h_t/h_x^2)\mathbf{A}]^l \boldsymbol{\psi}_0 = \boldsymbol{\psi}_l.
$$

$$(2.7.7)$$

Note that the matrix $\mathbf{A}$ is of tridiagonal form.

For the Laplace difference equation, we have the relation

$$
\frac{\phi_{k+1,j} - 2\phi_{kj} + \phi_{k-1,j}}{h_x^2} + \frac{\phi_{k,j+1} - 2\phi_{kj} + \phi_{k,j-1}}{h_y^2} = 0.
$$

$$(2.7.8)$$

By simple factoring, we have

$$
r^2(\phi_{k+1,j} + \phi_{k-1,j}) - \beta\phi_{kj} + \phi_{k,j+1} + \phi_{k,j-1} = 0,
$$

$$(2.7.9)$$

where $r^2 = h_y{}^2/h_x{}^2$ and $\beta = 2(1 + r^2)$.

We define the vector $\boldsymbol{\psi}_j$ as

$$\boldsymbol{\psi}_j = \begin{bmatrix} \phi_{1j} \\ \phi_{2j} \\ \vdots \\ \phi_{K-1,j} \end{bmatrix}. \tag{2.7.10}$$

The set of equations (2.7.9) is then

$$\mathbf{A}\boldsymbol{\psi}_j + \mathbf{I}\boldsymbol{\psi}_{j+1} + \mathbf{I}\boldsymbol{\psi}_{j-1} = \mathbf{0}, \tag{2.7.11}$$

where $\mathbf{A}$ is the matrix

$$\mathbf{A} = \begin{bmatrix} -\beta & r^2 & 0 & \dots & 0 & 0 \\ r^2 & -\beta & r^2 & \dots & 0 & 0 \\ \vdots & \vdots & \vdots & & \vdots & \vdots \\ 0 & 0 & 0 & \dots & r^2 & -\beta \end{bmatrix}. \tag{2.7.12}$$

We now define the extended vector $\boldsymbol{\psi}$

$$\boldsymbol{\psi} = \begin{bmatrix} \boldsymbol{\psi}_1 \\ \boldsymbol{\psi}_2 \\ \vdots \\ \boldsymbol{\psi}_{J-1} \end{bmatrix} = \begin{bmatrix} \phi_{11} \\ \phi_{21} \\ \vdots \\ \phi_{12} \\ \phi_{22} \\ \vdots \\ \phi_{K-1,J-1} \end{bmatrix}.$$

The set of equations (2.7.11) can then be written

$$\mathbf{B}\boldsymbol{\psi} = \mathbf{0}, \tag{2.7.13}$$

where

$$\mathbf{B} = \begin{bmatrix} \mathbf{A} & \mathbf{I} & \mathbf{0} & \dots & \mathbf{0} \\ \mathbf{I} & \mathbf{A} & \mathbf{I} & \dots & \mathbf{0} \\ \vdots & \vdots & \vdots & & \vdots \\ \mathbf{0} & & & \dots & \mathbf{I} & \mathbf{A} \end{bmatrix}. \tag{2.7.14}$$

Each of the elements of **B** is a $(K - 1)$ by $(K - 1)$ square submatrix. A matrix of the form of **B** is a block tridiagonal matrix. The procedure can obviously extended to difference equations with more unknowns and also to equations with variable coefficients and/or variable mesh spacing.

References

There are several books devoted to the calculus of finite differences. Particularly exhaustive treatments are included in references *1*, *2*, and *3*. Somewhat shorter treatments are found in *4* and *5*. Reference *5* also includes many other aspects of the difference calculus. The application of finite differences is not limited to approximating differential equations. Other uses for the calculus are described very cogently in *4* and *6*.

1. Jordan, C., "Calculus of Finite Differences." Chelsea, New York, 1947.
2. Milne-Thompson, L. M., "The Calculus of Finite Differences." Macmillan, London, 1933.
3. Fort, T., "Finite Differences and Difference Equations in the Real Domain." Oxford Univ. Press, London and New York, 1948.
4. Hildebrand, F. B., "Introduction to Numerical Analysis." McGraw-Hill, New York, 1956.
5. Hildebrand, F. B., "Methods of Applied Mathematics." Prentice-Hall, Englewood Cliffs, New Jersey, 1952.
6. Hamming, R. W., "Numerical Methods for Scientists and Engineers." McGraw-Hill, New York, 1962.

Problems

1. Prove the following:

$$\text{(a)} \qquad \Delta \sin(ax + b) = 2 \sin \frac{ah}{2} \cos \left(ax + b + \frac{ah}{2}\right),$$

$$\text{(b)} \qquad \Delta \cos(ax + b) = -2 \sin \frac{ah}{2} \sin \left(ax + b + \frac{ah}{2}\right).$$

2. Show that

$$f(x + nh) = f(x) + n\Delta f(x) + \frac{n(n - 1)}{2!} \Delta^2 f(x) + \dots + \Delta^n f(x).$$

3. Show that

$$\text{(a)} \qquad \sum \cos x = \frac{\sin(x - h/2)}{2 \sin h/2},$$

$$\text{(b)} \qquad \sum \sinh x = \frac{\cosh(x - h/2)}{2 \sinh h/2}.$$

4. Prove that the differentiation operator d/dx may be formally written

$$\frac{d}{dx} = \frac{2}{h} \sinh^{-1} \frac{\delta}{2}$$

and then develop expansion (2.3.17).

5. Find the solution to the following:

(a) $\quad \Delta^2 g_k + \Delta g_k - g_k = 0, \qquad \begin{cases} g(0) = 1, \\ g(1) = 2. \end{cases}$

(b) $\quad g(k + 3) - 8g(k) = 0.$

6. Find the solutions to the eigenvalue problem

$$\frac{\Delta^2 y_k}{h^2} + \lambda^2 y_k = 0, \qquad 0 \leqslant k \leqslant K$$

with boundary conditions

$$\Delta y_0 = 0; \qquad \nabla y_k = 0.$$

Show the convergence to the analytic solution.

7. An infinite medium, void of neutrons, has a constant scattering cross-section and a constant fission cross-section. There is no capture. The fission process produces 1 prompt neutron and another neutron delayed exactly τ secs. The total diffusion time of any neutron is exactly τ secs. One neutron is introduced at time $t = 0$ into the assembly.

[a] Derive an expression for the neutron population as a function of time.

[b] The assembly is to be scrammed when more than 10^{15} neutrons are present. When should scram occur?

8. Approximate the wave equation

$$\frac{\partial^2 \phi}{\partial t^2} = c^2 \frac{\partial^2 \phi}{\partial x^2}$$

with the difference approximation

$$\frac{\delta^2 \phi}{h_t^2} = c^2 \frac{\delta^2 \phi}{h_x^2}.$$

Solve the difference equation and compare the solutions with the analytic solution to the differential equation. Under what circumstances will the difference equation converge?

9. The determinant, Δ_N, of the N by N matrix

$$\begin{bmatrix} -\alpha & 1 & 0 & \cdots & & 0 \\ 1 & -\alpha & 1 & 0 & \cdots & \\ \vdots & & \vdots & \vdots & & \\ & & \vdots & \vdots & & \\ 0 & & \cdots & & 1 & -\alpha \end{bmatrix}$$

arises from applying the operator δ^2. By assuming $\Delta_0 = 1$, show the recurrence relation

$$\Delta_N = -\alpha \Delta_{N-1} - \Delta_{N-2}$$

is valid.

10. Derive a difference approximation to the Laplacian operator in r, z coordinates which is accurate to order h_z^2 and h_r^2.

11. By noting that the series $\sum_{k=0}^{K-1} e^{i\pi kn/K}$ is geometric, prove

$$\text{(a)} \quad \sum_{k=0}^{K-1} \sin \frac{k\pi n}{K} \sin \frac{k\pi m}{K} = 0, \qquad m \neq n,$$

$$\text{(b)} \quad \sum_{k=0}^{K-1} \cos \frac{k\pi n}{K} \sin \frac{k\pi m}{K} = 0, \qquad m = n.$$

[The other orthogonality relations given in Section 2.5 may be developed in a similar manner].

12. The purpose of this problem is to illustrate the construction of a difference equation by physical rather than mathematical means. Heat is transferred from a cylindrical fuel element of radius R_0 encased in cladding of uniform thickness a, centered in a cylindrical coolant channel of radius R_K. The coolant channel is assumed insulated at the outer boundary; the coolant mass flow rate and inlet temperature are assumed fixed. Calculate the temperature of the fuel, cladding, and coolant as functions of r and z, the radial and axial coordinates. Neglect any heating in the coolant or cladding as a result of neutron or photon irradiation. Assume thermal conductivities are independent of temperature in all materials; neglect axial heat flow; neglect any thermal resistance between cladding and fuel. Assume the heat source in the fuel depends only on axial position and that the coolant is completely turbulent.

(a) Write down the usual energy conservation equations and boundary conditions needed to solve the problem. Let η be the heat transfer coefficient between the cladding and the coolant, and k^f the fuel thermal conductivity.

(b) Solve the resulting equations analytically for the temperature as a function of r and z in the fuel, cladding, and coolant.

(c) Divide the assembly into a number of annuli such that the radius r_j of the jth one is given by $r_j = jh$. By performing energy balances directly on zones $j-1$, j, and $j+1$, show that

$$\frac{2k^f r_{j-1}}{h}(T_{j-1} - T_j) + \frac{2k^f r_j}{h}(T_{j+1} - T_j) = S(z)(r_j^2 - r_{j-1}^2),$$

where T_j is temperature at r_j and $S(z)$ is the heat source density. What happens at $j = 1$, i.e., how is the temperature of the centerline to be determined? Show that the above result is correct to first order.

(d) By using the cross-sectional area of flow at the average radius of an interval, show that

$$\frac{k^f}{h}(T_{j-1} - T_j)(r_{j-1} + r_j) + \frac{k^f}{h}(T_{j+1} - T_j)(r_j + r_{j+1}) = S(z)(r_j^2 - r_{j-1}^2).$$

Eliminate r_{j-1}, r_j, and r_{j+1} in terms of j and h. Show that the truncation error is of order h.

(e) As the next improvement, for the source use the volume between $r_j - h/2$ and $r_j + h/2$, and show that the heat flow equation is

$$\frac{k^f}{h}[(T_{j-1} - T_j)(r_{j-1} + r_j) + (T_{j+1} - T_j)(r_j + r_{j+1})] = S(z)(r_{j+\frac{1}{2}}^2 - r_{j-\frac{1}{2}}^2).$$

Eliminate the various r_j in terms of j and h. Show that the truncation error is of order h^2.

(f) Use central differences in the result of (a) and show that the result agrees with that (e).

(g) Determine the center temperature in (e) in terms of T_1 and $q(z)$ by evaluating $\lim_{r\to 0}[(1/r)(dT/dr)]$. Hint: Expand $(dT/dr)|_{r=0}$ in a Taylor series about $r = 0$. Show that

$$T_0 = T_1 + \frac{h^2 S(z)}{4k'} .$$

(h) How should the cladding be treated?

(i) How should the equations be generalized if the coefficients depend on r, z, and T?

III

NUMERICAL
SOLUTIONS OF EQUATIONS

In the previous chapter we reviewed the formation of difference equations as approximations to differential equations. The purpose of the current chapter is to discuss a variety of methods of obtaining numerical solutions to the approximating equations. As we shall presently see, the actual procedure adopted plays a profound influence on whether or not an approximate solution can be obtained.

For our present interest, we shall concentrate on numerical procedures suitable for digital computers. The reason for the emphasis is evident when one considers the labor involved in attempting to solve nontrivial problems with any degree of accuracy. We shall first consider the problem of numerical integration. Many of the results obtained can be carried over to solving ordinary differential equations. However, the major emphasis of the chapter will be upon solution of partial difference equations.

3.1 Numerical Integration

In the introductory example of Chapter II, we considered the problem of approximate integration. The results were obtained in terms of differences of first order. In this section we generalize the previous example. Consider the definite integral

$$I = \int_a^b dx f(x),$$ (3.1.1)

where $f(x)$ is known, either as an analytic expression or a table of values at points x_j. The basis for obtaining an approximate solution is to write the integral as

$$I = \int_a^b dx f(x) \approx \sum_j f(x_j) w_j \, \Delta x_j \, , \qquad (3.1.2)$$

where the w_j are weights associated with the integration process. The approximation (3.1.2) is known as a quadrature formula. One possible procedure for generating the quadrature formula is to expand $f(x)$ in a power series in x (if possible) and evaluate coefficients using known values of $f(x_j)$. The usual procedure in this vein leads to the so-called Lagrange interpolation formulas. The integration of the Lagrange formulas of various orders in turn lead to the Newton-Cotes integration formulas. We shall not proceed in this manner, but shall derive equivalent expressions directly in terms of difference operators.

In the previous chapter differential equations and difference equations were discussed. These were solved by integration. In particular, various differential operators were represented, sometimes approximately, by difference operators. In particular, Eq. (2.3.10) shows us an exact relation between the differential operator d/dx and the forward difference operator Δ. This relation can be exploited now to express the integral operator in terms of difference operators. Integration may be regarded as the inverse of differentiation. In principle, then, we need only to invert the operator $(1/h) \ln(1 + \Delta)$. To proceed we observe, again from the previous chapter, that

$$\Delta f_j = f(x_{j+1}) - f(x_j) = \frac{d}{dx_j} \int_{x_j}^{x_j+h} dx f(x) = \frac{d}{dx} \int_{x_j}^{x_{j+1}} dx f(x), \qquad (3.1.3)$$

so that from Eq. (2.3.10) we find

$$\int_{x_j}^{x_{j+1}} dx f(x) = \frac{h \Delta f_j}{\ln (1 + \Delta)} \qquad (3.1.4)$$

$$= h \left[1 + \frac{\Delta}{2} - \frac{\Delta^2}{12} + \cdots \right] f_j \, , \qquad (3.1.5)$$

the result desired.

Next we would like to derive several other integration formulas. The integral from x_j to x_{j+2} can be derived from the result just obtained, for example, by breaking up the region of integration into two parts, as follows:

$$\int_{x_j}^{x_{j+2}} dx f(x) = (1 + E) \int_{x_j}^{x_{j+1}} dx f(x) = 2h \left[1 + \Delta + \frac{\Delta^2}{6} - \frac{\Delta^4}{180} + \cdots \right] f_j \, , \qquad (3.1.6)$$

where the last equality has exploited our previous result (3.1.5) and Eq. (2.2.11).

We can also express these two results in terms of backward differences by merely expressing ∇ in terms of Δ. By Eqs. (2.2.11) and (2.2.12) we learn that

$$\Delta = \frac{\nabla}{1 - \nabla}. \tag{3.1.7}$$

This relation may be substituted into Eq. (3.1.4) to find that

$$\int_{x_j}^{x_{j+1}} dx f(x) = h \left[1 + \frac{\nabla}{2} + \frac{5}{12} \nabla^2 + \dots \right] f_j . \tag{3.1.8}$$

Again, by use of this result and the shift operator E expressed in terms of ∇ by Eq. (2.2.12), we find

$$\int_{x_j}^{x_{j+2}} dx f(x) = 2h \left[1 + \nabla + \frac{7}{6} \nabla^2 + \frac{4}{3} \nabla^3 + \dots \right] f_j . \tag{3.1.9}$$

Additional formulas are readily obtained for other difference operators and for different intervals of integration.

The significant feature of the integration formulas is the truncation error associated with termination of the expansions. If we cut off the expansion to order Δ^n, then the truncation error is given by the order of the next term, i.e., h^{n+1}. The coefficient h in these expansions then implies that the truncation error is of order h^{n+2}. Recall that the truncating of the approximation to a derivative at nth order yielded a truncation error of order h^n. We conclude that numerical integration formulas are more accurate than differentiation formulas of the same order, as indeed is usually true. The increased accuracy is easily under-stood geometrically when we realize that integration is a smoothing process, whereas differentiation tends to exaggerate fluctuations.

A formula of particular interest is readily obtained from Eq. (3.1.6) truncated to terms of order three. The resulting formula

$$\int_{x_j}^{x_{j+2}} dx f(x) = 2h \left[1 + \Delta + \frac{\Delta^2}{6} \right] f_j = \frac{h}{3} [f_j + 4f_{j+1} + f_{j+2}] + O(h^5) \tag{3.1.10}$$

is the well-known Simpson's rule.

We shall use Simpson's rule for a sample problem. If we desire to integrate $f(x)$ from a to b (Fig. 3.1.1), we divide the interval at J equally spaced points such that $x_1 = a$, $x_J = b$. We must choose J to be odd. The integration formula is then

$$\int_a^b dxf(x) = \int_{x_1}^{x_3} dxf(x) + \int_{x_3}^{x_5} dxf(x) + \dots + \int_{x_{J-2}}^{x_J} dxf(x), \quad (3.1.11)$$

or

$$\int_a^b dxf(x) = \frac{h}{3}[f_1 + 4f_2 + 2f_3 + \dots + f_J] = \sum_j f(x_j)w_j h. \quad (3.1.12)$$

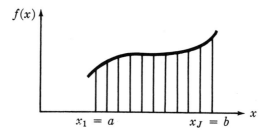

FIG. 3.1.1.   Equally spaced intervals of a curve for integration by Simpson's rule.

In each of the 3-point intervals, the function $f(x)$ is approximated as a parabola. It is readily apparent that the integration formula is indeed equivalent to a power series expansion of $f(x)$. The same is true for higher order expansion. An illustration of the accuracy of the formula is left for the problems.

3.2   Ordinary Differential Equations

The results of the previous section are readily adapted to the solution of ordinary differential equations. Thus, the simple equation

$$\frac{dy(x)}{dx} = f(x, y) \quad (3.2.1)$$

is equivalent to the indefinite integral

$$y(x) = y(a) + \int_a^x dxf(x, y). \quad (3.2.2)$$

The numerical solution of Eq. (3.2.1) may then be written in terms of differences. In order to advance a solution, it is usually convenient to use backward differences in order to use previously computed results. An approximation of the form

$$y_{j+1} = y_j + hg(\nabla)f(x_j, y_j),\qquad(3.2.3)$$

where g is some polynomial in ∇, is usually referred to as an Adams formula. We shall term such integration formulas explicit since all the quantities on the right-hand side are known by the time we try to evaluate the left-hand side. The truncation error in the integration formula is readily determined to be of $O(h^{n+2})$ where nth order differences are retained. In particular cases the order of the truncation error may be improved. Recall that the difference approximation $(h/2)(y_{i+1} - y_{i-1})$, was an approximation to the first derivative to $O(h^2)$. Similar formulas are obtainable for integration. For instance,

$$y_{j+1} = y_j + \int_{x_j}^{x_{j+1}} dx f(x, y) = y_j + h\left[1 + \frac{\nabla}{2} + \frac{5}{12}\nabla^2 + ...\right]f_j\qquad(3.2.4)$$

and

$$y_j = y_{j-1} + \int_{x_{j-1}}^{x_j} dx f(x, y) = y_{j-1} + h\left[1 - \frac{\nabla}{2} - \frac{1}{12}\nabla^2 + ...\right]f_j\qquad(3.2.5)$$

yield, together,

$$y_{j+1} = y_{j-1} + h[2 + \tfrac{1}{3}\nabla^2 + ...]f_j.\qquad(3.2.6)$$

Further formulas are readily obtainable for larger intervals. The truncation error, if we terminate before the ∇^2 term, is of $O(h^3)$. Either Eq. (3.2.4) or (3.2.5) is of $O(h^2)$ if truncated after the first term. The formula (3.2.5) is an example of an implicit formula since the right-hand side is to be evaluated at the same point as the left-hand side. Generally implicit formulas have less truncation error than corresponding explicit formulas. In the above example, note the coefficient of ∇^2 is smaller in the implicit formula. However, to use an implicit formula one must usually iterate to obtain the appropriate right-hand side.

Although the error term indicates a given truncation error, the actual error in computing may be increased since the values y_j, used to compute $f(x_j, y_j)$, are in error. Thus, the errors may propagate in a manner which reduces the order of approximation. As an extreme example, we reconsider the problem

$$\frac{dy}{dx} = -\alpha y,\qquad(3.2.7)$$

and use Eq. (3.2.4), terminated after first order differences. We have

$$y_{j+1} = y_j - \alpha h\left[\frac{3}{2}y_j - \frac{y_{j-1}}{2}\right].\qquad(3.2.8)$$

The solution of the difference equation yields the root pair

$$\beta_1 = \frac{1 - \frac{3}{2}\alpha h}{2} + \frac{1}{2}\sqrt{1 - \alpha h + \frac{9}{4}\alpha^2 h^2} \qquad (3.2.9a)$$

$$= 1 - \alpha h + \frac{\alpha^2 h^2}{2} + \frac{1}{4}\alpha^3 h^3 + \cdots \qquad (3.2.9b)$$

and

$$\beta_2 = \frac{1 - \frac{3}{2}\alpha h}{2} - \frac{1}{2}\sqrt{1 - \alpha h + \frac{9}{4}\alpha^2 h^2} \qquad (3.2.10a)$$

$$= -\tfrac{1}{2}\alpha h - \tfrac{1}{2}\alpha^2 h^2 - \tfrac{1}{4}\alpha^3 h^3 + \cdots . \qquad (3.2.10b)$$

The solution is then

$$y_j \approx c_0 \left(1 - \alpha h + \frac{\alpha^2 h^2}{2} + \frac{1}{4}\alpha^3 h^3\right)^j + c_1(-)^j \left(\frac{1}{2}\alpha h + \frac{\alpha^2 h^2}{2}\right)^j, \qquad (3.2.11)$$

$$y_j \approx c_0 \exp\left[-j\left(\alpha h - \frac{5}{12}\alpha^3 h^3\right)\right] + c_1 \left(\frac{-\alpha h}{2}\right)^j (1 + \alpha h)^j. \qquad (3.2.12)$$

Since the correction to the lowest order term in our result is $(-5/12)\,\alpha^2 h^2$ times that term, the solution is accurate to $O(h^2)$. A more important result is to note that the second solution, the parasitic solution, decreases in magnitude and hence the calculation is stable, for sufficiently small h. This result is in contrast to the earlier result (2.6.15). This result indicates a possible technique for combating instabilities in the numerical solution of differential equations. The two different difference equations, for the same problem, are

$$y_{j+1} + 2\alpha h y_j - y_{j-1} = 0 \qquad \text{(unstable)} \qquad (3.2.13)$$

and

$$y_{j+1} - \left(1 - \frac{3}{2}\alpha h\right) y_j - \frac{\alpha h}{2} y_{j-1} = 0 \qquad \text{(stable)}. \qquad (3.2.14)$$

Both approximations are accurate to $O(h^2)$, but the second is stable. In many problems it is possible to adjust coefficients in a difference relation to obtain a stable solution. Sometimes the adjustement in coefficients may increase the truncation error. Nevertheless, the adjustment may make a solution possible. We shall encounter the problem of instabilities in partial differential equations also and shall consider further techniques for obtaining a stable solution.[1]

In using higher order difference approximations to differential equations, a problem arises that does not occur in lowest order. The

---

[1] A very illustrative study of stability may be found in Reference 3.

high order difference equation requires the values of the dependent variable to be known at many more points than a low order difference equation in order to find the value of the dependent variable at the next point in the sequence. The boundary conditions, which must be known in order that the solution be specific, supply the value of the dependent variables at only a few points. Accordingly, in order to carry out the integration, using either an explicit or an implicit method, several values of the dependent variable must be computed initially. Several methods are of frequent use, and we outline only one.

A sufficient number of initial values of the dependent variables are assumed in order to construct the necessary differences for forward integration.

The assumed values of the dependent variable can be related to values at other points by means of the integration formulas, such as Eqs. (3.1.5), (3.1.6), (3.2.4), or (3.2.5). With the known boundary values, and the other assumed values, we may compute the value of each dependent variable assumed earlier by means of the relevant difference relation mentioned above.

In general, the first guess for the values of the dependent variable will not agree with those computed; the procedure is iterated until the assumed values and the computed values agree. After a consistent set of initial values are found, the integration proceeds in a straightforward manner.

Certain numerical integration formulas have been developed which have the advantage of being self-starting. Among the most widely known methods are the Runge-Kutta methods. The basic idea behind the Runge-Kutta formulas is to develop an integration formula for Eq. (3.2.1) of the form

$$y_{j+1} = y_j + h \sum_i \alpha_i f(x_i, y_i), \qquad (3.2.15)$$

where the α_i, x_i, y_i are chosen to make the integration formula agree with the Taylor series expansion of $y(x)$ to some order. The algebra involved in deriving the various formulas is quite involved (see Reference 2). We shall be content here to display an integration formula of 4th order:

$$y_{n+1} = y_n + (h/6)(k_1 + 2k_2 + 2k_3 + k_4), \qquad (3.2.16)$$

where

$$k_1 = f(x_n, y_n),$$
$$k_2 = f(x_n + h/2, y_n + k_1/2),$$
$$k_3 = f(x_n + h/2, y_n + k_2/2),$$
$$k_4 = f(x_n + h, y_n + k_3),$$

The set of formulas is accurate to order h^4.

In order to use the above-mentioned Runge-Kutta formula, one must evaluate the function $f(x, y)$ four different times for each point of the solution. This may constitute a serious drawback to a problem; however, with high-speed computers even the evaluation of involved functions is relatively simple. Equations such as (3.2.16) involve only two points initially and hence are completely self-starting.

Higher order Runge-Kutta methods require additional evaluation of constants, $(k_1, k_2, \text{etc.})$, and ultimately the effort involved makes their use impractical. A more serious drawback with the methods are the difficulties in finding expressions for the errors. With the explicit and implicit methods, the evaluation of the higher differences gave some estimate of the errors in the integration. With the Runge-Kutta methods, one normally does not keep a running check on the error, and hence additional computations are necessary.

In the numerical solution of differential equations of order higher than first order, methods may be derived in an analogous manner. Alternatively, the higher order equation may be reduced to a set of simultaneous first order equations and the methods considered thus far used. The choice of approach depends upon the equation involved and any particular properties that may be exploited. We shall indicate the reduction to simultaneous first order equations and then consider the direct derivation of an approximate integration formula for a particular second order equation.

The nth order differential equation

$$\frac{d^n y}{dx^n} \equiv \frac{d^n y}{dx^n} + g_{n-1}(x)\frac{d^{n-1}y}{dx^{n-1}} + \dots + g_0(x) = y(x) \qquad (3.2.17)$$

may be reduced by a simple change of variable. First we write (3.2.17) as

$$\frac{d^n y}{dx^n} \equiv y^n(x) = f(x, y, y', \dots, y^{n-1}), \qquad (3.2.18)$$

where prime denotes differentiation with respect to x. We define the variables $y_0, y_1, \dots, y_{n-1}$, by

$$\begin{aligned}
y_0(x) &= y, \\
y_1(x, y_0) &= y', \\
y_2(x, y_0, y_1) &= y'', \\
&\;\;\vdots \\
y_{n-1}(x, y_0, y_1, \dots, y_{n-2}) &= y^{(n-1)}.
\end{aligned} \qquad (3.2.19)$$

We then obtain the set of n first order equations by differentiation of Eq. (3.2.19)

$$y_0' = y_1(x, y_0),$$
$$y_1' = y_2(x, y_0, y_1),$$
$$y_2' = y_3(x, y_0, y_1, y_2),$$
$$\vdots$$
$$y_{n-1}' = f(x, y_0, y_1, y_2, ..., y_{n-1}). \tag{3.2.20}$$

Each equation of the set (3.2.20) may now be integrated in order by the first order integration formulas.

Frequently one encounters second order equations in which the first derivative does not occur, i.e.,

$$\frac{d^2y}{dx^2} + q(x)y = f(x). \tag{3.2.21}$$

A second order equation of the form

$$\frac{d^2u}{dx^2} + p(x)\frac{du}{dx} + g(x)u = s(x) \tag{3.2.22}$$

can be transformed into the form (3.2.21) by the change of variable

$$u = \exp\left(-\frac{1}{2}\int dx\, p\right) y. \tag{3.2.23}$$

The numerical integration of (3.2.21) can be accomplished by a double integration and by use of the expansions for functions of the difference operators. To this end, the double inverse of the differentiation operator d/dx is needed. Further, for our present purposes it will be convenient to express this operator in terms of the backwards difference operator, as in Eq. (2.3.14). Next we observe that, by repeated application of the technique used in obtaining Eq. (3.1.4),

$$y_{j+1} - y_j - hy_j' = \int_{x_j}^{x_{j+1}} dx'' \int_{x_j}^{x''} dx\, \frac{d^2y(x)}{dx^2}$$

$$= \frac{d^2}{dx^2} \int_{x_j}^{x_{j+1}} dx'' \int_{x_j}^{x''} dx\, y(x) = \left[\frac{\nabla}{1 - \nabla} - h\frac{d}{dx}\right] y_j. \tag{3.2.24}$$

From this last equality and Eq. (2.3.14), we find that

$$\int_{x_j}^{x_{j+1}} dx'' \int_{x_j}^{x''} dx\, y(x) = h^2 \left(\frac{1}{2} + \frac{\nabla}{6} + \frac{3}{24} \nabla^2 + ... \right) y_j \qquad (3.2.25)$$

and that

$$y_{j+1} = y_j + hy_j' + h^2 \left(\frac{1}{2} + \frac{\nabla}{6} + \frac{3}{24} \nabla^2 + ... \right) y_j''. \qquad (3.2.26)$$

Analogous implicit formulas and expressions using other difference operators are easily found.

Thus far we have considered only initial value problems. Frequently one encounters ordinary differential equations for which values of the dependent variable are given at the different boundaries of the domain of interest. It is possible to solve boundary value problems by the methods previously considered. Usually it is necessary to make an estimate of the starting slope and march to the far boundary. Any discrepancy between the computed and desired end condition must be eliminated by adjusting the starting slope. Pictorially the procedure is displayed in Fig. 3.2.1. We assume the function $y(a)$ and $y(b)$ known. The first trial is

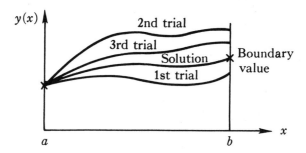

FIG. 3.2.1.   Trajectories for possible solutions of a boundary value problem by using different starting conditions.

a trajectory computed by some integration rule. The second trial results from correcting the initial slope. Trial three is a better one, while trial four would represent the solution. Except under the most extraordinary conditions, the solution of a boundary value problem by the means just described is iterative.

An alternative approach to the problem is to consider replacing derivatives with appropriate difference equations and solving the resultant set of simultaneous equations. This procedure has some advantages over the "trajectory" method mentioned above. For instance, the problem of extraneous solutions, which might contaminate a forward integration, can be controlled. Furthermore, for certain specific difference approximations, rapid methods for solving the simultaneous equations are possible. In later sections of this chapter, we shall discuss methods of solving boundary value problems in some detail.

3.3 Partial Differential Equations

The numerical solution of partial differential equations is usually considerably more difficult than the solution of ordinary differential equations. Different numerical procedures have evolved for different classes of partial differential equations. The most general second order, linear, partial differential equations can be written

$$A \frac{\partial^2 f}{\partial x^2} + 2B \frac{\partial^2 f}{\partial x \partial y} + C \frac{\partial^2 f}{\partial y^2} = F\left(x, y, \frac{\partial f}{\partial x}, \frac{\partial f}{\partial y}\right). \qquad (3.3.1)$$

An equation of the form (3.3.1) is termed elliptic, parabolic, or hyperbolic according to the nature of the discriminant, where

$$\Gamma = B^2 - AC. \qquad (3.3.2)$$

When $\Gamma > 0$ we call the equation hyperbolic, when $\Gamma = 0$ the equation is parabolic; and for $\Gamma < 0$ the equation is elliptic. If the coefficients A, B, and C depend upon position, then the nature of the equation may also depend upon position. It is possible, for instance, for an equation to be hyperbolic in some region and parabolic in another. If the equation is of one type, then the relations for Γ must hold everywhere. Classical examples of the three types of equations are:

(1) the wave equation

$$\frac{\partial^2 f}{\partial t^2} - \frac{\partial^2 f}{\partial x^2} = 0, \qquad (3.3.3)$$

which is hyperbolic; (2) the heat-flow equation

$$\frac{\partial f}{\partial t} - \frac{\partial^2 f}{\partial x^2} = 0, \qquad (3.3.4)$$

which is parabolic; (3) Laplace's equation

$$\frac{\partial^2 f}{\partial x^2} + \frac{\partial^2 f}{\partial y^2} = 0, \qquad (3.3.5)$$

which is elliptic.

Equations of the hyperbolic and parabolic type are usually associated with initial value problems, whereas elliptic equations are associated with boundary value problems.

The types of boundary conditions for a problem are classified in a rather simple manner. If the value of a function along some boundary is given, we speak of the condition as being a Dirichlet boundary condition. In particular, if the function is zero all along the boundary, the condition is termed homogeneous Dirichlet, otherwise it is an inhomogeneous Dirichlet condition. If the derivative of the function is specified along the boundary, the condition is termed a Neumann condition. It is possible to have homogeneous or inhomogeneous Neumann boundary conditions. If the boundary conditions contain values of the function and derivative, we speak of mixed boundary conditions.

For all of the examples to be considered subsequently, we shall be concerned with two properties of the numerical solution. First, we shall want to know if the solution of the finite difference approximation is a reasonable representation of the analytic solution. In other words, if the relevant mesh spacings are made smaller and smaller, does the difference solution approach the differential solution. If the difference solution does approach the differential solution, we say the approximation converges, and the study of this property is termed convergence. The second property of interest is the behavior of any errors introduced into the calculation, for instance by round-off. An error may grow in an unbounded fashion and destroy a solution. Such a situation is called an instability. The general study of error behavior is called the stability problem.

An example of the convergence problem was given in Section 2.6. We learned there that the approximation to the heat-flow equation was convergent under a stringent condition on the spacing ratio. It may happen that the coefficients of the particular harmonics which violate the convergence criterion are zero for certain initial conditions. In this case the difference solution would converge in principle to the differential solution. However, if a round-off error introduced the nonconvergent harmonics, the solution may degenerate. In this latter case, we would say the problem is convergent but unstable. The requirement for stability is exactly the same as the requirement for convergence in this particular example.

It is not necessarily true that the convergence and stability requirements are the same for a given problem. It has been shown (see Reference 6) however, that for certain difference approximations to initial value problems with a wide variety of boundary conditions, the stability and convergence requirements are the same. Proof of this important result is beyond the scope of this text. For our purpose we shall pay particular attention to the stability problem.

3.4 Hyperbolic Equations

3.4.1 THE WAVE EQUATION

For the study of hyperbolic equations, we consider the simple wave equation

$$\frac{\partial^2 \phi(x, t)}{\partial t^2} = c^2 \frac{\partial^2 \phi(x, t)}{\partial x^2}, \qquad a \leqslant x \leqslant b, \ 0 \leqslant t \tag{3.4.1}$$

with initial conditions

$$\phi(x, 0) = f_0(x), \qquad \frac{\partial \phi(x, 0)}{\partial t} = g_0(x). \tag{3.4.2}$$

Perhaps the simplest difference approximation is obtained by using central differences in space and time. The equations become

$$\frac{\phi_{j,k+1} - 2\phi_{j,k} + \phi_{j,k-1}}{h_t^2} = c^2 \frac{\phi_{j+1,k} - 2\phi_{j,k} + \phi_{j-1,k}}{h_x^2}, \tag{3.4.3}$$

where j denotes the space index, k the time index, h_t and h_x are the time and space mesh spacings respectively, assumed constant. We denote the ratio $c^2 h_t^2 / h_x^2 = r^2$, and factor Eq. (3.4.3) in the form

$$\phi_{j,k+1} = r^2 \left[\phi_{j+1,k} + \phi_{j-1,k} - 2\left(1 - \frac{1}{r^2}\right)\phi_{j,k} \right] - \phi_{j,k-1}. \tag{3.4.4}$$

Equation (3.4.4) is a 5-point difference relation and is shown schematically in Fig. 3.4.1.

We interpret the relation (3.4.4) as an algorithm to permit a march-out of the solution from $k = 0$ and $k = 1$ to later times. The procedure is explicit since all of the past values (smaller k) are known as we compute values along the time line $k + 1$.

The truncation error in the approximation is $O(h_t^2) + O(h_x^2)$. To study the stability of the approximation, there are several possible approaches. We shall discuss one procedure here and in the next section consider a more general technique. We note first that for $r^2 > 1$, Eq. (3.4.4) takes on an interesting character, i.e., the sign of the term in $\phi_{j,k}$ is positive.

We might expect that such an occurrence gives rise to some problems with the solution. To illustrate this fact, we consider the classical arguments presented by Courant *et al.* (see Reference 9).

The differential equation (3.4.1) is satisfied by any functions of the form

$$\phi_1(x, t) = q(x - ct), \tag{3.4.5}$$

$$\phi_2(x, t) = s(x + ct). \tag{3.4.6}$$

From the initial conditions we have

$$q(x) + s(x) = f_0(x), \tag{3.4.7}$$

$$-q'(x) + s'(x) = g_0(x). \tag{3.4.8}$$

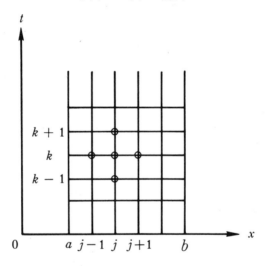

FIG. 3.4.1.   Five-point relation for difference approximation to the wave equation.

Differentiating and subtracting, we have

$$2q'(x) = f_0'(x) - g_0(x), \tag{3.4.9}$$

or

$$q(x) = \frac{1}{2} \left[f_0(x) - \int_0^x du \, g_0(u) \right] + C_1. \tag{3.4.10}$$

Similarly,

$$s(x) = \frac{1}{2} \left[f_0(x) + \int_0^x du \, g_0(u) \right] + C_2. \tag{3.4.11}$$

Any linear combination of $\phi_1(x, t)$ and $\phi_2(x, t)$ is a solution and therefore

$$\phi(x, t) = \frac{1}{2}\left[f_0(x + ct) + f_0(x - ct) + \int_{x-ct}^{x+ct} du\, g_0(u)\right] + C_3. \qquad (3.4.12)$$

The condition at $t = 0$ requires that $C_3 = 0$.

Equation (3.4.12) affords an interesting interpretation of the stability requirements. The lines $x + ct = $ constant and $x - ct = $ constant are lines along which the function f_0 is constant. These lines are called characteristics of the differential equation. At a given point, say x_0, t_0, the characteristics are given by

$$x - ct = x_1 \qquad (3.4.13)$$

$$x + ct = x_2. \qquad (3.4.14)$$

The characteristics are sketched in Fig. 3.4.2. The characteristics extend to the x axis at the points x_1 and x_2. The triangle with vertices at the points x_1, x_2, x_0 is called the region of determination of the solution at the point x_0, t_0. Notice that any initial conditions outside the interval

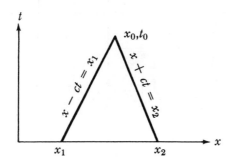

FIG. 3.4.2. Characteristics for the wave equation.

x_1 to x_2 is not in the region of determination of x_0, t_0. We see that the solution at x_0, t_0 is not dependent upon the data outside the interval x_1 to x_2. The slope of the characteristic is $1/c$.

In order to study the stability of our difference approximation as a function of the ratio r^2, we now consider the region of determination of the solution on the network approximating the domain of interest as shown in Fig. 3.4.3.

When $r^2 = 1$ the slope of the line bounding the region of determination is $1/c$. Hence the boundary lines intersect the x axis at the points x_1

and x_2. For $r^2 > 1$ the boundary lines have a slope greater than $1/c$ and define an interval within the interval x_1 to x_2 on the x axis. The converse result is obtained for $r^2 < 1$.

For the case $r^2 \leqslant 1$, the difference solution is determined by as much (or more) of the initial data as that which determines the analytic solution. We should expect that such a solution would be a reasonable representation of the analytic solution. On the other hand, for $r^2 > 1$

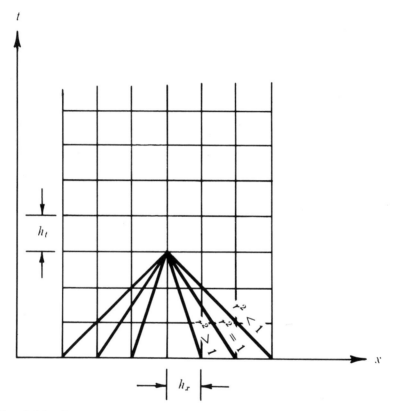

Fig. 3.4.3.   Regions of determination of the solution for various ratios of the spacing r^2.

the region of determination for the difference solution is smaller than that of the differential solution. This means that a portion of the data is not being used for the difference calculation that is necessary for the analytic solution. Consequently, we should expect that $r^2 > 1$ yields an unrealistic calculation. Indeed such is the case as we shall see.

Let us obtain the analytic solution of the difference equation (3.4.3). By the usual separation of variables, we have

$$\phi_{j,k} = R_j T_k .$$ (3.4.15)

Inserting in Eq. (3.4.3) and denoting the separation constant as $-(c\alpha/h_x)^2$, we have the difference equations

$$T_{k+1} - 2\left(1 - \frac{\alpha^2 r^2}{2}\right) T_k + T_{k-1} = 0,$$ (3.4.16)

and

$$R_{j+1} - 2\left(1 - \frac{\alpha^2}{2}\right) R_j + R_{j-1} = 0.$$ (3.4.17)

To simplify matters, we shall assume $\phi(a, t) = \phi(b, t) = 0$. The spatial solution is then of the form

$$R_j = A_n \sin \frac{n\pi j}{J},$$ (3.4.18)

with

$$\alpha_n^2/2 = \left(1 - \cos \frac{n\pi}{J}\right).$$ (3.4.19)

Using this result in Eq. (3.4.16), we have

$$T_{k+1} - 2\left[1 - r^2\left(1 - \cos \frac{n\pi}{J}\right)\right] T_k + T_{k-1} = 0.$$ (3.4.20)

For $r^2 \leqslant 1$ Eq. (3.4.20) has trigonometric solutions which are similar to the trigonometric solutions of the differential equation. However, for $r^2 > 1$ some solutions of (3.4.20) will be exponential and would fail to represent the analytic solution. In order for the procedure to be stable (and convergent in this case), we must have

$$r^2 \leqslant 1$$ (3.4.21)

or, equivalently,

$$\frac{c^2 h_t^2}{h_x^2} \leqslant 1.$$ (3.4.22)

The stability requirement (3.4.22) places an upper bound on the size of the time step for a given spatial mesh. In particular, if we decrease h_x (to reduce truncation error), we must also reduce the time increment. For particularly small meshes, the allowed maximum time step may be so small as to make the computation impractical.

In order to avoid the restriction, recourse is made to other difference approximations. For instance, the approximation

$$\frac{\phi_{j,k+1} - 2\phi_{j,k} + \phi_{j,k-1}}{h_t^2} = c^2 \frac{\phi_{j+1,k+1} - 2\phi_{j,k+1} + \phi_{j-1,k+1}}{h_x^2} \qquad (3.4.23)$$

which has a truncation error $O(h_x^2)$, $O(h_t)$. The point pattern for the equation is shown in Fig. 3.4.4. Notice that we cannot solve for the point $\phi_{j,k+1}$ explicitly in this case. In fact we must solve for the time line $k + 1$ at all j simultaneously. A difference equation such as (3.4.23) is called implicit since we cannot solve for each point explicitly.

The advantage of the formulation based on the difference relation (3.4.23) is that the equation is unconditionally stable. In order to prove this fact, we introduce a particularly simple means for studying stability in the next section.

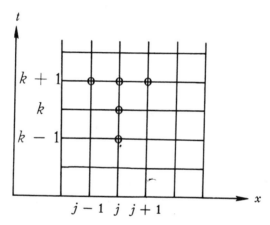

FIG. 3.4.4.   Five-point, implicit differencing pattern for the wave equation.

3.4.2   THE VON NEUMANN METHOD

To analyze the stability of a difference approximation, we must study the behavior of errors introduced into the computation. For a given difference equation, we may express the exact solution to the difference equation in the form

$$\phi(\text{exact}) = \phi(\text{computed}) + \epsilon(\text{error}). \qquad (3.4.24)$$

The error may be due to round-off, a computational mistake, etc. The propagation of errors through the computation is obviously governed by the original difference equation itself with one notable distinction. Since we presume initial values and boundary values are known, the initial and boundary values for the error are obviously zero. That is, the equation governing the propagation of errors is the homogeneous form of the defining difference equation.

For difference relations involving constant coefficients, the errors may be expanded in a finite Fourier series. Thus for example, in the difference approximation to the wave equation as given in Eq. (3.4.23), the spatial dependence of the error can be written

$$\epsilon_{jk} = \sum_n B_{nk} e^{in\theta_j}, \tag{3.4.25}$$

with $\theta_j \equiv \pi x_j / L_x$. The time dependence may be included by presuming a coefficient of the form

$$B_{nk} = A_n \zeta^k(n). \tag{3.4.26}$$

The error at any point j, k is expressed as

$$\epsilon_{jk} = \sum_n A_n \zeta^k(n) e^{in\theta_j}. \tag{3.4.27}$$

This expression for the error was first used by Von Neumann (see Reference 10). The problem of stability is studied by noting the behavior of the coefficients $\zeta(n)$. If any $\zeta(n)$ is such that

$$| \zeta(n)| > 1 \tag{3.4.28}$$

for any n, then we expect that the corresponding error harmonic would grow beyond limit for increasing k. To see this behavior we consider using the Von Neumann method for the difference approximation (3.4.3) and (3.4.23).

In the first case we have for the nth harmonic,

$$e^{in\theta_j}[\zeta^{k+1} - 2\zeta^k + \zeta^{k-1}] = r^2 \zeta^k [e^{in\theta_{j+1}} - 2e^{in\theta_j} + e^{in\theta_{j-1}}] \tag{3.4.29}$$

or

$$(\zeta - 2 + \zeta^{-1}) = -4r^2 \sin^2 \frac{n\theta_1}{2}. \tag{3.4.30}$$

Solutions of this equation obey the quadratic form

$$\zeta^2 - 2 \left(1 - 2r^2 \sin^2 \frac{n\theta_1}{2}\right) \zeta + 1 = 0. \tag{3.4.31}$$

We have for the roots

$$\zeta = [1 - 2r^2 \sin^2(n\theta_1/2)] \pm \sqrt{[1 - 2r^2 \sin^2(n\theta_1/2)]^2 - 1}. \quad (3.4.32)$$

For $r^2 > 1$ one of the roots is of absolute value greater than unity for large n. Consequently, we expect amplification of errors at successive time steps. Conversely, for $r^2 \leqslant 1$, we see there is no amplification of errors. Note that for $r^2 \leqslant 1$, the roots occur as complex pairs of magnitude unity. In such a case we speak of a linear instability. Obviously if errors are not diminished in magnitude, errors at successive steps may accumulate. For such cases the amount of round-off error may ultimately become the dominant factor in the calculation.

For the implicit difference relation, the error equation for the nth harmonic is easily seen to be

$$\left(1 + 4r^2 \sin^2 \frac{n\theta_1}{2}\right) \zeta^2 - 2\zeta + 1 = 0. \quad (3.4.33)$$

For any real r^2 the roots of this equation are complex conjugates of maximum magnitude unity. Hence the implicit relation is unconditionally stable.

In general, the Von Neumann method is conservative in predictions about stability. The range of values for the harmonic index n is taken to be $-\infty$ to $+\infty$ in the usual application of the method. For a problem in the finite domain, the actual number of Fourier harmonics needed to describe the error is finite. By a very careful analysis using the finite series, it is possible to generate very accurate stability criteria.

Although the method is strictly applicable to difference equations with constant coefficients, it is sometimes used heuristically for equations with variable coefficients. In later sections we shall show further application of the method.

3.5   Parabolic Equations

3.5.1   INTRODUCTION

In the previous chapter, we considered the analytic solution to the heat-flow equation and derived a convergence criterion. In this section we shall show the stability condition for the given difference equation is the same as the convergence criterion. We shall also discuss some implicit approximations to the heat-flow equation. We postpone discussion of the age diffusion equation (which is parabolic) until the discussion of multigroup methods in Chapter IV.

The stability of the explicit difference equation

$$\phi_{j,k+1} = \phi_{j,k} + \frac{h_t}{h_x^2} [\phi_{j+1,k} - 2\phi_{j,k} + \phi_{j-1,k}] \qquad (3.5.1)$$

or

$$\phi_{j,k+1} = r^2(\phi_{j+1,k} + \phi_{j-1,k}) + (1 - 2r^2)\phi_{j,k} \qquad (3.5.2)$$

with $r^2 = h_t/h_x^2$ is easily examined. Notice first that Eq. (3.5.2) is a 4-point expression with the point pattern as shown in Fig. 3.5.1. A

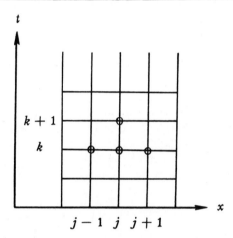

FIG. 3.5.1. Four-point difference relation for the heat-flow equation.

formula such as Eq. (3.5.2) is sometimes called a two-level formula in contrast to the hyperbolic difference equations which were all three-level. The starting conditions for a two-level formula require initial data only along one time line.

For a two-level formula, the Von Neumann method is quite simple. By substituting the trial function

$$\epsilon_{jk} = \zeta^k(n)e^{in\theta_j} \qquad (3.5.3)$$

into Eq. (3.5.2), we have

$$\zeta = 2r^2 \cos n\theta_1 + (1 - 2r^2). \qquad (3.5.4)$$

The growth factor ζ is bounded as

$$1 - 4r^2 \leqslant \zeta \leqslant 1. \qquad (3.5.5)$$

In order to keep the magnitude of $\zeta \leqslant 1$, we must require $r^2 \leqslant \frac{1}{2}$, or equivalently

$$h_t \leqslant \frac{h_x^2}{2} . \tag{3.5.6}$$

Equation (3.5.6) is precisely the same condition found earlier.

A wide variety of implicit approximations to the heat-flow equation have been studied. As usual, implicit relations are considered in order to overcome the restrictive condition imposed for stability of the simple explicit difference equation. Consider the following simple two-level approximation.

$$\frac{\phi_{j,k+1} - \phi_{jk}}{h_t} = \alpha \frac{\delta_x^2 \phi_{j,k+1}}{h_x^2} + (1 - \alpha) \frac{\delta_x^2 \phi_{jk}}{h_x^2}, \qquad 0 \leqslant \alpha \leqslant 1. \tag{3.5.7}$$

Notice that the second difference is applied along the time lines k and $k + 1$. The truncation error for the relation (3.5.7) is easily seen to be $O(h_t) + O(h_x^2)$. Formula (3.5.7) is a six-point formula and has the point pattern shown in Fig. 3.5.2.

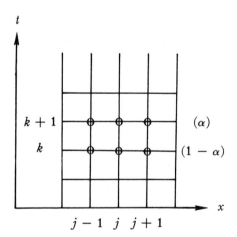

Fig. 3.5.2.   Six-point difference relation for an implicit approximation to the heat-flow equation.

The stability of Eq. (3.5.7) is studied by the Von Neumann method. By the usual process we have

$$\zeta - 1 = -4r^2\alpha\zeta \sin^2 \frac{n\theta_1}{2} - 4(1 - \alpha)r^2 \sin^2 \frac{n\theta_1}{2} . \tag{3.5.8}$$

Considering the extremum of the sine function, we find Eq. (3.5.8) factors into

$$r^2 \leqslant \frac{1}{2(1-2\alpha)}, \qquad 0 \leqslant \alpha < \tfrac{1}{2}, \tag{3.5.9}$$

and r^2 unrestricted for $\tfrac{1}{2} \leqslant \alpha \leqslant 1$. Note that in the limit $\alpha = 1$, the difference equation becomes a simple four-point implicit formula.

3.5.2 ALTERNATING-DIRECTION IMPLICIT METHOD

A very important method, first derived by Peaceman and Rachford (see Reference 11), will be considered in this section. The method is useful for solving two-dimensional parabolic equations (and also elliptic equations). We consider the simple heat-flow equation

$$\frac{\partial \phi}{\partial t} = \frac{\partial^2 \phi}{\partial x^2} + \frac{\partial^2 \phi}{\partial y^2}, \qquad 0 \leqslant x \leqslant a, \;\; 0 \leqslant y \leqslant b, \;\; t \geqslant 0, \tag{3.5.10}$$

with boundary conditions

$$\phi(0, y, t) = \phi(a, y, t) = 0,$$
$$\phi(x, 0, t) = \phi(x, b, t) = 0, \tag{3.5.11}$$
$$\phi(x, y, 0) = f(x, y).$$

The simple explicit difference equation is

$$\frac{\phi_{j,k,n+1} - \phi_{j,k,n}}{h_t} = \frac{\delta_x^2 \phi_{j,k,n}}{h_x^2} + \frac{\delta_y^2 \phi_{j,k,n}}{h_y^2}. \tag{3.5.12}$$

It is easily seen that the stability criterion for Eq. (3.5.12) is

$$\frac{h_t}{h_x^2} + \frac{h_t}{h_y^2} \leqslant \frac{1}{2}. \tag{3.5.13}$$

To derive a less restrictive condition, we consider the implicit equation

$$\frac{\Delta_t \phi_{j,k,n}}{h_t} = \frac{\delta_x^2 \phi_{j,k,n+1}}{h_x^2} + \frac{\delta_y^2 \phi_{j,k,n+1}}{h_y^2}. \tag{3.5.14}$$

It is easy to show that Eq. (3.5.14) is unconditionally stable; however, the solution requires the simultaneous solution of values along the entire plane of time $n + 1$. The basis of the Peaceman-Rachford method is to make the equations implicit along only one line at a time. Thus, we use the two difference equations

$$\frac{\Delta_t \phi_{j,k,n}}{h_t} = \frac{\delta_x^2 \phi_{j,k,n+1}}{h_x^2} + \frac{\delta_y^2 \phi_{j,k,n}}{h_y^2} \tag{3.5.15}$$

and

$$\frac{\Delta_t \phi_{j,k,n+1}}{h_t} = \frac{\delta_x^2 \phi_{j,k,n+1}}{h_x^2} + \frac{\delta_y^2 \phi_{j,k,n+2}}{h_y^2} \tag{3.5.16}$$

For simplicity we take $h_x = h_y$ and $h_t/h_x^2 = r^2$. Written in component form, the equations become

$$\phi_{j+1,k,n+1} - (2 + 1/r^2)\phi_{j,k,n+1} + \phi_{j-1,k,n+1}$$
$$= -\phi_{j,k+1,n} + (2 - 1/r^2)\phi_{j,k,n} - \phi_{j,k-1,n}, \tag{3.5.17}$$

$$\phi_{j,k+1,n+2} - (2 + 1/r^2)\phi_{j,k,n+2} + \phi_{j,k-1,n+2}$$
$$= -\phi_{j+1,k,n+1} + (2 - 1/r^2)\phi_{j,k,n+1} - \phi_{j-1,k,n+1}. \tag{3.5.18}$$

The two equations are used successively and hence the name alternating direction. The stability is analyzed in the usual manner. We assume an error function of the form

$$\epsilon_{j,k,n} = \zeta^n(m,l)e^{\iota m\theta_j}e^{\iota l\varphi_k}. \tag{3.5.19}$$

From Eq. (3.5.17) we have

$$\zeta(m, l)\left[\frac{1}{r^2} + 4\sin^2\frac{m\theta_1}{2}\right] = \left[\frac{1}{r^2} - 4\sin^2\frac{l\varphi_1}{2}\right] \tag{3.5.20}$$

or

$$\zeta(m, l) = \frac{\left(\dfrac{1}{r^2}\right) - 4\sin^2\dfrac{l\varphi_1}{2}}{\left(\dfrac{1}{r^2}\right) + 4\sin^2\dfrac{m\theta_1}{2}} \tag{3.5.21}$$

For some values of m, l, and r^2, the growth factor might be considerably greater than unity. Thus applying the implicit equation in only one direction is unstable in general. On the other hand, using the alternating equations we have

$$\zeta^2(m, l) = \frac{\left(\dfrac{1}{r^2}\right) - 4\sin^2\dfrac{l\varphi_1}{2}}{\left(\dfrac{1}{r^2}\right) + 4\sin^2\dfrac{l\varphi_1}{2}} \cdot \frac{\left(\dfrac{1}{r^2}\right) - 4\sin^2\dfrac{m\theta_1}{2}}{\left(\dfrac{1}{r^2}\right) + 4\sin^2\dfrac{m\theta_1}{2}} \tag{3.5.22}$$

For two successive steps the resulting growth is always bounded at unity. Consequently the alternating-direction method is unconditionally stable.

The second advantage of the method stems from the fact that the equations are implicit along one line at a time. The resulting equations are three-point relations. The matrix form of the equations along one line is tridiagonal and hence can be solved by the method of matrix factorization. The result is a very fast stable method for solving two-dimensional parabolic equations. In the discussion of iterative procedures, we shall return to the alternating-direction method and show its application to elliptic equations.

3.6 Elliptic Equations and Iterative Methods

3.6.1 INTRODUCTION

The treatment of initial-value problems involved the formation of a difference operator that permitted the initial conditions to be extended into the domain of interest of the problem. Such a procedure is generally not useful for elliptic equations where the boundary conditions are given over the entire region of interest. The numerical solution of elliptic equations is usually accomplished by solution of simultaneous equations with a variety of methods.

One possible means of solving a set of simultaneous equations is by the Gauss reduction scheme. Unfortunately the reduction process for N equations in N unknowns requires approximately N^3 operations. Furthermore, a certain amount of round-off in each operation may cause the solution to degenerate for large N. On the other hand, a direct reduction procedure is determinate in that a fixed number of steps are needed (in theory) to find the solution.

An alternative approach to the solution of elliptic equations is an iterative procedure. In general, iterative methods require an infinite number of steps to solve a problem exactly. However, for practical purposes it is usually possible to terminate an iteration after a finite number of steps which are fewer in number than those required for reduction methods. Furthermore, iterative procedures have certain advantages with respect to round-off over direct reduction. To make these matters clearer, we consider a simple introductory example.

We desire the solution of the problem

$$\frac{d^2y}{dx^2} = 0 \qquad (3.6.1)$$

with boundary conditions

$$y(0) = y_0; \qquad y(a) = y_a .$$

We divide the interval 0 to a into K subintervals of equal width h as in Fig. 3.6.1. For simplicity we replace the second derivative with a second

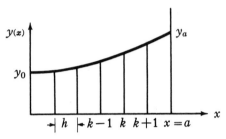

FIG. 3.6.1.   Simple mesh for the numerical solution of Laplace's equation.

central difference. We have then

$$y_{k-1} - 2y_k + y_{k+1} = 0, \qquad 1 \leqslant k \leqslant K - 1 . \qquad (3.6.2)$$

The set of equations (3.6.2) could be solved by reduction (in this case by matrix factorization, see Section 1.14) in a straightforward manner.

The iterative solution of the equations is achieved by first assuming a trial solution at all the interior points of the mesh. We then write Eq. (3.6.2) in the form

$$y_k = \frac{y_{k+1} + y_{k-1}}{2} . \qquad (3.6.3)$$

Equation (3.6.3) provides an algorithm for computing values of y_k in terms of its nearest neighbors. Let us denote the values of y_k for the initial trial with a superscript 0. To compute the "new" values of y_k from the "old," we might consider the rule

$$y_k^1 = \frac{y_{k+1}^0 + y_{k-1}^0}{2} \qquad (3.6.4)$$

and in general

$$y_k^p = \frac{y_{k+1}^{p-1} + y_{k-1}^{p-1}}{2} . \qquad (3.6.5)$$

The following important questions now occur:

1. Will the iteration rule (3.6.5) ever yield a solution?

2. How will we know when we have achieved a solution?
3. How long will it take?

We assume that the difference approximation itself has been adequate
for the problem.

To help answer these questions, let us denote the actual solution to
the difference equation as y_k^∞. We define the initial error, say ϵ_k^0, as

$$\epsilon_k^0 = y_k^0 - y_k^\infty \qquad (3.6.6)$$

and after p steps

$$\epsilon_k^p = y_k^p - y_k^\infty. \qquad (3.6.7)$$

The answer to the first question can be given in terms of the errors. Thus,
if the sequence ϵ_k^0, ϵ_k^1, ... , ϵ_k^p approaches zero, for all k, then the iteration
does yield a solution. To answer the second question is somewhat more
difficult in that we never know the errors (else we would also know the
solution). The usual test for determining when the solution has been
achieved is based upon the following criterion. We define a function,
say r_k, as

$$r_k^p = y_k^{p+1} - y_k^p. \qquad (3.6.8)$$

In terms of the errors we have

$$r_k^p = \epsilon_k^{p+1} - \epsilon_k^p. \qquad (3.6.9)$$

If r_k^p is small, for all k, then one assumes the approximate solution has
been found. Obviously this criterion is not always valid since a small
difference of errors does not necessarily imply small errors. A practical
way to be reasonably sure of convergence is to choose a sufficiently
small criterion and to iterate a few times perhaps beyond the criterion.
This second feature guards against the rate of convergence as a function
of the iteration index having a minimum. For example, the convergence
rate may initially increase only to later decrease. A minimum might
result while still far from converged.

The question of how long an iteration will take is very important,
and many different iteration methods have been devised to hasten the
rate at which a solution is obtained. We shall introduce a variety of
methods in later sections, and one of the criteria for judging the merit
of a method will be the rate of convergence.

3.6.2 STABILITY OF ITERATIONS

In this section we shall attempt to provide a unified basis for the study of iterative methods. We assume the set of simultaneous equations are written in the form

$$\mathbf{Ax} = \mathbf{y}, \tag{3.6.10}$$

where we further assume a solution does exist but otherwise do not restrict the matrix $\mathbf{A}$. The exact solution to the problem, say $\mathbf{x}^\infty$, is

$$\mathbf{x}^\infty = \mathbf{A}^{-1}\mathbf{y}. \tag{3.6.11}$$

We begin the iteration by considering a trial solution $\mathbf{x}^0$ and then operate on $\mathbf{x}^0$ to produce a new trial $\mathbf{x}^1$. We assume the iteration can be written

$$\mathbf{x}^1 = \mathbf{Bx}^0 + \mathbf{z}, \tag{3.6.12}$$

where the matrix $\mathbf{B}$ and the vector $\mathbf{z}$ are taken independent of the iteration index. Such an iteration is called stationary. The iterative procedure can be extended to successive trials in the form

$$\mathbf{x}^{\nu+1} = \mathbf{Bx}^\nu + \mathbf{z}. \tag{3.6.13}$$

The matrix $\mathbf{B}$ is called the iteration matrix, and the ability of achieving a solution and the corresponding rate of convergence are intimately related to the properties of the iteration matrix.

The properties we desire of our iteration are that the sequence of vectors $\mathbf{x}^\nu$ approach $\mathbf{x}^\infty$, and further, that iteration with $\mathbf{x}^\infty$ reproduces itself. In mathematical terms the last requirement is

$$\mathbf{x}^\infty = \mathbf{Bx}^\infty + \mathbf{z}. \tag{3.6.14}$$

Assuming Eq. (3.6.14) is valid, and defining the error vector $\boldsymbol{\epsilon}^\nu$ as

$$\boldsymbol{\epsilon}^\nu = \mathbf{x}^\nu - \mathbf{x}^\infty, \tag{3.6.15}$$

we have from Eq. (3.6.13)

$$\boldsymbol{\epsilon}^\nu = \mathbf{B}\boldsymbol{\epsilon}^{\nu-1}. \tag{3.6.16}$$

Equation (3.6.16) states that the error vector obeys the homogeneous form of the iteration equation. Now, if the sequence of vectors $\mathbf{x}^\nu$ is to approach $\mathbf{x}^\infty$, then the sequence of vectors $\boldsymbol{\epsilon}^\nu$ must approach zero. From Eq. (3.6.16) we have

$$\boldsymbol{\epsilon}^\nu = \mathbf{B}\boldsymbol{\epsilon}^{\nu-1} = \mathbf{B}^\nu\boldsymbol{\epsilon}^0. \tag{3.6.17}$$

We require

$$\lim_{p \to \infty} \epsilon^p = \lim_{p \to \infty} \mathbf{B}^p \epsilon^0 \to \mathbf{0}. \tag{3.6.18}$$

Let us now assume the matrix $\mathbf{B}$ has a complete set of eigenvectors, say $\mathbf{e}_i$, and corresponding eigenvalues λ_i. Since the eigenvectors are complete, we may expand ϵ^0 in the form

$$\epsilon^0 = \sum_i \alpha_i \mathbf{e}_i. \tag{3.6.19}$$

Operation on ϵ^0 by $\mathbf{B}$ yields ϵ^1 as

$$\epsilon^1 = \mathbf{B}\epsilon^0 = \sum_i \alpha_i \lambda_i \mathbf{e}_i. \tag{3.6.20}$$

By induction we have

$$\epsilon^p = \sum_i \alpha_i \lambda_i^p \mathbf{e}_i. \tag{3.6.21}$$

In order for the error vector to vanish, we must require[2]

$$|\lambda_i| < 1, \quad \text{all } i. \tag{3.6.22}$$

The above result is very important for our future considerations and is also quite general. We shall refer to Eq. (3.6.22) as the stability condition for iterative methods. If an eigenvalue, say λ_r, was of magnitude greater than unity, the iteration would diverge, and in our terminology is unstable. Even if the initial error vector were orthogonal to the eigenvector, say $\mathbf{e}_r$, of the eigenvalue λ_r, round-off in computations would introduce components along $\mathbf{e}_r$ and ultimately ruin the iteration.

The stability condition also provides a means of computing the convergence rate of an iteration. If the eigenvalues are ordered such that

$$1 > |\lambda_1| > |\lambda_2| > \dots > |\lambda_K|,$$

then for sufficiently large p, the error is approximately

$$\epsilon^p \approx \alpha_1 \lambda_1^p \mathbf{e}_1 = \alpha_1 e^{p \ln \lambda_1} \mathbf{e}_1. \tag{3.6.23}$$

The term $e^{\ln \lambda_1}$ is the decay factor for the errors. In particular we define

$$-\ln \lambda_1 = v, \tag{3.6.24}$$

---

[2] The requirement of completeness of the eigenvectors of $\mathbf{B}$ to derive condition (3.6.22) is over restrictive. By consideration of the Jordon canonical form, the same result can be achieved by any real matrix. See problem 7.

as the convergence rate of the iteration. For small λ_1 the convergence rate is large, meaning a rapid reduction of the error with increasing number of iterations. The worth of an iteration scheme is partly measured in terms of the factor v. We shall consider detailed examples later. We note, however, that in general v decreases for increasing number of unknowns for most iterations. That is, the larger the problem, the longer it takes to solve. In fact, for many methods convergence is reciprocally related to N^2, where N is the number of unknowns. That the relation goes as N^2 can be heuristically seen by the following argument. Since the eigenvalues must be distributed between -1 and $+1$, an increase in N should move the ones of largest magnitude toward the end points of the interval. Further, since there are more points to be solved, the number of operations grows with N. Thus we expect the convergence to be related somehow to N^2.

The above argument is strictly heuristic and not necessarily true. Later examples will be considered to illustrate the general behavior of the convergence factor.

Thus far our results have been derived by strictly algebraic considerations. It is interesting and instructive to consider a geometric interpretation of iterations. To this end, we introduce the residual vector $\mathbf{r}^p$ defined as

$$\mathbf{r}^p = \mathbf{x}^{p+1} - \mathbf{x}^p. \tag{3.6.25}$$

In terms of the error vector, Eq. (3.6.25) becomes

$$\mathbf{r}^p = (\mathbf{B} - \mathbf{I})\boldsymbol{\epsilon}^p. \tag{3.6.26}$$

Since the residual vector represents the error vector in a transformed space, the convergence criteria for the residuals are the same as for the errors. Furthermore, the asymptotic behavior is the same.

The residuals are calculable at any stage of the iteration. From the defining equation for the iteration (3.6.13), we have

$$\mathbf{r}^p = (\mathbf{B} - \mathbf{I})\mathbf{x}^p + \mathbf{z}. \tag{3.6.27}$$

We interpret Eq. (3.6.25) in the form

$$\mathbf{x}^{p+1} = \mathbf{x}^p + \mathbf{r}^p \tag{3.6.28}$$

as stating that the vector $\mathbf{x}^p$ is corrected by addition of a vector $\mathbf{r}^p$ which in turn is defined by an algorithm (3.6.27). Different iteration methods consist of different algorithms for computing the correction vector. Notice that if $\mathbf{r}^p$ is chosen to change only one component of $\mathbf{x}^p$, the vector $\mathbf{r}^{p+1}$ may still have all of its components changed since

$\mathbf{x}^{p+1}$ is transformed by an operator that is not diagonal. In any event, convergence of the solution requires that $\mathbf{x}^{\nu}$ approach a limit vector and $\mathbf{r}^{\nu}$ approach the null vector.

The change of the trial vector $\mathbf{x}^{\nu}$ by the correction vector $\mathbf{r}^{\nu}$ is called an iterate or one iteration. The change of each component separately is called a relaxation or displacement. Thus, after relaxing each component of $\mathbf{x}^{\nu}$, once and only once, we complete one iteration.

3.6.3 STATIONARY ITERATIONS

In this section we shall discuss several very common iteration methods and consider their stability properties. For each of the iteration methods introduced, we shall apply the method to the simple Laplace equation in the square.[3] That is, we consider the equation

$$\frac{\partial^2 \phi}{\partial x^2} + \frac{\partial^2 \phi}{\partial y^2} = 0, \qquad 0 \leqslant x \leqslant a, \ \ 0 \leqslant y \leqslant a \qquad (3.6.29)$$

with boundary conditions

$$\phi(0, y) = \phi(a, y) = 0,$$
$$\phi(x, 0) = 0, \qquad \phi(x, a) = f(x). \qquad (3.6.30)$$

For all iteration methods we use the difference equation

$$\frac{\delta_x^2 \phi}{h_x^2} + \frac{\delta_y^2 \phi}{h_y^2} = 0, \qquad h_x = h_y = h. \qquad (3.6.31)$$

A. Method of Simultaneous Displacements

Let us assume we are solving the matrix equation

$$\mathbf{Ax} = \mathbf{y}, \qquad (3.6.32)$$

where we assume a solution does exist. The matrix $\mathbf{A}$ is written in the form

$$\mathbf{A} = \mathbf{L} + \mathbf{D} + \mathbf{U}, \qquad (3.6.33)$$

where $\mathbf{L}$ is strictly lower triangular, $\mathbf{U}$ strictly upper triangular, and $\mathbf{D}$ diagonal. We assume $\mathbf{D} \neq \mathbf{0}$. We now define the iteration

$$(\mathbf{L} + \mathbf{U})\mathbf{x}^{\nu} + \mathbf{D}\mathbf{x}^{\nu+1} = \mathbf{y}, \qquad (3.6.34)$$

---

[3] The numerical solution of the two-dimensional Laplace equation is perhaps the most thoroughly studied problem in iterative analysis. The problem is sometimes referred to as the model problem.

or

$$\mathbf{x}^{p+1} = -\mathbf{D}^{-1}(\mathbf{L} + \mathbf{U})\mathbf{x}^{p} + \mathbf{D}^{-1}\mathbf{y}. \qquad (3.6.35)$$

The method of simultaneous displacements then consists in solving the difference equation by means of the iteration in Eq. (3.6.35).

We next observe that the method of iteration in consistent with a vector being a solution of our original Eq. (3.6.32) for if at some stage the correct answer were found, then, apart from round-off errors, iterating the solution does nothing more than give it back to us again. In particular, if at some stage $\mathbf{x}^{p}$ were the correct solution

$$\mathbf{x}^{p} = \mathbf{A}^{-1}\mathbf{y}, \qquad (3.6.36)$$

then by substituting this solution into the iteration scheme (3.6.35), we find that

$$\mathbf{x}^{p+1} = \mathbf{A}^{-1}\mathbf{y},$$

and we recover the original solution.

The important question of whether or not an arbitrary starting vector, say $\mathbf{x}^{0}$, will approach $\mathbf{A}^{-1}\mathbf{y}$ depends upon the iteration matrix $-\mathbf{D}^{-1}(\mathbf{L} + \mathbf{U})$. The eigenvalue spectrum of the iteration matrix must be such that $|\lambda_i| < 1$ for all i, where the λ_i are eigenvalues of the matrix. Thus, the roots of the equation

$$|-\mathbf{D}^{-1}(\mathbf{L} + \mathbf{U}) - \lambda\mathbf{I}| = 0 \qquad (3.6.37)$$

or, equivalently

$$|\mathbf{L} + \lambda\mathbf{D} + \mathbf{U}| = 0, \qquad (3.6.38)$$

must have magnitude less than unity.

In general the solution of (3.6.38) is quite difficult. However, for many cases of interest, it is possible to determine the nature of the eigenvalue spectrum without solving the secular equation. We assume that the problem is well posed in the sense that $\mathbf{A}$ is irreducible, otherwise we factor $\mathbf{A}$ into two separate problems. The iteration matrix can be written

$$\mathbf{D}^{-1}(\mathbf{L} + \mathbf{U}) = \begin{bmatrix} 0 & \dfrac{a_{12}}{a_{11}} & \dfrac{a_{13}}{a_{11}} & \cdots & \dfrac{a_{1n}}{a_{11}} \\ \dfrac{a_{21}}{a_{22}} & 0 & \dfrac{a_{23}}{a_{22}} & \cdots & \dfrac{a_{2n}}{a_{22}} \\ \vdots & \vdots & \vdots & & \vdots \\ \dfrac{a_{n1}}{a_{nn}} & & \cdots & & 0 \end{bmatrix}. \qquad (3.6.39)$$

By Gerschgorin's theorem, the spectral radius of $\mathbf{D}^{-1}(\mathbf{L} + \mathbf{U})$ is bounded by

$$|\lambda_{\max}| \leq \max_i \sum_j \left| \frac{a_{ij}}{a_{ii}} \right|. \tag{3.6.40}$$

Gerschgorin's theorem may be strengthened if the matrix (3.6.39) is irreducible. If the maximum value of the sum on the right-hand side of Eq. (3.6.40) is denoted ρ, then Gerschgorins' theorem states

$$|\lambda_{\max}| \leq \rho. \tag{3.6.41}$$

If, for any i, and for an irreducible matrix

$$\sum_j \left| \frac{a_{ij}}{a_{ii}} \right| < \rho, \tag{3.6.42}$$

then

$$|\lambda_{\max}| < \rho, \tag{3.6.43}$$

i.e., there is strict inequality.[4] As a consequence, we see that if the matrix $\mathbf{A}$ is such that

$$|a_{ii}| \geq \sum_j |a_{ij}| \qquad (j \neq i) \tag{3.6.44}$$

with inequality for some i, then the method of simultaneous displacements converges.

If the diagonal elements of $\mathbf{A}$ are such that (3.6.42) is true, then we say $\mathbf{A}$ has diagonal dominance. Consequently, for an irreducible matrix with diagonal dominance, the method of simultaneous displacements converges. Fortunately most elliptic difference equations of reactor interest have this property. Note that the condition is sufficient for convergence but not necessary. For instance, the matrix

$$\mathbf{A} = \begin{bmatrix} -1 & 2 \\ 2 & -5 \end{bmatrix} \tag{3.6.45}$$

does not have diagonal dominance, yet the iteration matrix

$$-\mathbf{D}^{-1}(\mathbf{L} + \mathbf{U}) = \begin{bmatrix} 0 & 2 \\ 2/5 & 0 \end{bmatrix} \tag{3.6.46}$$

has eigenvalues with magnitude less than unity.

[4] For proof see Reference 8, Chapter 1.

We now consider application of the method of simultaneous displacements to the model problem. The equation for the error function is the homogeneous form of the equation with homogeneous boundary conditions.[5] The iteration algorithm for the error $\epsilon_{j,k}^p$ is, from Eq. (3.6.34)

$$\epsilon_{j+1,k}^p + \epsilon_{j-1,k}^p - 2\epsilon_{j,k}^{p+1} + \epsilon_{j,k+1}^p + \epsilon_{j,k-1}^p - 2\epsilon_{j,k}^{p+1} = 0, \quad (3.6.47)$$

or

$$\epsilon_{j,k}^{p+1} = \tfrac{1}{4}[\epsilon_{j,k+1}^p + \epsilon_{j,k-1}^p + \epsilon_{j+1,k}^p + \epsilon_{j-1,k}^p]. \quad (3.6.48)$$

The stability of the iteration can be studied by examining the behavior of the various eigenfunctions of the iteration operator. From past results we know the error (with homogeneous boundary conditions) must be of the form

$$\epsilon_{j,k}^{(m,n)} = A(m, n) \sin \frac{n\pi j}{K} \sin \frac{m\pi k}{K}, \quad 1 \leqslant j, k \leqslant K - 1 \quad (3.6.49)$$

where (m, n) are the indices of the eigenfunction. If we assume $\epsilon_{j,k}^{(m,n)}$ is of the form (3.6.49) and insert in (3.6.48), we have

$$\epsilon_{j,k}^{p+1} = \frac{A(m, n)}{4} \left[\sin \frac{n\pi j}{K} \left(\sin \frac{m\pi(k + 1)}{K} + \sin \frac{m\pi(k - 1)}{K} \right) \right.$$
$$\left. + \sin \frac{m\pi k}{K} \left(\sin \frac{n\pi(j + 1)}{K} + \sin \frac{n\pi(j - 1)}{K} \right) \right]. \quad (3.6.50)$$

After an elementary reduction we have

$$\epsilon_{j,k}^{p+1} = A(m, n) \sin \frac{n\pi j}{K} \sin \frac{m\pi k}{K} \left[\frac{\cos \dfrac{m\pi}{K} + \cos \dfrac{n\pi}{K}}{2} \right] \quad (3.6.51)$$
$$= \zeta \epsilon_{j,k}^p . \quad (3.6.52)$$

The scale factor ζ determines the rate of growth or decay for the errors. For this case the errors all decay with differing rates for the different harmonics. The largest value of ζ occurs for $m = n = 1$ or $m = n = K - 1$. For such a case we have

$$\zeta = \cos \frac{\pi}{K} \approx 1 - \frac{\pi^2}{2K^2} . \quad (3.6.53)$$

The iteration converges with the convergence rate

$$v = \frac{\pi^2}{2K^2} . \quad (3.6.54)$$

[5] The argument below follows that of Frankel, Reference 12.

Notice that the convergence rate is proportional to K^2, the number of unknowns. For a mesh of 20 by 20 points, the convergence rate is approximately

$$v = 0.01234$$

and hence about 80 iterations are required to reduce the error by a factor of e.

Notice that the method of simultaneous displacements requires the vectors $\mathbf{x}^{\nu+1}$ and $\mathbf{x}^{\nu}$ in the computation simultaneously. This means that for a vector of N dimensions, $2N$ numbers must be retained. For large problems this condition may be important in working with digital computers.

The method of simultaneous displacements is easily described in terms of the residuals. By Eqs. (3.6.35) and (3.6.28) we have

$$\mathbf{r}^{\nu} = -\mathbf{D}^{-1}[\mathbf{A}\mathbf{x}^{\nu} - \mathbf{y}]. \qquad (3.6.55)$$

The quantity $\mathbf{A}\mathbf{x}^{\nu} - \mathbf{y}$ is a measure of the error in a given iteration. Some authors call $\mathbf{A}\mathbf{x}^{\nu} - \mathbf{y}$ the residual.

As a final note we remark that the method of simultaneous displacements is also called the Jacobi method or the Richardson method.

B. Method of Successive Displacements

The method of successive displacements (also called the Gauss-Seidel method or the Liebmann method) is quite similar to the previous scheme. We again consider the problem of solving the matrix equation (3.6.32). In this case we assume an iteration of the form

$$(\mathbf{L} + \mathbf{D})\mathbf{x}^{\nu+1} + \mathbf{U}\mathbf{x}^{\nu} = \mathbf{y} \qquad (3.6.56)$$

or

$$\mathbf{x}^{\nu+1} = -(\mathbf{L} + \mathbf{D})^{-1}\mathbf{U}\mathbf{x}^{\nu} + (\mathbf{L} + \mathbf{D})^{-1}\mathbf{y}, \qquad (3.6.57)$$

which is the iteration algorithm that defines the method of successive displacements.

As before, it is easily seen that if at some state $\mathbf{x}^{\nu} = \mathbf{A}^{-1}\mathbf{y}$, then $\mathbf{x}^{p+1} = \mathbf{A}^{-1}\mathbf{y}$.

We now consider the convergence properties of the iteration and derive expressions for the eigenvalues of the iteration operator. Assume $|\mathbf{D}| \neq 0$, and since $\mathbf{L}$ is strictly lower triangular, the matrix $(\mathbf{L} + \mathbf{D})^{-1}$ exists and is of the form

$$(\mathbf{L} + \mathbf{D})^{-1} = \mathbf{L}' + \mathbf{D}^{-1}, \qquad (3.6.58)$$

where $\mathbf{L}'$ is strictly lower triangular. Convergence of the iteration depends upon the eigenvalues of the iteration matrix, i.e., the roots λ of

$$| -(\mathbf{L} + \mathbf{D})^{-1}\mathbf{U} - \lambda\mathbf{I} | = 0 \qquad (3.6.59)$$

or

$$| \lambda\mathbf{L} + \lambda\mathbf{D} + \mathbf{U} | = 0. \qquad (3.6.60)$$

The roots of Eq. (3.6.60) must all have magnitude less than unity for convergence. It is usually difficult to solve for the roots explicitly; however, the rule concerning diagonal dominance of irreducible matrices applies for the method of successive displacement also.

In the method of successive displacements, we are always using the latest computed values for the unknown and hence the name successive displacement. It is interesting to compare the convergence rates of the method of simultaneous and successive displacements for the same problem. When the iteration matrices are non-negative, we shall prove shortly that the two methods converge or diverge together. Further, if they converge, then the successive displacements technique converges 'more rapidly.

To prove this result we consider first the method of simultaneous displacement. We assume that the iteration matrix is nonnegative which is possible if the matrices $\mathbf{L}$ and $\mathbf{U}$ have nonnegative elements and $\mathbf{D}$ has all negative nonzero components, or conversely, for instance. For the method of simultaneous displacements, the iteration matrix is then

$$-\mathbf{D}^{-1}(\mathbf{L} + \mathbf{U}) \equiv \mathbf{R} + \mathbf{T}, \qquad (3.6.61)$$

where $\mathbf{R}$ is strictly lower triangular and $\mathbf{T}$ strictly upper triangular. Similarly, the iteration matrix for the method of successive displacements is

$$-(\mathbf{L} + \mathbf{D})^{-1}\mathbf{U} \equiv (\mathbf{I} - \mathbf{R})^{-1}\mathbf{T}. \qquad (3.6.62)$$

The proof (from Reference 13) of divergence is straightforward. Let λ be the positive eigenvalue of $\mathbf{R} + \mathbf{T}$ of greatest magnitude, and similarly σ be the largest eigenvalue of $(\mathbf{I} - \mathbf{R})^{-1}\mathbf{T}$. Let $\mathbf{z}$ be the eigenvector corresponding to λ; that is,

$$(\mathbf{R} + \mathbf{T})\mathbf{z} = \lambda\mathbf{z}. \qquad (3.6.63)$$

Therefore

$$\left(\mathbf{I} - \frac{\mathbf{R}}{\lambda}\right)^{-1}(\mathbf{R} + \mathbf{T})\mathbf{z} = \lambda\left(\mathbf{I} - \frac{\mathbf{R}}{\lambda}\right)^{-1}\mathbf{z}. \qquad (3.6.64)$$

Now the matrix $(\mathbf{I} - \mathbf{R}/\lambda)^{-1}$ can be written

$$\left(\mathbf{I} - \frac{\mathbf{R}}{\lambda}\right)^{-1} = \mathbf{I} + \frac{\mathbf{R}}{\lambda} + \left(\frac{\mathbf{R}}{\lambda}\right)^2 + \cdots + \left(\frac{\mathbf{R}}{\lambda}\right)^m, \qquad (3.6.65)$$

where $\mathbf{R}$ is assumed $(m + 1)$ by $(m + 1)$. Thus terms beyond the mth power of $\mathbf{R}$ vanish, since $\mathbf{R}$ is strictly lower triangular. Note that all the elements of the sum are nonnegative in view of the hypothesis. Using the expansion (3.6.65) in Eq. (3.6.64), we have

$$\left(\mathbf{I} - \frac{\mathbf{R}}{\lambda}\right)^{-1} \mathbf{T}\mathbf{z} = \lambda\mathbf{z}. \qquad (3.6.66)$$

Thus λ is an eigenvalue of $(\mathbf{I} - \mathbf{R}/\lambda)^{-1}\mathbf{T}$. From the properties of nonnegative matrices, if $\lambda > 1$, then

$$\left(\mathbf{I} - \frac{\mathbf{R}}{\lambda}\right)^{-1} \mathbf{T} < (\mathbf{I} - \mathbf{R})^{-1}\mathbf{T}. \qquad (3.6.67)$$

Consequently $\sigma > \lambda > 1$, and the two iterations diverge together. If $\lambda = 1$, then $\sigma = 1$, while for $\lambda < 1$, $\sigma < \lambda < 1$, which proves the result.

Conversely we could reverse the arguments. Let σ be the largest positive eigenvalue of $(\mathbf{I} - \mathbf{R})^{-1}\mathbf{T}$ and $\mathbf{z}$ the corresponding eigenvector. Thus

$$(\mathbf{I} - \mathbf{R})^{-1}\mathbf{T}\mathbf{z} = \sigma\mathbf{z}, \qquad (3.6.68)$$

or

$$(\sigma\mathbf{R} + \mathbf{T})\mathbf{z} = \sigma\mathbf{z}. \qquad (3.6.69)$$

Therefore σ is also an eigenvalue of $\sigma\mathbf{R} + \mathbf{T}$. If $\sigma > 1$, then $\sigma\mathbf{R} + \mathbf{T} > \mathbf{R} + \mathbf{T}$ and $\sigma > \lambda > 1$. For $\sigma = 1$, then $\lambda = 1$. Finally if $\sigma < 1$

$$\sigma\mathbf{R} + \mathbf{T} < \mathbf{R} + \mathbf{T}. \qquad (3.6.70)$$

Therefore

$$\sigma < \lambda < 1. \qquad (3.6.71)$$

This last result is the important result as it shows that for nonnegative iteration matrices the method of successive displacements asymptotically converges faster than the method of simultaneous displacements.

For matrices which are not nonnegative, it is possible for one method to work and not the other, and vice versa (see problem 9).

We now illustrate the method by considering the model

$$\epsilon_{j,k}^{p+1} = \lambda_{m,n}\epsilon_{j,k}^p .$$ (3.6.72)

Stability requires that $|\lambda_{m,n}| < 1$ for all m, n. Using Eq. (3.6.72) in the difference equation (3.6.56) and factoring, we have

$$\lambda_{m,n}\epsilon_{j,k}^p = \tfrac{1}{4}[\epsilon_{j+1,k}^p + \lambda_{m,n}\epsilon_{j-1,k}^p + \epsilon_{j,k+1}^p + \lambda_{m,n}\epsilon_{j,k-1}^p].$$ (3.6.73)

Following Frankel (Ref. 12) we assume eigenfunctions of the form

$$\epsilon_{j,k}^{(m,n)} = A^j \sin \frac{n\pi j}{K} B^k \sin \frac{m\pi k}{K} ,$$ (3.6.74)

where A and B are assumed constants to be determined. Expanding the trigonometric functions in Eq. (3.6.73) yields the equation

$$\begin{aligned}
\lambda_{m,n}\epsilon_{j,k}^p = \frac{1}{4} \Big[& (A^{j+1} + \lambda_{m,n}A^{j-1})B^k \cos \frac{n\pi}{K} \\
& + (B^{k+1} + \lambda_{m,n}B^{k-1})A^j \cos \frac{m\pi}{K} \Big] \sin \frac{n\pi j}{K} \sin \frac{m\pi k}{K} \\
& + \frac{1}{4} \Big[(A^{j+1} - \lambda_{m,n}A^{j-1})B^k \sin \frac{n\pi}{K} \sin \frac{m\pi k}{K} \cos \frac{n\pi j}{K} \\
& + (B^{k+1} - \lambda_{m,n}B^{k-1})A^j \sin \frac{m\pi}{K} \sin \frac{n\pi j}{K} \cos \frac{m\pi k}{K} \Big] .
\end{aligned}$$ (3.6.75)

Since the error must be zero on the boundary, viz. at k or $j = 0$ or k or $j = K$, the terms in the cosine must vanish. Hence we require

$$\begin{aligned}
A^{j+1} - \lambda_{m,n}A^{j-1} &= 0 \\
B^{k+1} - \lambda_{m,n}B^{k-1} &= 0.
\end{aligned}$$ (3.6.76)

Therefore,

$$A^2 = B^2 = \lambda_{m,n} .$$ (3.6.77)

Equation (3.6.75) then becomes

$$\lambda_{m,n} = \frac{1}{4}\left(\cos \frac{n\pi}{K} + \cos \frac{m\pi}{K}\right)^2 .$$ (3.6.78)

The maximum value is again found for $m = n = 1$. Expanding we have

$$\lambda_{m,n} \approx 1 - \frac{\pi^2}{K^2}. \tag{3.6.79}$$

The asymptotic decay rate is then

$$v = \frac{\pi^2}{K^2}. \tag{3.6.80}$$

Notice that this rate is twice as large as for the method of simultaneous displacements (see Eq. (3.6.54)). Thus, we expect the method of successive displacements to take roughly half as long for the model problem as the method of simultaneous displacements. This result is consistent with the general result for nonnegative irreducible matrices since the Laplace difference equation (3.6.31) leads to a nonnegative irreducible iteration matrix.

In terms of the residuals the method of successive displacements becomes

$$\mathbf{x}^{p+1} = \mathbf{x}^p + \mathbf{r}^p, \tag{3.6.81}^*$$

where

$$\mathbf{r}^p = -(\mathbf{L} + \mathbf{D})^{-1}(\mathbf{A}\mathbf{x}^p - \mathbf{y}). \tag{3.6.82}$$

It is interesting to write out the component form of the residual for the model problem: we have

$$r^p_{j,k} = \tfrac{1}{4}[x^p_{j+1,k} + x^{p+1}_{j-1,k} + x^p_{j,k+1} + x^{p+1}_{j,k-1} - 4x^p_{j,k}]. \tag{3.6.83}$$

A similar result applies for the method of simultaneous displacements where all terms with superscript $p + 1$ are replaced by like terms with superscript p. Notice that the residual can be interpreted as the inbalance between the function $x^p_{j,k}$ and the value of the difference relation operating on the function at the pth iterate.

C. Successive Over-Relaxation

For both of the previous methods, the iteration algorithm could be written

$$\mathbf{x}^{p+1} = \mathbf{x}^p + \mathbf{r}^p \tag{3.6.84}$$

with different $\mathbf{r}^p$ for different methods. From the discussion above, we interpret the residual as correcting the function at each point, say j, k, so as to satisfy the difference equation. Obviously, if any neighboring point to j, k is changed, the residual also changes, as illustrated by Eq. (3.6.84). We might anticipate further changes in the function by over-correcting (or perhaps under-correcting) in hopes of speeding convergence of the iteration. The iteration might then be written

$$\mathbf{x}^{\nu+1} = \mathbf{x}^{\nu} + \alpha\mathbf{r}^{\nu}, \tag{3.6.85}$$

where α is a real number. For $\alpha > 1$ we speak of over-relaxation; for $\alpha < 1$ we speak of under-relaxation. The method of successive over-relaxation (also called the extrapolated Liebmann method) is defined (see problem 10) as

$$\mathbf{x}^{\nu+1} = \mathbf{x}^{\nu} + \alpha[(-\mathbf{D}^{-1}\mathbf{L}\mathbf{x}^{\nu+1} - \mathbf{D}^{-1}\mathbf{U}\mathbf{x}^{\nu} + \mathbf{D}^{-1}\mathbf{y}) - \mathbf{x}^{\nu}]. \tag{3.6.86}$$

The iteration can also be written

$$\mathbf{x}^{\nu+1} = (\mathbf{D} + \alpha\mathbf{L})^{-1}[(1 - \alpha)\mathbf{D} - \alpha\mathbf{U}]\mathbf{x}^{\nu} + \alpha(\mathbf{D} + \alpha\mathbf{L})^{-1}\mathbf{y}. \tag{3.6.87}$$

Notice for $\alpha = 1$ we recover the method of successive displacements. Again if $\mathbf{x}^{\nu} = \mathbf{A}^{-1}\mathbf{y}$, then the iteration yields $\mathbf{x}^{\nu+1} = \mathbf{A}^{-1}\mathbf{y}$, proving consistency.

To illustrate the utility of over-relaxation, consider again the model problem. The iteration algorithm for the errors is

$$\epsilon_{jk}^{\nu+1} = (1 - \alpha)\epsilon_{jk}^{\nu} + \frac{\alpha}{4}[\epsilon_{j+1,k}^{\nu} + \epsilon_{j-1,k}^{\nu+1} + \epsilon_{j,k+1}^{\nu} + \epsilon_{j,k-1}^{\nu+1}]. \tag{3.6.88}$$

We again try for the m, nth component of the error, an expression in the form

$$\epsilon_{jk}^{\nu} = A^{j} \sin \frac{m\pi j}{K} B^{k} \sin \frac{n\pi k}{K} \tag{3.6.89}$$

and also assume the form

$$\epsilon_{jk}^{\nu+1} = \lambda_{mn}\epsilon_{jk}^{\nu}. \tag{3.6.90}$$

Then we have, after the usual algebra,

$$\lambda_{mn} = (1 - \alpha) + \frac{\alpha}{2}\sqrt{\lambda_{mn}}\left(\cos\frac{m\pi}{K} + \cos\frac{n\pi}{K}\right). \tag{3.6.91}$$

The largest value of λ will occur for $m = n = 1$. Therefore let

$$\eta = \cos\frac{\pi}{K}. \tag{3.6.92}$$

We then have

$$\lambda_{11} = (1 - \alpha) + \alpha\eta(\lambda_{11})^{1/2}, \tag{3.6.93}$$

and

$$(\lambda_{11})^{1/2} = \frac{\alpha\eta + \sqrt{\alpha^2\eta^2 - 4(\alpha - 1)}}{2}, \tag{3.6.94}$$

for the largest real value of $(\lambda_{11})^{1/2}$. To study the behavior of λ as a function of α, note that for $\alpha = 1$, we have

$$\lambda_{11} = \eta^2, \tag{3.6.95}$$

which is consistent with Eq. (3.6.80). To find the slope of λ_{11} versus α, we write Eq. (3.6.93) in the form (with the subscript 11 suppressed)

$$(\lambda^{1/2})^2 = (1 - \alpha) + \alpha\eta\lambda^{1/2} \tag{3.6.96}$$

and differentiate with respect to α. We have

$$\frac{\partial\lambda^{1/2}}{\partial\alpha} = \frac{\eta\lambda^{1/2} - 1}{2\lambda^{1/2} - \alpha\eta}. \tag{3.6.97}$$

We also have from Eqs. (3.6.96) and (3.6.97)

$$\frac{\partial\lambda}{\partial\alpha} = -1 + \eta\lambda^{1/2} + \alpha\eta\left[\frac{\eta\lambda^{1/2} - 1}{2\lambda^{1/2} - \alpha\eta}\right], \tag{3.6.98}$$

or

$$\frac{\partial\lambda}{\partial\alpha} = -\frac{\lambda^{1/2} - \eta\lambda}{\lambda^{1/2} - \dfrac{\alpha\eta}{2}}. \tag{3.6.99}$$

At $\alpha = 1$, $\lambda^{1/2} = \eta$ with $\eta < 1$. Therefore, as α increases, λ decreases with ever steeper slope until the denominator vanishes. From Eq. (3.6.94) we see that the minimum λ occurs when

$$\alpha^2\eta^2 = 4(\alpha - 1) \tag{3.6.100}$$

or

$$\alpha = \frac{2 - 2\sqrt{1 - \eta^2}}{\eta^2} = \frac{2}{1 + \sqrt{1 - \eta^2}}. \tag{3.6.101}$$

With the above value of α, λ becomes

$$\lambda = \alpha - 1 = \frac{1 - \sqrt{1 - \eta^2}}{1 + \sqrt{1 - \eta^2}}. \tag{3.6.102}$$

To obtain an order of magnitude estimate we expand the expression for η to find

$$\alpha \approx \frac{2}{1 + \dfrac{\pi}{K}} , \qquad (3.6.103)$$

and with the given (optimum) α

$$\lambda \approx \frac{1 - \pi/K}{1 + \pi/K} \approx 1 - \frac{2\pi}{K} . \qquad (3.6.104)$$

Using the optimum over-relaxation factor, we have an asymptotic convergence rate of

$$v \approx \frac{2\pi}{K} . \qquad (3.6.105)$$

Notice that this decay rate is an enormous increase over that obtained for the method of successive displacements. For a 20 by 20 problem, the asymptotic decay rate is approximately

$$v = 0.314. \qquad (3.6.106)$$

This is greater than a factor of 10 better than the results obtained by using successive displacements. Such gains are characteristic of the method of successive over-relaxation with the optimum over-relaxation parameter.

It is interesting to study the behavior of the method as a function of the over-relaxation parameter. For a given η we consider various α's and λ's. At $\alpha = 0$, $\lambda = 1$, but this is evident since then no iteration occurs. The slope of the λ versus α curve grows steeper from $\alpha = 0$. As α increases from 1, λ decreases, the slope reaching minus infinity at the optimum α. Beyond the optimum α, λ begins to increase. Note that for α greater than the optimum, λ is complex. The derivative of the magnitude of λ is then

$$\frac{\partial |\lambda|}{\partial \alpha} = \frac{\partial}{\partial \alpha} \left[\frac{\alpha^2 \eta^2}{4} + \frac{1}{4} (4(\alpha - 1) - \alpha^2 \eta^2) \right] = 1, \qquad (3.6.107)$$

and hence the magnitude of λ increases linearly with α. The general shape of the λ versus α curve is shown in Fig. 3.6.2.

The results obtained thus far are more general than the derivation indicates. For difference approximations to a wide variety of elliptic equations, over-relaxation is very worth-while. It can be shown[6] that the results obtained previously for the asymptotic convergence rate and optimum over-relaxation factor apply to more general problems than the model problem. In particular, notice that the definition of η, Eq. (3.6.92), is the same as the largest eigenvalue for the method of simultaneous displacements, Eq. (3.6.53). The results, Eqs. (3.6.96) and (3.6.97), are actually expressed in terms of the eigenvalues of the method of simultaneous displacements.

In actual practice one seldom has available the eigenvalues η to predict accurately the optimum over-relaxation parameter. Usually an experimental approach is undertaken where one attempts to find the optimum factor by trial and error. The process of looking for the optimum factor is

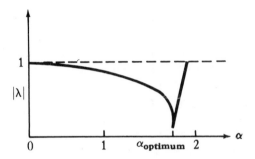

Fig. 3.6.2. Magnitude of the largest eigenvalue, λ, of the iteration operator versus the over-relaxation parameter.

time consuming, but the actual gain in convergence rate is usually so large that the total time of solution is significantly reduced. It is usually best to choose an α a little too large than a little too small, because the value of λ will then be closer to the minimum. In general, the optimum α is unknown so a small error will usually be made in choosing it.

3.6.4 NONSTATIONARY METHODS

Frequently it is possible to hasten the convergence of an iteration by considering nonstationary iterations. These are iteration methods in which the technique used depends upon the step of the iteration. In this section we shall consider several such techniques.

First, assume we have a convergent iteration with iteration matrix **B**. Since the iteration is convergent, the eigenvalues of **B**, say λ, are all

[6] See Forsythe and Wasow, Reference 5, for a very lucid discussion of the more general theory of successive over-relaxation.

less than one in magnitude. We assume we have a dominant eigenvalue, say λ_1. The errors are asymptotically given in the form

$$\epsilon^{\nu+1} \approx \lambda_1 \epsilon^{\nu}, \tag{3.6.108}$$

as shown in Section 3.6.2. Since the errors are not known at any stage of the iteration, we consider the residuals, which are known. The residuals obey the recurrence relation

$$\mathbf{r}^{\nu+1} = (\mathbf{B} - \mathbf{I})\mathbf{B}(\mathbf{B} - \mathbf{I})^{-1}\mathbf{r}^{\nu} = \mathbf{B}\mathbf{r}^{\nu}, \tag{3.6.109}$$

as may be seen from Eqs. (3.6.9) and (3.6.16). Consequently the asymptotic behavior of the residuals is also of the form

$$\mathbf{r}^{\nu+1} \approx \lambda_1 \mathbf{r}^{\nu}. \tag{3.6.110}$$

Once the residuals have assumed their asymptotic behavior (and this is measurable), we may predict the total of the future displacements. Thus

$$\mathbf{r}^{\nu+2} = \lambda_1^2 \mathbf{r}^{\nu}. \tag{3.6.111}$$

The total displacement, say $\mathbf{r}^t$, is then

$$\mathbf{r}^t = \mathbf{r}^{\nu} + \lambda_1 \mathbf{r}^{\nu} + \ldots + \lambda_1^{\infty} \mathbf{r}^{\nu} = \left(\frac{1}{1 - \lambda_1}\right)\mathbf{r}^{\nu}, \tag{3.6.112}$$

and the solution approximated as

$$\mathbf{x}^t = \mathbf{x}^{\nu} + \mathbf{r}^t. \tag{3.6.113}$$

We cannot expect the acceleration to yield the true answer since the factor $1/(1 - \lambda_1)$ will amplify harmonics other than the first. Nevertheless, the acceleration is frequently useful. The measurement of λ_1 is usually done experimentally. That is, one monitors the ratio

$$\frac{|\mathbf{r}^{p+1}|}{|\mathbf{r}^{p}|} \approx \lambda_1$$

for successive values of p. When the variation in the approximate value of λ_1 is small, then the acceleration may be attempted. The use of this technique for solving linear algebraic equations is analogous to a method for solving nonlinear algebraic equations, in which case the acceleration is known as Aitkens δ^2 method.

A. The Alternating Direction Method

The alternating direction implicit method of Peaceman and Rachford may also be applied to the iterative solution of elliptic equations. The following development is from Varga (Reference 8). We must require that the matrix operator be of block tridiagonal form and contain at most five nonzero elements per row. The basis of the method is to assume the iteration is analogous to a time variable. If we desire to solve the equation

$$\mathbf{Ax} = \mathbf{y}, \tag{3.6.114}$$

then we consider the equation

$$\frac{d\mathbf{x}}{dt} = \mathbf{Ax} - \mathbf{y}. \tag{3.6.115}$$

For any $\mathbf{x}$ satisfying Eq. (3.6.114), the derivative of $\mathbf{x}$ must be zero. Using a simple difference approximation we have

$$\frac{\mathbf{x}^{p+1} - \mathbf{x}^p}{\varDelta t_p} = \mathbf{Ax}^p - \mathbf{y}, \tag{3.6.116}$$

where $\varDelta t_p$ corresponds to a single time step. For elliptic equations in two dimensions, the spacing h^2 appears as a factor in the matrix $\mathbf{A}$, consequently the ratio $\varDelta t_p/h^2 = r_p{}^2$ is also a factor of $\mathbf{A}$. We now write $\mathbf{A}$ in the form

$$\mathbf{A} = (\mathbf{Y} + \mathbf{Z})/h^2, \tag{3.6.117}$$

where we assume $\mathbf{Y}, \mathbf{Z}$ symmetric and positive definite, and with at most three elements per row. The two matrices $\mathbf{Y}, \mathbf{Z}$ are taken to correspond to second differences in the two spatial dimensions y and z respectively. The iteration consists of time steps (iterations) in alternate directions and of the form

$$\mathbf{x}^{p+1} = \mathbf{x}^p + r_p^2[\mathbf{Yx}^{p+1} + \mathbf{Zx}^p - h^2\mathbf{y}], \tag{3.6.118}$$

and

$$\mathbf{x}^{p+2} = \mathbf{x}^{p+1} + r_p^2[\mathbf{Yx}^{p+1} + \mathbf{Zx}^{p+2} - h^2\mathbf{y}]. \tag{3.6.119}$$

The above equations can be written as

$$\mathbf{x}^{p+1} = (\mathbf{I} - r_p^2\mathbf{Y})^{-1}(\mathbf{I} + r_p^2\mathbf{Z})\mathbf{x}^p - h^2r_p^2(\mathbf{I} - r_p^2\mathbf{Y})^{-1}\mathbf{y}, \tag{3.6.120}$$

and

$$\mathbf{x}^{p+2} = (\mathbf{I} - r_p^2\mathbf{Z})^{-1}(\mathbf{I} + r_p^2\mathbf{Y})\mathbf{x}^{p+1} - h^2 r_p^2(\mathbf{I} - r_p^2\mathbf{Z})^{-1}\mathbf{y}, \qquad (3.6.121)$$

which define the iteration algorithm.

Before applying the iteration to the model problem, several comments are pertinent. We assume the factor r_p^2 may be a function of p, and in fact is chosen so as to speed convergence. However, r_p^2 must not vary in going from $\mathbf{x}^p$ to $\mathbf{x}^{p+2}$. That is, r_p^2 must be the same for the two alternating direction sweeps. Also, we take the operators $\mathbf{Y}$ and $\mathbf{Z}$ to be three-point relations so the rapid method of matrix factorization of Section 1.14 may be used.

The virtues of this method become evident by applying it to the model problem for which we can find an analytical relation. Applied to this problem, the method yields the error equations

$$[2 + (1/r_p^2)]\epsilon_{jk}^{p+1} - \epsilon_{j-1,k}^{p+1} - \epsilon_{j+1,k}^{p+1} = \epsilon_{j,k+1}^p + \epsilon_{j,k-1}^p - [2 - (1/r_p^2)]\epsilon_{jk}^p \quad (3.6.122)$$

and

$$[2 + (1/r_p^2)]\epsilon_{jk}^{p+2} - \epsilon_{j,k-1}^{p+2} - \epsilon_{j,k+1}^{p+2}$$
$$= \epsilon_{j+1,k}^{p+1} + \epsilon_{j-1,k}^{p+1} - [2 - (1/r_p^2)]\epsilon_{jk}^{p+1}. \quad (3.6.123)$$

From the results of Section 3.5, we can analytically find the eigenvalues of the two-step iteration to be

$$\lambda_{m,n} = \frac{(1/r_p^2) - 4\sin^2\dfrac{n\pi}{2K}\ (1/r_p^2) - 4\sin^2\dfrac{m\pi}{2K}}{(1/r_p^2) + 4\sin^2\dfrac{n\pi}{2K}\ (1/r_p^2) + 4\sin^2\dfrac{m\pi}{2K}}. \qquad (3.6.124)$$

It is evident from Eq. (3.6.124) that if r_p^2 (i.e., Δt_p) is properly chosen, we can make one eigenvalue equal to zero, and hence eliminate that error component by means of each two-step iteration. If the total number of unknowns is N, then in $2N$ steps the iterations will have converged quite precisely. However, in general it is not necessary to perform so many iterations; a sufficiently small error, though not zero error, can be found in rather fewer steps. To this end, an average factor r_p^2 is used to reduce significantly particular harmonics; the factor r_p^2 must be chosen, of course, so that other harmonics are not increased. Indeed, in the general problem, the most difficult part of the alternating direction method is the choice of a good average value for r_p^2. With enough average values the errors can be significantly reduced by using them cyclically.

Appropriate average factors $1/r_p{}^2$ can be easily found for the model problem. These will give an idea of the rate of convergence of the method. To find the appropriate average factors, we note from Eq. (3.6.124) that the values of $1/r_p{}^2$ found analytically in the model problem consist of a discrete spectrum between 0 and 4. Our present objective is to replace this spectrum with fewer, but representative, entries. We have two alternatives available: we can either choose the number of subintervals, or we can choose the error-reduction factor. In either case there is an optimum way of averaging over each subinterval in choosing a representative value of $1/r_p{}^2$ for this interval.

We note that all of the harmonics have factors of the form $\sin^2{(n\pi/2K)}$. Let

$$\bar{\beta}_n = \sin^2 \frac{n\pi}{2K}. \tag{3.6.125}$$

The factor $\bar{\beta}$ ranges from near zero, say a, to near unity, say b. We now subdivide the interval $a - b$ into subintervals β_i, $i = 0, 1, ..., I$, and such that

$$\sin^2 \frac{(K-1)\pi}{2K} = b = \beta_0 > \beta_1 > \beta_2 > ... > \beta_I = a = \sin^2 \frac{\pi}{2K}.$$

Suppose we desire to choose the factors $1/r_i{}^2$ such that an iteration with the given $1/r_i{}^2$ reduces all harmonics between β_i and β_{i+1} by a factor of at least α. We require then

$$\max \left| \frac{1/r_i^2 - 4\beta}{1/r_i^2 + 4\beta} \right| = \alpha, \qquad \beta_{i+1} \leqslant \beta \leqslant \beta_i. \tag{3.6.126}$$

Consequently, the best choice of the β_i is that for which the maximum occurs at the end points, i.e.,

$$-\frac{1/r_i^2 - 4\beta_i}{1/r_i^2 + 4\beta_i} = \frac{1/r_i^2 - 4\beta_{i+1}}{1/r_i^2 + 4\beta_{i+1}} = \alpha. \tag{3.6.127}$$

By eliminating $1/r_i{}^2$ from the equation, we find the intervals must be so chosen that

$$\beta_{i+1} = \left(\frac{1-\alpha}{1+\alpha}\right)^2 \beta_i \tag{3.6.128}$$

and therefore

$$\beta_i = \left(\frac{1-\alpha}{1+\alpha}\right)^{2i} b, \qquad i = 0, 1, ..., I. \tag{3.6.129}$$

Therefore, having selected the reduction factor α and knowing the interval in which the function β varies, we find the number of intervals needed and the widths of each. Note that for small α, many narrow intervals are needed, whereas for large α (but less than unity), few intervals are needed. Having found the interval widths, we use Eq. (3.6.127) to find r_i^2. The result is

$$\frac{1}{r_i^2} = 4b \left(\frac{1-\alpha}{1+\alpha}\right)^{2i+1}, \qquad i = 1, 2, ..., I, \qquad (3.6.130)$$

which are the average factors $1/r_i^2$ desired. With the appropriate values of r_i^2, one complete cycle of iterations reduces all the errors by at least α^2 as seen from Eq. (3.6.124).

To find the number of intervals needed to reduce each error by at least a factor of α^2, we must take a number of intervals (and hence iterations) given by Eq. (3.6.129) as

$$\beta_I \equiv \sin^2 \frac{\pi}{2K} = \left(\frac{1-\alpha}{1+\alpha}\right)^{2I} \sin^2 \frac{(K-1)\pi}{2K}. \qquad (3.6.131)$$

By the usual expansions, for K this becomes

$$\left(\frac{\pi}{2K}\right)^2 \approx \left(\frac{1-\alpha}{1+\alpha}\right)^{2I}$$

or

$$I = \frac{\ln K - \ln \frac{\pi}{2}}{\ln \left(\frac{1+\alpha}{1-\alpha}\right)} \approx \frac{\ln K}{2\alpha}. \qquad (3.6.132)$$

Therefore, to reduce the error by a factor of e, i.e., $\alpha = e^{-1/2}$, approximately $(.8)\ln K$ iterations are required. For $K = 100$ this means approximately 4 iterations. For comparison, the method of over-relaxation would require approximately 15 iterations. In general, the method is better than the method of over-relaxation by a factor of $(K/2)\ln K$, approximately.

The alternating direction method is admirable for the model problem. The large gain in convergence more than offsets the additional algebra due to the implicit nature of the equations. For more general problems, proof of the large gain in convergence has not been established. Nevertheless the method is used to good advantage for other two-dimensional problems.

B. Method of Steepest Descent

We consider again the matrix equation

$$\mathbf{A}\mathbf{x} = \mathbf{y} \tag{3.6.133}$$

and an associated iteration algorithm

$$\mathbf{x}^{p+1} = \mathbf{x}^p + \alpha_p \mathbf{z}^p, \tag{3.6.134}$$

where α_p is a scalar and $\mathbf{z}^p$ a correction vector. In the previously considered methods, the correction vector was obtained from the residuals in a straightforward manner. The method of steepest descent is derived by considering a geometric interpretation of the iteration. To this end we define the function

$$\mathbf{s}^p = \mathbf{A}\mathbf{x}^p - \mathbf{y}, \tag{3.6.135}$$

which is the amount by which the trial solution $\mathbf{x}^p$ fails to satisfy the original equation (3.6.133). The function

$$f(\mathbf{x}^p) = (\mathbf{s}^p)^T(\mathbf{s}^p) = (\mathbf{A}\mathbf{x}^p - \mathbf{y})^T(\mathbf{A}\mathbf{x}^p - \mathbf{y}) = \text{constant} \tag{3.6.136}$$

is the equation for an ellipsoid in the n dimensional space of the problem, n being the order of the operator $\mathbf{A}$. The center of the ellipsoid is the point $\mathbf{x} = \mathbf{A}^{-1}\mathbf{y}$. The solution of the matrix equations is then equivalent to finding the center of the ellipsoids defined by Eq. (3.6.136). At each step of the iteration, we desire a correction vector which will move us near the center of the ellipsoids. From elementary vector analysis, we know the direction of greatest change from a surface is the direction of the gradient vector. Hence a reasonable choice for $\mathbf{z}^p$ is the gradient of $f(\mathbf{x}^p)$.

To simplify the algebra we shall assume $\mathbf{A}$ is postive definite and symmetric. In this case $\mathbf{A}$ can be written

$$\mathbf{A} = \mathbf{B}^T\mathbf{B}, \tag{3.6.137}$$

an equation that has a solution since there are more elements in $\mathbf{B}$ than in $\mathbf{A}$. The original equation (3.6.133) is equivalent to

$$\mathbf{B}\mathbf{x} = \mathbf{u},$$
$$\mathbf{B}^T\mathbf{u} = \mathbf{y}. \tag{3.6.138}$$

We define the quadratic surface

$$f(\mathbf{x}) = (\mathbf{B}\mathbf{x} - \mathbf{u})^T(\mathbf{B}\mathbf{x} - \mathbf{u}) = \mathbf{x}^T\mathbf{A}\mathbf{x} - 2\mathbf{x}^T\mathbf{y} + \mathbf{u}^T\mathbf{u}. \tag{3.6.139}$$

This function vanishes for $\mathbf{x} = \mathbf{A}^{-1}\mathbf{y}$. The gradient to the surface is

$$\frac{df(\mathbf{x})}{dx_i} = 2(\mathbf{Ax} - \mathbf{y})_i , \qquad (3.6.140)$$

hence for $\mathbf{x} = \mathbf{x}^p$, the gradient is

$$\frac{df(\mathbf{x}^p)}{dx_i} = 2s_i^p . \qquad (3.6.141)$$

We take the correction $\mathbf{z}^p$ proportional to $\mathbf{s}^p$. The choice of α_p can be made in the following manner. We wish to add a correction to the approximate solution, in the direction $\mathbf{s}$, such that the magnitude of the function $f(\mathbf{x}^{p+1})$ is minimized. Thus we desire

$$\frac{\partial}{\partial \alpha}[f(\mathbf{x}^p + \alpha_p\mathbf{s}^p)] = 0. \qquad (3.6.142)$$

By simple operations we find

$$\alpha_p = -\frac{(\mathbf{s}^p)^T(\mathbf{s}^p)}{(\mathbf{s}^p)^T\mathbf{A}(\mathbf{s}^p)} . \qquad (3.6.143)$$

If one treats the method of steepest descent as a stationary problem with α_p the appropriate constant, then the method is the same as the method of simultaneous displacements. The convergence properties are thus similar to the same properties for simultaneous displacements. However, the geometric interpretation lends itself to a much improved gradient method which we consider next.

C. Method of Conjugate Gradients

The method of conjugate gradients is based upon the concept that along a line the shortest distance to a point (to be taken as the origin) is the perpendicular through that point to the line. In constructing a path to that point, we may proceed to the foot of the perpendicular along the line. The path to the origin may be traced in Fig. 3.6.3. Of course, only

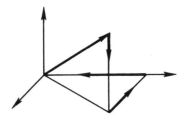

FIG. 3.6.3.   A typical path followed in the conjugate gradient procedure.

3 dimensions are illustrated in this figure. From this foot we never again have to travel in any direction with a component along the given line. Indeed, we need move only in a plane through the point and perpendicular to the given line. (This plane contains the original perpendicular, of course). In this plane, we may strike out in some arbitrary direction, which will be perpendicular to the original line. The shortest distance to the point from this arbitrary direction is again a new perpendicular to this direction (and also the original line) through the point. The previous process can then be repeated again. In a space of n dimensions, only n repetitions of this procedure are required to bring us precisely to the point desired—apart from round-off error.

The actual selection of the directions of correction is relatively simple. We desire that successive correction vectors be orthogonal to all previous corrections and further, we desire to minimize the error as much as possible at each step. We again consider the quadratic surface $f(\mathbf{x}^0)$ [as defined by Eq. (3.6.139)] and the gradient vector $\mathbf{s}^0$ [as defined by Eq. (3.6.140)]. We correct $\mathbf{x}^0$ in the direction $\mathbf{s}^0$ and such that $f(\mathbf{x}^1)$ is minimized. The vector from the origin to $\mathbf{x}^1$ lies in a plane orthogonal to $\mathbf{s}^0$. For the next correction we find the *component* of the gradient of $f(\mathbf{x}^1)$ which lies in the plane orthogonal to $\mathbf{s}^0$. We move along the correction vector to $\mathbf{x}^2$ a distance that minimizes $f(\mathbf{x}^2)$. We continue in this manner taking corrections as components of the gradient which are orthogonal to the previous directions of correction.

In general the process of orthogonalization of a set of vectors is quite complicated. Since we are dealing with projections of gradients, however, a remarkable simplification is possible. To illustrate, consider the starting vector $\mathbf{x}^0$ and the initial gradient $\mathbf{z}^0 = \mathbf{A}\mathbf{x}^0 - \mathbf{y}$. We choose $\mathbf{x}^1$ as in the steepest descent, i.e.,

$$\mathbf{x}^1 = \mathbf{x}^0 + \alpha_0 \mathbf{z}^0, \tag{3.6.144}$$

whence

$$\alpha_0 = -\frac{(\mathbf{z}^0)^T \mathbf{z}^0}{(\mathbf{z}^0)^T \mathbf{A} \mathbf{z}^0}. \tag{3.6.145}$$

For $\mathbf{z}^1$ we take the gradient

$$\mathbf{z}^1 = \mathbf{A}\mathbf{x}^1 - \mathbf{y} = \mathbf{z}^0 + \alpha_0 \mathbf{A} \mathbf{z}^0. \tag{3.6.146}$$

Note that $\mathbf{z}^1$ is orthogonal to $\mathbf{z}^0$ since

$$(\mathbf{z}^0)^T \mathbf{z}^1 = (\mathbf{z}^0)^T \mathbf{z}^0 + \alpha_0 (\mathbf{z}^0)^T \mathbf{A} \mathbf{z}^0 = 0 \tag{3.6.147}$$

for α_0 as in Eq. (3.6.145). If we take $\mathbf{x}^2$ in the form

$$\mathbf{x}^2 = \mathbf{x}^1 + \alpha_1\mathbf{z}^1 = \mathbf{x}^0 + \alpha_0\mathbf{z}^0 + \alpha_1\mathbf{z}^1, \tag{3.6.148}$$

then the gradient is

$$\mathbf{z}^2 = \mathbf{A}\mathbf{x}^2 - \mathbf{y} = \mathbf{z}^1 + \alpha_1\mathbf{A}\mathbf{z}^1, \tag{3.6.149}$$

and this vector is not orthogonal to $\mathbf{z}^0$ for any $\alpha_1 \neq 0$. We desire to correct $\mathbf{x}^2$ such that the vector $\mathbf{z}^2$ is orthogonal to $\mathbf{z}^0$ and $\mathbf{z}^1$. To this end it is convenient to write the residual in the form

$$\mathbf{z}^2 = a_1(\mathbf{z}^1 + b_0\mathbf{z}^0 + \alpha_1\mathbf{A}\mathbf{z}^1). \tag{3.6.150}$$

The orthogonality requires that

$$\alpha_1 = -\frac{(\mathbf{z}^1)^T\mathbf{z}^1}{(\mathbf{z}^1)^T\mathbf{A}\mathbf{z}^1} \tag{3.6.151}$$

and

$$b_0 = -\alpha_1\frac{(\mathbf{z}^0)^T\mathbf{A}\mathbf{z}^1}{(\mathbf{z}^0)^T\mathbf{z}^0}. \tag{3.6.152}$$

The correction is derived by substituting for $\mathbf{z}^i$ in the form $\mathbf{z}^i = \mathbf{A}\mathbf{x}^i - \mathbf{y}$. We have

$$\mathbf{A}\mathbf{x}^2 - \mathbf{y} = a_1(\mathbf{A}\mathbf{x}^1 - \mathbf{y} + b_0(\mathbf{A}\mathbf{x}^0 - \mathbf{y}) + \alpha_1\mathbf{A}\mathbf{z}^1). \tag{3.6.153}$$

Thus,

$$\mathbf{x}^2 = a_1[\mathbf{x}^1 + b_0\mathbf{x}^0 + \alpha_1\mathbf{z}^1] \tag{3.6.154}$$

for a_1 such that

$$a_1(1 + b_0) = 1. \tag{3.6.155}$$

Having computed $\mathbf{x}^2$ such that $\mathbf{z}^2$ is orthogonal to $\mathbf{z}^0$ and $\mathbf{z}^1$, we now consider correcting $\mathbf{x}^3$ such that $\mathbf{z}^3$ is orthogonal to $\mathbf{z}^0$, $\mathbf{z}^1$, $\mathbf{z}^2$. We expect $\mathbf{z}^3$ of the form

$$\mathbf{z}^3 = a_2(\mathbf{z}^2 + b_1\mathbf{z}^1 + c_0\mathbf{z}^0 + \alpha_2\mathbf{A}\mathbf{z}^2). \tag{3.6.156}$$

However, the coefficient c_0 must be zero since we have

$$\begin{aligned}(\mathbf{z}^0)^T\mathbf{z}^3 &= a_2(c_0(\mathbf{z}^0)^T\mathbf{z}^0 + \alpha_2(\mathbf{z}^0)^T\mathbf{A}\mathbf{z}^2) \\ &= a_2(c_0(\mathbf{z}^0)^T\mathbf{z}^0 + \alpha_2(\mathbf{z}^2)^T\mathbf{A}\mathbf{z}^0).\end{aligned} \tag{3.6.157}$$

Notice the vector $\mathbf{A}\mathbf{z}^0$ is a linear combination of $\mathbf{z}^1$ and $\mathbf{z}^0$. By the previous orthogonality $(\mathbf{z}^2)^T\mathbf{z}^0 = (\mathbf{z}^2)^T\mathbf{z}^1 = 0$. Hence $c_0 = 0$. In general one can show by the above argument that $\mathbf{z}^j$ consists only of terms in $\mathbf{z}^{j-1}$,

z^{j-2} and $\mathbf{A}z^{j-1}$. Consequently the expressions for the correction vectors and successive estimates are only three term recursions. The general rule is of the form

$$\mathbf{z}^j = a_{j-1}[\mathbf{z}^{j-1} + b_{j-2}\mathbf{z}^{j-2} + \alpha_{j-1}\mathbf{A}\mathbf{z}^{j-1}] \tag{3.6.158}$$

and

$$\mathbf{x}^j = a_{j-1}[\mathbf{x}^{j-1} + b_{j-2}\mathbf{x}^{j-2} + \alpha_{j-1}\mathbf{A}\mathbf{z}^{j-1}]. \tag{3.6.159}$$

The coefficients are computed in the form

$$\alpha_{j-1} = -\frac{(\mathbf{z}^{j-1})^T\mathbf{z}^{j-1}}{(\mathbf{z}^{j-1})^T\mathbf{A}\mathbf{z}^{j-1}}, \tag{3.6.160a}$$

$$b_{j-2} = -\frac{\alpha_{j-1}(\mathbf{z}^{j-1})^T\mathbf{A}\mathbf{z}^{j-2}}{(\mathbf{z}^{j-2})^T\mathbf{z}^{j-2}}, \tag{3.6.160b}$$

and

$$a_{j-1}(1 + b_{j-2}) = 1. \tag{3.6.160c}$$

By the orthogonality of the $\mathbf{z}^i$, we must have $\mathbf{z}^N = 0$ for N equal the dimension of the problem, and hence $\mathbf{x}^{N-1}$ is the desired solution.

The method of conjugate gradients is an N-step process which would yield an exact result if there were no round-off. With round-off an additional step may be necessary to correct the approximate solution. At each step we require something like N^2 operations (from the product $\mathbf{A}\mathbf{z}^i$) and N steps. Consequently, the total number of steps is proportional to N^3. For a sparse matrix the number of operations is much reduced.

3.6.5   EIGENVALUE PROBLEMS

Of frequent interest to nuclear engineers is the study of critical assemblies. The mathematical formulations of such problems lead to eigenvalue problems. In general, the nuclear engineer or physicist is interested in the smallest eigenvalue, that is, the first critical mode. Rarely is he concerned with the entire set of eigenvalues of a reactor system.

This limited interest greatly simplifies the numerical study of reactive assemblies. Although a variety of methods have been derived for generating the eigenvalues and eigenvectors of a matrix, many simplifications are possible when one is interested only in the largest or smallest eigenvalue. Hereafter we shall be concerned with criticality problems and assume we are interested in approximating the smallest eigenvalue of a given assembly.

For an introductory example, consider the simple one-group, one-region diffusion equation

$$\frac{d^2y}{dx^2} + B^2y = 0 \qquad (3.6.161)$$

with boundary conditions

$$y(0) = y(a) = 0.$$

The simple difference approximation

$$\delta^2 y_k + B^2 h^2 y_k = 0 \qquad (3.6.162)$$

can be easily solved analytically. We know the lowest mode has the solution

$$y_k = \sin \frac{k\pi}{K}, \qquad (3.6.163a)$$

$$B_1^2 = \frac{2}{h^2} \left(1 - \cos \frac{\pi}{K}\right), \qquad (3.6.163b)$$

where the subscript 1 is the mode index. For small h, the results (3.6.163a, b) approach the anlytic solution.

One approach to solving the problem is to write Eq. (3.6.162) in matrix form

$$\mathbf{A}\mathbf{y} = \lambda \mathbf{y}, \qquad (3.6.164)$$

where

$$\mathbf{A} = \begin{bmatrix} 2 & -1 & 0 & \cdots & 0 & 0 \\ -1 & 2 & -1 & \cdots & 0 & 0 \\ 0 & -1 & 2 & \cdots & 0 & 0 \\ \vdots & \vdots & \vdots & & \vdots & \vdots \\ 0 & 0 & 0 & \cdots & 2 & -1 \\ 0 & 0 & 0 & \cdots & -1 & 2 \end{bmatrix} \qquad (3.6.165)$$

and $\lambda = B^2 h^2$.

To generate the solution we might take a trial vector $\mathbf{y}^0$, operate with the matrix $\mathbf{A}$ repeatedly until we achieve a repeating distribution. This technique is called the power method. If we assume $\mathbf{A}$ has a complete set of eigenvectors, then we expand $\mathbf{y}^0$ in terms of the eigenvectors, say $\mathbf{e}_r$. We have

$$\mathbf{y}^0 = \sum_{r=1}^{n} a_r \mathbf{e}_r. \qquad (3.6.166)$$

Successive applications of the matrix $\mathbf{A}$ yield

$$\mathbf{y}^p = \mathbf{A}\mathbf{y}^{p-1} = \mathbf{A}^p\mathbf{y}^0 \tag{3.6.167}$$

$$= \lambda_1^p \left[a_1\mathbf{e}_1 + \sum_{r=2}^{n} a_r \left(\frac{\lambda_r}{\lambda_1}\right)^p \mathbf{e}_r \right]. \tag{3.6.168}$$

If $|\lambda_1| > |\lambda_2| \geqslant |\lambda_3| \geqslant ... \geqslant |\lambda_n|$, then ultimately we have

$$\mathbf{y}^{p+1} \approx a_1\lambda_1^p\mathbf{e}_1 . \tag{3.6.169}$$

We generate a repeating function which is the eigenvector $\mathbf{e}_1$ corresponding to the eigenvalue of largest magnitude. Unfortunately, we desire the eigenfunction corresponding to the smallest eigenvalue. There are several elementary methods of recasting the problem so that the smallest eigenvalue can be obtained. For instance, if we know the largest eigenvalue is bounded by some scalar, say β, then the matrix, $\beta\mathbf{I} - \mathbf{A}$, has eigenvalues, $\mu_r = \beta - \lambda_r$, and the largest μ_r corresponds to the smallest λ_r of $\mathbf{A}$.

Our primary concern in this section will be to consider the use of iteration methods for solving eigenvalue problems and some associated difficulties. We shall use the one-group diffusion equation in Cartesian coordinates as a model problem to illustrate techniques.

We consider first the basic eigenvalue problem

$$\mathbf{A}\mathbf{x} = \lambda\mathbf{x}, \tag{3.6.170}$$

where we assume we are interested in the smallest eigenvalue, say $\lambda_{\min}$. We write the basic equation in the form

$$(\mathbf{A} - \lambda\mathbf{I})\mathbf{x} = 0, \tag{3.6.171}$$

and again factor $\mathbf{A}$ into its upper, lower, and diagonal portions. The method of simultaneous displacements then gives the iteration rule

$$\mathbf{x}^{p+1} = -(\mathbf{D} - \lambda\mathbf{I})^{-1}(\mathbf{L} + \mathbf{U})\mathbf{x}^p, \tag{3.6.172}$$

provided $(\mathbf{D} - \lambda\mathbf{I})^{-1}$ exists (which it will unless $\mathbf{D}$ is the diagonal matrix some of whose elements are equal to λ). Define the iteration matrix as

$$\mathbf{B} = -(\mathbf{D} - \lambda\mathbf{I})^{-1}(\mathbf{L} + \mathbf{U}). \tag{3.6.173}$$

If all the eigenvalues of $\mathbf{B}$, say μ, are less than unity in magnitude, then the iteration (3.6.172) will always converge to the trivial solution.

On the other hand, if any eigenvalue of $\mathbf{B}$ is greater than unity, the
iteration diverges. To achieve a nontrivial, but finite, solution, we must
require that the largest eigenvalue of $\mathbf{B}$ be exactly unity.

The matrices formed from the difference approximations to elliptic
differential equations are frequently of a very special form called a
Stieltjes matrix. A Stieltjes matrix is a symmetric, positive definite,
irreducible matrix with nonpositive off-diagonal elements. The matrix
(3.6.165) is a typical example. We now let $\mathbf{A}$ be a Stieltjes matrix and
λ_r and $\mathbf{e}_r$ such that

$$\mathbf{A}\mathbf{e}_r = \lambda_r \mathbf{e}_r . \tag{3.6.174}$$

We then have

$$(\mathbf{A} - \lambda_r \mathbf{I})\mathbf{e}_r = 0,$$

$$(\mathbf{D} - \lambda_r \mathbf{I})\mathbf{e}_r = -(\mathbf{L} + \mathbf{U})\mathbf{e}_r ,$$

and finally

$$\mathbf{e}_r = -(\mathbf{D} - \lambda_r \mathbf{I})^{-1}(\mathbf{L} + \mathbf{U})\mathbf{e}_r . \tag{3.6.175}$$

Therefore, $\mathbf{e}_r$ is an eigenvector of $\mathbf{B}$ with eigenvalue unity. Now let
$\lambda_r = \lambda_{\min}$. In this case the matrix $\mathbf{B}$ is nonnegative and of the form

$$\mathbf{B} = - \begin{bmatrix} 0 & \dfrac{a_{12}}{a_{11} - \lambda_{\min}} & \dfrac{a_{13}}{a_{11} - \lambda_{\min}} & \cdots & \dfrac{a_{1n}}{a_{11} - \lambda_{\min}} \\ \dfrac{a_{21}}{a_{22} - \lambda_{\min}} & 0 & \dfrac{a_{23}}{a_{22} - \lambda_{\min}} & \cdots & \dfrac{a_{2n}}{a_{22} - \lambda_{\min}} \\ \vdots & \vdots & \vdots & & \vdots \\ & & & & 0 \end{bmatrix} \tag{3.6.176}$$

(see problem 13).

The eigenvector of $\mathbf{A}$ with eigenvalue $\lambda_{\min}$ is also an eigenvector of
$\mathbf{B}$ as defined in Eq. (3.6.176) and with eigenvalue unity, as may be seen
from Eq. (3.6.175). Since $\mathbf{A}$ is positive definite, the other eigenvalues
of $\mathbf{A}$ are greater than $\lambda_{\min}$. From the results of Section 1.13, if the
value of λ in Eq. (3.6.175) decreases from $\lambda_{\min}$, the spectral radius decreases from unity; conversely, if the value of λ increases from $\lambda_{\min}$, the spectral
radius increases. Hence the iteration using the method of simultaneous
displacements is admirably suited for finding the smallest eigenvalue of a
Stieltjes matrix. The eigenvalue of $\mathbf{A}$ may be found from the eigenvector
by Eq. (3.6.174).

In a manner similar to that above, it is also possible to show that the
methods of successive displacements and successive over-relaxation

(with appropriate relaxation parameters) provide a means of finding the smallest eigenvalue of a Stieltjes matrix.

The actual process of finding the eigenvalue and eigenvector is relatively complicated. Assuming we have no prior knowledge concerning the desired eigenvalue, it is probable that any guess will yield an iteration matrix that diverges or else converges to zero. Thus, our iteration must not only attempt to find a solution to the equations, but must also continually improve the approximation to the eigenvalue. In effect we have two concurrent iterations; one iteration to find the eigenvector and one iteration to find the eigenvalue.

The iteration techniques outlined earlier are suitable for finding the eigenvector, and we now consider techniques for locating the eigenvalue. Let the iteration be of the form

$$\mathbf{x}^{p+1} = \mathbf{B}\mathbf{x}^p. \tag{3.6.177}$$

We recall that the eigenvalues of $\mathbf{B}$, say γ, are related to the eigenvalues λ of the matrix $\mathbf{A}$, where $\mathbf{A}$ is the matrix we desire to solve. If we expand the trial solution $\mathbf{x}^0$ in terms of the eigenvectors of $\mathbf{B}$, say $\mathbf{v}_r$, with expansion coefficients a_r, then we have

$$\mathbf{x}^p = \sum_r a_r(\gamma_r)^p \mathbf{v}_r. \tag{3.6.178}$$

After a sufficient number of iterations, we have approximately

$$\mathbf{x}^p \approx \gamma_1 \mathbf{x}^{p-1}, \tag{3.6.179}$$

where γ_1 is the largest eigenvalue of $\mathbf{B}$. The approximate value of γ_1 may be obtained by comparing successive values of some component of the vector $\mathbf{x}$. Having obtained a value of γ_1, we can adjust the value of λ. Thus, from a previous result of this section concerning the matrix $\mathbf{B}$, if $\gamma_1 > 1$, we decrease λ, while if $\gamma_1 < 1$, we increase λ. The convergence of this method is dependent upon the ratio of the eigenvalues of $\mathbf{B}$. In general we have

$$\mathbf{x}^p = \gamma_1^p \left[\sum_r a_r \left(\frac{\gamma_r}{\gamma_1} \right)^p \mathbf{v}_r \right]. \tag{3.6.180}$$

If γ_2 is the second largest eigenvalue of $\mathbf{B}$, then the convergence is given by the factor $(\gamma_2/\gamma_1)^p$.

An alternative technique is to use Eq. (3.6.178) and compute the quantity

$$(\mathbf{x}^p)^T(\mathbf{x}^p) = (\mathbf{x}^p)^T \mathbf{B}\mathbf{x}^{p-1}. \tag{3.6.181}$$

After a sufficient number of iterations, we have

$$\frac{(\mathbf{x}^p)^T(\mathbf{x}^p)}{(\mathbf{x}^p)^T(\mathbf{x}^{p-1})} \approx \gamma_1. \tag{3.6.182}$$

Equation (3.6.182) is known as the Rayleigh quotient. If the eigenvectors of $\mathbf{B}$ are orthogonal, then the method converges faster than one in which a single component is examined. We have

$$(\mathbf{x}^p)^T(\mathbf{x}^p) = \sum_{r=1}^{R} a_r^2 \gamma_r^{2p} = \gamma_1^{2p} \sum_{r=1}^{R} a_r^2 \left(\frac{\gamma_r}{\gamma_1}\right)^{2p}$$

$$\tag{3.6.183}$$

$$(\mathbf{x}^p)^T(\mathbf{x}^{p-1}) = \sum_{r=1}^{R} a_r^2 \gamma_r^{2p-1} = \gamma_1^{2p-1} \sum_{r=1}^{R} a_r^2 \left(\frac{\gamma_r}{\gamma_1}\right)^{2p-1}$$

and hence

$$\frac{(\mathbf{x}^p)^T(\mathbf{x}^p)}{(\mathbf{x}^p)^T(\mathbf{x}^{p-1})} \approx \gamma_1 \left[\frac{a_1^2 + a_2^2 \left(\frac{\gamma_2}{\gamma_1}\right)^{2p}}{a_1^2 + a_2^2 \left(\frac{\gamma_2}{\gamma_1}\right)^{2p-1}}\right]. \tag{3.6.184}$$

The convergence to γ_1 is thus given by a factor $(\gamma_2/\gamma_1)^{2p}$, which is twice as fast as given by Eq. (3.6.180).

We now describe an equivalent procedure which is quite suited to eigenvalue problems. We assume an iteration of the form

$$\mathbf{x}^{p+1} = \mathbf{B}\mathbf{x}^p \tag{3.6.185}$$

and the initial trial solution $\mathbf{x}^0$. We define the scalar α_0 as

$$[(\mathbf{x}^0)^T(\mathbf{x}^0)]^{1/2} = \alpha_0. \tag{3.6.186}$$

We now compute $\mathbf{x}^1$ from the iteration rule (3.6.185) and also the factor

$$\alpha_1 = [(\mathbf{x}^1)^T(\mathbf{x}^1)]^{1/2}. \tag{3.6.187}$$

We now require that $\mathbf{x}^1$ be scaled as $\tilde{\mathbf{x}}^1$ such that

$$[(\tilde{\mathbf{x}}^1)^T(\tilde{\mathbf{x}}^1)]^{1/2} = \alpha_0. \tag{3.6.188}$$

Thus we multiply $\mathbf{x}^1$ by the factor $\sqrt{\alpha_0/\alpha_1} = \beta_1$. We continue in this manner generating the successive trial vectors and scaling the results by a factor

$$\beta_p = \sqrt{\frac{\alpha_0}{\alpha_p}}. \tag{3.6.189}$$

The factors α_p approach an asymptotic value γ_1 and at a rate dependent on $(\gamma_2/\gamma_1)^{2p}$, as may be seen from the discussion of the previous paragraph, which is applicable here. Thus we can approximately determine γ_1 by monitoring the quantity α. Furthermore, the scaling of the trial vectors prevents the solution from degenerating before we reach an asymptotic behavior even if $\gamma_1 \neq 1$. The advantage of this technique is consequently two-fold; a rapid convergence and a nondegenerating trial solution. The computation of the scale factors takes time, of course, but the increased convergence rate usually makes up for the additional computations.

To illustrate the steps in solving a simple problem, we consider the equation

$$\frac{\partial^2 \phi}{\partial x^2} + \frac{\partial^2 \phi}{\partial y^2} + B^2\phi = 0, \qquad 0 \leqslant x \leqslant a, \ 0 \leqslant y \leqslant a, \quad (3.6.190)$$

with boundary conditions

$$\phi(0, y) = \phi(a, y) = 0,$$
$$\phi(x, 0) = \phi(x, a) = 0. \qquad (3.6.191)$$

We desire the smallest critical buckling $B_{\min}$. We consider the difference approximation

$$-\frac{\delta_x^2 \phi_{j,k}}{h_x^2} - \frac{\delta_y^2 \phi_{j,k}}{h_y^2} - B^2\phi_{j,k} = 0. \qquad (3.6.192)$$

Let $h_x = h_y = h$. Denote the initial estimate of $B_{\min}$ as B_0. For simplicity, we use the method of simultaneous displacements. The iteration becomes

$$\phi_{j,k}^{p+1} = \frac{1}{4 - B^2h^2} [\phi_{j+1,k}^p + \phi_{j-1,k}^p + \phi_{j,k+1}^p + \phi_{j,k-1}^p]. \qquad (3.6.193)$$

The errors obey a similar iteration rule. The stability of the iteration can be studied by expanding the errors in the usual Fourier series. The resulting computation yields

$$\lambda_{mn} = \frac{2}{4 - B^2h^2} \left[\cos\frac{n\pi}{K} + \cos\frac{m\pi}{K}\right]. \qquad (3.6.194)$$

We again consider the first harmonic, i.e., $m = n = 1$. We have

$$\lambda_{11} = \frac{4\cos\dfrac{\pi}{K}}{4 - B^2h^2}. \qquad (3.6.195)$$

In order for the largest eigenvalue of the iteration matrix to be exactly unity, we require the buckling to be

$$B^2 = \frac{4}{h^2} \left[1 - \cos \frac{\pi}{K} \right], \qquad (3.6.196)$$

which is well known.

Note that for B^2 greater than the right-hand side of Eq. (3.6.196), the iteration diverges. Conversely for B less than the requisite quantity, the iteration converges to zero. Denote the proper value of B^2 [from Eq. (3.6.196)] as B_0^2. We then have

$$B^2 > B_0^2, \qquad \text{divergence;}$$
$$B^2 < B_0^2, \qquad \text{trivial solution;}$$
$$B^2 = B_0^2, \qquad \text{unique solution.}$$

The nuclear analyst recognizes the above three conditions as corresponding to a super-critical, sub-critical, and just critical reactor. Consequently, the iteration displays the same properties we expect the reactor to have. A generalization of this result to more involved equations and iteration methods is found in Birkhoff and Varga (Reference 14).

References

There are many excellent texts dealing with the numerical solution of equations. Particularly useful are *1, 2, 3,* and *4.* There are few elementary texts that deal with the numerical solution of partial differential equations in detail. One of the best texts is *5;* however, the level is above elementary. An excellent treatment of difference methods for parabolic and hyperbolic equations is *6;* again the level is not elementary. A very readable discussion of partial difference equations is found in Chapter III of *7.* An excellent survey of iterative methods, at a relatively advanced level, is *8.* Specific techniques are reviewed in many papers throughout the literature. Generalizations of results quoted in the text are cited.

1. Hildebrand, F. B., "Introduction to Numerical Analysis." McGraw-Hill, New York, 1956.

2. Kopal, Z., "Numerical Analysis." Wiley, New York, 1955.

3. Hamming, R. W., "Numerical Methods for Scientists and Engineers." MacGraw-Hill, New York, 1962.

4. Lanczos, C., "Applied Analysis." Prentice-Hall, Englewood Cliffs, New Jersey, 1956.

5. Forsythe, G. E., and Wasow, W. R., "Finite Difference Methods for Partial Differential Equations." Wiley, New York, 1960.

6. Richtmyer, R. D., "Difference Methods for Initial Value Problems." Wiley (Interscience), New York, 1957.

7. Hildebrand, F. B., "Methods of Applied Mathematics." Prentice-Hall, New York, 1952.

8. Varga, R. S., "Matrix Iterative Analysis." Prentice-Hall, Englewood Cliffs, New Jersey, 1962.

9. Courant, R., Friedrichs, K., and Lewy, H., Über die partiellen Differenzengleichungen der mathematischen Physik. *Math. Ann.* **100**, 32 (1928).

10. O'Brien, G. G., Hyman, M. A., and Kaplan, S., A study of the numerical solution of partial differential equations. *J. Math. Phys.* **29**, 223 (1951).

11. Peaceman, D. W., and Rachford, H. H. Jr., The numerical solution of parabolic and elliptic differential equations. *J. Soc. Ind. Appl. Math.* **3**, 28 (1955).

12. Frankel, S. P., Convergence rates of iterative treatments of partial differential equations. *Math. Tables Aids Comput.* **4**, 65 (1950).

13. Stein, P., and Rosenberg, R. L., On the solution of linear simultaneous equations by iteration. *J. London Math. Soc.* **23**, 111 (1948).

14. Birkhoff, G., and Varga, R. S., Reactor criticality and non-negative matrices. *J. Soc. Ind. Appl. Math.* **6**, 354 (1958).

Problems

1. Find the truncation error for the integration of $\sin x$ from $0 \leqslant x \leqslant \pi$ by Simpson's rule. Compare the result with the trapezoidal rule [i.e., truncate the integration at first differences].

2. Derive an integration formula over the interval x_j to x_{j+4} in terms of the central difference operator.

3. Discuss the stability of the numerical solution of the equation

$$\frac{d^2y}{dx^2} = y, \qquad y(0) = 0, \qquad y'(0) = 1.$$

Use an approximate difference quotient and also an integration formula.

4. Derive a difference approximation to the one-dimensional wave equation that is accurate to $0(h_t{}^4) + 0(h_x{}^4)$. Sketch the point pattern.

5. Analyze the stability and accuracy of the following approximation to the heat-flow equation.

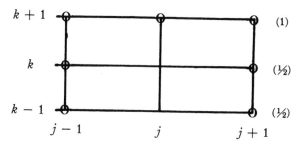

6. What order truncation error does the approximation

$$\left[\frac{\Delta - \nabla}{2h}\right]_t T_{j,k} = \frac{\delta^2}{h_x^2} T_{j,k}$$

have ? What stability criterion is applicable ?

7. Let the iteration operator **B** have the form

$$\mathbf{B} = \begin{bmatrix} \lambda_1 & 1 & 0 & 0 & 0 \\ 0 & \lambda_1 & 1 & 0 & 0 \\ 0 & 0 & \lambda_1 & 0 & 0 \\ 0 & 0 & 0 & \lambda_2 & 0 \\ 0 & 0 & 0 & 0 & \lambda_3 \end{bmatrix}, \qquad 1 > \lambda_1 > \lambda_2 > \lambda_3.$$

Prove the asymptotic behavior of the iteration is proportional to λ_1. How many iterations are necessary to achieve the asymptotic behavior ? Generalize the result.

8. It is desired to solve the Helmholtz equation

$$\delta^2\phi + k^2\phi = 0, \qquad (h_x = 1)$$

with $\phi(0) = \phi(4) = 0$. The mesh is shown below.

0   **1**   **2**   **3**   **4**

(a) Find the eigenvalues and eigenfunctions of the difference equation.

(b) Use the first eigenvalue from part (a) and the initial estimate $\phi(1) = \phi(2) = \phi(3) = 1$. Solve the problem by the method of simultaneous displacements and by successive displacements. Explain.

(c) Repeat using the second eigenvalue and explain.

9. Show that the method of simultaneous displacements converges, whereas the method of successive displacements diverges for the problem

$$\begin{bmatrix} 1 & 1 & -1 \\ 1 & 1 & -2 \\ 0 & 1 & 1 \end{bmatrix}\begin{bmatrix} x_1 \\ x_2 \\ x_3 \end{bmatrix} = \begin{bmatrix} y_1 \\ y_2 \\ y_3 \end{bmatrix}.$$

10. Derive Eq. (3.6.86) from the following considerations: the residual is defined as

$$\mathbf{r}^p = \mathbf{x}^{p+1/2} - \mathbf{x}^p$$

and $\mathbf{x}^{p+1/2}$ is the solution computed without over-relaxation, i.e.,

$$\mathbf{L}\mathbf{x}^{p+1} + \mathbf{D}\mathbf{x}^{p+1/2} + \mathbf{U}\mathbf{x}^p = \mathbf{y}.$$

By elimination of the intermediate solution, the desired algorithm is obtained.

11. Show that the difference approximation to the Laplace equation

$$\frac{\delta^2\phi_{j,k}}{h_x^2} + \frac{\delta^2\phi_{j,k}}{h_y^2} = 0$$

is unstable if the problem is treated as an initial value problem.

12. Consider a square mesh with $h_x = h_y = h$ and the difference equation from problem 11. If $\phi_{j,k}$ is changed by an amount $r_{j,k}$, derive an expression for the influence of the change at point $j + n$, $k + m$. Assume the iteration is the method of successive displacements and that j, k is relaxed before $j + n$, $k + m$.

13. Derive an expression for the growth factors of the Peaceman-Rachford iteration method for the Helmholtz equation in a rectangle.

14. Prove that **B** in Eq. (3.6.176) is nonnegative. Also: Examine the behavior of the spectral radius of **B** as a function of λ in place of $\lambda_{\min}$ and apply the Perron-Frobenius theorem of Chapter I.

IV

MULTIGROUP
DIFFUSION METHODS

One of the most important uses of numerical methods in nuclear engineering is in the calculation of reactor properties based on the multigroup formulation of diffusion theory. The multigroup equations arise as approximations to the well-known age-diffusion theory. It should be noted that the approximations inherent in age-diffusion theory are implicitly contained in the multigroup formulation.

There are also multigroup formulations based upon the transport theory, and we shall consider such problems in the next chapter. Our present interest will center on diffusion calculations. In this chapter we begin the study with a review of the age-diffusion equations and the adjoint equations. We then illustrate the construction of the multigroup difference equations and the resultant matrix formulation of the system.

4.1 Age-Diffusion Approximation

For time independent problems the general form of the age-diffusion equations is[1]

$$\frac{\partial q(\mathbf{r}, u)}{\partial u} = \nabla \cdot [D(\mathbf{r}, u) \nabla \phi(\mathbf{r}, u)] - \sigma_{\mathrm{a}}(\mathbf{r}, u) \phi(\mathbf{r}, u) + S(\mathbf{r}, u), \quad (4.1.1)$$

and

$$q(\mathbf{r}, u_{\mathrm{th}}) = -\nabla \cdot [D_{\mathrm{th}}(\mathbf{r}) \nabla \phi_{\mathrm{th}}(\mathbf{r})] + \sigma_{\mathrm{a}}^{\mathrm{th}}(\mathbf{r}) \phi_{\mathrm{th}}(\mathbf{r}) - S_{\mathrm{th}}(\mathbf{r}), \quad (4.1.2)$$

---

[1] See References 1 and 2 for derivation, etc. Note also that the macroscopic cross sections are denoted by σ to avoid confusion with summation operators. We shall follow this notation throughout the text.

where $(\mathbf{r}, u)$ denotes position and lethargy, the subscript "th" denotes the thermal group, $\phi(\mathbf{r}, u)$ is the flux of neutrons, $q(\mathbf{r}, u)$ is the slowing down density, $D(\mathbf{r}, u)$ is the diffusion coefficient, $\sigma_a(\mathbf{r}, u)$ is the macroscopic absorption coefficient, and $S(\mathbf{r}, u)$ is the number of neutrons made per unit volume per unit lethargy. The flux is the total distance traveled by neutrons in a unit volume per unit time; the slowing down density is the number of neutrons crossing the lethargy u per unit volume per unit time. The left-hand side of Eq. (4.1.1) thus represents the rate of increase of the slowing down density with lethargy. The terms of the right-hand side represent, respectively, the rate at which neutrons leak into a unit volume, the rate at which neutrons are absorbed per unit volume, and the rate at which they are created per unit time.

The model adopted for the slowing down process is the following: neutrons are born with lethargies greater than zero, but less than that of thermal energy, i.e., $0 < u < u_{th}$, where u_{th} is the lethargy at thermal cutoff. The slowing down equation applies between $u = 0$ and $u = u_{th}$. Above u_{th} we assume the slowing down density, q, is zero, and include all neutrons of lethargy greater than u_{th} as thermal neutrons of lethargy u_{th} precisely. (This model is sufficient for many practical cases.) We take $u = 0$ at an energy such that no neutrons are produced by any process at an energy above the reference energy, consequently $q(\mathbf{r}, 0) = 0$. We now see that the left-hand member of Eq. (4.1.2) is the rate at which neutrons become thermal per unit volume. The terms of the right-hand side represent the rate of loss of thermal neutrons per unit volume, the rate of absorption of neutrons per unit volume, and the rate at which they are created per unit volume. Thus, the two equations merely state that the rate of increase of neutrons is minus the rate of loss plus the rate of creation.

The source function, $S(\mathbf{r}, u)$, consists of fission sources plus extraneous sources. The fission source, say $S_f(\mathbf{r}, u)$, is given by

$$S_f(\mathbf{r}, u) = \nu \chi(u) \left[\int_0^\infty du'\, \sigma_f(\mathbf{r}, u')\, \phi(\mathbf{r}, u') + \sigma_f^{th} \phi_{th}(\mathbf{r}) \right]. \qquad (4.1.3)$$

We assume the fission spectrum, $\chi(u)$, independent of the lethargy, u', of the incident neutron, and we also assume the number of neutrons per fission, ν, to be independent of lethargy. The fission spectrum is normalized such that

$$\int_0^\infty du\, \chi(u) = 1. \qquad (4.1.4)$$

Consistent with the earlier approximations, we have

$$\int_0^\infty du\, \chi(u) = \int_0^{u_{th}} du\, \chi(u)\,. \tag{4.1.5}$$

The coupling relation between the flux and slowing down density is taken in the form

$$q(\mathbf{r}, u) = \xi\sigma_s(\mathbf{r}, u)\,\phi(\mathbf{r}, u)\,, \tag{4.1.6}$$

where ξ is the average logarithmic energy decrement. Equation (4.1.6) is strictly valid only for an infinite nonabsorbing medium. For simplicity we shall use Eq. (4.1.6); the results to be derived can always be modified for more realistic relationships. Since

$$q(\mathbf{r}, u) = 0,\qquad u < 0,\qquad u > u_{th}\,, \tag{4.1.7}$$

we could modify the integral in Eq. (4.1.3) to have limits of 0 and u_{th}. We shall use the infinite. range for later purposes. The thermal fissions could be included in the integral since

$$\phi_{th}(\mathbf{r}) = \int_0^\infty du\, \delta(u - u_{th})\,\phi_{th}(\mathbf{r}, u)\,. \tag{4.1.8}$$

We have assumed

$$\int_{u_{th}}^\infty du\, \chi(u) = 0, \tag{4.1.9}$$

consequently, the thermal source term consists of extraneous sources only.

By using the coupling relation, Eq. (4.1.6), we may express the basic age-diffusion equations entirely in terms of the flux or slowing down density. In terms of the flux we have

$$\frac{\partial}{\partial u}(\xi\sigma_s\phi) - \nabla\cdot[D\nabla\phi] + \sigma_a\phi - \nu\chi\int_0^\infty du'\,\sigma_f\phi - \nu\chi\sigma_f^{th}\phi_{th} = S_e\,, \tag{4.1.10}$$

and

$$-\xi\sigma_s\phi(\mathbf{r}, u_{th}) - \nabla\cdot[D_{th}\nabla\phi_{th}(\mathbf{r})] + \sigma_a^{th}\phi_{th}(\mathbf{r}) = S_{th}(\mathbf{r}). \tag{4.1.11}$$

The first term of Eq. (4.1.11) may be written

$$-\xi\sigma_s\phi(\mathbf{r}, u_{th}) = -\int_0^\infty du'\,\xi\sigma_s\phi(\mathbf{r}, u')\,\delta(u' - u_{th})\,. \tag{4.1.12}$$

The set of equations (4.1.10), (4.1.11), and (4.1.12) may be written in the matrix form

$$
\begin{bmatrix}
\dfrac{\partial}{\partial u}(\xi\sigma_s) - \nabla\cdot[D\nabla] + \sigma_a - \nu\chi\displaystyle\int_0^\infty du'\,\sigma_f; & -\nu\chi\sigma_f^{th} \\[2ex]
-\displaystyle\int_0^\infty du'\,\xi\sigma_s\delta(u' - u_{th}); & -\nabla\cdot[D_{th}\nabla] + \sigma_a^{th}
\end{bmatrix}
\begin{bmatrix}
\phi(\mathbf{r}, u) \\
\phi_{th}(\mathbf{r})
\end{bmatrix}
$$

$$
= \begin{bmatrix} S_e \\ S_{th} \end{bmatrix}. \tag{4.1.13}
$$

The operators are understood to operate on the appropriate argument. The set of equations may be written

$$
[\mathbf{A} - \nu\mathbf{B}][\boldsymbol{\psi}] = [\mathbf{S}], \tag{4.1.14}
$$

where $\mathbf{A}$ and $\mathbf{B}$ are formed by factoring the matrix above. The functions $\boldsymbol{\psi}$ and $\mathbf{S}$ are defined as

$$
\boldsymbol{\psi} = \begin{bmatrix} \phi(\mathbf{r}, u) \\ \phi_{th}(\mathbf{r}) \end{bmatrix}; \qquad
\mathbf{S} = \begin{bmatrix} S_e(\mathbf{r}, u) \\ S_{th}(\mathbf{r}) \end{bmatrix}. \tag{4.1.15}
$$

A similar formulation is possible in terms of the slowing down density and thermal flux. We shall find such a procedure useful when we consider the multigroup equations.

The set of equations (4.1.14) represents a coupled pair of integro-differential equations. The objective of the multigroup formulation is to reduce the pair of equations to a coupled *set* of differential equations, which are, in general, easier to solve.

The boundary conditions applied to the equations are the usual conditions, namely continuity of current and flux at interfaces, and vanishing of flux at extrapolated boundaries or return current at the actual boundaries. For different lethargies, the extrapolation distances are not all equal. We shall assume, however, that the extrapolation distance is a constant for all lethargy.

With the given boundary conditions, the equations are now defined. In the absence of extraneous sources, the equation (4.1.14) becomes

$$
\mathbf{A}\boldsymbol{\psi} = \nu\mathbf{B}\boldsymbol{\psi}, \tag{4.1.16}
$$

which is a generalized eigenvalue problem. For given collections of nuclear data and the geometry of the system, the operators $\mathbf{A}$ and $\mathbf{B}$ are completely defined. Solutions of the equation (4.1.16) exist only for certain values of ν, i.e., eigenvalues. The study of criticality is usually undertaken by finding a value of ν which is an eigenvalue of Eq. (4.1.16) and comparing with the experimentally determined value of ν, say ν_e. For $\nu > \nu_e$, the system would be subcritical, etc. Before we outline the computational steps, we first consider the system of adjoint equations.

4.2 Adjoint Equations

In Chapter I we discussed biorthogonal vectors and gave an illustration of the utility of the dual set of vectors. The adjoint function (importance function) plays a similar role in reactor calculations. The importance function is very useful in multigroup calculations and also in studying perturbation effects, etc.

In order to derive an adjoint set of functions, we review the formation of adjoint vectors in matrix algebra. For the matrix eigenvalue problem

$$\mathbf{A}\mathbf{x}_i = \lambda_i \mathbf{x}_i,\qquad(4.2.1)$$

the eigenvectors of

$$\mathbf{A}^T\mathbf{y}_j = \lambda_j \mathbf{y}_j\qquad(4.2.2)$$

form a biorthogonal set. The proof of biorthogonality was found in Section 1.12 from

$$\mathbf{y}_j^T\mathbf{A}\mathbf{x}_i - \mathbf{x}_i^T\mathbf{A}^T\mathbf{y}_j = 0.\qquad(4.2.3)$$

A similar procedure is possible for operators in continuous spaces. Consider an operator Θ with the corresponding eigenfunction equation

$$\Theta\psi_i = \lambda_i\psi_i.\qquad(4.2.4)$$

We shall assume the λ_i are all distinct and the ψ_i complete.[2] We define the adjoint operator Θ^* from the relation

$$\int_{\text{vol}} d(\text{vol})\,[\psi_j^*\Theta\psi_i - \psi_i\Theta^*\psi_j^*] = 0,\qquad(4.2.5)$$

where the ψ_j^* are the eigenfunctions of Θ^* with the associated eigenvalues γ_j, i.e.,

$$\Theta^*\psi_j^* = \gamma_j\psi_j^*.\qquad(4.2.6)$$

---

[2] In many problems of physics, it is not known whether or not the eigenfunctions of an operator are complete. Completeness is frequently assumed nevertheless.

The integration in Eq. (4.2.5) is over the entire volume in which the functions are defined. Equation (4.2.5) is merely a generalization of Eq. (4.2.3).

As a consequence of the definition of the adjoint operator, it is possible to show that the functions ψ_i and ψ_j^* form a biorthogonal set and further, that the operators Θ and Θ^* have the same eigenvalues. To prove the biorthogonality, we multiply Eq. (4.2.4) by ψ_j^* and integrate over the volume.

$$\int_{vol} d(vol)\psi_j^*\Theta\psi_i = \lambda_i \int_{vol} d(vol)\psi_j^*\psi_i . \tag{4.2.7}$$

Similarly, multiply Eq. (4.2.6), for the jth eigenfunction, by ψ_i and integrate over the volume to obtain

$$\int_{vol} d(vol)\psi_i\Theta^*\psi_j^* = \gamma_j \int_{vol} d(vol)\psi_j^*\psi_i . \tag{4.2.8}$$

By subtracting the resultant equations and use of Eq. (4.2.5), we have

$$0 = (\lambda_i - \gamma_j) \int_{vol} d(vol)\psi_j^*\psi_i . \tag{4.2.9}$$

For distinct eigenvalues we therefore conclude the eigenfunctions of the adjoint operator form a biorthogonal set of functions to the original set. Notice that if $\Theta = \Theta^*$, then the eigenfunctions are orthogonal amongst themselves; such operators are called self-adjoint.

We can now show that the eigenvalues λ_i and γ_i are equal. To this end, multiply Eq. (4.2.4) by ψ_j^* and integrate over all volume. We find that

$$\lambda_i\delta_{i,j} = \lambda_i \int_{vol} d(vol)\psi_j^*\psi_i$$

$$= \int_{vol} d(vol)\psi_j^*\Theta\psi_i = \int_{vol} d(vol)\psi_i\Theta^*\psi_j^* , \tag{4.2.10}$$

by Eqs. (4.2.5) and (4.2.7). We assume, without proof, that the ψ_j^* form a complete set and expand $\Theta^*\psi_j^*$ in this set

$$\Theta^*\psi_j^* = \sum_k a_{jk}\psi_k^* . \tag{4.2.11}$$

Substituting this relation into Eq. (4.2.10), we find that

$$\sum_k a_{jk} \int_{vol} d(vol)\psi_i\psi_k^* = a_{ji} = \lambda_i\delta_{ij} \tag{4.2.12}$$

by Eq. (4.2.10). If the expansion coefficients be inserted into Eq. (4.2.11), we learn that

$$\boldsymbol{\Theta}^* \boldsymbol{\psi}_j^* = \lambda_j \boldsymbol{\psi}_j^* . \tag{4.2.13}$$

Obviously from Eqs. (4.2.6) and (4.2.13) it follows that

$$\gamma_j = \lambda_j , \tag{4.2.14}$$

as was to be shown.

We now consider the construction of the adjoint age-diffusion equations, using the concepts and formalism introduced in this section. To this end, we shall have to generalize the previous matrix formalism slightly, in particular, Eqs. (4.1.13). Since we shall find it necessary to integrate over the variables $\mathbf{r}$ and u, the explicit dependence of the functions and operators upon $\mathbf{r}$ and u must be given. The thermal flux and thermal adjoint flux are represented by delta functions in keeping with the model previously introduced.

$$\phi_{\text{th}}(\mathbf{r}, u) = \phi_{\text{th}}(\mathbf{r}) \, \delta(u - u_{\text{th}}) ,$$

$$\phi_{\text{th}}^*(\mathbf{r}, u) = \phi_{\text{th}}^*(\mathbf{r}) \, \delta(u - u_{\text{th}}) .$$

The thermal diffusion equation, in terms of $\phi_{\text{th}}(\mathbf{r}, u)$, is written

$$- \int_0^\infty du' \, \xi \sigma_s \delta(u' - u_{\text{th}}) \, \phi(\mathbf{r}, u') - \int_0^\infty du' \, [\nabla \cdot (D_{\text{th}} \nabla) - \sigma_a^{\text{th}}] \, \phi_{\text{th}}(\mathbf{r}, u')$$

$$= S_{\text{th}} . \tag{4.2.15}$$

Similarly, the fission source in the slowing down equation is

$$\nu \chi(u) \int_0^\infty du' \, \sigma_f^{\text{th}} \phi_{\text{th}}(\mathbf{r}, u') = \nu \chi(u) \, \sigma_f^{\text{th}} \phi_{\text{th}}(\mathbf{r}) . \tag{4.2.16}$$

We define the vectors $\boldsymbol{\psi}$ and $\boldsymbol{\psi}^*$ as

$$\boldsymbol{\psi} = \begin{bmatrix} \phi(\mathbf{r}, u) \\ \phi_{\text{th}}(\mathbf{r}, u) \end{bmatrix} , \tag{4.2.17}$$

$$\boldsymbol{\psi}^* = \begin{bmatrix} \phi^*(\mathbf{r}, u) \\ \phi_{\text{th}}^*(\mathbf{r}, u) \end{bmatrix} . \tag{4.2.18}$$

The functional relation (4.2.5) may now be written in matrix form as

$$\int d\mathbf{r} \int_0^\infty du \left\{ [\phi^*(\mathbf{r}, u), \phi_{\text{th}}^*(\mathbf{r}, u)] \begin{bmatrix} a_{11} & a_{12} \\ a_{21} & a_{22} \end{bmatrix} \begin{bmatrix} \phi(\mathbf{r}, u) \\ \phi_{\text{th}}(\mathbf{r}, u) \end{bmatrix} \right\}$$

$$= \int d\mathbf{r} \int_0^\infty du \left\{ [\phi(\mathbf{r}, u), \phi_{\text{th}}(\mathbf{r}, u)] \begin{bmatrix} (a^*)_{11} & (a^*)_{12} \\ (a^*)_{21} & (a^*)_{22} \end{bmatrix} \begin{bmatrix} \phi^*(\mathbf{r}, u) \\ \phi_{\text{th}}^*(\mathbf{r}, u) \end{bmatrix} \right\}, \quad (4.2.19)$$

where $(a^*)_{ij}$ is the ijth element of the adjoint operator. The matrix elements a_{ij} are given in Eq. (4.1.13), (4.2.15) and (4.2.16). We desire to find the corresponding elements $(a^*)_{ij}$.

To find the adjoint, consider first the elements a_{11} and $(a^*)_{11}$. The element a_{11} is defined in Eq. (4.1.13). The contribution to the functional form above is then

$$\int d\mathbf{r} \int_0^\infty du\, \phi^*\, a_{11} \phi = \int d\mathbf{r} \int_0^\infty du\, \phi\, (a^*)_{11} \phi^*. \quad (4.2.20)$$

Consider first the leakage term. We recall the vector identity

$$\mathbf{\nabla} \cdot a\mathbf{x} = a\mathbf{\nabla} \cdot \mathbf{x} + \mathbf{x} \cdot \mathbf{\nabla} a, \quad (4.2.21)$$

where a is a scalar and $\mathbf{x}$ a vector. We have

$$\int d\mathbf{r} \int_0^\infty du\, \phi^* \mathbf{\nabla} \cdot [D\mathbf{\nabla}\phi] = \int d\mathbf{r} \int_0^\infty du[\mathbf{\nabla} \cdot (\phi^* D\mathbf{\nabla}\phi) - D\mathbf{\nabla}\phi \cdot \mathbf{\nabla}\phi^*]. \quad (4.2.22)$$

The first term in the brackets may be transformed to a surface integral, and, if we require the function ϕ^* to vanish on the surface, as the boundary conditions that partly determine this function, then the entire first term vanishes. The second term is again expanded using Eq. (4.2.21) to yield

$$-\int d\mathbf{r} \int_0^\infty du\, D\mathbf{\nabla}\phi \cdot \mathbf{\nabla}\phi^* = -\int d\mathbf{r} \int_0^\infty du[\mathbf{\nabla} \cdot (\phi D\mathbf{\nabla}\phi^*) - \phi\mathbf{\nabla} \cdot (D\mathbf{\nabla}\phi^*)].$$

$$(4.2.23)$$

The first term of the bracket again vanishes, since ϕ is zero on the boundary. Consequently we have

$$\int d\mathbf{r} \int_0^\infty du\, \phi^* \mathbf{\nabla} \cdot (D\mathbf{\nabla}\phi) = \int d\mathbf{r} \int_0^\infty du\, \phi\mathbf{\nabla} \cdot (D\mathbf{\nabla}\phi^*). \quad (4.2.24)$$

The operator $\mathbf{\nabla} \cdot (D\mathbf{\nabla})$ is thus self-adjoint.

The adjoint to the remaining terms in the element a_{11} may be found in a similar manner. By integration by parts, we find the adjoint to the derivative term, while we merely use the defining equation (4.2.20) to find the adjoint to the fission source term. Combining the results yields

$$(a^*)_{11} = -\xi\sigma_s \frac{\partial}{\partial u} - \nabla \cdot (D\nabla) + \sigma_a - \nu\sigma_f(u) \int_0^\infty du' \, \chi(u') \,. \qquad (4.2.25)$$

The salient features to note in Eq. (4.2.25) are the sign reversal in the derivative with respect to lethargy and the interchange of fission cross section and spectrum as the weighting function for the fission source. We shall have further comments on the implications later. Physically, the importance is the net number of neutrons ultimately produced in the system per unit time. The importance of a test particle is equal to the sum of the importances of its progeny. Various conservation equations can be written down from this basic concept (see Reference 3).

In a similar manner, it is easily shown that

$$(a^*)_{22} = \int_0^\infty du[-\nabla \cdot (D_{th}\nabla) + \sigma_a^{th}] \,. \qquad (4.2.26)$$

Note that the off-diagonal elements are transposed, however. From Eq. (4.2.19) we have

$$\int d\mathbf{r} \int_0^\infty du \, \phi^* a_{12} \phi_{th} = \int d\mathbf{r} \int_0^\infty du \, \phi_{th}(a^*)_{21}\phi^* \,, \qquad (4.2.27)$$

and similarly for a_{21} and $(a^*)_{12}$. By carrying out the detailed steps, we then have

$$-\xi\sigma_s \frac{\partial \phi^*(\mathbf{r}, u)}{\partial u} - \nabla \cdot [D\nabla\phi^*(\mathbf{r}, u)] + \sigma_a\phi^*(\mathbf{r}, u)$$

$$= \nu\sigma_f(u) \int_0^\infty du' \, \chi(u') \, \phi^*(\mathbf{r}, u') + \delta(u - u_{th}) \, \xi\sigma_s^{th}\phi_{th}^*(\mathbf{r}) \,, \qquad (4.2.28)$$

and

$$-\nabla \cdot [D_{th}\nabla\phi_{th}^*(\mathbf{r})] + \sigma_a^{th}\phi_{th}^*(\mathbf{r}) = \nu\sigma_f^{th} \int_0^\infty du'\chi(u') \, \phi^*(\mathbf{r}, u') \,. \qquad (4.2.29)$$

The solution of the age-diffusion equations and the adjoint equations can be obtained (in principle) by a method of successive approximations. We consider first the original equations in the form

$$\mathbf{A}\psi = \nu\mathbf{B}\psi \,. \qquad (4.2.30)$$

Denote the initial approximation as ψ_0. The homogeneous source terms in the equations are evaluated as

$$\nu_e\chi(u) \int_0^\infty du' \, \sigma_f(u') \, \phi_0(\mathbf{r}, u') \,,$$

and

$$\nu_e\chi(u)\sigma_t^{th}\phi_{0,th}(\mathbf{r}) \, ,$$

with ν_e the known number of neutrons per fission. Similarly, the source term for the thermal group is merely

$$\xi\sigma_s\phi_0(\mathbf{r}, u_{th}) \, .$$

Having obtained the sources, we solve the homogeneous form of Eq. (4.1.13). Denote this solution as ψ_1. Formally we solve Eq. (4.2.30) in the form

$$\psi_1 = \nu_e\mathbf{A}^{-1}\mathbf{B}\psi_0 \equiv \nu_e\mathbf{G}\psi_0 \, . \tag{4.2.31}$$

If ψ_0 were actually a solution of the homogeneous equations, then the eigenvalue ν would be given as

$$\frac{1}{\nu} = \frac{\int d(\text{vol}) \int_0^\infty du\, \psi_0\mathbf{G}\psi_0}{\int d(\text{vol}) \int_0^\infty du\, \psi_0\psi_0} \, . \tag{4.2.32}$$

We can compute an approximate value for ν even though ψ_0 may not be a solution using (4.2.31). The functional (4.2.32) becomes

$$\frac{\nu_e}{\nu} = \frac{\int d(\text{vol}) \int_0^\infty du\, \psi_0\psi_1}{\int d(\text{vol}) \int_0^\infty du\, \psi_0\psi_0} \, . \tag{4.2.33}$$

Successive iterations give successive estimates of ν from the functional

$$\frac{\nu_e}{\nu} = \frac{\int d(\text{vol}) \int_0^\infty du\, \psi_p\psi_{p+1}}{\int d(\text{vol}) \int_0^\infty du\, \psi_p\psi_p} \, , \tag{4.2.34}$$

where p is the iteration index, and ψ_p is the value of ψ on the pth iteration.

As shown in Section 3.6, the value of ν_e/ν will approach an asymptotic value which is the largest value of $1/\nu$ corresponding to the smallest eigenvalue ν, which we desire.

The use of the adjoint function will speed the convergence to the asymptotic value. First, if the adjoint equations are written in the form

$$\mathbf{A}^*\psi^* = \nu\mathbf{B}^*\psi^* \, , \tag{4.2.35}$$

and if we assume a trial solution ψ_0^*, we may carry out an iteration and compute ν according to

$$\frac{\nu_e}{\nu} = \frac{\int d(\text{vol}) \int_0^\infty du \, \psi_p^* \psi_{p+1}^*}{\int d(\text{vol}) \int_0^\infty du \psi_p^* \psi_p^*}. \tag{4.2.36}$$

The value of ν obtained by using the function and adjoint should agree after each iteration, but will not in general. Thus a check on the accuracy of the calculation is provided. More importantly, the adjoint function is biorthogonal to the original function. Consequently, we can use the functional

$$\frac{\nu_e}{\nu} = \frac{\int d(\text{vol}) \int_0^\infty du \, \psi_p^* \psi_{p+1}}{\int d(\text{vol}) \int_0^\infty du \psi_p^* \psi_p} \tag{4.2.37}$$

and expect a more rapid convergence. For instance, if ψ_p^* were exact, then regardless of the error in ψ_p and ψ_{p+1} the exact value for ν would be obtained, because ψ_p^* would be orthogonal to an error in ψ_p and ψ_{p+1} (see Section 3.6).

The adjoint is thus seen to be useful both as a check of the calculation and to speed convergence to the estimate of the multiplication. The procedure outlined above is simple in principle, but the actual calculations could not be performed except in extraordinary cases. The object of the multigroup method is to reduce the computational burden to a more tractable form.

4.3   Formation of Multigroup Equations

The multigroup equations are formed by dividing the lethargy space into discrete segments. The formation may be based upon the equation in terms of the slowing down density or the slowing down flux. We shall consider the difference in the two forms shortly. To begin we consider the slowing down equation (4.1.1) where we shall assume the reactor homogeneous in regions, and hence D and σ_a are not functions of position within a given region. We divide the lethargy interval $0 \leqslant u \leqslant u_{\text{th}}$ into G subintervals, and we denote the points of division u_g, $g = 0, 1, 2, ..., G$, such that $0 = u_0 < u_1 < ... < u_G = u_{\text{th}}$. The interval $u_g - u_{g-1}$ is denoted Δu_g. The intervals are not necessarily equally spaced. We integrate Eq. (4.1.1) from u_{g-1} to u_g obtaining

$$q(\mathbf{r}, u_g) - q(\mathbf{r}, u_{g-1}) = \int_{u_{g-1}}^{u_g} du [D \nabla^2 \phi(\mathbf{r}, u) - \sigma_a \phi(\mathbf{r}, u)] + \int_{u_{g-1}}^{u_g} du \, S(\mathbf{r}, u). \tag{4.3.1}$$

The source function is

$$S(\mathbf{r}, u) = \nu\chi(u)\,Q(\mathbf{r}) + S_{\mathrm{e}}(\mathbf{r}, u) \tag{4.3.2}$$

with

$$Q(\mathbf{r}) = \int_0^\infty du' \,\sigma_{\mathrm{f}}(u')\,\phi(\mathbf{r}, u') + \sigma_{\mathrm{f}}^{\mathrm{th}}\phi_{\mathrm{th}}(\mathbf{r}). \tag{4.3.3}$$

We now assume any external sources are separable in terms of space and lethargy dependence. Thus, we take

$$S_{\mathrm{e}}(\mathbf{r}, u) = S_{\mathrm{e}}(\mathbf{r})\,Z(u), \tag{4.3.4}$$

and compute the coefficients

$$\chi_g = \frac{1}{\Delta u_g} \int_{u_{g-1}}^{u_g} du\,\chi(u) \tag{4.3.5}$$

and

$$Z_g = \frac{1}{\Delta u_g} \int_{u_{g-1}}^{u_g} du\,Z(u)\,. \tag{4.3.6}$$

The integrated source function is then given as

$$\int_{u_{g-1}}^{u_g} du\,S(\mathbf{r}, u) = \nu\chi_g\Delta u_g Q(\mathbf{r}) + Z_g\Delta u_g S_{\mathrm{e}}(\mathbf{r})\,. \tag{4.3.7}$$

The remaining terms of Eq. (4.3.1) can be treated in different ways; we consider an analytic procedure first. We define the averages

$$\overline{\phi_g(\mathbf{r})} = \frac{\int_{u_{g-1}}^{u_g} du\,\phi(\mathbf{r}, u)}{\Delta u_g}\,, \tag{4.3.8}$$

and

$$\overline{\sigma_{\mathrm{a}g}} = \frac{\int_{u_{g-1}}^{u_g} du\,\sigma_{\mathrm{a}}(u)\,\phi(\mathbf{r}, u)}{\Delta u_g \overline{\phi_g}}\,. \tag{4.3.9}$$

A similar definition for $\bar{D}_g$ applies. Equation (4.3.1) may hence be written

$$q_g(\mathbf{r}) - q_{g-1}(\mathbf{r}) = \bar{D}_g\nabla^2\overline{\phi_g(\mathbf{r})}\,\Delta u_g - \overline{\sigma_{\mathrm{a}g}\phi_g(\mathbf{r})}\,\Delta u_g$$
$$+ \nu\chi_g Q(\mathbf{r})\,\Delta u_g + Z_g\Delta u_g S_{\mathrm{e}}(\mathbf{r}); \qquad (g = 1, 2, ..., G)\,. \tag{4.3.10}$$

The thermal group can be added to the above set of equations to give $G + 1$ simultaneous equations. The thermal group is given the subscript $G + 1$. The equation is

$$-D_{G+1}\nabla^2\phi_{G+1}(\mathbf{r}) + \sigma_{aG+1}\phi_{G+1}(\mathbf{r}) = q_G(\mathbf{r}) + S_e^{th}(\mathbf{r}). \qquad (4.3.11)$$

Before continuing we must obtain some relation between the average flux in a group and the slowing down density at the group boundaries. In order to construct such a relation, a number of approximations is possible. We shall discuss several of the most common presently, but first we consider an alternative form for the equations.

Notice that the average values of the coefficients are computed by flux weighting. As one proceeds in the computation obtaining more and more accurate approximations for the flux, the coefficients must be recomputed. This is a time consuming process, and we look for formulations that might be simpler to apply. However, the averages themselves as defined above are exact. Any simpler formulation that requires less computation will be less accurate. Consequently, we are trading accuracy for computational ease.

We recall that the slowing down density is, in general, a much more nearly constant function of the lethargy than the flux. If the basic equations are written in terms of the slowing down density, then the averages may be simplified. In terms of q, the basic equation is

$$\frac{\partial q(\mathbf{r}, u)}{\partial u} = \frac{D(u)}{\xi\sigma_s(u)}\nabla^2 q(\mathbf{r}, u) - \frac{\sigma_a(u)}{\xi\sigma_s(u)}q(\mathbf{r}, u) + S(\mathbf{r}, u). \qquad (4.3.12)$$

We integrate Eq. (4.3.12) from u_{g-1} to u_g and note that if $q(\mathbf{r}, u)$ is slowly varying with lethargy and if Δu_g small enough, then we may approximate the average of a product as the product of averages to an accuracy of $O(\Delta u)$. We define

$$\alpha_g = \int_{u_{g-1}}^{u_g} \frac{du}{\xi\sigma_s(u)}, \qquad (4.3.13)$$

$$D_g = \frac{1}{\alpha_g}\int_{u_{g-1}}^{u_g} du\,\frac{D(u)}{\xi\sigma_s(u)}, \qquad (4.3.14)$$

and

$$\sigma_{ag} = \frac{1}{\alpha_g}\int_{u_{g-1}}^{u_g} du\,\frac{\sigma_a(u)}{\xi\sigma_s(u)}. \qquad (4.3.15)$$

From the above equations we find the set of multigroup equations becomes approximately

$$q_g(\mathbf{r}) - q_{g-1}(\mathbf{r}) = \alpha_g[D_g\nabla^2\bar{q}_g - \sigma_{a_g}\bar{q}_g]$$

$$+ \nu\chi_g Q(\mathbf{r})\,\Delta u_g + Z_g\Delta u_g S_e(\mathbf{r}), \qquad (g = 1, 2, ..., G). \qquad (4.3.16)$$

To compare approximations, consider the term involving the diffusion coefficients, D_g and $\bar{D}_g$. By definition

$$\bar{D}_g = \frac{\int_{u_{g-1}}^{u_g} du\,D(u)\,\phi(\mathbf{r}, u)}{\int_{u_{g-1}}^{u_g} du\,\phi(\mathbf{r}, u)} = \frac{\int_{u_{g-1}}^{u_g} du\,D(u)\,q(\mathbf{r}, u)/\xi\sigma_s(u)}{\int_{u_{g-1}}^{u_g} du\,q(\mathbf{r}, u)/\xi\sigma_s(u)}. \qquad (4.3.17)$$

Obviously $\bar{D}_g = D_g$ if and only if $q(\mathbf{r}, u)$ is constant over the interval. If $q(\mathbf{r}, u)$ varies slightly, then the difference in accuracy of the two approximations is small, and we may use the simple second form. Henceforth, we shall use the simpler form of the equations as given in Eq. (4.3.16).

In order to relate the average slowing down density to the value at the end points, several standard approximations are possible, and we consider only two here. The approximations are

$$\overline{q_g}(\mathbf{r}) \approx q_g(\mathbf{r}) \qquad (4.3.18)$$

and

$$\overline{q_g}(\mathbf{r}) \approx \tfrac{1}{2}[q_g(\mathbf{r}) + q_{g-1}(\mathbf{r})]. \qquad (4.3.19)$$

That is, the function is constant and equal to its end value (4.3.18), or the function varies linearly in the interval. By considering the Taylor series expansion, it is apparent that the approximation (4.3.18) is accurate to order $\Delta u(\partial q_g/\partial u)$ whereas (4.3.19) is accurate to order $\Delta u(\partial q_g/\partial u - \partial q_{g-1}/\partial u)$ and may yield greater accuracy.

By use of the approximation in Eq. (4.3.18), the equations can be written in terms of the flux if we take

$$q_g(\mathbf{r}) = (\xi\sigma_s)_g\phi_g(\mathbf{r}). \qquad (4.3.20)$$

We then have

$$D_g\nabla^2\phi_g(\mathbf{r}) - \sigma_g\phi_g(\mathbf{r}) = -\frac{(\xi\sigma_s)_{g-1}}{(\xi\sigma_s)_g}\frac{\phi_{g-1}(\mathbf{r})}{\alpha_g} - \frac{1}{\alpha_g(\xi\sigma_s)_g}\int_{u_{g-1}}^{u_g} du\,S(\mathbf{r}, u),$$
$$(4.3.21)$$

with $\sigma_g = \sigma_{a_g} + (1/\alpha_g)$. The source integral is given by Eq. (4.3.7). If we take $q(\mathbf{r}, u)$ constant in each interval, the function $Q(\mathbf{r})$ becomes

$$Q(\mathbf{r}) = \sum_{g=1}^{G} \beta_g \phi_g(\mathbf{r}) + \sigma_f^{\text{th}} \phi_{\text{th}} \qquad (4.3.22)$$

from Eq. (4.3.9) with

$$\beta_g = (\xi\sigma_s)_g \int_{u_{g-1}}^{u_g} du \, \frac{\sigma_f(u)}{\xi\sigma_s(u)} . \qquad (4.3.23)$$

The expansion (4.3.22) is also accurate to $O(\varDelta u)$ and is consistent with earlier approximations. We define the function f_g as

$$f_g = - \frac{(\xi\sigma_s)_{g-1}}{(\xi\sigma_s)_g} \frac{\phi_{g-1}(\mathbf{r})}{\alpha_g}$$

$$- \frac{\nu\chi_g \varDelta u_g}{\alpha_g(\xi\sigma_s)_g} \left\{ \sum_{k=1}^{G} \beta_k \phi_k(\mathbf{r}) + \sigma_f^{\text{th}} \phi_{\text{th}} \right\} - \frac{Z_g \varDelta u_g}{\alpha_g(\xi\sigma_s)_g} S_e(\mathbf{r}) . \qquad (4.3.24)$$

Likewise, for the thermal group, we define

$$f_{G+1} = -(\xi\sigma_s)_G \phi_G(\mathbf{r}) - S_e^{\text{th}}(\mathbf{r}) . \qquad (4.3.25)$$

The entire set of multigroup equations (4.3.11) and (4.3.21) can be written

$$D_g \nabla^2 \phi_g(\mathbf{r}) - \sigma_g \phi_g(\mathbf{r}) = f_g(\mathbf{r}); \qquad (g = 1, 2, ..., G+1) . \qquad (4.3.26)$$

The truncation error associated with the equations is $O(\varDelta u)$. In considering the numerical solution of the set (4.3.26), we remark that similar equations are obtained for the second approximation to the average slowing down density, Eq. (4.3.19) (see problem 6).

The computational procedure for using the multigroup equations is straightforward. All of the coefficients can be computed once and for all when the energy groups are selected. A trial solution, say ψ_0, is assumed and the source terms f_g are computed. The basic diffusion equation for each group is solved to yield a new approximation, ψ_1. Note that the group equations must be solved in the order $g = 1$, $g = 2$, ..., $g = G + 1$. We shall consider the problem of the spatial dependence shortly; first we consider the formation of the adjoint multigroup equations.

4.4 Adjoint Multigroup Equations

The adjoint age-diffusion equations were given by Eqs. (4.2.28) and (4.2.29). We consider the lethargy interval divided into subintervals and integrate the basic equation (4.2.28) from u_{g-1} to u_g to obtain

$$-\phi_g^*(\mathbf{r}) + \phi_{g-1}^*(\mathbf{r}) = \int_{u_{g-1}}^{u_g} du \, \frac{D(u)}{\xi\sigma_s(u)} \nabla^2\phi^*(\mathbf{r}, u) + \int_{u_{g-1}}^{u_g} du \frac{\sigma_a(u)}{\xi\sigma_s(u)} \phi^*(\mathbf{r}, u)$$

$$+ \nu \int_{u_{g-1}}^{u_g} du \, \frac{\sigma_f(u)}{\xi\sigma_s(u)} Q^*(\mathbf{r}) + \phi_{th}^*(\mathbf{r}) \, \delta_{g,G}, \qquad (4.4.1)$$

where

$$Q^*(\mathbf{r}) = \int_0^\infty du' \, \chi(u') \phi^*(\mathbf{r}, u') . \qquad (4.4.2)$$

We again assume the reactor homogeneous by regions.

In order to perform the integrations, we must concern ourselves with appropriate averages for the integrands. To this end, assume $g \neq G$ and further that there is no leakage, absorption, or source. Then Eq. (4.4.1) merely states that

$$\phi_g^*(\mathbf{r}) = \phi_{g-1}^*(\mathbf{r}) . \qquad (4.4.3)$$

On the other hand, the adjoint slowing down density would obey the relation

$$(\xi\sigma_s)_g^{-1} \, q_g^*(\mathbf{r}) = (\xi\sigma_s)_{g-1}^{-1} \, q_{g-1}^*(\mathbf{r}) \qquad (4.4.4)$$

in the absence of sources, etc. Since the cross sections are not usually constant, we conclude that the adjoint flux is more nearly constant than the adjoint slowing down density. In order to use the simplest possible approximations to compute coefficients, we see we must deal with the adjoint flux instead of adjoint slowing down density in contradistinction to the basic equations.

We again define the average coefficients by Eqs. (4.3.13, 14, and 15) as previously computed in the last section. Further, we define the quantity

$$\zeta_g = \frac{1}{\Delta u_g} \int_{u_{g-1}}^{u_g} du \, \frac{\sigma_f(u)}{\xi\sigma_s(u)} . \qquad (4.4.5)$$

The equations (4.4.1) become

$$\phi_{n-1}^* - \phi_g^* = \alpha_g[D_g\nabla^2\bar{\phi}_g^*(\mathbf{r}) - \sigma_{a_g}\bar{\phi}_g^*(\mathbf{r})] + \nu\zeta_g\Delta u_g Q^*(\mathbf{r}) + \phi_{th}^*(\mathbf{r})\,\delta_{gG}\,.$$

(4.4.6)

Notice that the equation above is similar to Eq. (4.3.10), except for the sign reversal of the left-hand side and the appearance of the thermal adjoint flux in the equation. In carrying out computations for the adjoint flux, it is convenient to begin with the thermal group (index $G + 1$) and then compute in the direction of decreasing g. Thus the thermal group acts as a source for the distribution, and we follow neutrons moving down the lethargy scale. There is no limit to the lower end of the lethargy scale for the adjoint neutrons. However, due to leakage and absorption, the function ϕ^* continually decreases with u, and we introduce little error by ignoring adjoint neutrons of lethargy less than 0.

The relation between the average adjoint flux and the flux at lethargy interfaces is taken to be either

$$\overline{\phi_g^*} = \phi_{g-1}^*\,,$$

(4.4.7)

or

$$\overline{\phi_g^*} = \frac{\phi_g^* + \phi_{g-1}^*}{2}\,.$$

(4.4.8)

We consider the first form. The adjoint group equations are then

$$D_g\nabla^2\phi_{g-1}^* - \sigma_g\phi_{g-1}^* = f_g$$

(4.4.9)

with

$$f_g = -\frac{\phi_g^*}{\alpha_g} - \frac{\nu\zeta_g\Delta u_g}{\alpha_g}Q^*(\mathbf{r}) - \frac{\phi_{th}^*}{\alpha_g}\delta_{gG}\,,$$

(4.4.10)

where $\sigma_g = \sigma_{a_g} + 1/\alpha_g$. An expression similar to (4.4.9) is obtained for the approximation (4.4.8). The adjoint source terms may likewise be found as sums over g in terms of the ϕ_g^*.

The computation of the adjoint flux is similar to the computation of the flux, save for the direction of integration. Notice that the same coefficients are available for both the flux and adjoint flux. This provides an enormous simplification of the algebra.

4.5 Multigroup Difference Equations

In the earlier sections of this chapter, we obtained the multigroup equations by dividing the lethargy variable and obtaining a set of simultaneous differential equations. The next step in the process is to divide the spatial interval into discrete segments. The results will provide us with a set of simultaneous algebraic equations for which the methods introduced in other chapters are applicable.

The basic diffusion equation for each group is given in Eq. (4.3.26). The coefficients are assumed a constant within any given region, but may vary across boundaries. The differential operator for the leakage may be written

$$\mathbf{\nabla} \cdot [D_g \mathbf{\nabla} \phi_g] = \frac{1}{r^\rho} \left[\frac{d}{dr} \left(r^\rho D_g \frac{d\phi_g}{dr} \right) \right] \qquad (4.5.1)$$

$$\rho = 0, \text{ plane};$$

$$\rho = 1, \text{ cylinder};$$

$$\rho = 2, \text{ sphere}.$$

We consider the interval $0 \leqslant r \leqslant a$ and divide the interval into K subintervals and denote the interpolation points as r_k, $0 \leqslant k \leqslant K$. The spacings are denoted $\Delta r_k = r_{k+1} - r_k$, and are not necessarily equal. We do assume, however, that an interpolation point falls at each interface between regions. We now integrate Eq. (4.3.26) from $r_{k-1/2}$ to $r_{k+1/2}$ to obtain

$$r^\rho D_g \frac{\partial \phi_g}{\partial r} \bigg|_{r_{k+1/2}} - r^\rho D_g \frac{\partial \phi_g}{\partial r} \bigg|_{r_{k-1/2}}$$

$$= \int_{r_k}^{r_{k+1/2}} dr \, (\sigma_g \phi_g + f_g) r^\rho + \int_{r_{k-1/2}}^{r_k} dr (\sigma_g \phi_g + f_g) \, r^\rho . \qquad (4.5.2)$$

The material properties may be discontinuous at r_k, and hence the integral is factored into portions whose integrands are continuous.

Consider the integral on the right from r_k to $r_{k+1/2}$. We expand the integrand in a Taylor series and assume the interval sufficiently small that we may neglect all but the first term; thus we truncate to terms of order Δr. The integral is then

$$\int_{r_k}^{r_{k+1/2}} dr (\sigma_g \phi_g + f_g) \, r^\rho \approx [\sigma_g(r_k^+) \, \phi_g(r_k) + f_g(r_k^+)] \, r_k^\rho \frac{\Delta r_k}{2}, \qquad (4.5.3)$$

where the $+$ sign denotes the value of the factors obtained as $r \to r_k$ from the right. A similar result is obtained for the integral from $r_{k-1/2}$ to

r_k except that arguments r_k^- will be used to denote left-hand limits. For r_k not on an interface, the integral becomes

$$\int_{r_{k-1/2}}^{r_{k+1/2}} dr(\sigma_g \phi_g + f_g)\, r^\rho = [\sigma_g(r_k)\, \phi_g(r_k) + f_g(r_k)]\, r_k^\rho \left(\frac{r_{k+1} - r_{k-1}}{2}\right), \qquad (4.5.4)$$

which is merely the arithmetic average.

To eliminate the derivative terms, we use the simple approximation

$$\frac{\partial \phi}{\partial r}\bigg|_{r_{k+1/2}} = \frac{\phi_{k+1} - \phi_k}{r_{k+1} - r_k}, \qquad (4.5.5)$$

of accuracy $O(\Delta r)$. Using the difference approximation (4.5.5) in the left-hand side of Eq. (4.5.2), we obtain a 3-point difference equation

$$a_{g,k}\phi_{g,k+1} - b_{g,k}\phi_{g,k} + c_{g,k}\phi_{g,k-1} = w_{g,k}, \qquad (4.5.6)$$

where the coefficients are given by

$$a_{g,k} = \frac{r_{k+1/2}^\rho D_{g,k+1/2}}{\Delta r_k}, \qquad (4.5.7a)$$

$$c_{g,k} = \frac{r_{k-1/2}^\rho D_{g,k-1/2}}{\Delta r_{k-1}}, \qquad (4.5.7b)$$

$$w_{g,k} = \frac{r_k^\rho}{2}\,[\Delta r_k f_g(r_k^+) + \Delta r_{k-1} f_g(r_k^-)], \qquad (4.5.7c)$$

$$b_{g,k} = \frac{r_{k+1/2}^\rho D_{g,k+1/2}}{\Delta r_k} + \frac{r_{k-1/2}^\rho D_{g,k-1/2}}{\Delta r_{k-1}} + \frac{r_k^\rho}{2}\,[\sigma_g(r_k^+)\,\Delta r_k + \sigma_g(r_k^-)\,\Delta r_{k-1}]. \qquad (4.5.7d)$$

More accurate 3-point relations may be derived by considering the next order terms in the expansion of the integrands of Eq. (4.5.2). Even higher order expansions may be considered, but then the basic difference relation is no longer a 3-point formula. The derivation of the difference equation is similar to derivations considered earlier. Notice that to retain a 3-point difference approximation to the second derivative, we achieved accuracy of $O(\Delta r)$. Frequently variable coefficients have the effect of increasing the truncation error for an approximation which would otherwise be more accurate. A particular property of the present derivation is the symmetry of the coefficient matrix, that is $a_{g,k-1} = c_{g,k}$, as is readily shown. Properties of real symmetric matrices that can be exploited practically and theoretically are pointed out in Chapter I.

Further, much less time is consumed in computing their elements. If we take the usual boundary conditions that $\phi_0 = \phi_K = 0$, then an equation of the form (4.5.6) applies for each group and for $1 \leqslant k \leqslant K - 1$. Notice that the coefficients can be computed once and for all, and hence the entire set of equations is determined.

Analogous techniques are applicable to two dimensional reactors. Details are left for a problem. Similar procedures may be used to obtain difference equations for the adjoint flux.

4.6 Matrix Form of Multigroup Equations

In order to simplify the equations, it is convenient to consider the matrix form of the multigroup equations. We consider first the one dimensional case. To this end, we first reduce the spatial dependence to matrix form and then express the group dependence in matrix form. For a given group, the relevant difference equation was given by Eq. (4.5.6).

We define the flux vector ψ_g in the gth group, and $\mathbf{w}_g$ as

$$\psi_g = \begin{bmatrix} \phi_{g,1} \\ \phi_{g,2} \\ \vdots \\ \phi_{g,K-1} \end{bmatrix}, \tag{4.6.1}$$

and

$$\mathbf{w}_g = \begin{bmatrix} w_{g,1} \\ w_{g,2} \\ \vdots \\ w_{g,K-1} \end{bmatrix}, \tag{4.6.2}$$

where we take $\phi_{g,0} = \phi_{g,K} = 0$ (the extrapolated boundary) and similarly $w_{g,0} = w_{g,K} = 0$.

The set of equations for the gth group are then

$$\mathbf{A}_g \psi_g = \mathbf{w}_g \tag{4.6.3}$$

with

$$\mathbf{A}_g = \begin{bmatrix} -b_{g,1} & a_{g,1} & 0 & \cdots & \cdots & 0 \\ c_{g,2} & -b_{g,2} & a_{g,2} & \cdots & \cdots & 0 \\ \vdots & \vdots & \vdots & & & \vdots \\ & & & & c_{g,K-1} & -b_{g,K-1} \end{bmatrix}. \tag{4.6.4}$$

The vector $\mathbf{w}_g$ depends upon the source terms $f_g(\mathbf{r})$ which may be discontinuous across boundaries. From Eq. (4.3.24), the simplest form of f_g is

$$f_g = -\frac{(\xi\sigma_s)_{g-1}}{(\xi\sigma_s)_g}\frac{\phi_{g-1}}{\alpha_g} - \frac{\nu\chi_g\varDelta u_g}{\alpha_g(\xi\sigma_s)_g}\left\{\sum_{i=1}^{G+1}\beta_i\phi_i\right\} - \frac{Z_g\varDelta u_g S_e(\mathbf{r})}{\alpha_g(\xi\sigma_s)_g}, \qquad (4.6.5)$$

where $\beta_{G+1} = \sigma_f^{th}$.

The elements of the vector $\mathbf{w}_g$ involve the factor f_g at point k evaluated at the left- and right-hand limits. Since the flux is assumed continuous everywhere, the different limits affect only the coefficients. Thus, the vector $\mathbf{w}_g$ can be written

$$\mathbf{w}_g = -\mathbf{S}_g\boldsymbol{\psi}_{g-1} - \nu\sum_{g'=1}^{G+1}\mathbf{R}_{g'\to g}\boldsymbol{\psi}_{g'} - \mathbf{F}_g, \qquad (4.6.6)$$

where $\mathbf{S}_g$ is the matrix containing the slowing down factors, $\mathbf{R}_{g'\to g}$ is the fission source matrix, and $\mathbf{F}_g$ the extraneous source vector. Physically, we know that every element of $\mathbf{S}_g$, $\mathbf{R}_{g'\to g}$, and $\mathbf{F}_g$ is nonnegative for all g. The construction of the matrices is easily carried out. For $\mathbf{S}_g$ we have

$$\mathbf{S}_g = \begin{bmatrix} S_{g,1} & 0 & \cdots & 0 \\ 0 & S_{g,2} & \cdots & 0 \\ \vdots & \vdots & & \vdots \\ & & & S_{g,K-1} \end{bmatrix} \qquad (4.6.7)$$

with

$$S_{gk} = \frac{r_k^\rho}{\alpha_g}\frac{\varDelta r_k}{2}\frac{(\xi\sigma_s)_{g-1,k^+}}{(\xi\sigma_s)_{g,k^+}} + \frac{r_k^\rho}{\alpha_g}\frac{\varDelta r_{k-1}}{2}\frac{(\xi\sigma_s)_{g-1,k^-}}{(\xi\sigma_s)_{g,k^-}}. \qquad (4.6.8)$$

We have considered only scattering between adjacent groups thus far. Similarly,

$$\mathbf{F}_g = \begin{bmatrix} F_{g,1} \\ F_{g,2} \\ \vdots \\ F_{g,K-1} \end{bmatrix}, \qquad (4.6.9)$$

with

$$F_{g,k} = r_k^\rho\frac{\varDelta r_k}{2}\frac{Z_g\varDelta u_g}{\alpha_g(\xi\sigma_s)_{g,k^+}}S_e(r_{k^+}) + r_k^\rho\frac{\varDelta r_{k-1}}{2}\frac{Z_g\varDelta u_g}{\alpha_g(\xi\sigma_s)_{g,k^-}}S_e(r_k^-). \qquad (4.6.10)$$

The fission sources are

$$
\mathbf{R}_{g'\to g}\mathbf{\Psi}_{g'} =
\begin{bmatrix}
R_{g'\to g,1} & 0 & \cdots & 0 \\
 & R_{g'\to g,2} & \cdots & 0 \\
\vdots & \vdots & & \vdots \\
 & & & R_{g'\to g,K-1}
\end{bmatrix}
\begin{bmatrix}
\phi_{g',1} \\
\phi_{g',2} \\
\vdots \\
\phi_{g',K-1}
\end{bmatrix}
\tag{4.6.11}
$$

with

$$
R_{g'\to g,k} = \frac{\chi_g \Delta u_g}{\alpha_g(\xi\sigma_s)_{g,k^+}} r_k^p \frac{\Delta r_k}{2}\beta_{g,k^+} + \frac{\chi_g \Delta u_g}{\alpha_g(\xi\sigma_s)_{g,k^-}} r_k^p \frac{\Delta r_{k-1}}{2}\beta_{g,k^-}.
\tag{4.6.12}
$$

We remark that scattering beyond adjacent groups, e.g., inelastic scattering, may readily be included in the above matrices. The scattering matrix $\mathbf{S}_g$ contains the coefficients for scattering from group $g - 1$ to g. If we include transfer between more than adjacent groups, the scattering matrix is summed. The scattering contribution to the vector $\mathbf{w}_g$ may be written

$$
-\sum_{g'} \mathbf{S}_{g'\to g}\mathbf{\Psi}_{g'}
$$

with $\mathbf{S}_{g-1\to g} = \mathbf{S}_g$, where $\mathbf{S}_g$ is defined in Eq. (4.6.7).
The matrices $\mathbf{S}_{g'\to g}$ would be of the form

$$
\mathbf{S}_{g'\to g} =
\begin{bmatrix}
\sigma_{g'\to g,1} & 0 & \cdots & 0 \\
0 & \sigma_{g'\to g,2} & \cdots & 0 \\
\vdots & \vdots & & \vdots \\
0 & & & \sigma_{g'\to g,K-1}
\end{bmatrix}
\tag{4.6.13}
$$

where the $\sigma_{g'\to g,n}$ are transfer cross sections at space point n. Note that if down scattering only is permitted, $\mathbf{S}_{g'\to g} = 0$ for $g' > g$. The cross section for elastic transfer between nonadjacent groups may be found by considering the collision mechanics. If the mass of the scattering nucleus is known, and if the slowing down density is assumed constant within a group, then the transfer probabilities are readily computed (see problem 9). In the case of inelastic scattering, the cross section must be known from experiment or computed from a nuclear model, e.g., the optical model. Similarly, upscattering cross sections must be computed from a theoretical scattering model.

The matrices $\mathbf{S}_g$ and $\mathbf{R}_{g'\to g}$ are diagonal with respect to spatial indices since neutrons change their group at the point of nuclear interaction. Casting the spatial dependence of the multigroup difference equations

into matrix form has been completed; we turn next to the group dependence.

Define the extended vectors ψ and $\mathbf{w}$ as

$$\psi = \begin{bmatrix} \psi_1 \\ \psi_2 \\ \vdots \\ \psi_{G+1} \end{bmatrix}, \tag{4.6.14}$$

and

$$\mathbf{w} = \begin{bmatrix} \mathbf{w}_1 \\ \mathbf{w}_2 \\ \vdots \\ \mathbf{w}_{G+1} \end{bmatrix}. \tag{4.6.15}$$

The entire set of equations can be written

$$\mathbf{A}\psi = \mathbf{w} \tag{4.6.16}$$

with

$$\mathbf{A} = \begin{bmatrix} \mathbf{A}_1 & \mathbf{O} & \cdots & \mathbf{O} \\ \mathbf{O} & \mathbf{A}_2 & \cdots & \mathbf{O} \\ \vdots & \vdots & & \vdots \\ & & & \mathbf{A}_{G+1} \end{bmatrix}. \tag{4.6.17}$$

The vector $\mathbf{w}$ can be written in the form

$$\mathbf{w} = -\mathbf{S}\psi - \nu\mathbf{R}\psi - \mathbf{F}, \tag{4.6.18}$$

where the matrices $\mathbf{S}$, $\mathbf{R}$, and $\mathbf{F}$ are obvious. In the case of no extraneous
sources, we have

$$\mathbf{A}\psi = -(\mathbf{S} + \nu\mathbf{R})\psi \tag{4.6.19}$$

or

$$(\mathbf{A} + \mathbf{S})\psi = -\nu\mathbf{R}\psi .$$

We define

$$\mathbf{T} \equiv -(\mathbf{A} + \mathbf{S}) \tag{4.6.20}$$

and hence

$$\mathbf{T}\psi = \nu\mathbf{R}\psi . \tag{4.6.21}$$

Note that Eq. (4.6.21) is one of the same form as Eq. (4.2.30). Of course, the operators are significantly simpler in the finite difference approximation.

The matrix $\mathbf{T}$ has the form

$$\mathbf{T} = - \begin{bmatrix} \mathbf{A}_1 & \mathbf{O} & \mathbf{O} & \cdots & \mathbf{O} & \mathbf{O} \\ \mathbf{S}_2 & \mathbf{A}_2 & \mathbf{O} & \cdots & \mathbf{O} & \mathbf{O} \\ \vdots & \vdots & \vdots & \ddots & \vdots & \vdots \\ \mathbf{O} & \mathbf{O} & \mathbf{O} & \cdots & \mathbf{S}_{G+1} & \mathbf{A}_{G+1} \end{bmatrix}. \tag{4.6.22}$$

If we include scattering over adjacent groups, then $\mathbf{T}$ has the form

$$\mathbf{T} = - \begin{bmatrix} \mathbf{A}_1 & \mathbf{O} & & \cdots & & \mathbf{O} \\ \mathbf{S}_2 & \mathbf{A}_2 & \mathbf{O} & & \cdots & \mathbf{O} \\ \mathbf{S}_{1\to3} & \mathbf{S}_3 & \mathbf{A}_3 & \mathbf{O} & \cdots & \mathbf{O} \\ \vdots & \vdots & \vdots & \vdots & \vdots & \vdots \\ \mathbf{S}_{1\to G+1} & \mathbf{S}_{2\to G+1} & & \cdots & \mathbf{S}_{G+1} & \mathbf{A}_{G+1} \end{bmatrix}. \tag{4.6.23}$$

The off-diagonal submatrices are all diagonal, whereas the $\mathbf{A}_g$ are tridiagonal. It is easily shown that for either form $\mathbf{T}^{-1}$ exists and is nonnegative (problem 10). The basic equation is then

$$\frac{\psi}{\nu} = \mathbf{T}^{-1}\mathbf{R}\psi = \mathbf{G}\psi, \tag{4.6.24}$$

where $\mathbf{G}$ is nonnegative.

The matrix $\mathbf{R}$ represents the fission source terms and may have zeros in certain columns. In particular, the zeros occur for any column not in a fuel region. We may permute the rows and columns of $\mathbf{G}$ and the corresponding rows of ψ such that the equations take the form

$$\frac{\psi}{\nu} = \mathbf{G}'\psi \tag{4.6.25}$$

with

$$\mathbf{G}' = \begin{bmatrix} \mathbf{G}_{11} & \mathbf{G}_{12} \\ \mathbf{O} & \mathbf{G}_{22} \end{bmatrix} \tag{4.6.26}$$

The submatrices $\mathbf{G}_{11}$ and $\mathbf{G}_{22}$ are square; i.e., $\mathbf{G}'$ is reducible. The matrix $\mathbf{G}'$ is also nonnegative and hence possesses a largest eigenvalue which is positive. Furthermore, the eigenvector corresponding to the largest eigenvalue has nonnegative components. In other words, there is a smallest real ν for which the reactor is critical, and the corresponding flux mode is nowhere negative. If none of the columns of **R** is zero, then **G** is irreducible. We then conclude there is a smallest real ν for which the reactor is critical, and the corresponding flux mode is positive everywhere. Analogous results may be derived for higher dimension problems.

The adjoint equations may also be differenced and a similar eigenvalue relation obtained. It is important to notice that the formulation of the adjoint equations in Section 4.4 will produce a matrix eigenvalue equation of the form

$$\frac{\psi^*}{\nu} = \mathbf{G}^*\psi^* , \qquad (4.6.27)$$

but $\mathbf{G}^*$ will not be the transpose of matrix **G** as defined in Eq. (4.6.24). This circumstance occurs because we computed the adjoint of the age-diffusion equations and then formed the difference equations in energy and space, instead of vice versa. This phenomenon is another illustration of the noncommutability of the operation of computing the adjoint with other operations. However, if, in the formation of the multigroup adjoint equations, we have assumed q^* to be approximately constant from one group to another, instead of ϕ^*, then the **G** and $\mathbf{G}^*$ would be transposed.

4.7 Numerical Solution of the Multigroup Equations

The basic equations given in the last section may be solved by a variety of methods. The usual procedure is iterative, rather than direct inversion. As an example of the procedure, we outline the steps for one possible method.

Based upon the reactor materials and the relevant cross sections, the lethargy intervals are selected and the coefficients are computed. The coefficients may be computed by hand, graphically, or by numerical integration, depending upon the information and equipment available. An initial estimate of the flux in each group, say ψ_g^0, is made.[3] With the initial estimates and coefficients, the vectors $\mathbf{w}_g^0$ are computed using

---

[3] One of the many commonly used ways of estimating the flux in each group is to calculate it for an infinite assembly first. This calculation is performed explicitly very easily by starting from the group of highest energy and working down. The size of the thermal source of fission neutrons can be selected arbitrarily. Only the fission spectrum is important at this stage of the calculation, and this spectrum is known. By knowing the flux in all groups of higher energy than the one in question, the flux in the group of interest can be computed. The thermal flux so calculated will not in general agree with that assumed, because the composition of the infinite system assumed is not critical.

Eq. (4.6.6). Recall that the vectors $\mathbf{w}_g^0$ are the sources for the gth group. The flux in group 1, $\boldsymbol{\psi}_1^0$, is now corrected, i.e., we solve the diffusion equation

$$\mathbf{A}_1\boldsymbol{\psi}_1 = \mathbf{w}_1^0 \tag{4.7.1}$$

for the flux at all points of the reactor. For a one-dimensional problem, Eq. (4.7.1) might be solved by matrix factorization since $\mathbf{A}_1$ is then tridiagonal. (The equations could also be solved by inversion or iteration). Let the solution be denoted $\boldsymbol{\psi}_1^1$. In like manner, solve the diffusion equations

$$\mathbf{A}_g\boldsymbol{\psi}_g = \mathbf{w}_g^0 \tag{4.7.2}$$

in the remaining groups. The vector $\boldsymbol{\psi}^1$

$$\boldsymbol{\psi}^1 = \begin{bmatrix} \boldsymbol{\psi}_1^1 \\ \boldsymbol{\psi}_2^1 \\ \vdots \\ \boldsymbol{\psi}_{G+1}^1 \end{bmatrix} \tag{4.7.3}$$

represents the first iteration. It is convenient to rescale the vector $\boldsymbol{\psi}^1$ such that

$$(\zeta_1\boldsymbol{\psi}^1, \zeta_1\boldsymbol{\psi}^1) = (\boldsymbol{\psi}^0, \boldsymbol{\psi}^0), \tag{4.7.4}$$

where ζ_1 is the scale factor. The scaling, sometimes called renormalization, prevents the solution from diverging. With the new scaled vectors we recompute the source vectors in each group. Thus we find $\mathbf{w}_g^1$. With the corrected sources, we again solve the group diffusion equations at all points of the reactor to obtain $\boldsymbol{\psi}^2$, etc. After a sufficient number of iterations, say p, then $\boldsymbol{\psi}^p$ has converged, that is

$$|\boldsymbol{\psi}^{p+1} - \boldsymbol{\psi}^p| < \epsilon, \tag{4.7.5}$$

where ϵ is a convergence criterion, chosen by the user. In words, inequality (4.7.5) requires the flux on the $p + 1$st iteration to differ from that on the pth iteration by less than some arbitrarily chosen constant at all points of the reactor and in all speed groups. In testing for convergence one must be very careful in the application of the above inequality. The inequality merely states that the *difference* between two successive iterations be less than some quantity. It does *not* state that the error in any particular iteration is less than some criterion. Convergence may be slow, or the difference may have a maximum or minimum. The iteration process just described is sometimes called the "inner iteration."

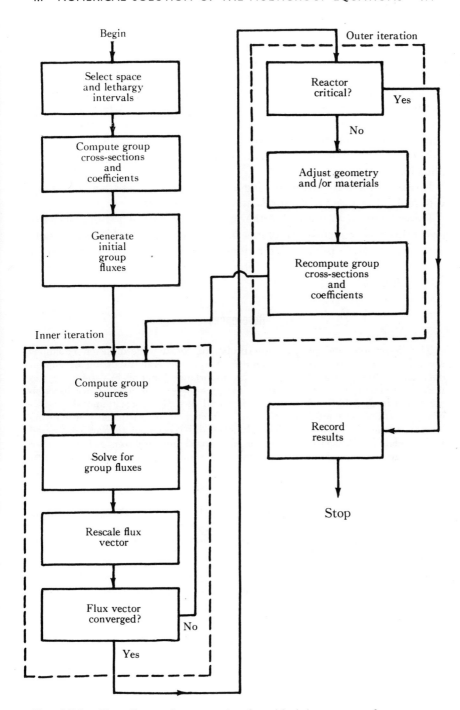

FIG. 4.7.1. Flow diagram for computing the critical size or mass of a reactor.

The scale factors ζ_μ will approach an asymptotic value determined by the state of the assembly. If $\zeta_\mu < 1$, then the flux is growing with each iteration; the assembly is supercritical. Similarly, for $\zeta_\mu > 1$, the assembly is subcritical. If the critical size of a reactor is sought, then the adjustable parameters are altered according to $1 - \zeta_\mu$. The adjustment of the gross properties is called an "outer iteration." After completing the outer iteration, the inner iterations are begun again. The process continues until the growth factors ζ_μ equal 1, which implies the system is critical. The scale factors ζ_μ are in fact the reciprocal of the multiplication factor.

It is convenient to outline the logic of the above process in a flow chart. Figure 4.7.1 is a pictorial representation of the steps.

It is important to recall that the method just outlined is one of many possibilities. Frequently programs are written for which there is only one inner iteration per outer iteration. Other variants exist, and we refer to some operating codes in the references for more detail (see References *10* through *14*).

References

The derivations and physical interpretations for the age-diffusion equations are exhaustively considered in *1* and *2*. A very general discussion of adjoint operators is found in *4*. The use of the importance function in reactor physics is well discussed in *1* and *2*. Further interpretations of the importance function are found in *3*. Additional discussion is found in *5*. The formation of the multigroup equations is considered in many references. For particularly interesting discussions, see *2*, *5*, *6*, and *7*. The multigroup difference equations are considered in *5* through *8*. The development in the text is predominantly from *5*. References *8* and *9* contain very rigorous discussions of the numerical solution of the multigroup difference equations. A brief list of particular multigroup codes is given in *10* through *13*. Reference *14* is an abstract of many different nuclear codes.

1. Weinberg, A. M., and Wigner, E. P., "The Physical Theory of Neutron Chain Reactors." Univ. of Chicago Press, Chicago, 1956.

2. Meghreblian, R. V., and Holmes, D. K., "Reactor Analysis." McGraw-Hill, New York, 1960.

3. Robkin, M. A., and Clark, M., Integral reactor theory; orthogonality and importance. *Nuclear Sci. Eng.* 8, 437 (1960).

4. Morse, P. M., and Feshbach, H., "Methods of Theoretical Physics." McGraw-Hill, New York, 1953.

5. Marchuk, G. I., "Numerical Methods for Reactor Calculations" (translation). Consultants Bureau, New York, 1959.

6. Ehrlich, R., and Hurwitz, H., Multigroup methods for neutron diffusion problems. *Nucleonics* 12, No. 2, 23 (1954).

7. Birkhoff, G., and Wigner, E. P., eds., "Proceedings of the Eleventh Symposium in Applied Mathematics." Am. Math. Soc., Providence, Rhode Island, 1961.

8. Birkhoff, G., and Wigner, E. P., eds., "Proceedings of the Eleventh Symposium in Applied Mathematics," pp. 164-189. Am. Math. Soc., Providence, Rhode Island, 1961.

9. Birkhoff, G., and Varga, R. S., Reactor criticality and non-negative matrices. *J. Soc. Ind. Appl. Math.* **6**, 354 (1958).

10. Wachspress, E. L., CURE: a generalized two-space dimension multigroup coding of the 704. KAPL-1724 (May, 1957).

11. Cadwell, W. R., Dorsey, J. P., Henderson, H. B., Liska, J. M., Mandell, J. P., and Suggs, M. C., PDQ-3: a program for the solution of the neutron diffusion equation in two dimensions on the IBM 704. WAPD-TM-179.

12. Brinkley, F. W., and Mills, C. B., A one dimensional intermediate reactor computing program. LA-2161 (May, 1959).

13. Stuart, R. N., Canfield, E. H., Dougherty, E. E., and Stone, S. P., Zoom, a one dimensional, multigroup neutron diffusion theory reactor code for the IBM 204. UCRL-5293 (November 1958).

14. Am. Nuclear Soc., Math. Comp. Div., "Abstract of Nuclear Codes," (M. Butler, ed.), No. 1-80 (1962).

Problems

1. Derive the critical equation from the age-diffusion equation for an infinite reactor with thermal fissions only. Interpret the results.

2. Generalize the results of problem 1 to an infinite reactor with fissions occurring at all lethargies between $0 \leqslant u \leqslant u_{\mathrm{th}}$.

3. Write the slowing down equation for an infinite medium in terms of the slowing down density, and derive an integral equation for the solution. Find the adjoint of the integral equation and show that solutions of the integral equations and its adjoint are biorthogonal.

4. For problem 3 above, derive the adjoint to the differential slowing down equation and then integrate the adjoint equation. Is the result the same as the adjoint equation in problem 3? Explain.

5. Derive the multigroup equations for a two-group approximation and express the criticality condition as a critical determinant.

6. Show that the multigroup equations obtained by using Eq. (4.3.19) are of the form of Eq. (4.3.26) with the following definitions:

$$f_g = -\frac{(\xi\sigma_\mathrm{s})_{g-1}}{(\xi\sigma_\mathrm{s})_g} \left[\left\{ \frac{D_g}{D_{g-1}} \sigma_{g-1} + \frac{2}{\alpha_g} - \sigma_{\mathrm{a}g} \right\} \phi_{g-1} - \frac{D_g}{D_{g-1}} f_{g-1} \right]$$

$$+ \frac{2\nu\chi_g \varDelta u_g}{\alpha_g(\xi\sigma_\mathrm{s})_g} \left[\sum_{k=1}^{G} \tau_k \phi_k(r) + \overset{\mathrm{th}}{\sigma_f} \phi_{\mathrm{th}}(r) \right] + \frac{2Z_g \varDelta u_g}{\alpha_g(\xi\sigma_\mathrm{s})_g} S_\mathrm{e}(r),$$

$$\sigma_g = \sigma_{\mathrm{a}g} + \frac{2}{\alpha_g},$$

and

$$\tau_k = \frac{1}{2}(\xi\sigma_\mathrm{s})_k \int_{u_{k-1}}^{u_k} du \, \frac{\sigma_f(u)}{\xi\sigma_\mathrm{s}(u)} \left\{ \frac{u - u_{k-1}}{\varDelta u_k} \right\}$$

$$+ \frac{1}{2}(\xi\sigma_\mathrm{s})_{k+1} \int_{u_k}^{u_{k+1}} du \, \frac{\sigma_f(u)}{\xi\sigma_\mathrm{s}(u)} \left\{ \frac{u_{k+1} - u}{\varDelta u_{k+1}} \right\} .$$

7. Consider the basic group diffusion equation (4.3.26 in text) in a two-region slab. Derive a difference approximation which is accurate to order $(\Delta x)^2$ in each region and across the interface.

8. Derive a five-point coefficient matrix for a two-dimensional diffusion problem in r, z coordinates. Show that the coefficient matrix is symmetric.

9. For elastic scattering, calculate $S_{i,j}$ in terms of the energies ϵ_i, ϵ_{i+1}, ϵ_j, and ϵ_{j+1}, assuming that the slowing down density is constant within a group, for the following cases:

    1. $\epsilon_{i+1} > \alpha\epsilon_j$

    2. $\epsilon_i > \alpha\epsilon_j$; $\alpha\epsilon_j > \epsilon_{i+1} > \alpha\epsilon_{j+1}$

    3. $\epsilon_i > \alpha\epsilon_j$; $\epsilon_{i+1} < \alpha\epsilon_{j+1}$

    4. $\alpha\epsilon_{j+1} < \epsilon_i < \alpha\epsilon_j$; $\epsilon_{i+1} < \alpha\epsilon_{j+1}$

    5. $\epsilon_i < \alpha\epsilon_{j+1}$

    6. $\epsilon_i < \alpha\epsilon_j$; $\epsilon_{i+1} > \alpha\epsilon_{j+1}$

where

$$\alpha = (M - 1)/(M + 1)^2$$

and M is the atomic mass. Suppose the groups are of width $\epsilon_i/\epsilon_{i+1} = \sqrt{10}$. Which cases apply to H, D, C, very heavy nuclides?

10. Show that the matrix $\mathbf{T}^{-1}$ [Eq. (4.6.23)] is nonnegative.

11. Show that the approximation $(\xi\sigma_s)_j^{-1}q_j = (\xi\sigma_s)_{j-1}^{-1}q_{j-1}$ leads to a matrix eigenvalue problem

$$\boldsymbol{\psi}^* = \nu\mathbf{G}^*\boldsymbol{\psi}^*$$

such that the $\mathbf{G}^*$ is the transpose of the corresponding eigenvalue problem for the flux.

The following sequence of problems provides an elementary discussion of the numerical solution of the reactor kinetics equations.

12. The infinite medium kinetics equations for G delayed groups may be written

$$\frac{dn(t)}{dt} = \frac{\rho - \beta}{\varLambda} n(t) + \sum_{i=1}^{G} \lambda_i C^i(t) ,$$

$$\frac{dC^i(t)}{dt} = \frac{\beta_i}{\varLambda} n(t) - \lambda_i C^i(t), \qquad i = 1, 2, ..., G ,$$

where n is the neutron density, C^i the ith delayed group precursor, ρ the reactivity, $\varLambda$ the generation time, λ_i the ith group decay factor, β_i the ith group fission yield fraction, and $\beta = \Sigma_i \beta_i$ the total delayed yield.

   (a) Define the vector

$$\boldsymbol{\psi} = \begin{bmatrix} n \\ C^1 \\ C^2 \\ \cdot \\ \cdot \\ \cdot \\ C^G \end{bmatrix}$$

and write the kinetics equation as the matrix equation

$$\frac{d\psi}{dt} = \mathbf{A}\psi .$$

(b) Let the eigenvalues and eigenvectors of $\mathbf{A}$ be defined as

$$\mathbf{A}\mathbf{e}_k = \omega_k \mathbf{e}_k .$$

Show that the analytic solution to the matrix equation in part (a) is

$$\psi(t) = \sum_k a_k e^{\omega_k t} \mathbf{e}_k .$$

What are the coefficients a_k?

(c) Approximating the derivative by a simple forward difference, we obtain the numerical approximation

$$\psi_{j+1} = \psi_j + \mathbf{A}\psi_j = [\mathbf{I} + \mathbf{A}]\psi_j .$$

What are the eigenvalues and eigenvectors of the above approximations? Are there any stability conditions imposed upon the approximation?

(d) For constant reactivity the numerical approximation can be written

$$\psi_{j+1} = e^{\mathbf{A}h}\psi_j .$$

If the Taylor series expansion of $e^{\mathbf{A}h}$ be truncated to order N, write the numerical approximation. What are the eigenvectors and eigenvalues of the approximation? Are any stability conditions imposed upon the time step?

13. The equations for the delayed neutron precursors and neutrons may be integrated directly in the form

$$C^i(t) = e^{-\lambda_i(t-t_j)}C^i(t_j) + \frac{\beta_i}{\Lambda} \int_{t_j}^t dt' e^{-\lambda_i(t-t')} n(t'), \qquad t_j \leqslant t' \leqslant t_{j+1}$$

and

$$n(t) = \int_{t_j}^t dt' \left(\frac{\rho - \beta}{\Lambda}\right) n(t') + \sum_i \lambda_i \int_{t_j}^t dt' C^i(t').$$

By eliminating the neutron precursors, a single integral equation of the form

$$n(t) = K_1 C^i(t_j) + \int_{t_j}^t dt' \, K_2 n(t')$$

is found.

(a) Derive the functions K_1 and K_2.

(b) Assume the reactivity is a small constant, i.e., $\rho \ll \beta$. If $n(t')$ is assumed constant such that $n(t') = n_j$, $t_j \leqslant t' \leqslant t_{j+1}$, derive the values of C^i_{j+1} and n_{j+1}. In matrix form we have

$$\psi_{j+1} = \mathbf{B}\psi_j .$$

(c) How are the eigenvalues of $\mathbf{B}$ (above) related to the eigenvalues of the matrix $\mathbf{A}$ in problem 12?

(d) Generalize part (b) by assuming $n(t')$ is a polynomial in $(t' - t_j)$ of degree N. To find expansion coefficients assume the integral equation for $n(t)$ above must agree with the polynomial at $N + 1$ points, $t_j, t_j + \Delta, ...,$ $t_j + N\Delta \equiv t_{j+1}$, where $\Delta = (t_{j+1} - t_j)/N$. Set up the simultaneous equations to be solved in matrix form.

14. The matrix $\mathbf{A}$ from problem 12 may be factored in the form

$$\mathbf{A} = \mathbf{L} + \mathbf{D} + \mathbf{U}$$

with $\mathbf{L}$ strictly lower triangular, $\mathbf{D}$ diagonal, and $\mathbf{U}$ strictly upper triangular. The kinetics equations can be written

$$\frac{d\boldsymbol{\psi}}{dt} - \mathbf{D}\boldsymbol{\psi} = (\mathbf{L} + \mathbf{U})\boldsymbol{\psi}.$$

(a) Assume a constant reactivity and integrate the above equation to obtain the matrix relation

$$\boldsymbol{\psi}(t) = e^{\mathbf{D}(t-t_j)}\boldsymbol{\psi}_j + \int_{t_j}^{t} dt' \, e^{\mathbf{D}(t-t')}(\mathbf{L} + \mathbf{U})\boldsymbol{\psi}(t').$$

(b) Assume $\boldsymbol{\psi}(t') = \boldsymbol{\psi}_j(t_j \leqslant t' \leqslant t_{j+1})$ and ·derive the matrix equation

$$\boldsymbol{\psi}_{j+1} = \mathbf{B}_0\boldsymbol{\psi}_j.$$

Show that $\mathbf{B}_0$ is nonnegative and irreducible. Also, show that for $\rho = 0$, the eigenvector of $\mathbf{A}$ of largest eigenvalue ($=0$) is an eigenvector of $\mathbf{B}$ with eigenvalue unity.

(c) Let ω_0 be the largest eigenvalue of $\mathbf{A}$ for any ρ (assumed constant). Show that the approximation

$$\boldsymbol{\psi}(t') = e^{\omega_0(t-t')}\boldsymbol{\psi}_j$$

yields a matrix equation of the form

$$\boldsymbol{\psi}_{j+1} = \mathbf{B}_1\boldsymbol{\psi}_j$$

where $\mathbf{B}_1$ is nonnegative, irreducible, and such that the eigenvector $\mathbf{e}_0$ is an eigenvector of $\mathbf{B}_1$ with eigenvalue $e^{\omega_0 h}$.

(d) What can you say about the stability of the methods using the matrices $\mathbf{B}_0$ or $\mathbf{B}_1$?

V

TRANSPORT METHODS

In the previous chapter we discussed the multigroup diffusion methods and their numerical solution. Frequently, however, greater accuracy than that provided by the diffusion equation is demanded by the physical problem. To this end, one turns to a more accurate relation known as the Boltzmann transport equation. Unfortunately this equation is much more complex and time consuming to solve either analytically or numerically than the diffusion equation.

In this chapter we consider several special numerical methods for solving the transport equation. Most of the methods considered can be applied to either neutrons or photons. However, some of them will be discussed only for neutrons and others only for gamma rays. The development to follow is limited to one dimensional problems. This limitation does not alter the basic approach in any of the methods; however, geometries with several dimensions lead to algebraic complexity.

We first consider the one group model of the transport equation. We shall derive the spherical harmonics expansion of the transport equation which leads directly to the P_N approximation. We then consider appropriate difference equations and alternative procedures for deriving the difference relations. The double P_N method is then discussed. The multigroup transport equations are then derived and an elementary discussion of group cross sections presented. Methods for treating transient problems are then reviewed. Finally we conclude the chapter with a discussion of the moments method.

The Monte Carlo method is also a way to determine the flow of neutrons and gamma rays. However, this method may be related directly to the transport problem and need not be based directly on the Boltzmann equation. For this reason and because the approach in the Monte Carlo method is so very different from that in any of the methods discussed in this chapter, we defer its discussion to the next chapter.

5.1 The P_N Approximation

The basic equation of neutron conservation is the linear Boltzmann equation.[1] For monoenergetic neutrons this equation is

$$\mathbf{\Omega} \cdot \nabla\phi(\mathbf{r}, \mathbf{\Omega}) + \sigma_t(\mathbf{r})\,\phi(\mathbf{r}, \mathbf{\Omega}) = \int_\Omega d\mathbf{\Omega}'\,\sigma_s(\mathbf{r}, \mathbf{\Omega}' \to \mathbf{\Omega})\,\phi(\mathbf{r}, \mathbf{\Omega}') + S(\mathbf{r}, \mathbf{\Omega}),$$

$$(5.1.1)$$

where $\phi(\mathbf{r}, \mathbf{\Omega})$ is the number of neutrons crossing a unit surface at $\mathbf{r}$ per unit time going in a unit solid angle centered in the direction $\mathbf{\Omega}$, $\sigma_t(\mathbf{r})$ is the total neutron cross section at $\mathbf{r}$, $\sigma_s(\mathbf{r}, \mathbf{\Omega}' \to \mathbf{\Omega})$ is the probability per unit length that a neutron at $\mathbf{r}$ and going in a direction $\mathbf{\Omega}'$ will undergo a collision and emerge going in a unit solid angle centered at $\mathbf{\Omega}$, and $S(\mathbf{r}, \mathbf{\Omega})$ is the number of neutrons created per unit volume at $\mathbf{r}$ going in a unit solid angle centered at $\mathbf{\Omega}$.

Except for a very few special, idealized cases, the Boltzmann equation cannot be solved analytically. The term involving the integral is the prime source of difficulty. Accordingly, it behooves us to seek various approximate solutions. Because the integral term involves the angular variable, approximations concerning the angular dependence are suggested. We shall elaborate several of those which have been devised. In particular we shall consider analytic approximations to which numerical procedures may be readily applied.

A particularly useful approximation of the Boltzmann equation is the so-called P_N or spherical harmonics approximation. The basis of the approximation is the expansion of all functions of the angular variable in terms of the spherical harmonics.[2] For one dimensional problems, a subset of the spherical harmonics, the Legendre polynomials, suffices. The Legendre polynomials are an orthogonal set of functions. The flux in the Boltzmann equation may be expanded in terms of these Legendre polynomials. The resulting set of equations separates into an infinite set of coupled differential equations. The spherical harmonic approximation is introduced by truncating the infinite set of differential equations at some order and treating them by either analytic or numerical methods. We shall illustrate the derivation for one dimensional plane geometry.

We first expand the scattering cross section, directional flux, and the source in Eq. (5.1.1). For an isotropic medium the scattering cross section is a function of only the angle between the vectors $\mathbf{\Omega}'$ and $\mathbf{\Omega}$, say θ_0. It is convenient to consider the variable $\cos\theta_0 \equiv \mu_0$, rather than

---

[1] For derivations and an elementary discussion, see Appendix A.
[2] For properties of the spherical harmonics, see Reference 4, pp. 1325–1328.

θ_0 itself. The scattering function can then be expanded in terms of the Legendre polynomials $P_n(\mu_0)$. Thus

$$\sigma_s(\mathbf{r}, \mathbf{\Omega}' \to \mathbf{\Omega}) = \frac{1}{2\pi} \sum \frac{2m+1}{2} \sigma_{s,m}(\mathbf{r}) P_m(\mu_0) , \qquad (5.1.2)$$

the factor $(2m+1)/4\pi$ being inserted for later convenience. From the orthogonality of the Legendre polynomials,[3] we have

$$\sigma_{s,n}(\mathbf{r}) = 2\pi \int_{-1}^{1} d\mu_0 \sigma_s(\mathbf{r}, \mathbf{\Omega}' \to \mathbf{\Omega}) P_n(\mu_0) . \qquad (5.1.3)$$

In slab geometry the flux $\phi(\mathbf{r}, \mathbf{\Omega})$ will be a function of position x and, since the medium is assumed isotropic, the angle between the x axis and $\mathbf{\Omega}$, say θ. It is again convenient to consider the variable $\cos \theta = \mu$. The directional flux is expanded in the form

$$\phi(x, \mu) = \sum_n \frac{2n+1}{2} \phi_n(x) P_n(\mu) , \qquad (5.1.4)$$

with

$$\phi_n(x) = \int_{-1}^{1} d\mu \phi(x, \mu) P_n(\mu) . \qquad (5.1.5)$$

Likewise, for the source we have

$$S(x, \mu) = \sum_n \frac{2n+1}{2} S_n(x) P_n(\mu) , \qquad (5.1.6)$$

with

$$S_n(x) = \int_{-1}^{1} d\mu \, S(x, \mu) P_n(\mu) . \qquad (5.1.7)$$

The expansions for the directional flux and directional source are functions of μ, whereas the scattering function is a function of μ_0. It is evident geometrically that μ and μ_0 are related as shown by Fig. 5.1.1. The angles θ, φ refer to the coordinates of $\mathbf{\Omega}$, whereas θ', φ' refer to the vector $\mathbf{\Omega}'$. The unit vectors $\mathbf{\Omega}$ and $\mathbf{\Omega}'$ may be written in terms of the unit coordinate vectors as

$$\mathbf{\Omega} = \cos \theta \, \mathbf{i} + \sin \theta \cos \varphi \mathbf{j} + \sin \theta \sin \varphi \mathbf{k}, \qquad (5.1.8a)$$

[3] See Appendix D (Eq. D.7) or Reference 3 or 4.

and

$$\Omega' = \cos \theta' \, \mathbf{i} + \sin \theta' \cos \varphi' \, \mathbf{j} + \sin \theta' \sin \varphi' \, \mathbf{k}. \qquad (5.1.8b)$$

The cosine of the angle θ_0 is then

$$\cos \theta_0 = \mu_0 = \cos \theta \cos \theta' + \sin \theta \sin \theta'(\cos \varphi \cos \varphi' + \sin \varphi \sin \varphi'), \quad (5.1.9a)$$

or

$$\mu_0 = f(\mu, \varphi; \mu', \varphi') . \qquad (5.1.9b)$$

To proceed further, the Legendre polynomials $P_n(\mu_0)$ with argument μ_0 must be expressed as functions of μ and μ'. To this end, the so-called addition theorem for Legendre polynomials is useful (Eq. D.3, Appendix D).

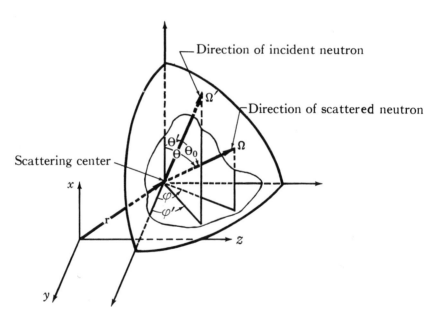

FIG. 5.1.1. Geometry of a scattering event

The scattering integral in the Boltzmann equation may be reduced to a function of x, μ only. The expansions (5.1.2) and (5.1.4), and the addition theorem may be used in the integrand of the integral in Eq. (5.1.1). Only the term $\beta = 0$ in the sum over β, which arises from the use of the addition theorem, contributes to the integral over φ'. Further, in the integration over μ', only the combination $m = n$ provides a nonvanishing contribution. By use of the expansions (5.1.4) and (5.1.6) in the remaining three terms of the Boltzmann equation, we find that

$$\sum_n \frac{2n+1}{2} \left[\mu P_n(\mu) \frac{d}{dx} \phi_n(x) + \sigma_t P_n(\mu) \phi_n(x) \right]$$

$$= \sum_n \frac{2n+1}{2} \left[\sigma_{s,n}(x) P_n(\mu) \phi_n(x) + S_n(x) P_n(\mu) \right]. \qquad (5.1.10)$$

To derive the equation for each harmonic, we multiply (5.1.10) by $P_N(\mu)$ and integrate over μ. The term in $\mu P_n(\mu)$ is eliminated by use of a recurrence relation for the Legendre polynomials (Eq. D.8, Appendix D). After some elementary algebra, we have

$$\frac{n+1}{2n+1} \frac{d}{dx} \phi_{n+1}(x) + \frac{n}{2n+1} \frac{d}{dx} \phi_{n-1}(x)$$

$$\sigma_t = \sigma_s + \sigma_e$$

$$+ \sigma_t \phi_n(x) = \left[\sigma_{s,n} \phi_n(x) + S_n(x) \right], \qquad n = 0, 1, \dots . \qquad (5.1.11)$$

Equations (5.1.11) represent an infinite set of coupled differential equations for the harmonics of the flux. Various order approximations are obtained by truncating the series at some fixed N. The truncation to order N consists of assuming all quantities with index $N + 1$ are zero. The first $N + 1$ equations are then used. The resulting set of equations are known as the P_N equations. The P_1 equations are

$$\frac{d}{dx} \phi_1(x) + \sigma_t \phi_0(x) = \sigma_{s,0} \phi_0(x) + S_0(x), \qquad (5.1.12a)$$

and

$$\frac{1}{3} \frac{d}{dx} \phi_0(x) + \sigma_t \phi_1(x) = \sigma_{s,1} \phi_1(x) + S_1(x). \qquad (5.1.12b)$$

The P_3 equations are

$$\frac{d}{dx} \phi_1(x) + \sigma_t \phi_0(x) = \sigma_{s,0} \phi_0(x) + S_0(x), \qquad (5.1.13a)$$

$$\frac{2}{3} \frac{d}{dx} \phi_2(x) + \frac{1}{3} \frac{d}{dx} \phi_0(x) + \sigma_t \phi_1(x) = \sigma_{s,1} \phi_1(x) + S_1(x), \qquad (5.1.13b)$$

$$\frac{3}{5} \frac{d}{dx} \phi_3(x) + \frac{2}{5} \frac{d}{dx} \phi_1(x) + \sigma_t \phi_2(x) = \sigma_{s,2} \phi_2(x) + S_2(x), \qquad (5.1.13c)$$

and

$$\frac{3}{7}\frac{d}{dx}\phi_2(x) + \sigma_t\phi_3(x) = \sigma_{s,3}\phi_3(x) + S_3(x) .\qquad (5.1.13d)$$

For illustrative purposes we shall use the P_3 equations. Higher order approximations are readily derived, and the results to be obtained subsequently are easily generalized.

Because more terms are used in the P_3 approximation than in the P_1 approximation, the angular distribution can be more accurately represented, and the answers will be more precise. The existence of more terms in the P_3 approximation than in the P_1 also implies that the boundary conditions can be more accurately approximated. Consistent with the increased accuracy with which the interior of a medium is treated, more accurate boundary conditions are required. Neutron conservation requires that the directional flux be continuous at an interface between two materials. If the directional fluxes in the adjoining media are denoted $\phi^I(x, \mu)$ and $\phi^{II}(x, \mu)$, then the continuity condition is

$$\phi^I(x, \mu) = \phi^{II}(x, \mu), \qquad -1 \leqslant \mu \leqslant 1 .\qquad (5.1.14)$$

In the P_N approximation, it is easily shown that condition (5.1.14) implies equality of each harmonic of the expansion (see problem 6). Thus, the boundary condition is

$$\phi_N^I(x) = \phi_N^{II}(x), \qquad \text{all } N .\qquad (5.1.15)$$

At a vacuum-matter interface (or black absorber), the proper boundary condition is

$$\phi(a, \mu) = 0, \qquad -1 \leqslant \mu \leqslant 0 ,\qquad (5.1.16)$$

where a is the boundary coordinate. Condition (5.1.16) cannot be satisfied in the P_N approximation for finite N. The x directional flux cannot be represented by a finite polynomial expansion. A frequently used boundary condition, which approximates condition (5.1.16), is the Marshak condition

$$\int_{-1}^{0} d\mu\, \phi(a, \mu)\, P_N(\mu) = 0, \qquad N \text{ odd.}\qquad (5.1.17)$$

At the opposite boundary for finite slabs, the Marshak condition is

$$\int_{0}^{1} d\mu\, \phi(-a, \mu)\, P_N(\mu) = 0, \qquad N \text{ odd} .\qquad (5.1.18)$$

$$\phi(a,\mu) = \frac{1}{2}\phi_o(x) + \frac{3}{2}\phi_1(x)\cdot\mu + \frac{5}{2}\phi_2(x)\cdot\frac{1}{2}(3\mu^2 - 1) + \cdots \left.\begin{array}{l} N=1 \\[4pt] N=3 \end{array}\right.$$

$\ell = 3$

We shall use the Marshak conditions in our discussion of the P_N method. It should be noted that other approximations have been suggested and applied.[4] In the next section we consider the double spherical harmonics method which was designed to permit better approximations to discontinuities in the angular distribution.

The application of Marshak's boundary conditions are facilitated by the following relations:[5]

$$\int_0^1 d\mu \, P_m(\mu) \, P_n(\mu)$$

$$= \begin{cases} \dfrac{1}{2m + 1}, & \text{if } m = n \\ 0, & \text{if } m - n \text{ is even, } (m - n \neq 0) \\ \dfrac{(-)^{i+k} m! \, n!}{2^{m+n-1}(n - m)(n + m + 1)(i!)^2(k!)^2}, & \text{if } m = 2k, \, n = 2i + 1 \end{cases}$$

The Marshak conditions in the P_3 approximation are derived in a straightforward manner. From the condition (5.1.17), we find that

$$\phi_0(a) - 2\phi_1(a) + \frac{5}{4}\phi_2(a) = 0, \tag{5.1.19a}$$

and

$$\phi_0(a) - 5\phi_2(a) + 8\phi_3(a) = 0. \tag{5.1.19b}$$

In like manner, at $x = -a$, we obtain

$$\phi_0(-a) + 2\phi_1(-a) + \frac{5}{4}\phi_2(-a) = 0, \tag{5.1.20a}$$

and

$$\phi_0(-a) - 5\phi_2(-a) - 8\phi_3(-a) = 0. \tag{5.1.20b}$$

The four conditions at the exterior boundaries, plus the continuity conditions at interfaces, complete the specification for the P_3 approximation. Four boundary conditions suffice, since Eqs. (5.1.13) represent a single fourth order equation. This point may be seen by solving each equation for one unknown (or derivatives of it) in terms of all the others. The result may be used to eliminate this unknown from all other equations, whereupon the process may be repeated again to eliminate another

---

[4] See Reference 1 for a more detailed discussion of boundary conditions.
[5] E. T. Whittaker and G. N. Watson, "Modern Analysis," Chapter 15. Cambridge Univ. Press, London and New York, 1940.

unknown. The boundary conditions (5.1.19) and (5.1.20) play an important role in designing numerical methods for treating the P_N equations. Before turning to the numerical methods, we first illustrate the reduction of the P_3 equations to a generalized eigenvalue problem for criticality studies. Once we have obtained the statement of the problem, it is evident that one can define an adjoint function and use the method of successive approximations as detailed in Chapter IV to solve for the flux.

For simplicity we define the coefficients

$$\sigma_i = \sigma_t - \sigma_{s,i}, \qquad i = 0, 1, 2, 3 . \tag{5.1.21}$$

We also define the vectors $\boldsymbol{\psi}(x)$ and $\mathbf{S}(x)$ as

$$\boldsymbol{\psi}(x) = \begin{bmatrix} \phi_0(x) \\ \phi_1(x) \\ \phi_2(x) \\ \phi_3(x) \end{bmatrix}, \tag{5.1.22}$$

and

$$\mathbf{S}(x) = \begin{bmatrix} S_0(x) \\ S_1(x) \\ S_2(x) \\ S_3(x) \end{bmatrix}. \tag{5.1.23}$$

The P_3 equations are then written in matrix form

$$\mathbf{A}\boldsymbol{\psi}(x) = \mathbf{S}(x), \tag{5.1.24}$$

with

$$\mathbf{A} = \begin{bmatrix} \sigma_0 & \dfrac{d}{dx} & 0 & 0 \\[2ex] \dfrac{1}{3}\dfrac{d}{dx} & \sigma_1 & \dfrac{2}{3}\dfrac{d}{dx} & 0 \\[2ex] 0 & \dfrac{2}{5}\dfrac{d}{dx} & \sigma_2 & \dfrac{3}{5}\dfrac{d}{dx} \\[2ex] 0 & 0 & \dfrac{3}{7}\dfrac{d}{dx} & \sigma_3 \end{bmatrix}. \tag{5.1.25}$$

The boundary conditions (5.1.19) and (5.1.20) are readily written in matrix form.

For criticality studies there is no external source, only fission. To an excellent approximation the fission neutron angular distribution is isotropic in laboratory coordinates and further, the fission cross section is independent of the initial neutron direction. The source is therefore

$$S(x, \mu) = \nu \int_{-1}^{1} d\mu' \, \sigma_f(x) \, \phi(x, \mu') = \nu\sigma_f(x) \, \phi_0(x) \,. \tag{5.1.26}$$

The expansion coefficients for the source are then

$$S_0(x) = \nu\sigma_f(x) \, \phi_0(x) \,, \tag{5.1.27a}$$

and

$$S_1(x) = S_2(x) = S_3(x) = 0 \,. \tag{5.1.27b}$$

The P_3 equations are then

$$\mathbf{A}\psi(x) = \nu\mathbf{B}\psi(x) \,, \tag{5.1.28}$$

with

$$\mathbf{B} = \begin{bmatrix} \sigma_f(x) & 0 & \cdots & 0 \\ 0 & 0 & & \cdot \\ \vdots & \vdots & & \cdot \\ 0 & 0 & \cdots & 0 \end{bmatrix} \,. \tag{5.1.29}$$

Equation (5.1.28) is the general eigenvalue equation we set out to find. For higher order P_N approximations, the formulation is exactly parallel to the above.

We now consider numerical procedures for solving the equations (5.1.28). The continuous space x, μ has been replaced by the x, N space where N is a discrete variable. In order to derive appropriate difference equations for the harmonics, we again divide the interval $-a \leqslant x \leqslant a$ into discrete points x_j such that $x_0 = -a$, $x_J = a$. We again assume the mesh chosen so that all interfaces lie on an interpolation point. The discrete mesh appears as shown in Fig. 5.1.2.

To derive appropriate difference equations, we must consider the boundary conditions applicable to the problem. We note from Eqs. (5.1.19) that if any two functions $\phi_n(a)$ are fixed, then the remaining two

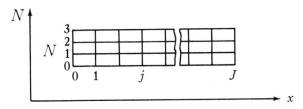

FIG. 5.1.2.   Discrete mesh for the numerical approximation to the P_3 equations.

$\phi_n(a)$ are determined. Likewise for Eqs. (5.1.20). As an example, let us fix $\phi_2(a)$ and $\phi_3(a)$; then $\phi_0(a)$ and $\phi_1(a)$ are determined. We now integrate in the direction a to $-a$ to compute $\phi_0(-a)$ and $\phi_1(-a)$. But then $\phi_2(-a)$ and $\phi_3(-a)$ are determined, and hence we should integrate in the direction $-a$ to a to find new values of $\phi_2(a)$ and $\phi_3(a)$. Thus a circular path through the mesh is implied, and our difference equations will be derived on this basis. Note that the implied direction of integration says nothing whatsoever about the neutron direction.

We now derive a set of difference equations based upon the above discussion. For the harmonics $\phi_0(x)$ and $\phi_1(x)$, we integrate over the interval x_j to x_{j-1}. For the equation in $\phi_0(x)$ we have

$$\int_{x_j}^{x_{j-1}} dx \frac{d}{dx} \phi_1(x) + \int_{x_j}^{x_{j-1}} dx \sigma_0(x) \phi_0(x) = \int_{x_j}^{x_{j-1}} dx S_0(x) . \tag{5.1.30}$$

We shall use the double subscript notation

$$f_n(x_j) = f_{n,j} . \tag{5.1.31}$$

The coefficient $\sigma_0(x)$ is constant over the interval x_j to x_{j-1} and is denoted $\sigma_{0,j}$. The spacing interval x_j to x_{j-1} is denoted Δ_j. To terms accurate to $O(\Delta_j^2)$ we have

$$\phi_{1,j-1} - \phi_{1,j} + \sigma_{0,j} \frac{\Delta_j}{2} (\phi_{0,j-1} + \phi_{0,j}) = \frac{\Delta_j}{2} (S_{0,j-1} + S_{0,j}) . \tag{5.1.32}$$

The equation for $\phi_1(x)$ is treated in the same manner; we have

$$\frac{1}{3} (\phi_{0,j-1} - \phi_{0,j}) + \frac{2}{3} (\phi_{2,j-1} - \phi_{2,j}) + \sigma_{1,j} \frac{\Delta_j}{2} (\phi_{1,j-1} + \phi_{1,j}) = 0 . \tag{5.1.33}$$

The above difference relations are used for $1 \leqslant j \leqslant J$.

For the harmonics $\phi_2(x)$ and $\phi_3(x)$, we integrate from x_j to x_{j+1}. The difference equations are

$$\frac{2}{5} (\phi_{1,j+1} - \phi_{1,j}) + \frac{3}{5} (\phi_{3,j+1} - \phi_{3,j}) + \sigma_{2,j+1} \frac{\Delta_{j+1}}{2} (\phi_{2,j+1} + \phi_{2,j}) = 0 ,$$

$$\tag{5.1.34}$$

and

$$\frac{3}{7} (\phi_{2,j+1} - \phi_{2,j}) + \sigma_{3,j+1} \frac{\Delta_{j+1}}{2} (\phi_{3,j+1} + \phi_{3,j}) = 0 . \tag{5.1.35}$$

Equations (5.1.34) and (5.1.35) are used for $0 \leqslant j \leqslant J - 1$.

The direction of integration is shown in Fig. 5.1.3.

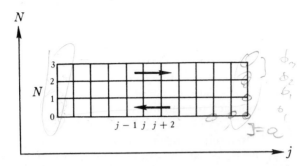

FIG. 5.1.3.   Directions of integration through a mesh for the integration of the P_3 equations.

There are numerous iteration procedures that can be used with the set of difference equations just derived. We outline one possible procedure below which is analogous to the method of successive displacements. First we assume an initial distribution for the $\phi_{n,j}$ consistent with the boundary conditions. The source is computed at each space point. Starting at $j = J$, we solve Eq. (5.1.32) in the form

$$\phi_{0,j-1}^1 = \frac{S_{0,j-1}^0 + S_{0,j}^0 + (2/\Delta_j)(\phi_{1,j}^0 - \phi_{1,j-1}^0)}{\sigma_{0,j}} - \phi_{0,j}^1, \qquad (5.1.36)$$

where the superscript is the iteration index. Equation (5.1.33) is written as

$$\phi_{1,j-1}^1 = \frac{2}{3\Delta_j\sigma_{1,j}}(\phi_{0,j}^1 - \phi_{0,j-1}^1) + \frac{4}{3\Delta_j\sigma_{1,j}}(\phi_{2,j}^0 - \phi_{2,j-1}^0) - \phi_{1,j}^1. \qquad (5.1.37)$$

Equations (5.1.36) and (5.1.37) are used for $1 \leqslant j \leqslant J$. The analogous equations for the second and third harmonic are

$$\phi_{2,j+1}^1 = \frac{4}{5\Delta_{j+1}\sigma_{2,j+1}}(\phi_{1,j}^1 - \phi_{1,j+1}^1) + \frac{6}{5\Delta_{j+1}\sigma_{2,j+1}}(\phi_{3,j}^0 - \phi_{3,j+1}^0) - \phi_{2,j}^1, \qquad (5.1.38)$$

and

$$\phi_{3,j+1}^1 = \frac{6}{7\Delta_{j+1}\sigma_{3,j-1}}(\phi_{2,j}^1 - \phi_{2,j+1}^1) - \phi_{3,j}^1. \qquad (5.1.39)$$

The iteration may be repeated for the previously calculated source S^0, i.e., multiple inner iterations, or the source may be recomputed from the newly found fluxes before continuing. The source is rescaled so that

$$\alpha^2(S_{0,j}^1, S_{0,j}^1) = (S_{0,j}^0, S_{0,j}^0) . \tag{5.1.40}$$

The scale factor α^2 will approach an asymptote after a sufficient number of outer iterations to permit modifications of the assembly properties to achieve criticality. The process described above is merely indicative of the types of procedures that are possible.

An alternative approach to the numerical solution of the P_N equations of great merit has been considered by Marchuk (Reference 5, Chapter 13) and Gelbard *et al.* (Reference 6). We shall adopt Marchuk's formulation. It turns out that the P_N equations can be reduced to a form identical to that of the multigroup equations. We shall illustrate this reduction for one case. The reduction then enables us to extend the use of any one of the many already existing multigroup diffusion codes to higher order spherical harmonic approximations.

Consider the P_N approximation to any order with N odd. The sources are assumed isotropic. The equations are of the form

$$\frac{d}{dx}\phi_1(x) + \sigma_0\phi_0(x) = S_0(x) ,$$

$$\alpha_1 \frac{d}{dx}\phi_2(x) + \beta_1 \frac{d}{dx}\phi_0(x) + \sigma_1\phi_1(x) = 0 ,$$

$$\vdots$$

$$\alpha_{N-1} \frac{d}{dx}\phi_N(x) + \beta_{N-1} \frac{d}{dx}\phi_{N-2}(x) + \sigma_{N-1}\phi_{N-1}(x) = 0 ,$$

and

$$\beta_N \frac{d}{dx}\phi_{N-1} + \sigma_N\phi_N(x) = 0 . \tag{5.1.41}$$

We define the vectors $\boldsymbol{\psi}_e(x)$ and $\boldsymbol{\psi}_o(x)$ as

$$\boldsymbol{\psi}_e(x) = \begin{bmatrix} \phi_0(x) \\ \phi_2(x) \\ \vdots \\ \phi_{N-1}(x) \end{bmatrix} , \tag{5.1.42}$$

and

$$\boldsymbol{\psi}_o(x) = \begin{bmatrix} \phi_1(x) \\ \phi_3(x) \\ \vdots \\ \phi_N(x) \end{bmatrix} . \tag{5.1.43}$$

The vector $\psi_e(x)$ contains only even harmonics of the flux, whereas $\psi_o(x)$ contains only odd harmonics. The set of equations (5.1.41) may be written

$$\mathbf{A}_1 \frac{d}{dx}\psi_o(x) + \mathbf{B}_1\psi_e(x) = \mathbf{S}(x),$$ (5.1.44a)

and

$$\mathbf{A}_2 \frac{d}{dx}\psi_e(x) + \mathbf{B}_2\psi_o(x) = \mathbf{0},$$ (5.1.44b)

where the definitions of the matrices are evident upon comparison of Eqs. (5.1.41) and (5.1.44). It is easily seen that the matrices $\mathbf{B}_1$ and $\mathbf{B}_2$ are diagonal and nonsingular, whereas $\mathbf{A}_1$ and $\mathbf{A}_2$ are tridiagonal with all diagonal elements zero. Note also that $\mathbf{A}_1$ and $\mathbf{A}_2$ are not functions of x, whereas $\mathbf{B}_1$ and $\mathbf{B}_2$ are functions of x in general. The matrix $\mathbf{B}_2$ possesses an inverse and hence, from Eq. (5.1.44b),

$$\psi_o(x) = -\mathbf{B}_2^{-1}\mathbf{A}_2 \frac{d}{dx}\psi_e(x).$$ (5.1.45)

Using the above expression for $\psi_o(x)$ in (5.1.44a), we have

$$-\frac{d}{dx}(\mathbf{A}_1\mathbf{B}_2^{-1}\mathbf{A}_2)\frac{d}{dx}\psi_e(x) + \mathbf{B}_1\psi_e(x) = \mathbf{S}(x).$$ (5.1.46)

The set of equations (5.1.46) are in the same form as the multigroup diffusion equations. In the above case, the harmonic index plays the role of a group index. For the P_3 equations, analogous to a two-group diffusion problem, we have

$$-\frac{d}{dx}\begin{bmatrix} 1 & 0 \\ \dfrac{2}{5} & \dfrac{3}{5} \end{bmatrix}\begin{bmatrix} \dfrac{1}{3\sigma_1} & \dfrac{2}{3\sigma_1} \\ 0 & \dfrac{3}{7\sigma_3} \end{bmatrix}\frac{d}{dx}\begin{bmatrix} \phi_0(x) \\ \phi_2(x) \end{bmatrix} + \begin{bmatrix} \sigma_0 & 0 \\ 0 & \sigma_2 \end{bmatrix}\begin{bmatrix} \phi_0(x) \\ \phi_2(x) \end{bmatrix} = \begin{bmatrix} S_0(x) \\ 0 \end{bmatrix}.$$ (5.1.47)

In detail the equations are

$$-\frac{d}{dx}\left[\frac{1}{3\sigma_1}\frac{d}{dx}(\phi_0 + 2\phi_2)\right] + \sigma_0\phi_0(x) = S_0(x),$$ (5.1.48)

and

$$-\frac{d}{dx}\left[\frac{2}{15\sigma_1}\frac{d}{dx}\phi_0(x)\right] + \left(\frac{4}{15\sigma_1} + \frac{9}{35\sigma_3}\right)\frac{d}{dx}\phi_2(x) + \sigma_2\phi_2(x) = 0.$$ (5.1.49)

The numerical integration of Eqs. (5.1.48) and (5.1.49) may be done as outlined in Chapter IV.

A practical advantage of the formulation of the P_N equations as multigroup type equations is that a standard multigroup diffusion program is readily used for P_N calculations.

5.2 Double P_N Approximation

The P_N equations yield quite accurate approximations to the total flux in the interior of a reactor. They should, because the angular distribution deep inside a homogeneous medium is nearly isotropic and because the spherical harmonics method corresponds to an expansion in increasingly higher orders of anisotropy [see Eq. (5.1.4)]. The angular distribution deep within a reactor is nearly isotropic essentially because leakage processes, which are anisotropic by nature, do not enter importantly into the neutron balance and because nuclear processes, such as fission, tend to be isotropic. Elastic scattering by heavy elements, a predominant process, is isotropic; for the light elements scattering is somewhat anisotropic. However, after a few anisotropic scatterings the angular distribution is nearly isotropic. Consequently, in many cases the angular distribution predicted is therefore good in the interior. However, near strong discontinuities in material properties, such as the region near a strong absorber or vacuum boundaries, the angular distribution is usually much more anisotropic. The discontinuities impose step function changes upon the angular flux. The approximation of a step function by polynomials requires many harmonics, in particular the P_3 approximations would hardly be adequate to represent a discontinuity.

The essential idea of the method developed by Yvon (Reference 7) is to use a separate expansion over each region within which the angular distribution is smoothly and slowly varying, instead of one expansion for all angles. Thus, a discontinuity in the angular distribution can be accurately approximated by using a separate expansion on each side of the discontinuity, the discontinuity being represented by a corresponding discontinuity in the expansion coefficients. In particular, the directional flux is expanded into two series of Legendre polynomials for problems involving an interface between two media. As might be expected, the method of Yvon is very good for such problems. We shall discuss the method briefly and reduce the equations to a group diffusion form from which the numerical procedures remaining are evident. Our notation is that of Ziering and Schiff (see Reference 8). We assume slab geometry and isotropic sources and scattering.

We begin with the one group transport equation for slabs

$$\mu \frac{d\phi(x, \mu)}{dx} + \sigma_t \phi(x, \mu) = \frac{1}{2} \int_{-1}^{1} d\mu' \sigma_s(x) \phi(x, \mu') + \frac{S(x)}{2}. \qquad (5.2.1)$$

We expand the directional flux in terms of the half-range polynomials

$$P_n^+(\mu) = P_n(2\mu - 1), \qquad 0 \leqslant \mu \leqslant 1,$$
$$= 0, \qquad\qquad \mu < 0, \tag{5.2.2a}$$

$$P_n^-(\mu) = P_n(2\mu + 1), \qquad -1 \leqslant \mu \leqslant 0,$$
$$= 0, \qquad\qquad \mu > 0, \tag{5.2.2b}$$

where $P_n(2\mu \pm 1)$ is the Legendre polynomial of order n. The orthogonality relations are

$$\int_0^1 d\mu P_n^+(\mu)\, P_m^+(\mu) = \int_{-1}^0 d\mu P_n^-(\mu)\, P_m^-(\mu) = \frac{1}{2n+1}\, \delta_{nm}. \tag{5.2.3}$$

The half-range polynomials obey the recurrence relation

$$2(2n+1)\,\mu\, P_n^\pm(\mu) = (n+1)\, P_{n+1}^\pm(\mu) \pm (2n+1)\, P_n^\pm(\mu) + n P_{n-1}^\pm(\mu), \tag{5.2.4}$$

a relation that follows from the full range Legendre polynomial recurrence relations. The flux expansion is of the form

$$\phi(x, \mu) = \sum_n (2n+1)\, [P_n^+(\mu)\, \phi_n^+(x) + P_n^-(\mu)\, \phi_n^-(x)], \tag{5.2.5}$$

where

$$\phi_n^-(x) = \int_{-1}^0 d\mu \phi(x, \mu)\, P_n^-(\mu), \tag{5.2.6a}$$

$$\phi_n^+(x) = \int_0^1 d\mu\, \phi(x, \mu)\, P_n^+(\mu). \tag{5.2.6b}$$

In view of Eqs. (5.2.2) and (5.2.5), ϕ_n^+ may be regarded as describing the directional flux for $\mu > 0$, and $\phi_n^-(x)$, for $\mu < 0$. If we insert the expansion (5.2.5) into (5.2.1) we have

$$\sum_n (2n+1)\,\mu\, \left[P_n^+(\mu)\, \frac{d}{dx}\phi_n^+(x) + P_n^-(\mu)\, \frac{d}{dx}\phi_n^-(x) \right]$$
$$+ \sigma_t \sum_n (2n+1)[P_n^+(\mu)\, \phi_n^+(x) + P_n^-(\mu)\, \phi_n^-(x)]$$
$$= \tfrac{1}{2}\sigma_s(x)[\phi_0^+(x) + \phi_0^-(x)] + S_0(x). \tag{5.2.7}$$

We multiply by $P_n^+(\mu)$ and integrate over the interval $0 \leqslant \mu \leqslant 1$.

Again, we multiply Eq. (5.2.7) by $P_N^{\pm}(\mu)$ and integrate with respect to μ over the interval from ± 1 to 0. After some algebra we find

$$(N + 1)\frac{d}{dx}\phi_{N+1}^{\pm}(x) + N\frac{d}{dx}\phi_{N-1}^{\pm}(x) \pm (2N + 1)\frac{d}{dx}\phi_N^{\pm}(x)$$

$$+ 2(2N + 1)\sigma_t\phi_N^{\pm}(x) = [\sigma_s(x)(\phi_0^+(x) + \phi_0^-(x)) + 2S_0(x)]\delta_{N0}. \qquad (5.2.8)$$

The equations for the double P_1 expansion which we denote by $P_1^{\pm}$ are

$$\frac{d}{dx}\phi_1^+(x) + \frac{d}{dx}\phi_0^+(x) + 2\sigma_t\phi_0^+(x) = \sigma_s(x)(\phi_0^+(x) + \phi_0^-(x)) + 2S_0(x),$$
$$(5.2.9a)$$

$$3\frac{d}{dx}\phi_1^+(x) + \frac{d}{dx}\phi_0^+(x) + 6\sigma_t\phi_1^+(x) = 0, \qquad (5.2.9b)$$

and

$$\frac{d}{dx}\phi_1^-(x) - \frac{d}{dx}\phi_0^-(x) + 2\sigma_t\phi_0^-(x) = \sigma_s(x)(\phi_0^+(x) + \phi_0^-(x)) + 2S_0(x), \qquad (5.2.9c)$$

$$-3\frac{d}{dx}\phi_1^-(x) + \frac{d}{dx}\phi_0^-(x) + 6\sigma_t\phi_1^-(x) = 0. \qquad (5.2.9d)$$

Note that the expansions in $\phi_N^+(x)$ are coupled only through the zeroth harmonic. For anisotropic scattering the coupling occurs in the higher order terms also.

The method of Yvon makes it possible to satisfy certain types of boundary conditions exactly. As an example, consider a plane slab in the region $-a \leqslant x \leqslant a$. At $x = -a$, $\phi(-a, \mu) = 0$, $0 \leqslant \mu \leqslant 1$; at $x = +a$, $\phi(a, \mu) = 0$, $-1 \leqslant \mu \leqslant 0$. Thus, from Eq. (5.2.6) we learn that the proper boundary conditions are $\phi_n^+(-a) = 0 = \phi_n^-(a)$ all n. Since $\phi_n^{\pm}(x) = 0$ for $n \geqslant N + 1$, and since we can both require and satisfy $\phi_n^+(-a) = 0 = \phi_n^-(a)$, the boundary conditions can be precisely satisfied. Because the only approximation is the truncation, Yvon's method might be expected to give quite accurate results for this type of problem, as is in fact the case. However, the $P_N^{\pm}$ equations are usually as accurate as the P_{2N+1} equations, particularly with regard to the angular distribution.

The set of equations (5.2.9) are readily reduced to a formal multigroup type set of equations. To this end, we add and subtract the Eqs. (5.2.9a, c) and (5.2.9b, d) to obtain the set of equations

$$\frac{d}{dx}(\phi_1^+ + \phi_1^-) + \frac{d}{dx}(\phi_0^+ - \phi_0^-) + 2\sigma_0(\phi_0^+ + \phi_0^-) = 4S_0 \,,$$

$$\frac{d}{dx}(\phi_1^+ - \phi_1^-) + \frac{d}{dx}(\phi_0^+ + \phi_0^-) + 2\sigma_t(\phi_0^+ - \phi_0^-) = 0 \,,$$

$$3\frac{d}{dx}(\phi_1^+ - \phi_1^-) + \frac{d}{dx}(\phi_0^+ + \phi_0^-) + 6\sigma_t(\phi_1^+ + \phi_1^-) = 0 \,,$$

$$3\frac{d}{dx}(\phi_1^+ + \phi_1^-) + \frac{d}{dx}(\phi_0^+ - \phi_0^-) + 6\sigma_t(\phi_1^+ - \phi_1^-) = 0 \,,$$

$$(5.2.10)$$

with $\sigma_0 = \sigma_t - \sigma_s$. We define the vectors

$$\psi_e(x) = \begin{bmatrix} (\phi_0^+ + \phi_0^-) \\ (\phi_1^+ - \phi_1^-) \end{bmatrix}, \qquad (5.2.11a)$$

and

$$\psi_o(x) = \begin{bmatrix} (\phi_0^+ - \phi_0^-) \\ (\phi_1^+ + \phi_1^-) \end{bmatrix}. \qquad (5.2.11b)$$

The set of equations (5.2.10) is then

$$\mathbf{A}_1 \frac{d}{dx}\psi_e(x) + \mathbf{B}_1\psi_o(x) = \mathbf{O} \,, \qquad (5.2.12a)$$

and

$$\mathbf{A}_2 \frac{d}{dx}\psi_o(x) + \mathbf{B}_2\psi_e(x) = \mathbf{S}(x) \,. \qquad (5.2.12b)$$

The matrix elements are evident. From the first of Eqs. (5.2.12) we have

$$\psi_o(x) = -\mathbf{B}_1^{-1}\mathbf{A}_1 \frac{d}{dx}\psi_e(x) \,, \qquad (5.2.13)$$

and hence

$$-\mathbf{A}_2 \frac{d}{dx}\left[\mathbf{B}_1^{-1}\mathbf{A}_1 \frac{d}{dx}\psi_e(x) \right] + \mathbf{B}_2\psi_e(x) = \mathbf{S}(x) \,, \qquad (5.2.14)$$

which is the desired form of the equations. The difference equations for the set (5.2.14) are readily formed by methods considered earlier.

While Yvon's method has not had extensive application, because of its rapid convergence it is useful for treating problems involving sharp changes in material properties for plane boundaries or problems involving the interaction of two plane boundaries.

5.3 Multigroup Transport Methods

The derivation of the multigroup transport equations is very similar to the procedure adopted in Chapter IV for the multigroup diffusion equations. The basic purpose of this section is to reduce the lethargy dependent Boltzmann equation to a coupled set of transport equations which apply to each lethargy group separately. Once the coupled equations have been found, the remainder of the numerical treatment will be omitted. Instead, various procedures for finding the probabilities for neutron transfer from different groups and angles are considered.

The Boltzmann equation with lethargy dependence may be written[6]

$$\mathbf{\Omega} \cdot \nabla\phi(\mathbf{r}, u, \mathbf{\Omega}) + \sigma_t\phi(\mathbf{r}, u, \mathbf{\Omega})$$

$$= \int_{u'} du' \int_{\mathbf{\Omega}'} d\mathbf{\Omega}' [\sigma_s(\mathbf{r}; u', \mathbf{\Omega}'; u, \mathbf{\Omega}) \phi(\mathbf{r}, u', \mathbf{\Omega}')] + S(\mathbf{r}, u, \mathbf{\Omega}), \qquad (5.3.1)$$

where $\phi(\mathbf{r}, u, \mathbf{\Omega})$ is the number of neutrons of lethargy u per unit lethargy crossing a unit surface at $\mathbf{r}$ per unit time going in a unit solid angle centered in the direction $\mathbf{\Omega}$, and $\sigma_s(\mathbf{r}; u', \mathbf{\Omega}'; u, \mathbf{\Omega})$ is the probability per unit path length that a neutron at $\mathbf{r}$ and going in a direction $\mathbf{\Omega}'$ with a lethargy u' is scattered into a unit solid angle centered at $\mathbf{\Omega}$ and a unit lethargy interval centered at u. The remaining symbols are evident from Section 5.1.

The construction of the multigroup equations proceeds as in diffusion theory. We divide the lethargy range into G groups of arbitrary width and label the initial and final lethargies as $0 = u_0$, $u_{\text{th}} = u_G$. The thermal group is indexed by $G + 1$. Let $\Delta u_g = u_g - u_{g-1}$. We then integrate Eq. (5.3.1) from u_{g-1} to u_g to obtain

$$\mathbf{\Omega} \cdot \nabla\overline{\phi^g}(\mathbf{r}, \mathbf{\Omega}) + \overline{\sigma_t^g}(\mathbf{r}, \mathbf{\Omega})\overline{\phi^g}(\mathbf{r}, \mathbf{\Omega}) = \overline{Q^g}(\mathbf{r}, \mathbf{\Omega}) + \overline{S^g}(\mathbf{r}, \mathbf{\Omega}), \qquad g = 1, 2, ..., G.$$

$$(5.3.2)$$

We let

$$Q(\mathbf{r}, u, \mathbf{\Omega}) = \int du' \int d\mathbf{\Omega}' \, \sigma_s(\mathbf{r}; u', \mathbf{\Omega}'; u, \mathbf{\Omega}) \phi(\mathbf{r}, u', \mathbf{\Omega}') . \qquad (5.3.3)$$

---

[6] The derivation of (5.3.1) is in Appendix A.

The averages are all weighted by the appropriate flux. Thus, for $\sigma_t(\mathbf{r}, u)$ we use

$$\overline{\sigma_t^g}(\mathbf{r}, \mathbf{\Omega}) = \int_{u_{g-1}}^{u_g} du \sigma_t(\mathbf{r}, u) \, \phi(\mathbf{r}, u, \mathbf{\Omega}) \Big/ \int_{u_{g-1}}^{u_g} du \phi(\mathbf{r}, u, \mathbf{\Omega}) , \qquad (5.3.4)$$

whereas for $Q(\mathbf{r}, u, \mathbf{\Omega})$ we use

$$\overline{Q^g}(\mathbf{r}, \mathbf{\Omega}) = \int_{u_{g-1}}^{u_g} du Q(\mathbf{r}, u, \mathbf{\Omega}) \, \phi(\mathbf{r}, u, \mathbf{\Omega}) \Big/ \int_{u_{g-1}}^{u_g} du \phi(\mathbf{r}, u, \mathbf{\Omega}). \qquad (5.3.5)$$

The thermal equation may be added to the set (5.3.2) in the form

$$\mathbf{\Omega} \cdot \nabla \phi^{G+1}(\mathbf{r}, \mathbf{\Omega}) + \sigma_t^{G+1}(\mathbf{r}) \phi^{G+1}(\mathbf{r}, \mathbf{\Omega}) = Q^{G+1}(\mathbf{r}, \mathbf{\Omega}) + S^{G+1}(\mathbf{r}, \mathbf{\Omega}) . \qquad (5.3.6)$$

The set (5.3.2) plus the thermal group equation and the boundary conditions furnish a multigroup transport formulation which is rigorous. The remaining steps are approximate, and each step is taken to reduce the complexity of the problem. The first problem is obtaining the appropriate group constants. Obviously weighting with the flux and even the directional flux is a time consuming process. Many alternative procedures have been suggested including: (1) use of infinite media spectra to eliminate iterative determination of group constants; (2) use of the fission spectrum as the weighting function; (3) use of diffusion theory spectra; (4) constant flux within groups and hence unweighted cross sections. We do not specify any procedure at the moment, but assume the group constants may be specified at the beginning of the computation.

The second problem is the relation of the average flux to the flux at the lethargy interfaces. A full range of possibilities exists as in diffusion theory. We shall use only one approximation, namely

$$\overline{\phi^g}(\mathbf{r}, \mathbf{\Omega}) = \phi(\mathbf{r}, u_g, \mathbf{\Omega}) \equiv \phi^g(\mathbf{r}, \mathbf{\Omega}) , \qquad (5.3.7)$$

which is accurate only to order Δu. Likewise for the other variables.

The group equations are then

$$\mathbf{\Omega} \cdot \nabla \phi^g(\mathbf{r}, \mathbf{\Omega}) + \sigma_t^g(\mathbf{r}) \phi^g(\mathbf{r}, \mathbf{\Omega}) = Q^g(\mathbf{r}, \mathbf{\Omega}) + S^g(\mathbf{r}, \mathbf{\Omega}), \qquad g = 1, 2, ..., G + 1. \qquad (5.3.8)$$

Note that the angular dependence of σ_t^g has been dropped; σ_t^g must be only slightly dependent on $\mathbf{\Omega}$ as may be seen from Eq. (5.3.4), if the multigroup approximation (5.3.7) is a good one, since the total cross section itself is nearly independent of $\mathbf{\Omega}$.

The set of Eqs. (5.3.8) is the multigroup transport equations desired. The nature of the inhomogeneities will be considered in the remainder of this section. We shall describe a few ways of calculating them in detail. To this end, we observe that the set of equations (5.3.8) is equivalent to the assumption

$$\int_{u_{g-1}}^{u_g} du K(u) = \alpha^g K^g, \tag{5.3.9}$$

where α^g is a constant which depends upon the weighting function assumed for the lethargy dependent constants, and $K(u)$ is a lethargy dependent variable. For instance,

$$\int_{u_{g-1}}^{u_g} du \sigma_t(\mathbf{r}, u) \phi(\mathbf{r}, u, \mathbf{\Omega}) = \alpha^g \sigma_t^g(\mathbf{r}) \phi^g(\mathbf{r}, \mathbf{\Omega}). \tag{5.3.10}$$

The terms of particular interest are the inhomogeneous terms $Q^g(\mathbf{r}, \mathbf{\Omega})$ and $S^g(\mathbf{r}, \mathbf{\Omega})$. We consider first the scattering source $Q^g(\mathbf{r}, \mathbf{\Omega})$. From Eq. (5.3.9) we have

$$\alpha^g Q^g(\mathbf{r}, \mathbf{\Omega}) = \int_{u_{g-1}}^{u_g} du Q(\mathbf{r}, u, \mathbf{\Omega}). \tag{5.3.11}$$

The integration over u' may be written as a sum

$$\int du' \sigma_s(\mathbf{r}; u', \mathbf{\Omega}'; u, \mathbf{\Omega}) \phi(\mathbf{r}, u', \mathbf{\Omega}') = \sum_{g'=1}^{G+1} \alpha^{g'} \sigma_s^{g'}(\mathbf{r}; \mathbf{\Omega}'; u, \mathbf{\Omega}) \phi^{g'}(\mathbf{r}, \mathbf{\Omega}'), \tag{5.3.12}$$

where $\sigma_s^{g'}(\mathbf{r}, \mathbf{\Omega}'; u, \mathbf{\Omega})$ is the probability that a neutron at $\mathbf{r}$ going in the direction $\mathbf{\Omega}'$ in the group g' will suffer a scattering in going a unit distance and be scattered into a unit solid angle centered at $\mathbf{\Omega}$ and a unit lethargy centered at u. The integration of (5.3.12) over the interval u_{g-1} to u_g yields

$$\alpha^g \sum_{g'=1}^{G+1} \alpha^{g'} \sigma_s^{g', g}(\mathbf{r}, \mathbf{\Omega}'; \mathbf{\Omega}) \phi^{g'}(\mathbf{r}, \mathbf{\Omega}'), \tag{5.3.13}$$

and hence

$$Q^g(\mathbf{r}, \mathbf{\Omega}) = \sum_{g'=1}^{G+1} \alpha^{g'} \int d\mathbf{\Omega}' \, \sigma_s^{g', g}(\mathbf{r}, \mathbf{\Omega}'; \mathbf{\Omega}) \phi^{g'}(\mathbf{r}, \mathbf{\Omega}'), \tag{5.3.14}$$

where $\sigma_s^{g', g}$ is the probability of transfer from group g' with direction $\mathbf{\Omega}'$

to group g with direction $\mathbf{\Omega}$. The nature of the coefficient $\sigma_s^{g',g}$ depends upon the materials within the assembly and the nature of the scattering law. For instance, if no upscattering is permitted, then

$$\sigma_s^{g',g} = 0, \quad \text{if } g' > g . \tag{5.3.15}$$

For elastic scattering of heavy elements, then, only terms for g' near g enter.

We now consider the source term $S^g(\mathbf{r}, \mathbf{\Omega})$. We again have

$$\int_{u_{g-1}}^{u_g} du S(\mathbf{r}, u, \mathbf{\Omega}) = \alpha^g S^g(\mathbf{r}, \mathbf{\Omega}) . \tag{5.3.16}$$

The source will consist of fission sources plus extraneous sources. The fission sources are

$$S_f(\mathbf{r}, u, \mathbf{\Omega}) = \nu\chi(u) \int du' \int_{\Omega'} d\mathbf{\Omega}' \sigma_f(\mathbf{r}; u', \mathbf{\Omega}'; u, \mathbf{\Omega}) \phi(\mathbf{r}, u', \mathbf{\Omega}') . \tag{5.3.17}$$

The integration over u' is replaced by a summation to yield

$$S_f(\mathbf{r}, u, \mathbf{\Omega}) = \nu\chi(u) \int_{\Omega'} d\mathbf{\Omega}' \sum_{g'=1}^{G+1} \alpha^{g'} \sigma_f^{g'}(\mathbf{r}, \mathbf{\Omega}'; u, \mathbf{\Omega}) \phi^{g'}(\mathbf{r}, \mathbf{\Omega}') . \tag{5.3.18}$$

We then have

$$S_f^g(\mathbf{r}, \mathbf{\Omega}) = \nu\chi_g \sum_{g'=1}^{G+1} \alpha^{g'} \int_{\Omega'} d\mathbf{\Omega}' \sigma_f^{g',g}(\mathbf{r}, \mathbf{\Omega}'; \mathbf{\Omega}) \phi^{g'}(\mathbf{r}, \mathbf{\Omega}') . \tag{5.3.19}$$

The equations (5.3.14) and (5.3.19) imply that the right-hand side of Eq. (5.3.8) is

$$Q^g(\mathbf{r}, \mathbf{\Omega}) + S^g(\mathbf{r}, \mathbf{\Omega}) = \sum_{g'=1}^{G+1} \int_{\Omega'} d\mathbf{\Omega}' T^{g',g}(\mathbf{r}; \mathbf{\Omega}'; \mathbf{\Omega}) \phi^{g'}(\mathbf{r}, \mathbf{\Omega}') + S_e^g(\mathbf{r}, \mathbf{\Omega}) ,$$

where S_e^g is the external source and

$$T^{g',g}(\mathbf{r}; \mathbf{\Omega}'; \mathbf{\Omega}) = \alpha^{g'}[\sigma_s^{g',g} + \nu\chi_g \sigma_f^{g',g}] .$$

$T^{g',g}(\mathbf{r}; \mathbf{\Omega}'; \mathbf{\Omega})$ is called the transfer kernel for the multigroup equations. Physically $T^{g',g}(\mathbf{r}; \mathbf{\Omega}'; \mathbf{\Omega})$ is the probability that a neutron appears in group g going in a unit solid angle centered at $\mathbf{\Omega}$ as a result of a neutron in group g' at $\mathbf{r}$ going a unit distance in a unit solid angle centered at $\mathbf{\Omega}'$.

The function $T^{g',g}$ may be constructed after the relevant scattering laws and cross section weighting factors have been chosen. As an example, consider the case of isotropic scattering and fission in the laboratory coordinates. The scattering kernel is then of the form

$$T^{g',g}(\mathbf{r}; \mathbf{\Omega}'; \mathbf{\Omega}) = \frac{1}{4\pi} T^{g',g}(\mathbf{r}).$$
(5.3.20)

It is frequently useful to expand the transfer kernel in Legendre polynomials. If the cosine of the angle between $\mathbf{\Omega}'$ and $\mathbf{\Omega}$ is μ_0, then we expand $T^{g',g}$ in the form

$$T^{g',g}(\mathbf{r}; \mathbf{\Omega}'; \mathbf{\Omega}) = \frac{1}{2\pi} \sum_n \frac{2n+1}{2} T_n^{g',g}(\mathbf{r}) P_n(\mu_0).$$
(5.3.21)

The zeroth harmonic contains the isotropic components while the remaining harmonics include the anisotropic moments.

The angular and spatial variations are separable under certain conditions, e.g., for isotropic media. The transfer kernel may then be written

$$T^{g',g}(\mathbf{r}; \mathbf{\Omega}'; \mathbf{\Omega}) = C^{g',g}(\mathbf{r}) f^{g',g}(\mathbf{\Omega}' \to \mathbf{\Omega}).$$
(5.3.22)

$C^{g',g}(\mathbf{r})$ is the probability that a neutron appear in group g as a result of a neutron in group g' at $\mathbf{r}$ going a unit distance. For one group problems, the coefficient is merely $C(\mathbf{r})$, the mean number of neutrons per collision. We shall make frequent use of Eq. (5.3.22) in the remainder of this chapter.

5.4 Discrete Ordinate Methods

In Section 5.1 we considered approximate solutions to the transport equation by use of an expansion in terms of Legendre polynomials. In particular the angle variable was eliminated from the equation in favor of harmonic coefficients. We now consider an alternative treatment of the angular dependence called the discrete ordinate method. We will merely outline the procedure for developing discrete ordinate approximations. In the next section we specialize to a particular method, the S_N method. The reason for the emphasis on the S_N method is due to its wide use in transport calculations.

For simplicity we consider the one group transport equation in slab geometry with isotropic scattering

$$\mu \frac{d}{dx} \phi(x, \mu) + \sigma_t(x) \phi(x, \mu) = \frac{c(x)}{2} \int_{-1}^{1} d\mu' \, \phi(x, \mu') + S_e(x, \mu).$$
(5.4.1)

We have used the transfer kernel of the previous section, and hence the source $S_e(x, \mu)$ is external.

Rather than expand the flux, we divide the μ interval into a discrete number of intervals instead, hence the name discrete ordinate. Let the interpolation points be denoted as μ_n, $n = 0, 1, ..., N$. The directional flux is to be evaluated at the points μ_n and interpolated in between. We denote directional fluxes $\phi(x, \mu_n) = \phi_n(x)$. Note the subscript n now refers to a given direction, not an index for an expansion.

The transfer integral is now approximated by a quadrature formula of the form

$$\int_{-1}^{1} d\mu' \phi(x, \mu') = \sum_{n'} w_{n'} \phi_{n'}(x),$$
(5.4.2)

where the $w_{n'}$ are weighting factors. The Boltzmann equation is applied to each group separately in the form

$$\mu_n \frac{d}{dx} \phi_n(x) + \sigma_t(x) \phi_n(x) = \frac{c(x)}{2} \sum_{n'} w_{n'} \phi_{n'}(x) + S_e(x, \mu_n), \quad n = 0, 1, ..., N.$$
(5.4.3)

In order to avoid discontinuities the interpolation points are so chosen that $\mu_n \neq 0$, all n.

A variety of quadrature formulas have been proposed and used. In particular, for interfaces where the directional flux may be discontinuous at $\mu = 0$, double expansions in μ space are recommended. The most frequently suggested method for such problems is Gauss quadrature. This method has significant advantages regarding the accuracy of the approximation. The use of the Gaussian quadrature was suggested by Wick (Reference 9).

In the elementary integration formulas considered in Chapter III, it was indicated that N point integration formulas approximated the integrand as a polynomial of degree $N - 1$. The Gaussian integration formula has the property of being accurate to order $2N$, i.e., approximating the integrand as a polynomial of degree $2N - 1$. The remarkable feature of this quadrature is that only N points are needed for the integrand. In order to derive the Gaussian quadrature, we consider the following problem. Suppose we have a polynomial $f_{2N-1}(x)$ of degree $2N - 1$. Is it possible to find another polynomial, of degree $N - 1$, $g_{N-1}(x)$, which agrees with $f_{2N-1}(x)$ at N points, say x_j, $j = 1, 2, ..., N$, and such that

$$\int_{-1}^{1} dx\, f_{2N-1}(x) = \int_{-1}^{1} dx\, g_{N-1}(x),$$
(5.4.4)

for properly chosen x_j? If the above question can be answered in the affirmative, then the integration of $g_{N-1}(x)$ can be replaced by a summation which gives exactly the value of the integral. In other words, it is then possible to approximate an integral with an N-point formula which has a truncation error of order $2N$.

The proof that such an integration formula is possible is simple. Since $f_{2N-1}(x)$ is of order $2N - 1$ and $g_{N-1}(x)$ coincides with $f_{2N-1}(x)$ at N points x_n, we have

$$f_{2N-1}(x) = g_{N-1}(x) + (x - x_1)(x - x_2) \dots (x - x_N)\, G_{N-1}(x)\,, \qquad (5.4.5)$$

where $G_{N-1}(x)$ is a polynomial of degree $N - 1$. If we integrate Eq. (5.4.5) from $-1 \leqslant x \leqslant 1$ and apply (5.4.4), then we must have

$$\int_{-1}^{1} dx(x - x_1)(x - x_2) \dots (x - x_N)\, G_{N-1} = 0\,. \qquad (5.4.6)$$

If the integration formula is to be valid for all $f_{2N-1}(x)$, then $G_{N-1}(x)$ is arbitrary. Hence each power of x in $G_{N-1}(x)$ which appears in (5.4.6) must vanish separately. That is,

$$\int_{-1}^{1} dx(x - x_1)(x - x_2) \dots (x - x_N)\, x^n = 0, \qquad n = 0, 1, \dots, N - 1\,. \quad (5.4.7)$$

The coefficient of x^n in the above integral is a polynomial of degree N, and Eq. (5.4.7) states that this polynomial must be orthogonal to all polynomials of lower degree, over the interval $-1 \leqslant x \leqslant 1$. It is well known that the Legendre polynomials satisfy this criterion. Therefore, if the interpolation points are the zeros of the Legendre polynomial of degree N, then Eq. (5.4.7) and thus Eq. (5.4.4) are true. But then we have

$$\int_{-1}^{1} dx\, f_{2N-1}(x) = \sum_{j=1}^{N} w_j f_{2N-1}(x_j)\,, \qquad (5.4.8)$$

which is exact. We now consider finding the w_j. First consider $f_{2N-1}(x) = $ constant. Then

$$\sum_{j=1}^{N} w_j = 2\,. \qquad (5.4.9)$$

By continuing in this manner we arrive at a set of N simultaneous equations of the form

$$
\begin{bmatrix}
1 & 1 & \cdots & 1 \\
x_1 & x_2 & \cdots & x_N \\
x_1^2 & x_2^2 & \cdots & x_N^2 \\
\cdot & \cdot & & \cdot \\
\cdot & \cdot & & \cdot \\
\cdot & \cdot & & \cdot \\
x_1^N & & \cdots & x_N^N
\end{bmatrix}
\begin{bmatrix}
w_1 \\
w_2 \\
\cdot \\
\cdot \\
\cdot \\
w_N
\end{bmatrix}
=
\begin{bmatrix}
c_1 \\
c_2 \\
\cdot \\
\cdot \\
\cdot \\
c_N
\end{bmatrix},
\qquad (5.4.10)
$$

where the c_n are readily formed by inserting various powers of x into Eq. (5.4.8). Since the rows of the square matrix in Eq. (5.4.10) are linearly independent, the inverse matrix always exists, and the w_j may be found by solving Eq. (5.4.10). In fact it is readily shown that the weight factors are always positive (see problem 10). There are several other formulas that can be used to derive the weight coefficients w_j (see, for instance, Reference 10, pp. 362–367).

The example we have used to derive the Gaussian integration formula was a particularly simple one. There exist many Gaussian formulas for different intervals of integration, and for more complicated integrands. We will not have occasion to use the more general formulas (for further details, see References 10 and 11).

To reiterate, the advantage of the Gaussian quadrature is the high order truncation error. A disadvantage is the location of the interpolation points. The intervals are not equally spaced in general, and for this reason the Gaussian type formula is rarely used for deriving difference approximations. Nevertheless for integration over the angular coordinate, the method is frequently used. It can be shown (see Reference 2, pp. 268–271) that for spherically symmetric scattering the discrete ordinate method using Gaussian quadrature is equivalent to the spherical harmonics method.

The discrete ordinate equations, Eqs. (5.4.3), are readily reduced to finite difference equations by standard techniques. In the next section a particular example of the formation of the spatial difference equations will be given in conjunction with the S_N method. As a final word on the discrete ordinate method, we remark that anisotropic scattering can be incorporated into the equations, and multigroup problems considered. The discrete ordinate method is widely used for one dimensional problems; its use in multidimensional problems seems to have been limited.

5.5 The S_N Method

The S_N method is a special case of the discrete ordinate method and was originated by B. G. Carlson (see Reference *12*). The characteristic feature of the S_N method is the assumption of linear variation of the directional flux between interpolation points in both the angular and spatial variations. We shall derive the equations in a straightforward manner for spherical geometry in the multigroup model. Consideration is then given to a variant of the S_N method, called the discrete S_N method, also proposed by Carlson (Reference *13*).

The transport equation for a given energy group g in spherical geometry is[7]

$$\mu \frac{\partial}{\partial r} \phi^g(r, \mu) + \frac{1}{r}(1 - \mu^2) \frac{\partial}{\partial \mu} \phi^g(r, \mu) + \sigma_t^g \phi^g(r, \mu) = S^g(r), \qquad (5.5.1)$$

where μ is the cosine of the angle between the neutron direction and the radius vector where we have assumed all sources are isotropic. An isotropic source is not an essential feature of the S_N method but it greatly simplifies the analysis. The extension to include anisotropies is direct but detailed, and we shall not consider such problems here. The interval $-1 \leqslant \mu \leqslant 1$ is divided into N segments, usually of equal width, $\varDelta_n$. The interpolation points are then defined as $\mu_n = -1 + 2n/N$ so that $\mu_0 = -1$ and $\mu_N = 1$. The directional flux is assumed to vary linearly between the interpolation points, and hence

$$\phi^g(r, \mu) = \frac{\mu - \mu_{n-1}}{\mu_n - \mu_{n-1}} \phi^g(r, \mu_n) + \frac{\mu_n - \mu}{\mu_n - \mu_{n-1}} \phi^g(r, \mu_{n-1}), \qquad (5.5.2)$$

for $\mu_{n-1} \leqslant \mu \leqslant \mu_n$. A representative directional flux distribution is shown in Fig. 5.5.1 for an S_4 approximation.
Here

$$\phi_n(x) = \phi(r, \mu_n). \qquad (5.5.2a)$$

The linear approximation in Eq. (5.5.2) may be substituted into Eq. (5.5.1) and the result integrated from μ_{n-1} to μ_n. The integration yields

$$\left[a_n \frac{d}{dr} + \frac{b_n}{r} + \sigma_t^g\right] \phi_n^g(r) + \left[\bar{a}_n \frac{d}{dr} - \frac{b_n}{r} + \sigma_t^g\right] \phi_{n-1}^g(r) = c_n S^g(r),$$

$$(n = 1, 2, ..., N) \qquad (5.5.3)$$

---

[7] For derivation see Appendix A.

with

$$a_n = \frac{1}{3}(2\mu_n + \mu_{n-1}), \qquad \bar{a}_n = \frac{1}{3}(\mu_n + 2\mu_{n-1})$$

$$b_n = \frac{2}{3\Delta_n}(3 - \mu_n^2 - \mu_n\mu_{n-1} - \mu_{n-1}^2),$$

and

$$c_n = 2.$$

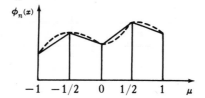

FIG. 5.5.1. S_4 approximation to the directional flux distribution. The dashed line represents the directional flux; the solid line, the S_N approximation.

The set of equations (5.5.3) consists of N equations in the $N + 1$ unknowns $\phi_n^g(r)$. The $N + 1$st equation is obtained by setting $\mu = -1$ and writing the transport equation, Eq. (5.5.1), directly. We have

$$-\frac{d}{dr}\phi_0^g(r) + \sigma_t^g\phi_0^g(r) = S^g(r). \tag{5.5.4}$$

The above equation may be included in the set (5.5.3) by choosing the constants

$$a_0 = -1,$$

$$b_0 = 0,$$

$$\phi_{-1}^g(r) = 0,$$

$$c_0 = 1.$$

It is evident that the approximations made are accurate to order $(\Delta\mu^2)$. The spatial dependence is obtained in the same manner. We divide the interval $0 \leqslant r \leqslant R$ into J segments of width $\Delta_j = r_j - r_{j-1}$, which are not assumed equal. As usual the division is such that interfaces lie on interpolation points. We order the points such that $r_0 = 0$, $r_J = R$. The mesh in $r - \mu$ space for any energy group is shown in Fig. 5.5.2.

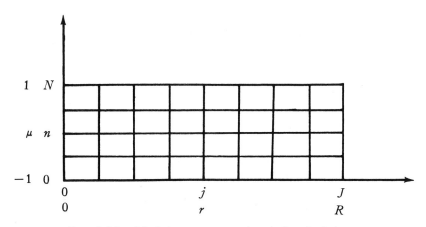

FIG. 5.5.2.   Mesh in $r - \mu$ space for an S_4 calculation.

In order to perform the spatial integrations, it is important to consider the direction of neutron motion. For the line $\mu = -1$, i.e., $n = 0$, the neutrons move from large r to small r. For reduced truncation error, we should perform the spatial integration in the direction of neutron travel (see problem 11).

To derive the appropriate difference equations for n such that $\mu_n \leqslant 0$, we integrate from r_j to r_{j-1}. Conversely, for $\mu_n > 0$, we integrate from r_{j-1} to r_j. Let Δ_j be defined as $\Delta_j = r_j - r_{j-1}$. To terms of order Δ_j^2 we approximate integrals as

$$\int_{r_{j-1}}^{r_j} dr f(r) = \frac{f(r_{j-1}) + f(r_j)}{2} \Delta_j . \tag{5.5.5}$$

The terms in $1/r$ are integrated by assuming an average value $1/\langle r_j \rangle$. The simplest choice is $\langle r_j \rangle = (r_j + r_{j-1})/2 = \bar{r}_j$. Another choice is

$$\langle r_j \rangle = \frac{\overline{r_j^2}}{\bar{r}_j} = \frac{2(r_j^3 - r_{j-1}^3)}{3(r_j^2 - r_{j-1}^2)} . \tag{5.5.6}$$

The difference equations for $n = 0, 1, ..., N/2$ are found by integrating from r_j to r_{j-1}. Using Eq. (5.5.5) and any suitable approximation for $\langle r_j \rangle$ in Eqs. (5.5.3) and (5.5.4), we have, after some algebra,

$$\left[-a_n + \frac{b_n}{\langle r_j \rangle} \frac{\Delta_j}{2} + \sigma_t^g \frac{\Delta_j}{2} \right] \phi_{n,j-1}^g + \left[a_n + \frac{b_n}{\langle r_j \rangle} \frac{\Delta_j}{2} + \sigma_t^g \frac{\Delta_j}{2} \right] \phi_{n,j}^g$$

$$+ \left[-\bar{a}_n - \frac{b_n}{\langle r_j \rangle} \frac{\Delta_j}{2} + \sigma_t^g \frac{\Delta_j}{2} \right] \phi_{n-1,j-1}^g$$

$$+ \left[\bar{a}_n - \frac{b_n}{\langle r_j \rangle} \frac{\Delta_j}{2} + \sigma_t^g \frac{\Delta_j}{2} \right] \phi_{n-1,j}^g = \frac{c_n \Delta_j}{2} [S_{j-1}^g + S_j^g]. \qquad (5.5.7)$$

Equation (5.5.7) may be used to compute successive iterates for the flux $\phi_{n,j-1}^g$. The usual iteration algorithm is analogous to the method of successive displacements. We drop the group index g and use superscript p for the iteration index. Equation (5.5.7) is then used in the form

$$\phi_{n,j-1}^{p+1} = a_{n,j}(S_{j-1}^p + S_j^p) - b_{n,j}\phi_{n,j}^{p+1} - c_{n,j}\phi_{n-1,j-1}^{p+1} - d_{n,j}\phi_{n-1,j}^{p+1}, \qquad (5.5.8)$$

where the coefficients are evident. Equation (5.5.8) applies for $j = J, J - 1, ..., 1$, and $n = 0, 1, ..., N/2$. For $n = 0$ the coefficients $c_{n,j}$ and $d_{n,j}$ are to be taken as zero.

An analogous equation is obtained for neutrons heading away from the reactor center; that is, for $n > N/2$. Without considering the details the basic difference equation is seen to be of the form

$$\phi_{n,j}^{p+1} = a_{n,j}'(S_{j-1}^p + S_j^p) - b_{n,j}'\phi_{n,j-1}^{p+1} - c_{n,j}'\phi_{n-1,j-1}^{p+1} - d_{n,j}'\phi_{n-1,j}^{p+1}. \qquad (5.5.9)$$

The iteration algorithm is similar to Eq. (5.5.8).

The boundary conditions to be used in conjunction with Eqs. (5.5.8) and (5.5.9) are simple. If there are any neutrons incident upon the external boundary, then the values $\phi_{n,J}$ are determined for $n \leqslant N/2$. For a vacuum boundary the $\phi_{n,J}$ are zero for $n \leqslant N/2$. At the center the directional fluxes are continuous and hence

$$\phi_{n,0} = \phi_{N-n,0}, \qquad 0 \leqslant n \leqslant \frac{N}{2}. \qquad (5.5.10)$$

A mesh for a single group, with boundary conditions, and the difference equation point pattern is shown in Fig. 5.5.3.

The source function $S^g(r)$ consists of scattering, fission, and extraneous sources. Thus

$$S^g(r, u) = \int_0^{u\,\text{th}} du'\sigma_s(r, u' \to u)\,\phi(r, u')$$

$$+ \nu\chi(u)\int_0^{u\,\text{th}} du'\sigma_f(r, u')\,\phi(r, u') + S_e^g(r, u), \qquad (5.5.11)$$

where the isotropic assumption has been used. The integrals over lethargy are replaced by summations over the group index g'. Thus, Eq. (5.5.11) is written

$$S^g(r, u) = \sum_{g'=1}^{G+1} [\sigma_s^{g',g}(r) + \nu\chi^g\sigma_f^{g',g}]\,\phi^g(r) + S_e^g(r, u). \qquad (5.5.12)$$

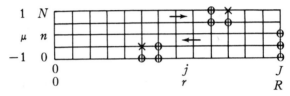

FIG. 5.5.3.   The $r - \mu$ mesh for an S_4 calculation in a sphere. The boundary conditions are shown as heavy dots. The 4-point difference equations are shown with directional arrows for the path of the computation. The points marked with a cross are to be computed using the points marked with a circle.

The scalar flux $\phi^g(r)$ is determined from the angular components as

$$\phi^g(r) = \frac{1}{2}\int_{-1}^{1} d\mu\,\phi^g(r, \mu) = \sum_{n=0}^{N} w_n\phi_n^g(r) \qquad (5.5.13)$$

where, for a uniform μ spacing,

$$w_0 = w_N = \frac{\Delta}{4}, \qquad (5.5.14a)$$

$$w_n = \frac{\Delta}{2}, \qquad n = 1, 2, ..., N - 1. \qquad (5.5.14b)$$

The spatial integration of $S^g(r)$ is carried out as before; we omit the details.

The entire calculational procedure for the S_N method is now evident. We again consider a criticality problem. The coefficients for the desired energy groups, angular segments, and spatial regions are computed in advance. To estimate the source an initial estimate of the scalar flux in each group is made. Note that only the scalar fluxes are needed, not the directional fluxes. After the source has been computed the directional fluxes in each group are computed, first for $\mu_0(= -1)$, then μ_1, etc., up to $\mu_{N/2}$ in the direction $r = R$ to $r = 0$. The boundary conditions are invoked to yield starting values for $\mu_{(N/2)+1}$, etc., and the integration is from $r = 0$ to $r = R$. After a group has been iterated once, we may go to the next group or recompute the source and recalculate the same group. Both procedures are used in practice. After every group has been iterated, the source may be recomputed and scaled appropriately. The entire procedure may be written in matrix form as a generalized eigenvalue problem (see problem 15).

The discrete S_N is a simplification of the original S_N . For the discrete S_N the $r - \mu$ space is again divided into segments r_j and μ_n . The spacing in μ will again be assumed uniform. We define

$$\Delta_j = r_j - r_{j-1}, \qquad j = 1, 2, ..., J, \qquad (5.5.15a)$$

and

$$\Delta_n = \mu_n - \mu_{n-1}, \qquad n = 1, 2, ..., N. \qquad (5.5.15b)$$

Next we consider the cell $\Delta_j \Delta_n$ and the average directional flux in the cell, say $\bar{\phi}_{n,j}$.[8] As before, the flux is assumed linear in both r and μ directions. The average flux is then given as

$$\bar{\phi}_{n,j} = \frac{\phi_{n,j} + \phi_{n,j-1} + \phi_{n-1,j} + \phi_{n-1,j-1}}{4}. \qquad (5.5.16)$$

The objective of the discrete S_N method is to re-express $\bar{\phi}_{n,j}$ in terms of average values of the directional flux at the midpoints $\bar{r}_j = (r_j + r_{j-1})/2$ and $\bar{\mu}_n = (\mu_n + \mu_{n-1})/2$. The resulting equations are simpler in detail than the original S_N equations and are also somewhat easier to derive. We define

$$\phi_n = \frac{\phi_{n,j} + \phi_{n,j-1}}{2}, \qquad (5.5.17a)$$

and

$$\phi_j = \frac{\phi_{n,j} + \phi_{n-1,j}}{2}. \qquad (5.5.17b)$$

The average flux over the cell is then

$$\bar{\phi}_{n,j} = \frac{\phi_n + \phi_{n-1}}{2} = \frac{\phi_j + \phi_{j-1}}{2}. \qquad (5.5.18)$$

---

[8] The group index is omitted in the following since the results apply to each group.

Equation (5.5.18) is intuitively obvious since ϕ_n and ϕ_j represent midpoint values on the cell boundaries.

The difference equations are now found in terms of ϕ_n and ϕ_j by averaging the Boltzmann equation over the cell $\varDelta_n \varDelta_j$. Each term of Eq. (5.5.1) may be treated separately. The first term is then

$$\frac{1}{\varDelta_n \varDelta_j} \int_{\mu_{n-1}}^{\mu_n} d\mu \int_{r_{j-1}}^{r_j} dr\, \mu \frac{d}{dr} \phi(r, \mu) = \frac{1}{\varDelta_j} \bar{\mu}_n [\phi_j - \phi_{j-1}], \qquad (5.5.19a)$$

where we have assumed $\phi(r_j, \mu) \approx \phi(r_j, \bar{\mu}_n)$. This approximation is valid to order $\varDelta \mu$. The second term is

$$\frac{1}{\varDelta_n \varDelta_j} \int_{r_{j-1}}^{r_j} dr \int_{\mu_{n-1}}^{\mu_n} d\mu \left[\frac{(1 - \mu^2)}{r} \frac{d}{d\mu} \phi(r, \mu) \right] = \frac{b_n}{\varDelta_n} \frac{1}{\langle r_j \rangle} [\phi_n - \phi_{n-1}], \quad (5.5.19b)$$

where b_n is the average of the quantity $(1 - \mu^2)$, $\langle r_j \rangle$ is the average radius, usually taken as Eq. (5.5.6). The removal term is readily written as

$$\frac{1}{\varDelta_n \varDelta_j} \int_{\mu_{n-1}}^{\mu_n} d\mu \int_{r_{j-1}}^{r_j} dr \sigma(r) \phi(r, \mu) = \sigma_j \left[\frac{\phi_j + \phi_{j-1}}{2} \right] \qquad (5.5.19c)$$

with σ_j the midpoint value of $\sigma(r)$. For the source, assumed isotropic, we have

$$\frac{1}{\varDelta_n \varDelta_j} \int_{\mu_{n-1}}^{\mu_n} d\mu \int_{r_{j-1}}^{r_j} dr\, S(r) = S_j, \qquad (5.5.19d)$$

with S_j the midpoint value of $S(r)$.

Collecting terms the difference equation is then

$$\bar{\mu}_n [\phi_j - \phi_{j-1}] + \frac{b_n}{\varDelta_n} \frac{\varDelta_j}{\langle r_j \rangle} [\phi_n - \phi_{n-1}] + \varDelta_j \sigma_j \left[\frac{\phi_j + \phi_{j-1}}{2} \right] = \varDelta_j S_j. \quad (5.5.20)$$

The term in ϕ_n may be eliminated by use of Eq. (5.5.18). Substituting and collecting terms we have

$$\left(\bar{\mu}_n + \frac{b_n}{\varDelta_n} \frac{\varDelta_j}{\langle r_j \rangle} + \frac{\sigma_j \varDelta_j}{2} \right) \phi_j + \left(-\bar{\mu}_n + \frac{b_n}{\varDelta_n} \frac{\varDelta_j}{\langle r_j \rangle} + \frac{\sigma_j \varDelta_j}{2} \right) \phi_{j-1}$$

$$= \varDelta_j S_j + \frac{2 b_n}{\varDelta_n} \frac{\varDelta_j}{\langle r_j \rangle} \phi_{n-1}. \quad (5.5.21)$$

Equation (5.5.21) is the desired difference relation. Note that, in contrast to the original S_N method, this equation is only 3-point in terms of the unknowns. As before an additional equation is obtained for $\mu = -1$. The mesh pattern is actually triangular shaped for the discrete S_N as shown in Fig. 5.5.4.

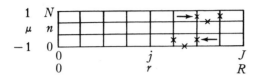

FIG. 5.5.4. Mesh point pattern for the discrete S_N method. The arrows indicate the direction of integration.

The procedure for solving the discrete S_N equations is very similar to the original S_N method. For a criticality problem the scalar flux must be estimated, which gives the source term. The integration is started along the line $\bar{\mu}_0 = -1$. The ϕ_{j-1} are evaluated from $j = J$ to $j = 1$. At $j = J$ the boundary condition of zero incident flux is used. Once the line $\bar{\mu}_0$ is computed, the lines $\bar{\mu}_1, \bar{\mu}_2, \ldots, \bar{\mu}_{(N/2)}$ are computed in turn. Note that the values of ϕ_n are readily found by linear interpolation. For $\bar{\mu}_n$, $n > N/2$, the direction of integration reverses. As before, the boundary conditions at $j = 0$ are

$$\phi_0(\bar{\mu}_n) = \phi_0(\bar{\mu}_{N-n}) .$$ (5.5.22)

The source is computed as

$$S_j = \frac{1}{N} \sum_n A_{n,j} \phi_n ,$$ (5.5.23)

where the matrix $A_{n,j}$ represents the scattering plus fission processes, averaged over the interval $j - 1$ to j.

The proper value of b_n to be used is determined by the condition that the net outflow of neutrons from the element Δ_j be equal to the source strength in that element. The neutron current, $J(r)$, is defined as

$$J_j = \int_{-1}^{1} d\mu \, \mu \, \phi(r_j , \mu) = \frac{1}{N} \sum_{n=1}^{N} \bar{\mu}_n \phi_j .$$ (5.5.24)

Integration of the Boltzmann equation over μ yields

$$\frac{d}{dr} J(r) + \frac{2}{r} J(r) + \sigma\phi(r) = S(r) .$$ (5.5.25)

Integrating over the interval Δ_j then yields

$$J_j - J_{j-1} + \frac{\Delta_j}{\langle r_j \rangle} [J_j + J_{j-1}] + \sigma_j \Delta_j \bar{\phi}_j = \Delta_j S_j. \tag{5.5.26}$$

Equation (5.5.26) is the difference equation for the integral over the element. The difference equation (5.5.21) is the equation in the interval Δ_n. Therefore, if we sum Eq. (5.5.21) over all n, the resulting sum must equal Eq. (5.5.26). It suffices to define b_n to obey the relation (see problem 17),

$$b_n - b_{n-1} = -\Delta_n(\bar{\mu}_m + \bar{\mu}_{m-1}). \tag{5.5.27}$$

Note that $b_0 = 0$, and hence the b_n are readily evaluated by recursion.

Further modifications of the discrete S_N have been suggested by Carlson and are discussed in Reference *13*.

5.6 Time Dependent Transport Methods

All of the numerical procedures for the transport equation considered thus far may be generalized to include transient effects. We consider examples in one-group slab geometry. The time dependent transport equation is (see Appendix A)

$$\frac{1}{v} \frac{\partial \phi}{\partial t} + \mu \frac{\partial \phi}{\partial x} + \sigma_t \phi = S. \tag{5.6.1}$$

The time dependent equation is readily transformed into the time dependent P_N equations. By the methods considered in Section 5.1, we obtain, for the P_3 equations,

$$\frac{1}{v} \frac{\partial \phi_0}{\partial t} + \frac{\partial \phi_1}{\partial x} + \sigma_t \phi_0 = \sigma_{s,0} \phi_0 + S_0, \tag{5.6.2a}$$

$$\frac{1}{v} \frac{\partial \phi_1}{\partial t} + \frac{2}{3} \frac{\partial}{\partial x} \phi_2 + \frac{1}{3} \frac{\partial}{\partial x} \phi_0 + \sigma_t \phi_1 = \sigma_{s,1} \phi_1 + S_1, \tag{5.6.2b}$$

$$\frac{1}{v} \frac{\partial \phi_2}{\partial t} + \frac{3}{5} \frac{\partial}{\partial x} \phi_3 + \frac{2}{5} \frac{\partial}{\partial x} \phi_1 + \sigma_t \phi_2 = \sigma_{s,2} \phi_2 + S_2 \tag{5.6.2c}$$

$$\frac{1}{v} \frac{\partial \phi_3}{\partial t} + \frac{3}{7} \frac{\partial}{\partial x} \phi_2 + \sigma_t \phi_3 = \sigma_{S,3} \phi_3 + S_3. \tag{5.6.2d}$$

We define the vectors

$$\psi = \begin{bmatrix} \phi_0 \\ \phi_1 \\ \phi_2 \\ \phi_3 \end{bmatrix}, \qquad (5.6.3a)$$

$$\mathbf{S} = \begin{bmatrix} S_0 \\ S_1 \\ S_2 \\ S_3 \end{bmatrix}. \qquad (5.6.3b)$$

The P_3 equations may then be written

$$\frac{1}{v}\frac{\partial}{\partial t}\psi + \mathbf{A}\frac{\partial}{\partial x}\psi + \sigma_t\psi = \mathbf{B}\psi + \mathbf{S}, \qquad (5.6.4)$$

with

$$\mathbf{A} = \begin{bmatrix} 0 & 1 & 0 & 0 \\ 1/3 & 0 & 2/3 & 0 \\ 0 & 2/5 & 0 & 3/5 \\ 0 & 0 & 3/7 & 0 \end{bmatrix}, \qquad (5.6.5a)$$

$$\mathbf{B} = \begin{bmatrix} \sigma_{s,0} & 0 & 0 & 0 \\ 0 & \sigma_{s,1} & 0 & 0 \\ 0 & 0 & \sigma_{s,2} & 0 \\ 0 & 0 & 0 & \sigma_{s,3} \end{bmatrix}. \qquad (5.6.5b)$$

In the absence of external sources, Eq. (5.6.4) becomes

$$\frac{1}{v}\frac{\partial}{\partial t}\psi + \mathbf{A}\frac{\partial}{\partial x}\psi + \sigma\psi = \nu\mathbf{B}'\psi, \qquad (5.6.6)$$

where $\mathbf{B}'$ includes the fission sources, and σ the cross sections.
One simple difference approximation for Eq. (5.6.6) is

$$\frac{\psi_j^{l+1} - \psi_j^l}{v\Delta t} + \mathbf{A}\frac{(\psi_{j+1}^l - \psi_{j-1}^l)}{2\Delta x} + \sigma\psi_j^l = \nu\mathbf{B}'\psi_j^l, \qquad (5.6.7)$$

with j the space index, l the time index, and

$$\psi_j^l = \begin{bmatrix} \phi_0(x_j, t_l) \\ \phi_1(x_j, t_l) \\ \phi_2(x_j, t_l) \\ \phi_3(x_j, t_l) \end{bmatrix}. \qquad (5.6.8)$$

The difference equation (5.6.7) is explicit in time and has truncation error $O(\Delta t) + O(\Delta x^2)$.

To study the stability of the procedure, we consider a generalization of the Von Neumann method. We recall that the Von Neumann method was based upon a Fourier expansion of the form

$$\phi(x_j, t_l) = \sum_n (\xi_n)^l \, e^{\iota \beta_n x_j} . \tag{5.6.9}$$

The difference equation for the function $\phi(x_j, t_l)$ was used to find the behavior of the amplification factor ξ_n. In the case of equation (5.6.7), the difference equation relates to vectors and hence a generalization of the expansion (5.6.9) is needed. Obviously an expansion of the form

$$\boldsymbol{\psi}_j^l = \sum_n \mathbf{u}_n^l \, e^{\iota \beta_n x_j} \tag{5.6.10}$$

is necessary. In the particular problem considered here, each vector $\mathbf{u}_n$ consists of four components. To study stability the difference relation is used to relate the vectors $\mathbf{u}_n^{l+1}$ and $\mathbf{u}_n^l$. In general, a relation of the form

$$\mathbf{u}_n^{l+1} = \mathbf{C}(\Delta x, \Delta t) \, \mathbf{u}_n^l \tag{5.6.11}$$

is found. The quantity $\mathbf{C}(\Delta x, \Delta t)$ is a matrix called the amplification matrix. Stability depends upon the eigenvalues of the amplification matrix.

Equation (5.6.7) will serve as a useful example of the generalization of the Von Neumann method. Inserting the expansion (5.6.10) into the difference equation, we find, for a particular index n,

$$\frac{(\mathbf{u}_n^{l+1} - \mathbf{u}_n^l)}{v\Delta t} \, e^{\iota \beta_n x_j} + \frac{\mathbf{A}(e^{\iota \beta_n \Delta x} - e^{-\iota \beta_n \Delta x})}{2\Delta x} \, \mathbf{u}_n^l \, e^{\iota \beta_n x_j} + \boldsymbol{\sigma} \mathbf{u}_n^l \, e^{\iota \beta_n x_j} = v \mathbf{B}' \mathbf{u}_n^l \, e^{\iota \beta_n x_j} . \tag{5.6.12}$$

Collecting terms and transposing, we have

$$\mathbf{u}_n^{l+1} = \left[\mathbf{I} + v\Delta t(v\mathbf{B}' - \boldsymbol{\sigma}) - \iota \frac{v\Delta t}{\Delta x} \sin \beta_n \Delta x \, \mathbf{A} \right] \mathbf{u}_n^l . \tag{5.6.13}$$

The quantity in brackets is the amplification matrix, $\mathbf{C}(\Delta x, \Delta t)$.

To find the eigenvalues of the amplification matrix, we consider the following simplification. Let the ratio $\Delta t/\Delta x$ be a fixed quantity, say α. In the limit of very small Δt, the amplification matrix is then

$$\mathbf{C}(\Delta x, 0) = [\mathbf{I} - \iota \alpha \sin \beta_n \Delta x \, \mathbf{A}] . \tag{5.6.14}$$

The matrix $\mathbf{A}$ has at least one nonzero eigenvalue, say λ_0. Hence $\mathbf{C}(\Delta x, 0)$ has an eigenvalue with magnitude given by

$$|\gamma_0| = \sqrt{1 + \alpha^2 \sin^2 \beta_n \Delta x \lambda_0^2} \geqslant 1 , \qquad (5.6.15)$$

and hence the difference relation (5.6.7) is unstable.

Richtmyer (Reference *14*, pp. 132–134) has shown that Eq. (5.6.7) is stable for a fixed ratio $\Delta t/(\Delta x)^2$. The stability criterion is then eventually found to be of the form

$$\Delta t \leqslant K(\Delta x)^2 , \qquad (5.6.16)$$

with K some constant. The increment in t is too small for practical use.

An alternative difference relation for the P_N equations has been suggested by Friedrichs (Reference *14*, pp. 135–136). In this method the vector ψ_j^l, in Eq. (5.6.7), is replaced by the spatial average, i.e.,

$$\psi_j^l = \frac{1}{2}(\psi_{j+1}^l + \psi_{j-1}^l) . \qquad (5.6.17)$$

The resulting difference equation is then

$$\frac{2\psi_j^{l+1} - \psi_{j+1}^l - \psi_{j-1}^l}{2v\Delta t} + \frac{\mathbf{A}(\psi_{j+1}^l - \psi_{j-1}^l)}{2\Delta x}$$

$$+ \frac{\sigma}{2}(\psi_{j+1}^l + \psi_{j-1}^l) = \frac{v\mathbf{B}'}{2}(\psi_{j+1}^l + \psi_{j-1}^l) . \qquad (5.6.18)$$

The difference equation (5.6.18) is explicit and the amplification matrix is readily found. Inserting the Fourier expansion for ψ_j^l we have, for the nth harmonic,

$$\frac{\mathbf{u}_n^{l+1} - \cos \beta_n \Delta x \mathbf{u}_n^l}{v\Delta t} + \frac{\mathbf{A}}{\Delta x} \iota \sin \beta_n \Delta x \, \mathbf{u}_n^l + \sigma \cos \beta_n \Delta x \, \mathbf{u}_n^l = v\mathbf{B}' \cos \beta_n \Delta x \, \mathbf{u}_n^l .$$
$$(5.6.19)$$

The amplification matrix is then

$$\mathbf{C}(\Delta x, \Delta t) = \left[(\mathbf{I} + v\Delta t(v\mathbf{B}' - \sigma)) \cos \beta_n \Delta x - \frac{v\Delta t}{\Delta x} \mathbf{A} \iota \sin \beta_n \, \Delta x \right] . \qquad (5.6.20)$$

For small $v\Delta t$ and fixed $\Delta t/\Delta x$ we have

$$\mathbf{C}(\Delta x, 0) = [\mathbf{I} \cos \beta_n \, \Delta x - \iota \alpha \mathbf{A} \sin \beta_n \, \Delta x] . \qquad (5.6.21)$$

Let λ_0 be the largest eigenvalue of $\mathbf{A}$. The eigenvalues of $\mathbf{C}(\varDelta x, 0)$ are bounded by unity provided

$$\alpha\lambda_0 \leqslant 1 , \tag{5.6.22}$$

and therefore

$$\varDelta t \leqslant \frac{\varDelta x}{\lambda_0 v} \tag{5.6.23}$$

is the stability condition.[9]

Time dependent problems in the S_N method are solved in a less straightforward manner than considered thus far. In particular, the time dependent difference equations are derived by consideration of the direction of particle flow. Recall from Eqs. (5.5.3) et seq. that the coefficient a_n has the properties

$$a_n > 0, \qquad \mu_n > 0 ;$$
$$a_n < 0, \qquad \mu_n \leqslant 0 .$$

Furthermore, $|a_n|$ increases as $|\mu_n|$ increases. The distance that a particle travels radially in a time $\varDelta t$ is dependent upon $|a_n|$. We define the quantity

$$\varDelta_l = t_{l+1} - t_l , \tag{5.6.24}$$

and consider two cases of particle flow:

$$(a) \qquad |a_n| < \frac{\varDelta_j}{v_g \varDelta_l} , \tag{5.6.25a}$$

$$(b) \qquad |a_n| > \frac{\varDelta_j}{v_g \varDelta_l} , \tag{5.6.25b}$$

where $\varDelta_j$ is the space increment and v_g the group speed. The two cases are illustrated in Fig. 5.6.1.

The directional flux at point C must be determined from values at points A, B, D which are assumed known. We consider the two cases separately.

Case a: In this case the coefficient $|a_n|$ is small, i.e., $|\mu_n|$ small and hence the neutron does not travel far along the radius vector in a time $\varDelta_l$. The direction line EC intersects the line AB. We assume the variation of the directional flux is linear in time as well as space and angle. The interpolation points AB should be used for the evaluation of the flux at C.

---

[9] We have neglected the effect of terms of $O(\varDelta t)$ in the eigenvalue. Richtmyer, in Reference *14*, shows that a more general condition of the form $1 + O(\varDelta t)$ is sufficient and in some cases necessary.

Case b: In this case $|a_n|$ is large and hence the neutron travels a large distance along the radius vector in a time Δ_l. The direction line EC intersects the line DA. The interpolation points DA should be used to evaluate the flux at C.

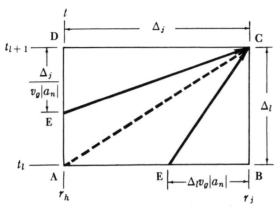

FIG. 5.6.1.   The relation of the increments of integration in the $r - t$ plane for different neutron directions.

Notice that the meaning of r_h depends upon the sign of a_n. For $a_n > 0$ neutrons move out along the radius vector and

$$r_h = r_{j-1} .$$

For $a_n < 0$ neutrons move inward and hence

$$r_h = r_{j+1} .$$

In order to approximate the time and space derivatives, we consider the one group, time-dependent analog of Eq. (5.5.3). We have

$$\left(\frac{1}{v}\frac{\partial}{\partial t} + a_n \frac{\partial}{\partial r}\right)\phi_n(r, t) + \left(\frac{1}{v}\frac{\partial}{\partial t} + \bar{a}_n \frac{\partial}{\partial r}\right)\phi_{n-1}(r, t) = R_n(r, t) \qquad (5.6.26)$$

with $R_n(r, t)$ given as

$$R_n(r, t) = c_n S(r, t) - \left(\frac{b_n}{r} + \sigma_t\right)\phi_n(r, t) + \left(\frac{b_n}{r} - \sigma_t\right)\phi_{n-1}(r, t) . \qquad (5.6.27)$$

Consider the case a; that is, the EC intersects the line AB. The space derivative should be evaluated at points AB along time line t_l. The time derivative should be evaluated along the space line r_j from points BC. From the approximation of linearity, we have then

$$\frac{\partial}{\partial r}\phi_n(r, t) = \frac{\phi_n(r_j, t_l) - \phi_n(r_h, t_l)}{\Delta_j}, \tag{5.6.28a}$$

and

$$\frac{\partial}{\partial t}\phi_n(r, t) = \frac{\phi_n(r_j, t_{l+1}) - \phi_n(r_j, t_l)}{\Delta_l}. \tag{5.6.28b}$$

Conversely, for case b, where the line EC interesects AD, we should use the following:

$$\frac{\partial}{\partial r}\phi_n(r, t) = \frac{\phi_n(r_j, t_{l+1}) - \phi_n(r_h, t_{l+1})}{\Delta_j} \tag{5.6.29}$$

and

$$\frac{\partial}{\partial t}\phi_n(r, t) = \frac{\phi_n(r_h, t_{l+1}) - \phi_n(r_h, t_l)}{\Delta_l}. \tag{5.6.30}$$

We shall indicate the details for case a. With the above derivatives, Eq. (5.6.26) becomes

$$\frac{1}{v\Delta_l}[\phi_n(r_j, t_{l+1}) - \phi_n(r_j, t_l)] + \frac{a_n}{\Delta_j}[\phi_n(r_j, t_l) - \phi_n(r_h, t_l)]$$

$$+ \frac{1}{v\Delta_l}[\phi_{n-1}(r_j, t_{l+1}) - \phi_{n-1}(r_j, t_l)]$$

$$+ \frac{\bar{a}_n}{\Delta_j}[\phi_{n-1}(r_j, t_l) - \phi_{n-1}(r_h, t_l)] = R_n(r, t). \tag{5.6.31}$$

One possible approach is to evaluate $R_n(r, t)$ at r_j, t_l and solve Eq. (5.6.31) for $\phi_n(r_j, t_{l+1})$.

An alternative procedure is usually used however. In particular, the quantity $R_n(r, t)$ is evaluated at the midpoint of the time-space interval. This makes the resulting equations implicit, but a simple iteration reduces the effort. The midpoint values are given as

$$R_n(\bar{r}, \bar{t}) = c_n \frac{[S(r_h, t_l) + S(r_j, t_{l+1})]}{2}$$

$$- \left(\frac{b_n}{\langle r_j \rangle} + \sigma_t\right) \frac{[\phi_n(r_h, t_l) + \phi_n(r_j, t_{l+1})]}{2}$$

$$+ \left(\frac{b_n}{\langle r_j \rangle} - \sigma_t\right) \frac{[\phi_{n-1}(r_h, t_l) + \phi_{n-1}(r_j, t_{l+1})]}{2}. \tag{5.6.32}$$

Inserting Eq. (5.6.32) into (5.6.31) and solving for $\phi_n(r_j, t_{l+1})$ yields

$$\phi_n(r_j, t_{l+1}) = \frac{1}{1 + (v\Delta_l/2)(b_n/\langle r_j \rangle + \sigma_t)} \left\{ \left[1 - \frac{v\Delta_l a_n}{\Delta_j}\right] \phi_n(r_j, t_l) \right.$$

$$+ v\Delta_l \left[\frac{a_n}{\Delta_j} - \frac{b_n}{2\langle r_j \rangle} - \frac{\sigma_t}{2}\right] \phi_n(r_h, t_l)$$

$$- \left[1 - \frac{v\Delta_l}{2}\left(\frac{b_n}{\langle r_j \rangle} - \sigma_t\right)\right] \phi_{n-1}(r_j, t_{l+1}) + \left[1 - \frac{v\Delta_l \bar{a}_n}{\Delta_j}\right] \phi_{n-1}(r_j, t_l)$$

$$+ v\Delta_l \left[\frac{\bar{a}_n}{\Delta_j} + \frac{b_n}{2\langle r_j \rangle} - \frac{\sigma_t}{2}\right] \phi_{n-1}(r_h, t_l)$$

$$\left. + \frac{v\Delta_l c_n}{2} [S(r_j, t_{l+1}) + S(r_h, t_l)] \right\}. \tag{5.6.33}$$

Notice that the only implicit term in Eq. (5.6.33) is the source term. The usual procedure for using equation (5.6.33) is to assume $S(r_j, t_{l+1})$ equals $S(r_j, t_l)$ and compute tentative values for $\phi_n(r_j, t_{l+1})$. The tentative values are then used to recompute $S(r_j, t_{l+1})$, and the final values of $\phi_n(r_j, t_{l+1})$ are computed. The difference expression for case b is readily found to be of the same form.

Although the equation (5.6.33) appears formidable, the coefficients are computed only once. The relation is actually a 5-point equation, save for the source terms, and is easy to use.

No proof of the stability of the S_N difference method has been found thus far. Based upon many experiments at Los Alamos and elsewhere, the method is usually considered to be stable.

5.7 Moments Method

The last method we shall discuss for treating the Boltzmann equation is the moments method, also called the Spencer-Fano method. The moments method is an expansion technique for solving the transport equation in infinite media. The method has been devised to treat the difficult problem of neutron and gamma-ray deep penetration (see References *15–21*). As will be noted in Chapter VI, the Monte Carlo treatment of the deep penetration problem is difficult since the expected penetration is small. Direct numerical integration is also difficult for the deep penetration problem since the number of spatial points required is usually very large. The moments method is semi-analytic in nature; the angle, space, and energy variations are treated by polynomial expansion. The series are truncated to obtain the solution. In general the numerical aspects of the method are simple. The method illustrates the general principle that the analytic work should be carried as far as possible before resorting to the numerics.

We shall apply the method here to the gamma-ray problem and treat the algebraically much more complex neutron problem in Appendix C. Before entering the details, we first outline the motivations for each of the steps involved. Consider the case of a plane shield with an incident plane source of monoenergetic photons. The angular dependence of the flux is to be approximated by a polynomial. The particular expansion polynomials are the Legendre polynomials, $P_n(\mu)$, as used in the spherical harmonics method. By using the series expansion for the directional flux, an infinite series of equations for the expansion coefficients results. Note that the expansion coefficients will be functions of position and energy. In general, shielding calculations are performed in order to find the nondirectional flux at any point, and hence the zeroth moment of the expansion is of primary interest. The nondirectional flux is next expanded in a simple power series x^n, $n = 0, 1, \dots$, to compute the coefficients of the spatial powers, which are in turn functions of energy. The resultant expression is then solved for the coefficients. With these preliminary remarks, we now move into the details.

The transport equation for photons is (see Appendix A)

$$\mathbf{\Omega} \cdot \nabla \phi(\mathbf{r}, \Lambda, \mathbf{\Omega}) + \sigma(\mathbf{r}, \Lambda) \phi(\mathbf{r}, \Lambda, \mathbf{\Omega})$$

$$= \frac{1}{2\pi} \int_0^\Lambda d\Lambda' \int_{4\pi} d\mathbf{\Omega}' K(\Lambda', \Lambda) \, \delta[1 + (\Lambda' - \Lambda) - \mathbf{\Omega}' \cdot \mathbf{\Omega}] \, \phi(\mathbf{r}, \Lambda', \mathbf{\Omega}')$$

$$+ S(\mathbf{r}, \Lambda, \mathbf{\Omega}), \qquad (5.7.1)$$

where $K(\Lambda', \Lambda)$ is given by Eq. (A.40).

The first step in the analysis is to expand the directional flux in the Legendre polynomials. The details of method have been indicated in Section 5.1 so we shall merely state the result of the transformation. For plane geometry we have

$$\phi(x, \Lambda, \mu) = 2\pi \phi(\mathbf{r}, \Lambda, \mathbf{\Omega}), \qquad (5.7.2)$$

and

$$\phi(x, \Lambda, \mu) = \sum_{n=0}^{\infty} \frac{2n + 1}{2} \phi_n(x, \Lambda) P_n(\mu), \qquad (5.7.3a)$$

with

$$\phi_n(x, \Lambda) = \int_{-1}^{1} d\mu \, \phi(x, \Lambda, \mu) P_n(\mu). \qquad (5.7.3b)$$

By inserting (5.7.3a) into the transport equation and following the steps outlined before, we obtain

$$\frac{n+1}{2n+1} \frac{d}{dx} \phi_{n+1}(x, \Lambda) + \frac{n}{2n+1} \frac{d}{dx} \phi_{n-1}(x, \Lambda) + \sigma(x, \Lambda) \phi_n(x, \Lambda)$$

$$= S_n(x, \Lambda) + \int_0^\Lambda d\Lambda' P_n(1 + \Lambda' - \Lambda) K(\Lambda', \Lambda) \phi_n(x, \Lambda') . \qquad (5.7.4)$$

Note that the argument of the Legendre polynomial is given in terms of Λ, Λ' by virtue of the Compton relation (A.36).

We now desire to eliminate the spatial dependence to find an equation for coefficients as functions of energy only. To this end, we expand $\phi_n(x, \Lambda)$ in a power series in x. We define the expansion coefficients $\phi_{jn}(\Lambda)$ as

$$\phi_{jn}(\Lambda) = \alpha_j \int_{-\infty}^\infty dx \, x^j \phi_n(x, \Lambda) , \qquad (5.7.5)$$

where the coefficient α_j will be obtained subsequently. These coefficients are arbitrary to this point, but will be chosen to simplify the equation that determines the moments. To find an equation relating the $\phi_{jn}(\Lambda)$, we multiply both sides of Eq. (5.7.4) by $\alpha_j x^j$ and integrate. To treat the left-hand side, we consider the general expression

$$\alpha_j \int_{-\infty}^\infty dx \, x^j \frac{d}{dx} \phi_n(x, \Lambda) = \alpha_j \left[x^j \phi_n(x, \Lambda) \Big|_{-\infty}^\infty - \int_{-\infty}^\infty dx \, \phi_n(x, \Lambda) j x^{j-1} \right] , \qquad (5.7.6)$$

where we have integrated by parts. In order to continue, we must require that $x^j \phi_{n'+1}(x, \Lambda)$ vanish at $\pm \infty$. Therefore, we must assume we have an infinite medium. (This assumption of an infinite medium is one of the most serious limitations of the moments method.) Then we find that

$$\alpha_j \int_{-\infty}^\infty dx \, x^j \frac{d}{dx} \phi_n(x, \Lambda) = -\frac{j \alpha_j}{\alpha_{j-1}} \phi_{j-1,n}(\Lambda) . \qquad (5.7.7)$$

In order to integrate the term $\sigma(x, \Lambda) \phi_n(x, \Lambda)$, we make the second major assumption of the moments method, i.e., the medium is homogeneous so that $\sigma(x, \Lambda)$ is only a function of Λ. We then have

$$\alpha_j \int_{-\infty}^\infty dx \, x^j \sigma(\Lambda) \phi_n(x, \Lambda) = \sigma(\Lambda) \phi_{j,n}(\Lambda) . \qquad (5.7.8)$$

To find the right-hand side, we recall that the source was assumed plane and monoenergetic, i.e., $S_n(x, \Lambda) = S_n(\Lambda) \delta(x) = S_n \delta(\Lambda - \Lambda_0) \delta(x)$.

Hence

$$\alpha_j \int_{-\infty}^{\infty} x^j S_n(x, \Lambda) \, dx = \alpha_j S_n \delta(\Lambda - \Lambda_0) \, \delta_{j0} . \qquad (5.7.9)$$

Finally, the last term of the right-hand side is

$$\int_0^\Lambda d\Lambda' P_n(1 + \Lambda' - \Lambda) \, K(\Lambda', \Lambda) \, \alpha_j \int_{-\infty}^{\infty} dx \, x^j \phi_n(x, \Lambda')$$

$$= \int_0^\Lambda d\Lambda' P_n(1 + \Lambda' - \Lambda) \, K(\Lambda', \Lambda) \, \phi_{jn}(\Lambda') . \qquad (5.7.10)$$

Collecting terms and transposing, we have

$$\sigma(\Lambda) \phi_{jn}(\Lambda) = \alpha_j S_n \delta(\Lambda - \Lambda_0) \, \delta_{j0}$$

$$+ \int_0^\Lambda d\Lambda' P_n(1 + \Lambda' - \Lambda) \, K(\Lambda', \Lambda) \, \phi_{jn}(\Lambda')$$

$$+ \frac{1}{2n+1} \frac{j\alpha_j}{\alpha_{j-1}} [(n+1) \phi_{j-1,n+1}(\Lambda) + n\phi_{j-1,n-1}(\Lambda)] . \qquad (5.7.11)$$

To find the coefficient α_j from a dimensional analysis of each term of Eq. (5.7.11), we note that α_j/α_{j-1} must have the dimensions of $(\text{length})^{-1}$. We now choose the arbitrary coefficients α_j : the choice

$$\frac{j\alpha_j}{\alpha_{j-1}} = \sigma(\Lambda_0) \equiv \sigma_0 \quad j \geqslant 1 , \qquad \alpha_0 = \sigma_0 , \qquad (5.7.12)$$

leads to a simple result. We find that

$$\alpha_j = \frac{(\sigma_0)^{j+1}}{j!} . \qquad (5.7.13)$$

Finally we have

$$\sigma(\Lambda) \phi_{jn}(\Lambda) = \int_0^\Lambda d\Lambda' P_n(1 + \Lambda' - \Lambda) \, K(\Lambda', \Lambda) \, \phi_{jn}(\Lambda')$$

$$+ \frac{\sigma_0^{j+1}}{j!} S_n \delta(\Lambda - \Lambda_0) \, \delta_{j0} + \frac{\sigma_0}{2n+1} [(n+1) \phi_{j-1,n+1}(\Lambda) + n\phi_{j-1,n-1}(\Lambda)] .$$

$$(5.7.14)$$

To compute $\phi_{jn}(\Lambda)$ requires some simple numerical steps; however, before considering the actual computation, we first discuss the properties of the Eq. (5.7.14).

Of primary importance is the nature of the coupling between various coefficients. Notice that $\phi_{jn}(\Lambda)$ is a function only of the coefficients with indices j, n; $j - 1$, $n - 1$; and $j - 1$, $n + 1$. Thus the coefficients for a given j, n can be computed without truncation of a series in contradistinction to the usual P_n method. This result greatly simplifies application of

the moments method since computations with higher order approximations merely require calculation of the additional coefficients.

We can exploit a feature of the present problem to greatly simplify the
numerical analysis. The integral term involves integration from
$\Lambda' = 0$ to Λ, i.e., the range of integration is limited due to the fact that
photons only down scatter in energy. The evaluation of the $\phi_{jn}(\Lambda)$ can
consequently be accomplished without iteration.

We now consider the detailed steps in evaluating the coefficients
$\phi_{jn}(\Lambda)$. For simplicity we assume the source is isotropic, and hence
$S_n = 0$, $n \neq 0$. The coefficients at $\Lambda = \Lambda_0$ are found as described
below.

Figure 5.7.1 displays the order in which the coefficients may be found.
From this figure it is seen that

$$\phi_{jn}(\Lambda_0) \neq 0 \qquad \text{if } j \geqslant n \text{ and if } j + n = \text{even integer},$$

$$\phi_{jn}(\Lambda_0) = 0 \qquad \text{if } j < n \text{ or } j + n = \text{odd integer}.$$

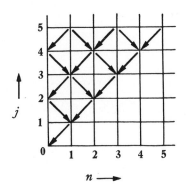

FIG. 5.7.1. The j, n plane for $\Lambda = \Lambda_0$ showing the linkage between nodes
according to Eq. (5.7.14). Nonzero points for a plane, monoenergetic, isotropic
source are indicated by arrows pointing away from or towards points. The arrows
indicate the relationships between nodes. The value of ϕ_{jn} at the node (n, j) may
be found from the $\phi_{j'n'}$ at the nodes at the heads of the arrows pointing away
from the node (n, j).

In deriving these results, it is simplest to start with the case of $j = 0$
and determine all $\phi_{0,n}$ using Eq. (5.7.14). Next we examine $\phi_{1,n}$, all n,
with Eq. (5.7.14) and so on. Of course, one does not compute more
$\phi_{jn}(\Lambda_g)$ than are needed. To this end, we remark that symmetries can
frequently be exploited to reduce the number of nonzero coefficients.

In order to find further values, we must approximate the integral
term in Eq. (5.7.14). The kernel $P_n(1 + \Lambda' - \Lambda)K(\Lambda', \Lambda)$ is a simple

polynomial in Λ' which can be accurately approximated. If a series of values of Λ, say Λ_g, be picked, then the integral can be written

$$\int_{\Lambda_0}^{\Lambda} d\Lambda' P_n(1 + \Lambda' - \Lambda) K(\Lambda', \Lambda) \phi_{jn}(\Lambda') \approx \sum_{g'=0}^{g} H_n(g', g) \phi_{jn}(g') , \qquad (5.7.15)$$

where the $H_n(g', g)$ are weighting coefficients and depend upon the quadrature formula used. As an example, for the first step we shall use the trapezoidal rule, and Simpson's rule for each step thereafter. Thus, we have

$$\int_{\Lambda_0}^{\Lambda_1} d\Lambda' P_n(1 + \Lambda' - \Lambda) K(\Lambda', \Lambda) \phi_{jn}(\Lambda')$$

$$\approx [P_n(1 + \Lambda_0 - \Lambda_1) K(\Lambda_0, \Lambda_1) \phi_{jn}(\Lambda_0) + P_n(1) K(\Lambda_1, \Lambda_1) \phi_{jn}(\Lambda_1)] \frac{\Delta\Lambda}{2} ,$$
$$(5.7.16)$$

in which we note that $P_n(1) = 1$ and $K(\Lambda_1, \Lambda_1) = 2\pi(1)(e^2/mc^2)^2$ [see Eq. (A.40)]. Similarly, for an even number of intervals of integration, we can use Simpson's rule and find

$$\int_{\Lambda_0}^{\Lambda_g} d\Lambda' P_n(1 + \Lambda' - \Lambda) K(\Lambda', \Lambda) \phi_{jn}(\Lambda')$$

$$\approx \frac{\Delta\Lambda}{3} [P_n(1 + \Lambda_0 - \Lambda_g) K(\Lambda_0, \Lambda_g) \phi_{jn}(\Lambda_0)$$

$$+ 4P_n(1 + \Lambda_1 - \Lambda_g) K(\Lambda_1, \Lambda_g) \phi_{jn}(\Lambda_1) + \dots$$

$$+ P_n(1) K(\Lambda_g, \Lambda_g) \phi_{jn}(\Lambda_g)] . \qquad (5.7.17)$$

We remark that for $\Lambda' < \Lambda - 1$, the kernel $K(\Lambda', \Lambda)$ is zero, and hence the integration is significantly simplified.

Regardless of the quadrature formula used, it is always possible to write the integral in Eq. (5.7.16) in the form

$$\int_{\Lambda_0}^{\Lambda_g} d\Lambda' P_n(1 + \Lambda' - \Lambda) K(\Lambda', \Lambda) \phi_{jn}(\Lambda')$$

$$\approx H_n(g, g) \phi_{jn}(\Lambda_g) + \sum_{g'=0}^{g-1} H_n(g', g) \phi_{jn}(\Lambda_g) , \qquad (5.7.18)$$

and hence solve Eq. (5.7.14) in the form

$$\phi_{jn}(\Lambda_g) = \frac{1}{\sigma(\Lambda) - H_n(g, g)} \left\{ \sum_{g'=0}^{g-1} H_n(g', g) \phi_{jn}(\Lambda_{g'}) + \frac{\sigma_0^{j+1}}{j!} S_n \delta(\Lambda_g - \Lambda_0) \delta_{j0} \right.$$

$$\left. + \frac{\sigma_0}{2n+1} [(n+1) \phi_{j-1,n+1}(\Lambda) + n\phi_{j-1,n-1}(\Lambda)] \right\} . \qquad (5.7.19)$$

The weighting coefficients are universal and may be computed once and for all, or else generated when needed. The computational process is straightforward; one first computes for $g = 0$. One then goes to $g = 1$ and computes the needed portion of the j, n plane. The details are as before.

To this point the analysis has been on obtaining the expansion coefficients $\phi_{jn}(\Lambda_g)$. We now address ourselves to the problem of deriving expressions for the flux in terms of the $\phi_{jn}(\Lambda_g)$. In particular, we consider the calculation of $\phi_n(x, \Lambda_g)$. One possibility is a simple polynomial expansion of the form

$$\phi_n(x, \Lambda_g) = \sum_{j=0}^{J} \alpha_{j,n}(\Lambda_g)\, x^j , \qquad (5.7.20)$$

where the $\alpha_{j,n}$ are to be determined from the known moments $\phi_{j,n}(\Lambda_g)$. An expansion such as Eq. (5.7.20) is limited to a certain range of x since for very deep penetrations the number of terms necessary becomes prohibitive.

A better approach is to assume the spatial behavior of the flux is given predominantly by some function of $f(x)$; then we may assume an expansion in the form

$$\phi_n(x, \Lambda_g) = f(x) \sum_{j=0}^{J} \alpha_{j,n}(\Lambda_g)\, x^j , \qquad (5.7.21)$$

where the summation represents a modulation of the predominant behavior. The hope is that for a properly chosen $f(x)$, we need only a few terms in the series expansion. In practice it is convenient to use an expansion in the form

$$\phi_n(x, \Lambda_g) = f(x) \sum_{j=0}^{J} b_{j,n}(\Lambda_g)\, p_j(x) , \qquad (5.7.22)$$

where the $p_j(x)$ are polynomials of degree j in x. The purpose is to select the $p_j(x)$ as orthogonal polynomials with respect to the weighting function $f(x)$, i.e.,

$$\int dx\, p_j(x)\, f(x)\, p_k(x) = \delta_{jk} . \qquad (5.7.23)$$

Such a choice facilitates the calculation of the coefficients $b_{n,j}$. (We remark that not all weight functions possess a set of orthogonal polynomials; however, an adjoint set of polynomials $p_j^*(x)$ may be defined such that a relation similar to Eq. (5.7.23) exists.)

As an example of the utility of the above approach, we consider the following physically reasonable case: for deep penetrations the flux to first order is given by the unscattered contribution, and so we use the weighting function

$$f(x) = e^{-\sigma_0 x}; \qquad x > 0;$$
$$f(x) = 0; \qquad x < 0; \qquad (5.7.24)$$

where the quantity σ_0 is the total macroscopic cross section at the energy of the source, assumed monoenergetic, in the expansion (5.7.23). The orthogonal expansion polynomials are then the Laguerre polynomials $L_j(\sigma_0 x)$. (See Appendix D.)

To determine the coefficients $b_{j,n}(\Lambda_g)$, we proceed as follows: we rewrite Eq. (5.7.22) in the form

$$\phi_n(x, \Lambda_g) = e^{-\sigma_0 x} \sum_{j=0}^{J} b_{j,n}(\Lambda_g) L_j(\sigma_0 x) . \qquad (5.7.25)$$

We multiply by $L_k(\sigma_0 x)$ and integrate to obtain

$$b_{j,n}(\Lambda_g) = \int_0^\infty dx \, \phi_n(x, \Lambda_g) L_j(\sigma_0 x) . \qquad (5.7.26)$$

We recall that the coefficients $\phi_{j,n}(\Lambda_g)$ are defined as

$$\phi_{j,n}(\Lambda_g) = \frac{\sigma_0^{j+1}}{j!} \int_0^\infty dx \, \phi_n(x, \Lambda_g) x^j . \qquad (5.7.27)$$

Obviously we can expand $L_j(\sigma_0 x)$ in terms of x and find the relation between $b_{j,n}(\Lambda_g)$ and the $\phi_{j,n}(\Lambda_g)$. Without performing the details, it is evident that a relation of the form

$$b_{j,n}(\Lambda_g) = \sum_{k=0}^{j} \gamma_k \phi_{k,n}(\Lambda_g) , \qquad (5.7.28)$$

is obtained, where the γ_k are known. Equation (5.7.26) is then the desired result. Other expansions give rise to different series, but are computed the same way.

The procedures for testing the expansions are very interesting. The first crude test is to see if higher terms in j contribute significantly. After the magnitude of $b_{j,n}$ is sufficiently small, the series is truncated. The amount of truncation error acceptable depends upon the nature of the problem under investigation.

A second procedure is to study the effect of the weighting function for a fixed number of terms. Let us assume the weight function $e^{-\sigma_0 x}$ has been used and the number of terms J determined by some truncation criterion. If J is sufficiently large, then the results should be relatively independent of σ_0. That is, for a large enough number of terms, the weight function may be varied and the computed results should still agree to within a small tolerance. In practice, the coefficient σ_0 is modified to $\alpha \sigma_0$, and α is varied near $\alpha = 1$ (hence the test is called an α test). In the region of α where the results are the same to within a small error, one concludes the expansion is valid. Further variations and applications of the moments method are found in the references.

References

There are several excellent books that deal with the neutron transport equation, the spherical harmonics expansion, and other procedures. References *1*, *2*, and *3* are particularly recommended. The spherical harmonics and other orthogonal series are considered in *4*. The remaining references relate to special items discussed in the text. An excellent collection of the coefficients for use in the S_n method for various geometries may be found in reference *13*. Reference *14* contains an excellent discussion of the solution of transient problems involving the transport equation. References *15–21* contain both the basic derivation of the moments method and many detailed examples of the use of the technique.

1. Davison, B., "Neutron Transport Theory." Oxford Univ. Press, London and New York, 1956.
2. Weinberg, A. M., and Wigner, E. P., "The Physical Theory of Neutron Chain Reactors." Univ. of Chicago Press, Chicago, 1958.
3. Meghreblian, R. V., and Holmes, D. K., "Reactor Analysis." McGraw-Hill, New York, 1960.
4. Morse, P. M., and Feshbach, H., "Methods of Theoretical Physics," Vol. II. McGraw-Hill, New York, 1953.
5. Marchuk, G. I., "Numerical Methods for Nuclear Reactor Calculations" (translation). Consultants Bureau, New York, 1959.
6. Gelbard, E., Davis, J., and Pearson, J., *Nuclear Sci. Eng.* **5**, 36 (1959).
7. Yvon, J. J., *Nuclear Eng.* **4**, 305 (1957).
8. Ziering, S., and Schiff, D., *Nuclear Sci. Eng.* **3**, 635 (1958).
9. Wick, G. C., *Zeits. Phys.* **121**, 702 (1943).
10. Kopal, Z., "Numerical Analysis." Chapman and Hall, London, 1955.
11. Hildebrand, F. B., "Introduction to Numerical Analysis." McGraw-Hill, New York, 1956.
12. Carlson, B., Solution of the transport equation by S_n approximation. LA-1891 (1955).
13. Carlson, B., Numerical solution of neutron transport problems. *Proc. Symp. Appl. Math.* **11**, 219–232.
14. Richtmeyer, R. D., "Difference Methods for Initial-Value Problems." Wiley (Interscience), New York, 1957.

15. Spencer, L. V., and Fano, U., *J. Research Natl. Bur. of Standards* **46**, 446 (1951).
16. Goldstein, H., and Wilkins, Jr., J. E., Calculations of the penetration of gamma rays. NYO-3075 (1954).
17. Goldstein, H., "The Attenuation of Gamma Rays and Neutrons in Reactor Shields," U.S. Government Printing Office, Washington, D.C.
18. Certaine, J., A solution of the neutron transport equation. Introduction and Part I. NYO-3081 (1954).
19. Certaine, J., A solution of the neutron transport equation. Part II: NDA Univac Moment Calculations. NYO-6268 (1955).
20. Certaine, J., A solution of the neutron transport equation. Part III: Reconstruction of a function from its moments. NYO-6270 (1956).
21. Fano, U., Spencer, L. V., and Berger, M. J., Penetration and diffusion of X-rays. *Encyclopedia of Physics* **38**, Part 2. Springer, Berlin.

Problems

1. Show that

$$\phi_1^{\pm 1}(\mathbf{r}, t, v) = \sqrt{\frac{3}{8\pi}} \left[\pm J_x(\mathbf{r}, t, v) - i J_y(\mathbf{r}, t, v) \right],$$

$$\phi_1^0(\mathbf{r}, t, v) = \sqrt{\frac{3}{4\pi}} J_z(\mathbf{r}, t, v),$$

$\mathbf{J}(\mathbf{r}, t, v)$ being the current of neutrons at point $\mathbf{r}$, at time t of speed v, as defined by Eq. (A.11). Express the directional flux in terms of the scalar flux and the current. This expression is accurate, of course, only to zeroth and first order.

2. Derive the diffusion equation from the P_1 approximation.

3. Derive the spherical harmonic expansion in three dimensions. To this end, expand the directional flux as follows:

$$\phi(\mathbf{r}, t, v, \mathbf{\Omega}) = \sum_{n=0}^{\infty} \sum_{k=-n}^{n} Y_n^k(\mu, \varphi) \phi_n^k(\mathbf{r}, t, v).$$

Expand the source rate density similarly. Prove that

$$\mathbf{\Omega} \cdot \mathbf{\nabla} = \sin \theta \cos \varphi \, \frac{\partial}{\partial x} + \sin \theta \sin \varphi \, \frac{\partial}{\partial y} + \cos \theta \, \frac{\partial}{\partial z}$$

Next, show that

$$- \left[\frac{1}{v} \frac{\partial}{\partial t} + \sigma(v) \right] \phi_l^m(\mathbf{r}, t, v) + S_l^m(\mathbf{r}, t, v)$$

$$+ 2\pi \int_0^\infty dv' f_l(v', v) c(v') \sigma(v') \phi_l^m(\mathbf{r}, t, v')$$

$$= \frac{1}{2}\left[\frac{\partial}{\partial x} - \iota\frac{\partial}{\partial y}\right]$$

$$\times \left[-\sqrt{\frac{(l-m+2)(l-m+1)}{(2l+3)(2l+1)}}\,\phi_{l+1}^{m-1} + \sqrt{\frac{(l+m)(l+m-1)}{(2l+1)(2l-1)}}\,\phi_{l-1}^{m-1}\right]$$

$$+ \frac{1}{2}\left[\frac{\partial}{\partial x} + \iota\frac{\partial}{\partial y}\right]$$

$$\times \left[\sqrt{\frac{(l+m+2)(l+m+1)}{(2l+3)(2l+1)}}\,\phi_{l+1}^{m+1} - \sqrt{\frac{(l-m)(l-m-1)}{(2+1)(2l-1)}}\,\phi_{l-1}^{m+1}\right]$$

$$+ \frac{\partial}{\partial z}\left[\sqrt{\frac{(l+m+1)(l-m+1)}{(2l+3)(2l+1)}}\,\phi_{l+1}^{m} + \sqrt{\frac{(l+m)(l-m)}{(2l+1)(2l-1)}}\,\phi_{l-1}^{m}\right],$$

where

$$-l \leqslant m \leqslant l, \qquad f_l(v', v) = \int_{-1}^{1} d(\cos\Theta_0)\, P_l(\cos\Theta_0)\, f(v', v, \Theta_0),$$

and $f(v', v, \Theta_0)$ is the probability of a neutron of speed v' being scattered through the angle Θ_0 in the laboratory system and emerging with a speed v. The following relations will be useful in the above derivation:

$$N_n^k P_n^k(\mu)\,\frac{e^{\iota\varphi(k+1)}}{2}\,\sin\theta$$

$$= \frac{1}{2}\left[\sqrt{\frac{(n+k+2)(n+l+1)}{(2n+3)(2n+1)}}\,Y_{n+1}^{k+1}(\Omega) - \sqrt{\frac{(n-k)(n-k-1)}{(2n+1)(2n-1)}}\,Y_{n-1}^{k+1}(\Omega)\right].$$

$$N_n^k P_n^k(\mu)\,\frac{e^{\iota\varphi(k-1)}}{2}\,\sin\theta$$

$$= \frac{1}{2}\left[-\sqrt{\frac{(n-k+2)(n-k+1)}{(2n+1)(2n+3)}}\,Y_{n+1}^{k-1}(\Omega) + \sqrt{\frac{(n+k-1)(n+k)}{(2n+1)(2n-1)}}\,Y_{n-1}^{k-1}(\Omega)\right].$$

$$N_n^k P_n^k e^{\iota k\varphi}\cos\theta$$

$$= \sqrt{\frac{(n+k)(n-k)}{(2n+1)(2n-1)}}\,Y_{n-1}^{k}(\Omega) + \sqrt{\frac{(n+k+1)(n-k+1)}{(2n+3)(2n+1)}}\,Y_{n+1}^{k}(\Omega).$$

$$N_n^k = \sqrt{\frac{(2n+1)(n-k)!}{4\pi(n+k)!}}.$$

$$Y_n^k(\mu, \varphi) = N_n^k P_n^k(\mu)e^{\iota k\varphi}.$$

4. Find the propagation constants in the P_1 and P_3 approximations for one dimensional problems. In other words, find κ in the solutions $\phi_l = c_l e^{\kappa\sigma z}$ of the homogeneous parts of the P_1 or P_3 equations. Express the directional flux in terms of ϕ_0 and ϕ_1 in the P_1 approximation and in terms of ϕ_0, ϕ_1, ϕ_2, and ϕ_3 in the P_3 approximation.

5. Find the flux in the P_3 approximation for an infinite, isotropic plane source at $z = 0$ in an infinite medium.

6. Show that the condition (5.1.14) implies equality of each coefficient of the expansion (5.1.4).

7. Find the directional flux in the P_3 approximation and the extrapolation length for a nonabsorbing, isotropically scattering, homogeneous medium that fills the half space to the right of the origin. Vacuum occupies the space to the left of the origin. The extrapolation distance is the distance from the interface at which the *asymptotic* component of the nondirectional flux extrapolates linearly to zero. Assume a source of neutrons far to the right in the scattering medium. This source creates a current that travels towards the left.

8. Show that the second order double P_n approximation is as follows:

$$
\begin{cases}
D_{\pm}\phi_0^{\pm} + \dfrac{1}{2}\dfrac{d}{dx}\phi_1^{\pm} = \dfrac{1}{2}\sigma_s[\phi_0^+ + \phi_0^-] + S_0\,, \\[2ex]
\dfrac{1}{2}\dfrac{d\phi_0^{\pm}}{dx} + 3D_{\pm}\phi_1^{\pm} + \dfrac{d}{dz}\phi_2^{\pm} = 0, \\[2ex]
\dfrac{d}{dx}\phi_1^{\pm} + 5D_{\pm}\phi_2^{\pm} = 0,
\end{cases}
$$

where $D_{\pm} = \pm\frac{1}{2}\,d/dx + \sigma$; and

$$
\left[3D_{\pm}^3 - \frac{9}{20}D_{\pm}\frac{d^2}{dx^2}\right]\phi_0^{\pm} = \left[3D_{\pm}^2 - \frac{1}{5}\frac{d^2}{dx^2}\right]\left[\sigma_s \frac{(\phi_0^+ + \phi_0^-)}{2} + S_0\right],
$$

and

$$
\left[\frac{d^6}{dx^6} + (24\sigma_s - 84\sigma)\,\sigma\,\frac{d^4}{dx^4} + \left(420\sigma - \frac{860}{3}\sigma_s\right)\sigma^3\frac{d^2}{dx^2}\right.
$$

$$
\left. + 400(\sigma_s - \sigma)\,\sigma^5\right]\frac{[\phi_0^+ + \phi_0^-]}{2} = \left[-24\sigma^2\frac{d^4}{dx^4} + \frac{860}{3}\sigma^4\frac{d^2}{dx^2} - 400\sigma^6\right]S_0\,.
$$

9. Solve Milne's problem in the P_1^+ approximation. The Milne problem consists of a pure scatterer filling half of all space and a vacuum in the other half of all space. Mono-energetic neutrons are incident upon the interface from the medium and leak out. The problem is to find the directional flux within the medium. Suppose that the medium fills the right half of all space. Note that the solution of an ordinary differential equation with constant coefficients consists of a linear combination of exponentials with arguments that must be determined plus a particular solution. This particular solution is a linear function of x, because the coefficient of $\phi_0^+ + \phi_0^-$ vanishes in our present case. Assume then the solution in the form

$$
\phi = c_1 + c_2 x + c_3 e^{-\kappa x}.
$$

(a) Show that the characteristic equation for the roots is $\kappa = \sqrt{12}\,\sigma$.

(b) Why may one of the coefficients c_1, c_2, c_3 be arbitrarily chosen? Pick $c_2 = 1$.

(c) What boundary conditions must be satisfied? Express these conditions in terms of $\phi_0^\pm(0)$, $\phi_1^\pm(0)$, where $x = 0$ is the plane of the interface.

(d) Find the c_i.

(e) Choose $\phi_0^\pm(x) = B_{10}^\pm + B_{20}^\pm \sigma x + B_{30}^\pm e^{-\kappa x}$; $\phi_1^\pm(x) = B_{11}^\pm + B_{21}^\pm \sigma x + B_{31}^\pm e^{-\kappa x}$.

Show that:

$$B_{21}^\pm = 0, \qquad B_{20}^\pm = 1$$

$$B_{10}^\pm = c_1 \mp \frac{1}{2}$$

$$B_{11}^\pm = -\frac{1}{6}$$

$$B_{30}^\pm = \frac{(\mp \kappa/2 + \sigma)\, c_3 \sigma}{(\mp \kappa/2 + \sigma)^2 - \kappa^2/12}$$

$$B_{31}^\pm = \frac{(\kappa/6)\, c_3 \sigma}{(\mp \kappa/2 + \sigma)^2 - \kappa^2/12}$$

$$\begin{cases} B_{30}^+ + B_{10}^+ = 0 \\ B_{31}^+ + B_{11}^+ = 0 \end{cases}$$

(f) Find c_1, c_3, B_{30}^-, B_{31}^- and show that

$$n = 0.71132 + \sigma x - 0.13397 \exp(-3.464\sigma x),$$

$$n^-(0, \mu) = \frac{1}{4\pi}\left[c_1 + \frac{1}{2} + B_{30}^- + 3(2\mu + 1)\left(-\frac{1}{6} + B_{31}^-\right)\right].$$

10. Show that the weight factors w_j in Eq. (5.4.10) are positive.

11. Show that the truncation error in the S_n method is reduced by spatially integrating in the direction in which the neutrons travel. Consider the problem of neutron penetration of a thick slab on which a current J_i is incident, in which S is the source density, and from which a current J_e emerges. Let E be the attenuation of neutrons through the slab. Relate J_e, J_i, E, and S to each other for the two directions and consider the errors resulting in the answer for small errors in the independent variables.

12. Show that in the S_2 approximation in which the intervals are equal

n	ϕ_n	ϕ_{n-1}	μ_n	a_n	$\bar{a}_n$	b_n	c_n	Equation
0	ϕ_0	0	-1	-1		0	1	(5.5.8)
1	ϕ_1	ϕ_0	0	$-\dfrac{1}{3}$	$-\dfrac{2}{3}$	$\dfrac{4}{3}$	2	(5.5.8)
2	ϕ_2	ϕ_1	$+1$	$\dfrac{2}{3}$	$\dfrac{1}{3}$	$\dfrac{4}{3}$	2	(5.5.9)

and in the S_4 approximation in which all intervals are equal

n	ϕ_n	ϕ_{n-1}	μ_n	a_n	$\bar{a}_n$	b_n	c_n	Equation
0	ϕ_0	0	-1	-1		0	1	(5.5.8)
1	ϕ_1	ϕ_0	$-\dfrac{1}{2}$	$-\dfrac{2}{3}$	$-\dfrac{5}{6}$	$\dfrac{5}{3}$	2	(5.5.8)
2	ϕ_2	ϕ_1	0	$-\dfrac{1}{6}$	$-\dfrac{1}{3}$	$\dfrac{11}{3}$	2	(5.5.8)
3	ϕ_3	ϕ_2	$+\dfrac{1}{2}$	$+\dfrac{1}{3}$	$\dfrac{1}{6}$	$\dfrac{11}{3}$	2	(5.5.9)
4	ϕ_3	ϕ_3	$+1$	$+\dfrac{5}{6}$	$\dfrac{2}{3}$	$\dfrac{5}{3}$	2	(5.5.9)

13. Find the coefficients a_{nj}, b_{nj}, c_{nj}, d_{nj}, a'_{nj}, b'_{nj}, c'_{nj}, d'_{nj} in Eqs. (5.5.8) and (5.5.9).

14. The modifications due to anisotropic scattering are to be explored in this problem. Let us assume one dimensional geometry and let this one spatial dimension be specified by r. The source S will be a function $S(r, \mu)$ of both r and the cosine μ between the radius vector $\mathbf{r}$ and the velocity $\mathbf{v}$ of the neutron, and we assume there are no external sources not proportional to the flux. Define

$$P_{n,\alpha} = \int_{\mu_{n-1}}^{\mu_n} d\mu' P_\alpha(\mu')$$

$$\sigma_{s\alpha}^{g'g} = \int_{-1}^{1} d\bar{\mu}\, \sigma_{s\alpha}^{g'g}(\bar{\mu})\, P_\alpha(\bar{\mu}).$$

Let $a_{\alpha n'}$ be a coefficient such that

$$\phi_\alpha^l(r) = \sum_{n'=0}^{\alpha} a_{\alpha,n'}\phi_{n'}^l(r),$$

where $\phi_\alpha^l(r)$ is a spherical harmonic component of the directional flux as given by Eq. (5.1.4) and $\phi_n^l(r)$ is an S_n component of the directional flux as given by Eqs. (5.5.2) and (5.5.2a). In other words, $[a_{\alpha n}]$ is the matrix transforming the S_n components of the directional flux into the spherical harmonic components. Show that

$$S_n^g(r) = \frac{1}{4\pi} \sum_{g'} \int_{\mu_{n-1}}^{\mu_n} d\mu \int_{-1}^{1} d\mu' \int_{0}^{2\pi} d\varphi'\, \sigma_s^{g'g}(\bar{\mu})\phi^{g'}(r, \mu')$$

$$= \sum_{g'} \sum_{\alpha=0}^{\infty} \sum_{n'=0}^{\alpha} P_{n\alpha}\sigma_s^{g'g}\, \frac{2\alpha+1}{4}\, a_{\alpha n'}\phi_{n'}^{g'}(r), \qquad n = 0, 1, 2, ..., N.$$

Show for the S_2 approximation that

$$
\begin{bmatrix} S_0^{g'g}(r) \\[2mm] S_1^{g'g}(r) \\[2mm] S_2^{g'g}(r) \end{bmatrix} = \begin{bmatrix} 1 & -1 & 1 \\[2mm] 1 & -\dfrac{1}{2} & 0 \\[2mm] 1 & -\dfrac{1}{2} & 0 \end{bmatrix} \begin{bmatrix} \sigma_{s0}^{g'g} & 0 & 0 \\[2mm] 0 & \sigma_{s1}^{g'g} & 0 \\[2mm] 0 & 0 & \sigma_{s2}^{g'g} \end{bmatrix} \begin{bmatrix} \dfrac{1}{8} & 1 & \dfrac{1}{8} \\[2mm] -\dfrac{1}{4} & 0 & \dfrac{1}{4} \\[2mm] \dfrac{5}{32} & -\dfrac{5}{16} & \dfrac{5}{32} \end{bmatrix} \begin{bmatrix} \phi_0^g(r) \\[2mm] \phi_1^g(r) \\[2mm] \phi_2^g(r) \end{bmatrix} ,
$$

where $S_n^{g'g}(r)$ is such that

$$ S_n^g(r) = \sum_{g'} S_n^{g'g}(r). $$

Note that $S_o^{g'g}(r) = S^{g'g}(r, -1)$. This source is now used in the S_n approximation as the source term.

15. Formulate the S_n method in matrix form as a generalized eigenvalue problem.

16. Construct a flow diagram of the S_2 method of calculating the critical size of a sphere consisting of two different material regions, a multiplicative core and a nonmultiplicative reflector. Use 15 zones in the core and 10 in the reflector, and 3 speed groups. Test for convergence by use of a source at the center. Assume all data needed are in fast memory. In each box where a calculation is to be made, indicate the symbol for the quantity to be calculated and write the formula number in the box used to calculate the symbol. The logic, control, tests used, transfers, and the like are to be indicated on the flow diagram. Do not diagram the calculation of the formulas themselves.

17. Show that Eq. (5.5.26) is satisfied upon summing Eq. (5.5.21) over all n if the b_n satisfy Eq. (5.5.27).

18. Work out the time independent S_n method for plane geometry. Develop the time dependent S_n method for spherical geometry.

19. Find a dual between the time dependent S_n method for the transport equation for infinitely long cylindrical geometry and the time dependent, multispeed transport equation for spherical geometry. Establish a duality between the time independent transport equation for an infinite cylinder and the time independent multispeed transport equation for spherical geometry.

20. The purpose of this problem is the development of the S_n method for cylindrical geometry. Note the expression for $\mathbf{\Omega} \cdot \nabla \phi$ from problem 3 of Appendix A. Assume an isotropic source density $S(r, z, t, v)$. Show that

$$ S(r, z, t, v) = \frac{1}{2\pi} \sum_{g'} \sigma^{g'g} \int_{-1}^{1} d\mu' \int_{-1}^{1} \frac{d\eta' \phi(r, z, \eta', t, v^{g'}, \mu')}{\sqrt{1 - \eta'^2}} . $$

Write down the appropriate time independent transport equation for cylindrical geometry and establish a dual between it, suitably quantized, and the time dependent, multispeed, transport equation for spherical geometry by putting related variables into correspondence. Use the Gauss quadrature formula for the angle variable not treated by the S_n approximation. Determine the order of the Gauss quadrature, i.e., the number of roots required and the order of the corresponding Legendre polynomial, to be consistent with the S_n approximation.

VI

THE MONTE CARLO METHOD

6.1 Introduction

The Monte Carlo method is a statistical method for solving deterministic or statistical problems. Statistical estimates are found for quantities of interest. The estimate is obtained by the repetitive playing of a game. The game played is an analog of the physical problem of interest. The game is specified by a set of deterministic rules related to and sets of probabilities governing the occurrences of physical phenomena of interest.

A very simple example will illustrate the nature of the Monte Carlo method. Consider the problem of determining whether or not a conventional die is unbiased, i.e., whether or not it is loaded in favor of one or more faces. A physical determination of any bias could be made by measurements of various types. For instance, measuring the sides to see if the die was a true cube, locating the center of mass, and measuring the principal moments of inertia. The measurements lead to a deterministic answer regarding the bias or lack of bias. An alternative procedure is empirical in nature. Suppose the die is rolled many times and the occurrence of various faces in the upright position recorded. A statistical determination of the probability of obtaining any particular face will permit an analysis of any bias in the die. This second procedure could be termed a Monte Carlo study.

The above example is trivial in theory but serves to illustrate the conceptual simplicity of the Monte Carlo method. There are several points to consider in the example which are universal to all Monte Carlo studies. First, although the problem has a deterministic solution, a statistical procedure was adopted which consisted of the repetitive playing of a game. The game was so constructed that the desired result could be found. In the example, the game to be played is straightforward.

In more complicated problems the analog to be constructed is more complex. In any case, it is characteristic of the Monte Carlo method that one replaces a deterministic problem by an analog which consists of a reasonably straightforward game to be played many times.

The second point about the example is the method of playing the game, i.e., rolling the die. Obviously, if the results are to be meaningful the actual roll of the die must be random, i.e., the process of rolling must not favor any particular face of the die. In more complex problems, it may be necessary to play the game according to some given probability distribution function.

Third, the desired results are found by statistical study. We should expect variations and fluctuations in the answers obtained. If the die was unbiased, we expect the mean occurrence of any particular face to be $1/6$. However, the mean value will only be approached asymptotically. The statistical nature of the results is inherent in all Monte Carlo problems.

Our second example concerns the transport of neutrons within a reactor. In this case the reactor's construction may be simulated within a digital computer. The neutrons within the reactor may traverse or attempt to traverse various materials, such as the moderator, fuel elements, cladding, and so forth. When penetrating these materials, the neutron may experience various nuclear events, such as elastic collision, fissions, absorption, and so on. The sequence of events experienced by each neutron is called its history. Interesting pertinent details may be recorded during the history of each neutron, and when enough histories have been followed, a census of these details recorded earlier may be compiled into statistical averages over the population studied. In following a particle we shall use Newton's laws to determine its trajectory. Neutrons, being neutral, move in straight lines with constant velocity. During the course of motion, the neutron may experience a nuclear collision. In such an encounter, only the probabilities with which various events take place are known. To decide which of them occurs, a random number is used (see Section 6.2 for definition, etc.). For example, one random number may be used to decide between a radiative capture and an elastic scattering, and a second random number may be used to determine the direction of the emergent neutron if an elastic scattering occurred. Conservation of momentum and energy may then be used to find the speed and energy of the emergent neutron.

The Monte Carlo method is tremendously flexible in that almost any physical effect and problem can be treated. It is applicable to transport problems, the evaluation of multiple integrals, the composition of music, problems in economics, and war games. However, the Monte Carlo method is not well adapted to the direct study of problems in which many particles simultaneously interact, e.g., the mutually induced oscillation of electrons and ions in a plasma. The use of the Monte Carlo method is indicated for problems involving complicated geometries, for the study of systems only a few mean free paths in size, for the calculation of the effects of beam holes or control elements, for the computations of resonance escape probabilities, and the like.

In spite of its power, the Monte Carlo method should only be used where there is no other method available. Because of the use of random numbers, the Monte Carlo method is seldom as accurate in practice as other nonstatistical methods. Since the statistical fluctuations decrease only as the square root of the number of particles studied and because a large number of histories must be followed, a large amount of computer time is needed to get reasonable accuracy. Further, the logic of a coded program for a problem of some complexity is more intricate than that for almost any other coded program.

It is usually difficult to estimate the accuracy of a Monte Carlo calculation. The fluctuations in the results found after a large number of histories may be used to this end, but extreme care must be used to be sure the fluctuations are truly random. Each neutron must be followed for many lifetimes. Several generations are required to erase statistical fluctuations in an earlier population, such as an arbitrarily selected initial distribution.

The aim of this chapter is to illustrate the Monte Carlo method, particularly as applied to problems of reactor analysis. In order to understand the method, it is necessary to consider the problem of constructing the analog, selection from distributions, and some elementary statistics. In the next sections we consider the selection from the various distributions. We then review some basic statistics and the central limit theorem upon which most Monte Carlo studies are based. Next, we consider some examples of constructing the analog to certain problems. Finally, we consider some techniques for modifying the basic game in order to improve the method.

6.2 Random Numbers

In almost all Monte Carlo studies it is necessary to use numbers obtained from the random distribution, i.e., random numbers. Consider the interval $a \leqslant x \leqslant b$. The random distribution function for the interval is defined as

$$f(x)\, \varDelta x = \frac{1}{b-a}\, \varDelta x, \tag{6.2.1}$$

i.e., a flat distribution. Since any value of x in this distribution is as likely as any other x, the distribution is called random. A number selected from the distribution (6.2.1) is called a random number. It is usually convenient to consider random numbers in the interval $0 \leqslant x \leqslant 1$, in which case

$$f(x) = 1 . \tag{6.2.2}$$

The selection of numbers from the distribution (6.2.2) may be accomplished in several ways in a digital computer. One consists in storing a large table of random numbers, which are obtained otherwise than by machine. Usually so many random numbers are required that insufficient memory space exists to hold a table.

Arithmetic procedures are used almost exclusively at present. The procedures all involve arithmetic operations with numbers and do not generate truly random numbers. The numbers computed by such methods are called pseudorandom since each of the techniques yields predictable chains of numbers and hence cannot be truly random. However, the methods do generate numbers which are approximately random as determined by their distribution function, the occurrence of particular digits, digit pairs, etc. The methods do provide large chains of numbers which can be assumed random. Furthermore, the predictability of a sequence of numbers is not really a disadvantage, since this predictability permits rerunning of problems for testing or debugging purposes.

One of the many methods of generating random numbers will be discussed: the congruential multiplicative method. This method is the most frequently used. Successive random numbers are generated by the algorithm

$$x_{n+1} = \alpha x_n (\bmod N) , \tag{6.2.3}$$

where n is the iterate number, α is a scale factor, and N is an integer.

The selection of the parameters α, x_0, and N is based upon the following observations. First, the integer N is taken to be a little larger than the digit capacity of the computer so that all of the x_n are scaled between $0 \leqslant x_n \leqslant 1$, for convenience. The scale factor should be so chosen that the period of the string x_n is very long. The selection of appropriate scale factors may be studied by classical methods of number theory. Such a study is well beyond the scope of this book (see, however, Reference 11). For binary machines α is usually taken to be

$$\alpha = 5^g , \tag{6.2.4}$$

where g is the largest odd integer for which α is less than a full word in the machine. If the machine has p binary bits, if the appropriate value of α is chosen, and if $x_0 = 1$ (mod 5), then it can be shown that the resultant string of pseudorandom numbers has a period of approximately 2^{p-2} (Reference *11*). For a 36 bit machine the period is of the order of 10^{10}, which seems adequate for most purposes. Strings of different length may be found by modifying various factors in the multiplicative algorithm (6.2.3).

6.3 Distribution Functions

Decisions in Monte Carlo problems must often be made not on the basis that some phenomenon surely occurs, but rather that the given phenomenon occurs in accord with a given distribution function. The distribution of occurrences of an event is usually a more complicated function than the simple flat or random distribution. In this section we discuss methods of selection from distribution functions. We consider first a few elementary definitions and then techniques for selection.

Distribution functions are of two types: integral and differential probability distributions. The probability $f(x)\Delta x$ that the random variable x has a value between x and $x + \Delta x$ is called the differential distribution function and also the probability distribution function, and is frequently abbreviated as p.d.f. If the variable is defined in the range $a \leqslant x \leqslant b$, then $f(x)$ must be such that

$$\int_a^b dx f(x) = 1 . \tag{6.3.1}$$

The probability $F(x)$ that the random variable x' is less than x is called the integral distribution function or the cumulative distribution function, sometimes abbreviated as c.d.f. The c.d.f. is defined as

$$F(x) = \int_a^x dx' f(x') . \tag{6.3.2}$$

Obviously, since the probability that something happens is unity,

$$F(b) = \int_a^b dx' f(x') = 1 . \tag{6.3.3}$$

An example of a p.d.f. and the corresponding c.d.f. is shown in Fig. 6.3.1.
Since a probability is always positive, i.e., since

$$F(x) \geqslant 0, \qquad a \leqslant x \leqslant b , \tag{6.3.4}$$

it follows that $F(x)$ is a monotonically increasing function of x. Since the probability that x takes on some value less than or equal to a is zero, then $F(x)$ must be zero for $x \leqslant a$, as Eq. (6.3.2) indicates.

Distribution functions of more than one variable may be defined by analogous means. Thus, if $f(x, y)$ is the p.d.f. for the random variables $a \leqslant x \leqslant b, c \leqslant y \leqslant d$, then

$$F(x, y) = \int_a^x dx' \int_a^y dy' f(x', y') . \qquad (6.3.5)$$

The function $f(x, y)$ is called the joint p.d.f., whereas $F(x, y)$ is called the joint c.d.f. Many related distribution functions may be defined from the joint distribution functions.

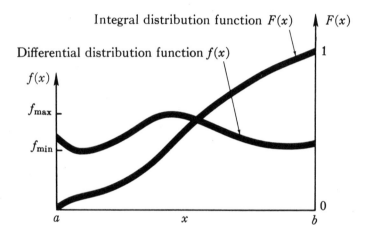

FIG. 6.3.1. Differential and integral distribution functions of one variable.

The selection of a variable distributed according to a given probability distribution is of central interest in Monte Carlo investigations. One of the several ways is as follows: If $f(x)$ and $F(x)$ represent the p.d.f. and c.d.f. respectively of a random variable x, also called a stochastic variable, if κ is a random number distributed between 0 and 1, and if x is such that

$$F(x) = \kappa , \qquad (6.3.6)$$

then for each κ there is a corresponding x, and the variable x is distributed according to the distribution $f(x)$. To prove this statement let $p(\kappa) = 1$ denote the probability distribution function for the random variable κ. For each κ in the range κ to $\kappa + \Delta\kappa$ there is a corresponding x in the range x to $x + \Delta x$. Denote the probability distribution for x as $g(x)$. We now show that for x as given by Eq. (6.3.6), the p.d.f., $g(x)$, is in fact $f(x)$. We have

$$g(x)\, \Delta x = p(\kappa)\, \Delta \kappa = \Delta \kappa = F(x + \Delta x) - F(x) , \qquad (6.3.7)$$

and hence

$$g(x) = \frac{dF(x)}{dx} = f(x) . \qquad (6.3.8)$$

Therefore, the stochastic variable

$$x = F^{-1}(\kappa) \qquad (6.3.9)$$

is distributed according to the p.d.f. $f(x)$. Further, the function F^{-1} always exists.

As an example of the use of the above result, consider the distribution

$$f(x) = \alpha e^{-\alpha x}, \qquad 0 \leqslant x \leqslant \infty . \qquad (6.3.10)$$

The corresponding c.d.f. is

$$F(x) = 1 - e^{-\alpha x} . \qquad (6.3.11)$$

To generate values of x distributed according to Eq. (6.3.10), we first generate a random number κ and compute x by the prescription

$$x = -(1/\alpha) \ln(1 - \kappa) . \qquad (6.3.12)$$

Note that if κ is randomly distributed from 0 to 1, then $1 - \kappa$ is randomly distributed from 1 to 0; hence we might as well use the formula

$$x = -(1/\alpha) \ln \kappa . \qquad (6.3.13)$$

In many cases the cumulative distribution function $F(x)$ is so complicated that computation of the stochastic variable $x = F^{-1}(\kappa)$ is impractical. A large table of values of $F(x)$ stored in the computer is particularly useful in such a case. For a given random number κ, the corresponding value of x may be found by interpolation if necessary. If κ is such that $F(x_{j-1}) \leqslant \kappa \leqslant F(x_j)$, then linear interpolation yields

$$x = x_j - \frac{F(x_j) - \kappa}{F(x_j) - F(x_{j-1})} (x_j - x_{j-1}) . \qquad (6.3.14)$$

This linear approximation assumes x is uniformly distributed in the interval x_{j-1} to x_j (see problem 1).

A method of selection from differential distributions is the rejection method. We shall introduce it for one dimensional distributions and then illustrate for three dimensions. Let the p.d.f. be given as shown in Fig. 6.3.1. The maximum value of $f(x)$ is denoted by f_{max}, the minimum by f_{min}. Consider the rectangle bounded by a, b, f_{max}, and f_{min}. The area of the rectangle is denoted by A. For any given random number κ, the random numbers

$$s(\kappa) = (b - a)\kappa + a,$$

$$g(\kappa) = (f_{max} - f_{min})\kappa + f_{min} \qquad (6.3.15)$$

are uniformly distributed over the intervals a to b and f_{min} to f_{max}, respectively. For any two random numbers κ_1, κ_2, the associated pair $s(\kappa_1), g(\kappa_2)$ define a point randomly distributed over the rectangle. If $g > f(s)$, then the point lies above the curve of $f(x)$ and is rejected. Two new random numbers κ_3, κ_4 are found and new values of s, g are computed. Sooner or later a pair of numbers is found such that $g < f(s)$, in which case the value of s is accepted. Geometrically it is evident that the values of s accepted are distributed according to the function $f(x)$.

The relative efficiency, E, with which the values of s are accepted is given by

$$E = 1/A. \qquad (6.3.16)$$

The average number of trials needed to find an acceptable value is merely $1/E$ as may readily be seen (see problem 2). If the area A is very large compared with one, the rejection method is very inefficient. For distribution functions with large peaks, either other methods must be used or the rejection method must be modified. In general it is desirable to select from a cumulative distribution, since such a method is 100 % efficient, i.e., every κ yields an x from $f(x)$. In the usual case where F^{-1} is very difficult to compute or not explicitly known, then table look-up is used. In particular, for multidimensional distributions, table look-up is the only practical procedure. The rejection method is attractive in those cases where the efficiency is high.

The determination of the direction cosines of an isotropically scattered neutron provides a useful example of the rejection method. A neutron is isotropically scattered if the probability of passing through any one element of area of a sphere circumscribed about the point of scattering equals the probability of the neutron being scattered through any other element of equal area. Let θ be the colatitude angle and φ the azimuthal angle of the scattered neutron. Then elements of area for which $\Delta\cos\theta$ and $\Delta\varphi$ are equal will be of equal area ΔA:

$$\Delta A = \Delta \cos \theta \, \Delta\varphi . \tag{6.3.17}$$

If, now, the values of $\cos \theta$ and φ are chosen randomly and independently, then the probability of $\cos \theta$ lying in the range $\Delta \cos \theta$ and φ lying in the range $\Delta\varphi$ is

$$f(\theta, \varphi) \, \Delta \cos \theta \Delta\varphi = \frac{\Delta \cos \theta}{2} \frac{\Delta\varphi}{2\pi} , \tag{6.3.18}$$

since $-1 \leqslant \cos\theta \leqslant 1$ and $0 \leqslant \varphi \leqslant 2\pi$. For the randomly selected values of $\cos \theta$ and φ, we have

$$f(\theta, \varphi) \, \Delta A = \frac{1}{4\pi} \Delta A , \tag{6.3.19}$$

which is quite independent of either θ or φ, the condition for isotropic scattering. Thus, isotropic scattering is equivalent to $\cos\theta$ and φ being randomly distributed variables.

A number of rejection techniques are in use for the determination of the direction cosines of a random scattering. Only one will be described here, two others being left for the problems. Since a random direction is characterized by a random azimuth, such an azimuth may be selected by choosing the coordinates of a point within a unit circle randomly. If η_1 and η_2 are random numbers in the interval between -1 to $+1$, then this pair is accepted if

$$\eta_1^2 + \eta_2^2 \leqslant 1 , \tag{6.3.20}$$

for then these random numbers may be considered to describe a point within the unit circle. Otherwise, they are rejected, for they will then describe a randomly selected point within the circumscribed unit square outside the circle. Further pairs are generated until one is acceptable. The efficiency of selecting a random azimuth is seen to be $(\pi/4)1^2/1^2 = 78\,\%$. The cosine of the colatitude angle is randomly selected by identifying it with a third random number η_3 lying in the interval between -1 and $+1$. The direction cosines are then given by

$$\alpha_d = \eta_1[(1 - \eta_3^2)/(\eta_1^2 + \eta_2^2)]^{1/2} ,$$
$$\beta_d = \eta_2\alpha_d/\eta_1 , \tag{6.3.21}$$
$$\gamma_d = \eta_3 .$$

A second example of the use of the rejection technique is provided by a frequently used method of calculating the logarithm $\ln \eta_1$ of a random number. Basically the procedure consists in selecting a subinterval from the interval between 0 and 1 and of selecting a number within the subinterval chosen, both the subintervals and the number within the subinterval being chosen such that the logarithm of a random number η_1 is computed.

The subintervals are selected as follows: Let H be some number between 0 and 1. Subdivide the interval from 0 to 1 starting at 1, by marking the points $1 - H, (1 - H)^2, (1 - H)^3$, and so on, as shown in Fig. 6.3.2. Number the subintervals as illustrated, the first being labeled as 0. The length of the nth interval is then

$$(1 - H)^n - (1 - H)^{n+1} = H(1 - H)^n . \tag{6.3.22}$$

In particular the length of the 0th interval is H.

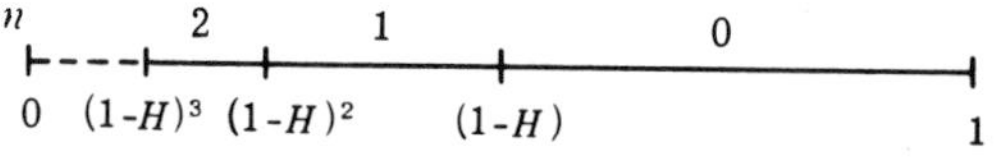

Fig. 6.3.2. Logarithmic division of the unit interval.

Now consider the following. The probability that a random number between 0 and 1 will lie within the 0th interval is H and that it lie outside this interval is $1 - H$. The probability that a series of n random numbers all between 0 and 1 not lie within the 0th interval is $(1 - H)^n$ and that the next, the $(n + 1)$st random number, lies within the 0th interval is $(1 - H)^n H$. On the other hand, the probability that a random number between 0 and 1 lie in the nth interval equals its length. Equation (6.3.22) then merely states that the probability that a random number lie within the nth interval is equal to the probability that n random numbers in sequence lie outside the 0th interval while the $(n + 1)$st random number lies inside the 0th interval. A subinterval is chosen according to the equality by determining the least number of random numbers required before one of them lies inside the 0th interval.

Attention is now turned toward determining the point of interest within the subinterval selected. If κ_2 is a random number between 0 and 1, then $(1 - H\kappa_2)$ is a random number between $1 - H$ and 1. For the particular values of n just found, the number $(1 - H)^n(1 - H\kappa_2)$ ranges completely over and only over the nth interval from $(1 - H)^{n+1}$ to $(1 - H)^n$. Since the nth interval has been chosen with a probability equal to its length by the indirect procedure mentioned above, the ensemble of numbers

$$\kappa_1 = (1 - H)^n(1 - H\kappa_2) \qquad (6.3.23)$$

is randomly distributed from 0 to 1, i.e., is a random number in the interval from 0 to 1.

The ease with which $\ln \kappa_1$ can be calculated justifies the labor in getting it.

$$\ln \kappa_1 = n \ln(1 - H) + \ln(1 - H\kappa_2) \qquad (6.3.24)$$

by Eq. (6.3.23). We may rewrite the argument of the second logarithm to facilitate convergence of a power series expansion:

$$\ln \kappa_1 = n \ln(1 - H) + \ln \left[\left(1 - \frac{H\kappa_2}{2 - H\kappa_2}\right)\left(1 + \frac{H\kappa_2}{2 - H\kappa_2}\right)^{-1} \right],$$

$$= n \ln(1 - H) - \frac{2\kappa_2 H}{2 - \kappa_2 H} \sum_{k=1}^{\infty} \frac{1}{2k + 1} \left(\frac{H\kappa_2}{2 - H\kappa_2}\right)^{2k}, \qquad (6.3.25)$$

$$= n \ln(1 - H) - \frac{2\kappa_2 H}{2 - \kappa_2 H}.$$

The present rejection method may be summarized as follows:

1. Choose a number H. Compute $\ln(1 - H)$ once and for all.

2. Generate a number of random numbers and select the first random number such that $1 - H \leqslant \kappa_3 \leqslant 1$, counting the number $n + 1$ of trials required.

3. Generate one more random number, κ_2.

4. Compute $\ln \kappa_1$ from Eq. (6.3.25).

If $H = 0.2$, then the efficiency of the method of selecting the first acceptable random number is 20 % and the error introduced by truncating the power series at one term is less than 0.5 %.

6.4 Statistical Estimation

Results of Monte Carlo calculations are inevitably expressed as average values of variables determined from many trials of some game. In order to understand whether or not a given analog game will yield the desired results and how accurate the results are, it is necessary to consider the statistical basis of the calculation. Some elementary statistical quantities are defined below, and the important central limit theorem is discussed.

Let $f(x)$ be a probability distribution function in the interval $-\infty$ to $+\infty$. If $g(x)$ is an integrable function of x, then the mean value

$$\langle g \rangle = \int_{-\infty}^{\infty} dx\, g(x)f(x) \qquad (6.4.1)$$

exists and is known as the expected value of $g(x)$. The expected value is merely the first moment of $g(x)$ about the origin. The second moment about the origin is

$$\langle g^2 \rangle = \int_{-\infty}^{\infty} dx\, g^2(x)f(x) . \qquad (6.4.2)$$

The variance is defined to be the second moment of $g(x)$ about its mean

$$V = \int_{-\infty}^{\infty} dx(g(x) - \langle g \rangle)^2 f(x) = \langle g^2 \rangle - \langle g \rangle^2 . \qquad (6.4.3)$$

The square root of the variance is called the standard deviation.

If N values of the random variable x are chosen from the p.d.f. $f(xs$ and denoted as x_i, $i = 1, 2, ..., N$, then an estimate of $\langle g \rangle$ is given a)

$$\bar{g} = \frac{1}{N} \sum_i g(x_i) . \qquad (6.4.4)$$

How good an estimate $\bar{g}$ is of $\langle g \rangle$ depends upon the number of trials N and upon the variance of $g(x)$. A bound for the estimate is given by the central limit theorem. This theorem states in part that

$$\operatorname*{Lim}_{N \to \infty} \text{ probability} \left\{ \langle g \rangle + \frac{\alpha \sqrt{V}}{\sqrt{N}} \leqslant \bar{g} \leqslant \langle g \rangle + \frac{\beta \sqrt{V}}{\sqrt{N}} \right\} = \frac{1}{\sqrt{2\pi}} \int_{\alpha}^{\beta} e^{t^2/2} , \qquad (6.4.5)$$

where α and β are constants. It is assumed that the events leading to the statistical average are independent of each other. Thus, the probability that $\bar{g}$ lie within an interval $\pm \sqrt{V}/\sqrt{N}$ of $\langle g \rangle$ is approximately 60 %, while the probability that $\bar{g}$ lie within $\pm 3\sqrt{V}/\sqrt{N}$ is approximately 99 %.

Relation (6.4.5) is an analytic statement of a rather intuitive concept, viz., that the more trials one uses in computing an average the more accurate the average is. The central limit theorem states that if many estimates of $\langle g \rangle$ are obtained, each estimate of $\langle g \rangle$ involving N trials, then the variable $\bar{g}$ is normally distributed about $\langle g \rangle$ to terms of accuracy $O(1/\sqrt{N})$.[1] Equation (6.4.5) is the limiting form of the theorem as $N \to \infty$.

For a given estimate $\bar{g}$ the mean square error, i.e., the variance V of $\bar{g}$ is

$$V(\bar{g}) = \langle (\bar{g} - \langle g \rangle)^2 \rangle = \langle \bar{g}^2 \rangle - \langle g \rangle^2 . \tag{6.4.6}$$

We are interested in $V(\bar{g})$ as a measure of the accuracy of $\bar{g}$. By Eq. (6.4.4), we have

$$\langle \bar{g}^2 \rangle = \frac{1}{N^2} \left\langle \sum_i g(x_i) \sum_j g(x_j) \right\rangle = \frac{1}{N^2} \left\langle \sum_i g^2(x_i) + \sum_{\substack{i;j \\ i \neq j}} g(x_i) g(x_j) \right\rangle . \tag{6.4.7}$$

Note that

$$\left\langle \frac{1}{N} \sum_i g^n(x_i) \right\rangle = \langle \overline{g^n} \rangle = \langle g^n \rangle . \tag{6.4.8}$$

(See proof below for $N = 1$.) By Eqs. (6.4.2) and (6.4.7) we have

$$\langle \bar{g}^2 \rangle = \frac{1}{N^2} [N \langle g^2 \rangle + N(N-1) \langle g \rangle^2] = \frac{\langle g^2 \rangle}{N} + \frac{N-1}{N} \langle g \rangle^2 . \tag{6.4.9}$$

The variance of $\bar{g}$ is thus

$$V(\bar{g}) = \frac{1}{N} [\langle g^2 \rangle - \langle g \rangle^2] = \frac{V}{N} . \tag{6.4.10}$$

The fractional square error associated with a given estimate $\bar{g}$ is

$$\epsilon^2 = \frac{1}{N} \left[\frac{\langle g^2 \rangle}{\langle g \rangle^2} - 1 \right] . \tag{6.4.11}$$

The magnitude of the error decreases as $1/\sqrt{N}$; thus to reduce the error by a factor of 10 requires 100 times as many trials. This is the essence of the difficulty with and the disadvantage of using the Monte Carlo method.

In many cases the first and second moments of $g(x)$ are unknown. In such cases the statistical data may be used to find approximate expressions for the moments. The expected value of $\bar{g}$, i.e., $\langle \bar{g} \rangle$, is given as

$$\langle \bar{g} \rangle = \frac{1}{N} \left\langle \sum_i g(x_i) \right\rangle = \frac{1}{N} \sum_i \int_{-\infty}^{\infty} dx_i f(x_i) g(x_i) = \frac{1}{N} \sum_{i=1}^{N} \langle g \rangle = \langle g \rangle . \tag{6.4.12}$$

[1] See remarks concerning the references at the end of the chapter.

The estimate $\bar{g}$ is said to be an unbiased estimate of $\langle g \rangle$ since the expected value of $\bar{g}$ is $\langle g \rangle$. However,

$$\langle \bar{g}^2 \rangle \neq \langle g \rangle^2 :$$

for from Eq. (6.4.9) we have

$$\langle g \rangle^2 = \frac{N}{N-1} \left[\langle \bar{g}^2 \rangle - \frac{\langle g^2 \rangle}{N} \right], \tag{6.4.13}$$

and hence $\bar{g}^2$ is not an unbiased estimate of $\langle g \rangle^2$. Obviously $\langle \overline{g^2} \rangle = \langle g^2 \rangle$, and hence, by Eq. (6.4.10), $V(\bar{g})$ can be approximated by

$$V(\bar{g}) \approx \frac{1}{N-1} [\overline{g^2} - \bar{g}^2], \tag{6.4.14}$$

while the fractional error may be approximated by

$$\epsilon^2 \approx \frac{1}{N-1} \left[\frac{\overline{g^2}}{\bar{g}^2} - 1 \right]. \tag{6.4.15}$$

For large N the bias is unimportant, i.e., $N - 1 \approx N$. Equations (6.4.14) and (6.4.15) may also be derived by finding the expected value of the sample variance

$$V_s = \frac{1}{N} \sum_i (g(x_i) - \bar{g})^2 \tag{6.4.16}$$

(see problem 5).

As a very elementary example of the application of the above formulas, we consider the die rolling problem. If the die is unbiased, the probability of rolling any face is $1/6$. Let the true probability of rolling a particular face be p, which will not equal $1/6$ if the die is biased. For N rolls with x successes an estimate of p is

$$\bar{p} = x/N. \tag{6.4.17}$$

The probability of obtaining x successes in N rolls is

$$f(x) = p^x (1-p)^{N-x} \frac{N!}{x!(N-x)!}. \tag{6.4.18}$$

Equation (6.4.18) follows by noting that the probability of x straight successes followed by $N - x$ failures is merely $p^x(1 - p)^{N-x}$. All possible distinct permutations then yield Eq. (6.4.18). The distribution (6.4.18) is the well-known binomial distribution.

The sample mean $\bar{p}$ is given by

$$\bar{p} = \langle x \rangle / N, \tag{6.4.19}$$

where

$$\langle x \rangle = \sum_{x=0}^{N} x f(x). \tag{6.4.20}$$

But

$$\langle x \rangle = \sum_{x=1}^{N} p^x (1-p)^{N-x} \frac{N!}{(x-1)!(N-x)!}$$

$$= Np \sum_{x=1}^{N} p^{x-1}(1-p)^{N-x} \frac{(N-1)!}{(x-1)!(N-x)!}. \tag{6.4.21}$$

With the substitution $y = x - 1$, the second form of Eq. (6.4.21) yields

$$\langle x \rangle = Np \sum_{y=0}^{N-1} p^y (1-p)^{N-1-y} \frac{(N-1)!}{y!(N-1-y)!} = Np, \tag{6.4.22}$$

since the sum is unity. We then have by Eq. (6.4.19)

$$\bar{p} = p, \tag{6.4.23}$$

as we expect.

It is easily shown that the variance of the binomial distribution is

$$V = Np(1-p) \tag{6.4.24}$$

(see problem 12). According to Eq. (6.4.10), the variance in $\bar{x}$ is then

$$V(\bar{x}) = p(1-p), \tag{6.4.25}$$

while the variance in $\bar{p}$ is

$$V(\bar{p}) = p(1-p)/N. \tag{6.4.26}$$

The magnitude of the fractional error is thus

$$|\epsilon| = \sqrt{(1-p)/Np}. \tag{6.4.27}$$

As expected intuitively we can improve the error in an estimate $\bar{p}$ by taking more trials, i.e., rolling the die more times. Notice that for small p the fractional error may be quite large; thus we need many trials and many successes for a reduced error.

In the case of neutron penetration through a shield, the probability of penetration may be so small that the error indicates the standard Monte Carlo method cannot be profitably used. In this case and certain others, it is necessary to modify the game being played so that p is increased. The objective is to reduce the variance by altering the game and hence such modifications are collectively known as variance reduction methods. We consider several such procedures in Section 6.6.

6.5   Analogs of Two Simple Problems

In this section we shall illustrate the problem of constructing a statistical game to simulate a deterministic problem by two examples. In all of the examples the utility of variance reduction techniques will become apparent.

Numerical integration by statistical procedures will serve as our first example. The rejection techniques of Section 6.3 will be applied. If the integral

$$I = \int_a^b dx \, s(x) \tag{6.5.1}$$

is to be evaluated, then a rectangle which bounds the function $s(x)$ in the interval a to b is constructed. For the moment we shall assume $s(x) \geqslant 0$ in the interval a to b. If the maximum of $s(x)$ is known to be $s_{\max}$, then the bounding rectangle is as shown in Fig. 6.5.1.

The Monte Carlo game to be played consists of generating points randomly distributed over the rectangle and of counting each point

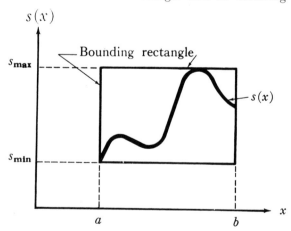

FIG. 6.5.1.   The function $s(x)$ and the bounding rectangle.

that lands beneath the curve $s(x)$. If the total number of successes is n out of N trials, then obviously

$$I = n/N \tag{6.5.2}$$

is the statistical estimate of the area. From the results of the previous section we know the fractional error associated with I is given by

$$|\epsilon| = \sqrt{(1-p)/Np} \tag{6.5.3}$$

with p defined as the ratio of I to the total area. Clearly, if p is very small, as might occur if $s(x)$ had a tall, thin peak, then the number of trials required for reasonable accuracy is prohibitive by the straightforward application of this method.

Frequently an integral of the form

$$I = \int_a^b dx\, g(x) f(x) \tag{6.5.4}$$

occurs, where

$$\int_a^b dx f(x) = 1. \tag{6.5.5}$$

Every definite integral may be factored into the form (6.5.4) and hence the integral may be interpreted to be the expected value of g, i.e.,

$$I = \langle g \rangle, \tag{6.5.6}$$

and a Monte Carlo game to evaluate I would consist of picking values of x_i distributed according to $f(x)$ and computing

$$\bar{g} = \frac{1}{N} \sum_i g(x_i). \tag{6.5.7}$$

Equation (6.5.1) is a special case of Eq. (6.5.4) with

$$f(x) = 1/(b-a), \tag{6.5.8a}$$

$$g(x) = (b-a)\, s(x). \tag{6.5.8b}$$

However, the two methods differ with regard to the scoring procedure. In the first game a score of 0 or 1 is tallied depending upon whether or not a random variable is greater than or less than $s(x_i)$. In the second game a score of $g(x_i)$ is tallied for every point x_i. The two different games obviously produce the same asymptotic values for the integral and standard deviation. The second method is somewhat more general in that it lends itself readily to variations which can be exploited to reduce the variance. We shall consider such ideas later.

Although the discussion has considered functions of only one variable, it is evident that the procedures carry over to multidimensional integrals. Indeed one would hardly consider using the Monte Carlo method for problems in fewer than three dimensions since classical methods of numerical integration are both feasible and accurate in such cases. Classical methods are slow and cumbersome for integrals involving many dimensions because of the large amount of data that must be stored and the large amount of calculation that must be performed.

Boundary value problems can also be solved by statistical sampling methods. We shall now discuss a classical statistical solution to an ordinary differential equation as our second example. First we consider the ordinary differential equation

$$\frac{d^2y}{dx^2} + 2g(x)\frac{dy}{dx} = 0 \tag{6.5.9}$$

with $g(x) > 0$ for x in the interval $0 \leqslant x \leqslant a$. The boundary conditions are

$$y(0) = y_0, \tag{6.5.10a}$$

$$y(a) = y_a. \tag{6.5.10b}$$

As usual, we divide the interval into $K + 1$ segments numbered $0, 1, ..., K$. The differential equation is replaced by a simple difference approximation

$$\frac{\delta^2 y_k}{h^2} + 2g_k\frac{\Delta y_k}{h} = 0, \tag{6.5.11}$$

which yields

$$y_k = \frac{1 + 2g_k h}{2(1 + g_k h)}y_{k+1} + \frac{1}{2(1 + g_k h)}y_{k-1}$$

$$= a_k y_{k+1} + b_k y_{k-1}, \qquad k = 1, 2, ..., K - 1. \tag{6.5.12}$$

Notice that $a_k + b_k = 1$ for all k.

A statistical game may now be constructed to find the values of y_k, the game being called a random walk. Consider a unit element at point k. We interprete the quantities a_k, b_k as the probability of the element moving to point $k + 1$ or $k - 1$, respectively. If a unit element at k is allowed to move randomly through the mesh, then sooner or later the element will arrive at point 0 or K. Depending upon which boundary the element reaches first, a score of y_0 or y_a is tallied, and the game is terminated. Let the score tallied, whichever boundary is reached, be denoted by s_1. Another element is started from point k and allowed to move through the mesh until a boundary is reached and a score s_2 tallied. After N games, the mean value for y_k is

$$\overline{y_k} = \frac{1}{N} \sum_i s_i. \tag{6.5.13}$$

The actual playing of the game is very simple. Starting at the point k, we compute the probability a_k, or look it up in a table. A random number r between 0 and 1 is generated. If $r < a_k$, then $k + 1$ replaces k, i.e., the element moves to the right one place. Conversely, if $r > a_k$, then $k - 1$ replaces k, i.e., the element moves to the left one place. After each move a test must be made to see if a boundary has been reached. In such a case, an appropriate score is tallied, and the game is terminated. Otherwise, the process is repeated until a boundary is reached.

It is easy to show that the mean value computed by Eq. (6.5.13) does approach the analytic solution of the difference equation (6.5.12). The proof that $\bar{y}_k$ approaches y_k is developed as follows (see Reference 7): Let $v_m(k, K)$ be the probability of an element starting at point k and reaching point K before reaching 0 in m or fewer moves. Similarly let $v_m(k, 0)$ be the probability of reaching point 0 before reaching point K in m or fewer moves. Let $v_m(k)$ be the mean score attained in a game of m or fewer moves, the rules of scoring being as follows:

1. Nothing is added to the tally if neither $k = 0$ nor $k = K$ is reached.

2. y_0 is added to the tally if $k = 0$ is reached in m or fewer moves before $k = K$ is reached.

3. y_a is added to the tally if $k = K$ is reached in m or fewer moves before $k = 0$ is reached.

Obviously we have
$$v_m(k) = y_0 v_m(k, 0) + y_a v_m(k, K). \tag{6.5.14}$$

From the definition of $v_m(k)$ and from Eq. (6.5.13), we have[2]
$$\bar{y}_k = \lim_{m \to \infty} v_m(k). \tag{6.5.15}$$

To show that $\bar{y}_k$ approaches the analytic solution, we must show
$$\lim_{m \to \infty} v_m(k) = y_k. \tag{6.5.16}$$

---

[2] The probability of spending an infinite number of moves without reaching a boundary is zero (see Reference 7).

Thus, we must show that $\lim_{m \to \infty} v_m(k)$ exists and further that the limit obeys the difference equation (6.5.12). We first show that the limit exists.

Consider the function $v_m(k, 0)$. Obviously $v_m(k, 0)$ is bounded by unity for all m. Therefore, if we can show $v_m(k, 0) \geqslant v_{m-1}(k, 0)$, then a limit to the sequence certainly exists. The function $v_m(k, 0)$ is related to $v_{m-1}(k + 1, 0)$ and $v_{m-1}(k - 1, 0)$ by the recurrence relation

$$v_m(k, 0) = a_k v_{m-1}(k + 1, 0) + b_k v_{m-1}(k - 1, 0). \qquad (6.5.17)$$

Equation (6.5.17) follows since an element at point k can only go to $k \pm 1$ in one move. The probability of reaching point 0 from point k in m moves thus consists of two parts: the probabilities of reaching point 0 from the two points $k \pm 1$ in $m - 1$ moves. The coefficients a_k, b_k are the probabilities of travel from k to $k + 1$, $k - 1$ respectively.

Consider the case $m = 1$; we have

$$v_0(k, 0) = 0, \qquad k = 1, 2, ..., K - 1,$$

but

$$v_1(1, 0) = b_1,$$
$$v_1(k, 0) = 0, \qquad k = 2, 3, ..., K - 1.$$

And then

$$v_2(1, 0) = b_1,$$
$$v_2(2, 0) = b_2 b_1,$$
$$v_2(k, 0) = 0, \qquad k = 3, 4, ..., K - 1.$$

Therefore, by an obvious induction,

$$v_m(k, 0) \geqslant v_{m-1}(k, 0), \qquad \text{all } k.$$

This result is also evident by stating it in words. Similarly,

$$v_m(k, K) \geqslant v_{m-1}(k, K), \qquad \text{all } k.$$

Since the sequences $v_m(k, 0)$ and $v_m(k, K)$ are bounded and monotonic, they possess limits, say $v(k, 0)$ and $v(k, K)$. Consequently $\lim_{m \to \infty} v_m(k)$ exists and is denoted by $v(k)$. To prove that $v(k)$ obeys the difference equation, we use Eq. (6.5.17) in the definition of $v_m(k)$, Eq. (6.5.14). We have

$$v_m(k) = y_0[a_k v_{m-1}(k + 1, 0) + b_k v_{m-1}(k - 1, 0)]$$
$$+ y_n[a_k v_{m-1}(k + 1, K) + b_k v_{m-1}(k - 1, K)],$$
$$= a_k v_{m-1}(k + 1) + b_k v_{m-1}(k - 1). \qquad (6.5.18)$$

Taking limits, we then have

$$v(k) = a_k v(k+1) + b_k v(k-1), \qquad (6.5.19)$$

which is the desired result.

As a practical matter one would not solve the differential equation (6.5.9) by the random walk method just considered. Obviously the time required to achieve reasonable accuracy is much greater than a straight-forward iterative solution. However, for problems in higher dimensions the random walk process becomes more attractive. This is particularly true since the random walk method holds out the possibility of computing the solution in a particular region of a problem without considering the solution elsewhere. Further, in problems involving many dimensions, the length of each individual game and the number of required games are a slowly varying function of the number of dimensions in contrast to conventional iteration methods.

To illustrate the random walk in two dimensions, we outline the steps for solving Laplace's equation in a square. The relevant difference equation is

$$\phi_{j,k} = \tfrac{1}{4}[\phi_{j+1,k} + \phi_{j-1,k} + \phi_{j,k+1} + \phi_{j,k-1}]. \qquad (6.5.20)$$

The boundary conditions are assumed known for $k = 0, K$ all j, and $j = 0, J$ all k.

The random walk is initiated at point j, k. A random number is generated, and the probability of going in any one of the four directions used to locate the next mesh point. The walk continues until a boundary is reached, say point m, n. The score $\phi_{m,n}$ is tallied and another game is begun. The mean tally

$$\bar{\phi}_{j,k} = \sum_{m,n} \phi_{m,n} \qquad (6.5.21)$$

is the desired result. Proofs of the scoring procedure and generalizations are found in the references (for particulars, see References 6 and 7).

Random walk problems also show the need of modifying the game or the scoring procedure in some way so as to reduce the variance. For instance, a given walk may take many many steps only to reach a boundary point which contributes little or nothing to the total score. Conversely, an element may oscillate back and forth for a long time before finally reaching a boundary. There is an evident need for improvement of the random walk method outlined above.

6.6   Monte Carlo Calculation of the Fast Fission Factor

In this section we discuss a straightforward application of the Monte Carlo method to a typical reactor problem. Many nuclear calculations require studies of neutrons or photons as they pass through matter. The example considered here is sufficiently general to illustrate many of the aspects of particle processing and is representative of a simple application of the Monte Carlo method. Before outlining the computational steps, we first discuss some general procedures for handling transport problems.

In running time-independent Monte Carlo problems, it is often very convenient to introduce a periodic interval, called a census time, at which the population may be surveyed, statistics compiled and published, or certain changes made in the parameters characterizing a problem. In time-dependent problems, a census period is essential. Censuses are also very useful in reducing the variance in a problem: the use of census periods insures the processing of a representative selection of particles present at the beginning of the census period. If no census were used, then the whole calculation might consist of a study of only one initial particle and its progeny. Thus, the initial distribution would be very poorly represented. Other uses of census periods will be mentioned in the next section. In general the census period should be $1/2$ to 2 lifetimes of the particle: shorter times waste machine time because many operations are performed only once per census period, longer times may result in a great change in the number of neutrons in the population. This is bad for reasons that will become clear in the next section. At a census statistics may be compiled and published on the results achieved.

In addition to the optional but advised use of census times, Monte Carlo studies in particle motion involve the following essential steps:

1. The selection of a neutron from a population of neutrons. "Selection" means that the six coordinates, $\mathbf{r}$, $\mathbf{v}$, characterizing a neutron are assigned to one to be studied. In a multiplicative problem the initial population may be roughly estimated and selected somewhat arbitrarily from whatever may be known about the problem. It has been the authors' experience with a number of diverse problems of this class that accurate initial populations hasten the convergence to the final answer only a little for reasons that will become clear later. In a problem involving the detailed study of only a small part of a system, the macroscopic features of the population must be accurately found so that the microscopic features can be accurately determined by the Monte Carlo method.

2. In the digital computer the neutron is followed until it dies, more or less as it would diffuse, interact, moderate its energy, alter its direction,

and so on in the actual system. The neutron is said to die whenever it gets captured, escapes from the system, reaches the end of a census period, or in some problems gets below a certain energy. In any event the coordinates characterizing the interesting properties of the neutron surrounding its death will be recorded; at the end of a census period the coordinates $\mathbf{r}$, $\mathbf{v}$ characterizing a neutron will certainly be recorded.

3. If any neutrons have been born in a fission or $(n, 2n)$ event, these will be followed to their death. It is advisable in order to save memory space to follow the one most recently born to its death first.

4. After the original neutron and all its progeny of all generations have been followed to their death, a new neutron will be selected from the population present at the beginning of the census period. It and its progeny are followed to their deaths. This process is repeated until as many of the initial population have been studied as desired.

5. If the problem is nonmultiplicative, it is terminated at this point. If the problem is multiplicative, a new census period may be begun until as many as desired have been examined. The data recorded at the end of the previous census period are used as the population for the beginning of the new census period.

With these general remarks about particle transport, we now consider the problem of the calculation of the fast fission factor for an infinite single fuel rod in a unit cell, as shown in Fig. 6.6.1. The fuel rod consists

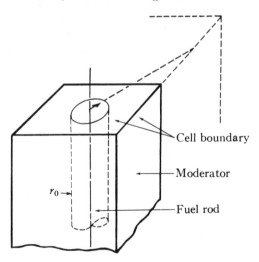

FIG. 6.6.1. Idealized unit cell with associated fuel and moderator regions for the calculation of the fast fission effect.

of U^{235} and U^{238} with N^{25} and N^{28} atoms per unit volume, respectively. The moderator will be taken as a single material with atomic density N^{mod}. Various macroscopic cross sections will be denoted by σ_{se}, σ_{si}, σ_c, and σ_f for elastic scattering, inelastic scattering, capture, and fission. Where necessary a superscript will be used to identify nuclear species. The thermal neutron flux is denoted by $\phi_{th}(\mathbf{r})$ in the fuel. The approach taken in this section for the present problem will be somewhat naive. Refinements to reduce variance will be discussed in the next section. If the total number of neutrons produced by thermal fission is denoted by N_0 and if ΔN neutrons are produced by fast fission, then the final computation of the fast fission factor ϵ_f is

$$\epsilon_f = 1 + \frac{\Delta N}{N_0} . \tag{6.6.1}$$

We now consider the details of the computation. In this problem it is assumed that the macroscopic behavior of $\phi_{th}(\mathbf{r})$ is known. This distribution may be sampled by any of the methods discussed in Section 6.3 to determine the location at which the fission neutron is born. On the average two and a fraction neutrons are born in fission. Therefore, in the Monte Carlo method, two neutrons are certainly created in every fission, and a third is created a fraction of the time equal to the fraction above two neutrons born in fission on the average. If 2.4 neutrons are born in fission, then 40 % of the time a third neutron is made: if a random number $\kappa < 0.40$, an additional neutron is made, otherwise not.

The selection of the energy of the fission neutrons is next considered. In the problem at hand, since only neutrons of energy greater than about 1 Mev can cause a fission in U^{238}, only a fraction of the fission spectrum is of interest. Let

$$\alpha = \int_0^{1 \text{ Mev}} dE \chi(E) , \tag{6.6.2}$$

where $\chi(E)$ is the fission spectrum so normalized that

$$\int_0^\infty dE \chi(E) = 1 . \tag{6.6.3}$$

Fairly accurate analytic expressions exist for the fission spectrum; these expressions could be used to select an energy E. However, table look-up is more frequently employed because of the cost in computer time to compute the transcendental functions involved and because the table can be of modest size. The neutron energy is selected then in accord with any of the methods outlined in Section 6.3. In this problem, if the random number κ used to select the neutron energy is less than α, the neutron is not processed at all, because it can induce no fast fissions. The direction of the fission neutron may be selected again according to the procedure outlined in Section 6.3, since the angular distribution of fission neutrons is isotropic.

The details of particle motion through the medium can be very complicated when irregular boundaries exist. In general the parameters characterizing the direction in which a particle moves change as the particle moves. Cartesian coordinates have the great advantage that the direction cosines do not change for particles moving in straight lines as the particle moves. For this reason Cartesian coordinates are used even in problems having other than rectangular symmetries, even spherical.

After the neutron has been selected by choice of the parameters characterizing it, one must decide whether it gets to a boundary, experiences a nuclear collision, or reaches the end of the census period. The event that is predicted to occur first is, of course, the one that is actually taken to happen in the Monte Carlo calculation. To effect this decision a random number must be generated to determine the total number of mean free paths l the neutron goes before a collision is experienced. If the total macroscopic cross section is denoted by σ, then the probability of a collision in an element Δl located l mean free paths from the present position of the neutron with no collision in between is

$$p(l)\,\Delta l = \exp\left(-l\sigma\right)\sigma\Delta l \,. \tag{6.6.4}$$

The c.d.f. may be calculated by integrating Eq. (6.6.4). The number of mean free paths the neutron goes is then decided by identifying the resulting c.d.f. with a random number, as mentioned in Section 6.3. Thus,

$$l = -\frac{1}{\sigma}\ln\kappa\,, \tag{6.6.5}$$

where κ is a random number between 0 and 1.[5]

---

[5] The logarithm of κ may be computed either by the rejection technique mentioned in Section 6.3 or by the following method. Multiply the random number by such a power p of 2 that the product κ_1 lies between $\frac{1}{2}$ and 1.

$$\kappa_1 = 2^p\kappa \tag{6.6.6}$$

and

$$\ln\kappa = a(\kappa_1 - \tfrac{1}{2}) + b(\kappa_1 - \tfrac{1}{2})^2 + c(\kappa_1 - \tfrac{1}{2})^3 + d(\kappa_1 - \tfrac{1}{2})^4 - (p+1)\ln 2,$$

where $a = 1.994884$, $b = -1.8851356$, $c = 1.8053480$, $d = -0.9400432$ have been so chosen to make the truncated power series expansion a best fit over the interval $0 \leqslant 2(\kappa_1 - \tfrac{1}{2}) \leqslant 1$ to $\ln\left[1 + 2(\kappa_1 - \tfrac{1}{2})\right]$

The distance to the nearest boundary must be computed. Unfortunately, to determine this quantity the distance to all boundaries must usually be computed. For example, in Fig. 6.6.1 although we can see that the neutron is within the fuel rod, this fact is not usually "known" to the computer, so it must calculate the distance not only to the cylinder and the north wall, but also to the projection of the east wall. (In this problem it would be practical to keep track of which region the neutron is in, but in more complicated geometries this is usually not the case. It is also usually very time consuming to determine by testing which region of several the neutron may be in if the region is unknown. However, a method that is especially suited to complex geometries will be given later.)

A simple method for calculating the distance to a boundary is now considered. The essential idea is to characterize the geometrical surface by some simple vector equation. For example, if $\mathbf{n}$ is a unit vector along the axis of our cylinder, then the cylinder is characterized by the statement that

$$(\mathbf{n} \times \mathbf{r}')^2 = \mathbf{r}_0^2 , \tag{6.6.7}$$

where $\mathbf{r}'$ is a vector from the origin on the axis of the cylinder to the point of the cylinder at which the neutron will hit the cylinder.

$$\mathbf{r}' = \mathbf{r} + L\boldsymbol{\Omega} , \tag{6.6.8}$$

where $\mathbf{r}$ is the vector from the origin to the present position of the neutron which goes in the direction specified by the unit vector $\boldsymbol{\Omega}$. L is the distance from the neutron to the point of impact with the bounding cylinder. Now from Eqs. (6.6.7) and (6.6.8), we learn that

$$(\mathbf{n} \times \mathbf{r}')^2 = (\mathbf{r} + L\boldsymbol{\Omega})^2 - (\mathbf{n} \cdot \mathbf{r} + L\mathbf{n} \cdot \boldsymbol{\Omega})^2 . \tag{6.6.9}$$

Upon equating this expression to $\mathbf{r}_0^2$ according to Eq. (6.6.7) and solving for L, we find

$$L = \left((\mathbf{n} \cdot \mathbf{r})(\mathbf{n} \cdot \boldsymbol{\Omega}) - (\mathbf{r} \cdot \boldsymbol{\Omega}) \pm \left\{ [(\mathbf{n} \cdot \mathbf{r})(\mathbf{n} \cdot \boldsymbol{\Omega}) - (\mathbf{r} \cdot \boldsymbol{\Omega})]^2 \right. \right.$$
$$\left. + [1 - (\mathbf{n} \cdot \boldsymbol{\Omega})^2][\mathbf{r}_0^2 + (\mathbf{n} \cdot \mathbf{r})^2 - \mathbf{r}^2] \right\}^{1/2} \right) [1 - (\mathbf{n} \cdot \boldsymbol{\Omega})^2]^{-1} , \tag{6.6.10}$$

the desired relation. The plus sign is used if the neutron is inside the cylinder and the minus sign is used if it is outside. Figure 6.6.2 illuminates some of the vector relations. In the case of a sphere the distance to the boundary is given by

$$L = -\boldsymbol{\Omega} \cdot \mathbf{r} \pm \sqrt{(\boldsymbol{\Omega} \cdot \mathbf{r})^2 + \mathbf{r}'^2 - \mathbf{r}^2} , \tag{6.6.11}$$

where the origin is taken at the center of the sphere, the association of the $+$ and $-$ signs being as for the cylinder. The distance to a plane boundary is given by

$$L = (\mathbf{r}' - \mathbf{r}) \cdot \mathbf{n}/(\mathbf{\Omega} \cdot \mathbf{n}), \qquad (6.6.12)$$

where $\mathbf{n}$ is a unit vector perpendicular to the plane through the point of reference. The distance to the closest boundary is selected, and the transit time computed from the known speed with which the neutron travels. In the present example, a neutron upon reaching a plane surface would be reflected there in the calculation, since then the next cell into which the neutron would penetrate in the actual system would be correctly simulated by the one at hand in the calculation.

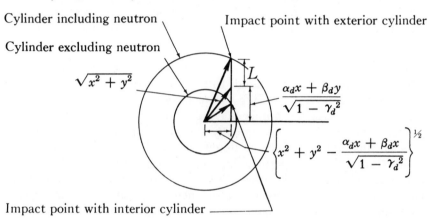

Cylinder including neutron

Impact point with exterior cylinder

Cylinder excluding neutron

$\sqrt{x^2 + y^2}$

L

$\dfrac{\alpha_d x + \beta_d y}{\sqrt{1 - \gamma_d^2}}$

$\left\{ x^2 + y^2 - \dfrac{\alpha_d x + \beta_d x}{\sqrt{1 - \gamma_d^2}} \right\}^{1/2}$

Impact point with interior cylinder

FIG. 6.6.2. Distances to two boundaries in cylindrical geometry. The plane is perpendicular to the axis of the cylinder. All lines and points are projected onto the plane. The view is along the z axis.

The neutron will eventually experience a collision. At a collision several decisions must be made. The material with which the neutron collides is found as follows: Define

$$\Xi_i = \sigma_i \Big/ \sum_{j=1}^{N} \sigma_j , \qquad (6.6.13)$$

where σ_i is the total macroscopic cross section for element i. The quantity Ξ_i may be regarded as the fraction of the unit interval occupied by the element i. The element may be selected by generating a random number κ and finding the largest i for which

$$\sum_{j=1}^{i-1} \Xi_j \leqslant \kappa . \qquad (6.6.14)$$

Once the element has been selected, the nature of the collision is determined. The variation of cross sections with energy is usually so complicated that table look-up is the only practical procedure for specifying cross sections as functions of energy. A random number is then used to determine the type of collision. The various types of collisions that one might consider are as follows:

1. *Capture.* In this case the particle history is terminated and another neutron is picked up.

2. *Fission.* In this case the particle history is terminated and appropriate data concerning the vital statistics of the neutron causing fission are recorded. The energy and location of the neutron inducing fission are likely to be of interest in this connection, or one particle can be added to the appropriate energy group tally and to the appropriate spatial zone tally.

3. *Inelastic scattering.* In this event the energy and direction of the scattered particle must be found. In this connection tables of the cross sections for inelastic scattering between various groups g and g' are required. One random number may be used to select the energy of the scattered neutron and consequently the group in which this neutron falls. In this problem, if the scattered neutron has an energy below the fission threshold, the particle history is terminated, and if desired, appropriate statistics recorded. Since inelastic scattering is important chiefly only for heavy elements, the neutrons may be assumed isotropically scattered in the laboratory system. The direction cosines may then be chosen as described in Section 6.3.

4. *Elastic scattering.* This case is the one that most frequently occurs. The energy of the scattered neutron can be found from Eq. (B.8) once the cosine of the scattering angle in the center-of-mass system is known. As always, if the energy of the scattered neutron is less than the fission threshold of U^{238}, the particle history is terminated. If the scattering is isotropic, then, the direction cosines in the center-of-mass frame with its axes parallel to the corresponding axes of the laboratory system may be found by the method indicated in Section 6.3. The direction cosines referred to the laboratory system may then be found by Eqs. (B.21). One the other hand, if the scattering is anisotropic, then the cosine of the angle of scattering must be found from the scattering law and the azimuth chosen randomly about the direction of the incident neutron by the method mentioned in Section 6.3. The scattering law is usually made available to the computer in the form of a table. The direction cosines thus found are transformed from the center-of-mass frame with

its z axis along the direction of the incident neutron to those of the center-of-mass frame with its axes parallel to the corresponding ones of the laboratory frame by Eqs. (B.30). These in turn are transformed to those referred to the laboratory frame by Eqs. (B.21).

Once the particle directional and energy parameters are found after the collision, the computer proceeds to find the times to the next boundary crossing, census, and collision.

It is evident from this problem that, since $\Delta N/N_0$ is on the order of a few percent and since the fuel rods are at most on the order of a mean free path in thickness, many neutrons must be processed per fast fission, and hence very few histories contribute to the result. Large variance is the consequence. Variance reduction methods will be considered in Section 6.7.

It is further evident from the discussion above that in a problem involving a complicated geometry, many boundaries must be checked for each possible boundary crossing and that in checking the distances to curved boundaries, a great amount of calculation is required. Since many histories must be followed to get reasonable accuracy and since the Monte Carlo method is inherently capable of handling complicated geometries, it behooves us to find some more efficient way to treat such geometries (see Reference *10*). Two facts may be exploited to this end:

1. The probability of crossing boundaries more removed than three mean free paths is quite low.

2. Tests for the crossing of planes perpendicular to the Cartesian coordinate axes are very simple since they involve only a comparison of the coordinates of the particle with the corresponding ones describing the orthogonal planes. Accordingly, a substantial amount of computer time can be saved if the system is subdivided by a set of planes orthogonal to the coordinate axes. Orthogonal planes are circumscribed around every curved surface with a diameter of curvature one mean free path or more, thus dividing the system into a number of geometrical parts each of which will be called a zone. Some of the boundaries of a zone may be purely mathematical, some may be physical. Parts of the system physically small compared with a mean free path can often be treated sufficiently well by homogenization. To further facilitate the determination of boundary crossings, certain orthogonal planes may be chosen as block boundaries. These should include at least six zones along any edge. The block within which the neutron is located is first determined, a matter that can be executed with great speed in view of the easy comparisons involved. The zone within which the neutron is found is determined by

examining the boundaries of all those and only those zones within this block. Orthogonal planes located too closely together defeat the very purpose for which they are installed in the system; orthogonal planes located too far apart will not be very effective in simplifying the search for the zone within which the neutron is located. About three mean free paths apart is approximately optimum for many problems.

Approximate expressions for the distance to a curved boundary that are less than this actual distance can often be used to expedite the calculations. If a boundary crossing based upon the use of the approximate expression is predicted, the prediction can be checked by a calculation with the exact expression.

6.7   Variance Reduction Methods

In the preceding example we have observed the need for modifying a game or scoring procedure in order to reduce the variance or error. A number of variance reducing methods have been examined in the literature partly because of the obvious need for them and partly for their mathematical appeal. We shall display a few of these methods. However, the reader is strongly cautioned against their indiscriminate use. Normally, the lowest possible variance is desired with a given amount of machine time. Complicated variance reduction schemes can cost so much time that a lower variance results by avoiding their use and by using the time saved to follow more histories. It has been the authors' experience in many problems that the reduction of variance by elaborate weighting, for example by assigning different weights to different regions of space and/or to different speed groups, should *only* be used when mandatory. These cases will make themselves obvious, and the way in which the weighting should be carried out in such cases is usually very obvious from rough calculations or physical intuition. For example, a problem involving huge attenuation through shields is one that can be handled *only* by suitable weighting. Again, weighting should not be used, for example, in criticality studies of light water systems.

The importance sampling method is the first variance reduction method to be discussed. The basic idea here is to play a game so modified that the variance is reduced by selecting from a distribution other than that suggested by the problem. The technique is perhaps best illustrated by the problem of calculating by the Monte Carlo method an integral

$$\langle g \rangle = \int_a^b dx \, g(x) f(x) \qquad (6.7.1)$$

with $f(x)$ a p.d.f. A statistical estimate of $\langle g \rangle$ is

$$\bar{g}_1 = (1/N) \sum_i g(x_i), \tag{6.7.2}$$

where the x_i are chosen from $f(x)$. Let us now consider modifying the integrand in the form

$$\langle g \rangle = \int_a^b dx\, g(x) \frac{f(x)}{f^*(x)} f^*(x) \tag{6.7.3}$$

with $f^*(x)$ a p.d.f. such that $g(x)f(x)/f^*(x)$ exists everywhere in the interval $a \leqslant x \leqslant b$.

Obviously, either form gives the same expected value. The statistical estimate

$$\bar{g}_2 = (1/N) \sum_i g(x_i) f(x_i)/f^*(x_i) \tag{6.7.4}$$

has the expected value $\langle g \rangle$ when the x_i are chosen from $f^*(x)$. We now compare the variance associated with $\bar{g}_1$ and $\bar{g}_2$. By Eq. (6.4.10), the variance for the first method is given by

$$V_1(\bar{g}_1) = (1/N) \int_a^b dx (g(x) - \langle g \rangle)^2 f(x)$$

$$= (1/N) \left[\int_a^b dx\, g^2(x) f(x) - \langle g \rangle^2 \right], \tag{6.7.5}$$

whereas the variance for the second method is given by

$$V_2(\bar{g}_2) = (1/N) \int_a^b dx \left(\frac{g(x)f(x)}{f^*(x)} - \langle g \rangle \right)^2 f^*(x)$$

$$= (1/N) \left[\int_a^b dx\, \frac{g^2(x)f^2(x)}{f^*(x)} - \langle g \rangle^2 \right]. \tag{6.7.6}$$

In general, the two variances V_1 and V_2 differ. The objective is to choose an $f^*(x)$ which makes V_2 smaller than V_1. If $g(x) \geqslant 0$ in $a \leqslant x \leqslant b$, then

$$f^*(x) = g(x)f(x)/\langle g \rangle \tag{6.7.7}$$

would yield an answer of zero variance. This result is hardly surprising since knowledge of the optimum $f^*(x)$ requires knowledge of the answer. The example does show, however, the possibility of making a very good choice of $f^*(x)$.

In general the choice of $f^*(x)$ is a difficult matter. Clearly the wrong choice can increase the variance. Intuitively a distribution $f^*(x)$ is desired that concentrates on the portion of the interval which contributes most to the integral, i.e., is the most important to the integral, whence the name of the method.

A special case of importance sampling is the so-called splitting method or Russian roulette. In this method it is recognized that some regions of velocity-configuration space may be more important and contribute more heavily to the final answer than others. Accordingly, these regions should be studied more intensively than those of lesser importance. Consequently the concept of particles carrying weight is introduced, and important regions are studied by many particles having little weight, whereas unimportant regions are studied by few particles having high weight. For example, in a problem in which the attenuation through a shield is being investigated, the particles near the exit face would have a much lower weight than those near the entrance face, since the neutrons near the exit face contribute much more heavily to the final answer that neutrons near the entrance face.

Each particle followed may in general represent many neutrons, since restrictions on the use of machine time usually limit the number of histories followed to less than 10,000, 1000 being frequently followed. The number of neutrons n is related to the weight W of N particles by

$$n = CWN, \qquad \text{(6.7.8)}$$

growing of separate things into one.

where C is some proportionality constant. This constant needs to be evaluated only in problems involving the accretion and depletion of nuclear matter. This equation governs the reweighting process, for in this process neutrons must be conserved. Thus if for some reason the weight of a particle is to be changed from W to W', then W/W' particles must be followed after the reweighting for each one followed prior to the reweighting in order that the number of neutrons be unchanged. If W/W' is larger than one, then W/W' particles are created with the same relevant coordinates $\mathbf{r}, \mathbf{v}$ as the particle previously being followed. Should W/W' be an integer plus a fraction, then $[W/W']$ particles are always created, where $[W/W']$ is the greatest integer less than W/W', and an extra particle is followed $W/W' - [W/W']$ of the time. To this end, an extra particle is followed if a random number κ, scaled between 0 and 1, is less than $W/W' - [W/W']$. The case of W/W' less than 1 is merely a special case of that already discussed. The resulting game is called splitting if $W/W' > 1$ and Russian roulette if $W/W' < 1$.

Variance can be reduced by avoidance of gaming where possible. The use of weights gives a way of reducing the gaming. For example, if a particle experiences a nuclear event, scattering, fission, and capture may occur with the probabilities σ_s/σ, σ_f/σ, and σ_c/σ, respectively. After the event a particle with weight $\nu\sigma_f W/\sigma$ is recorded in memory with the coordinates $\mathbf{r}, \mathbf{v}$ of the parent; this particle's history would be followed later. The death weight $W(\sigma_c + \sigma_f)/\sigma$ would be tallied, if desired, and a particle of weight $W\sigma_s/\sigma$ and coordinates $\mathbf{r}, \mathbf{v}$ would be followed. Death then can now come to a particle in such a game only by Russian roulette and by being lost from the system. Further, it will be noted that if a number of nuclides are present, the particle experiences an event with an average nuclide if the macroscopic cross sections, σ, are used with no loss of information and with a reduction of variance. Of course, with this method of gaming, the angular distributions for anisotropic scattering of the different nuclides must be compiled into a composite $f(\theta)$ by means of the macroscopic cross section:

$$f(\theta) = \sum_i \sigma_i f(\theta)_i \Big/ \sum_i \sigma_i , \qquad (6.7.9)$$

where $f(\theta)_i$ is the angular distribution for the ith nuclide. Likewise, for all other distributions, such as the fission spectra, the spectra resulting from elastic or inelastic scattering, and so forth.

If such a weighting procedure is used, then it is advisable to introduce weight standards for each of the various regions of velocity-configuration space to broadly limit the range over which the weights of the particles may vary for several reasons (see Reference *10*).

1. It is inadvisable to reweight the particles at each game because of the increased variance introduced by the gaming. If certain facts are definitely known, such as the relative probability with which various nuclear events may occur, the use of these facts will avoid the playing of a game and the introduction of variance.

2. Since importances are only approximately known in any case, it makes no sense to control the weights of the particles very closely by reweighting at each game.

3. The control of the weights within broad limits will reduce variance by preventing the computer from wasting time in following particles whose weight has been reduced to a very low value.

It seems reasonable then to control the weight of a particle within a factor of two; whenever the weight of the particle exceeds the weight standard by a factor of two, it is split until the weight is reduced to within this factor; whenever the weight is less than the weight standard, a game of Russian roulette is played with its life at stake with the odds in favor of life given by the ratio of its weight to the weight standard.

Two rather definite rules emerge from experience in the use of weight standards.

1. All weight standards should be equal unless it is mandatory that they be different in order to get an answer with reasonably low variance. Attenuation and perturbation problems require the use of weight standards; criticality studies do not.

2. The use of weight standards in different regions of velocity-configuration space differing by a factor of less than 8 or so in criticality calculations wastes machine time and violates the very reason for which weighting was introduced.

Calculation of the attenuation in shields provides an illuminating example of the use of importance sampling by the use of weights. If no weights were used, then even a study of a million histories might result in no particles penetrating the shield if its attenuation were in excess of a million. The variance would be enormous. In a shield problem, splitting planes are often inserted in such a way that the population of particles studied is maintained approximately constant (see Fig. 6.7.1).

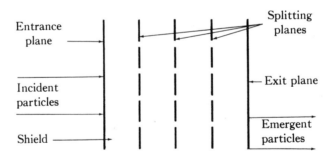

FIG. 6.7.1.   Particle splitting boundaries in a plane slab shield.

The weight standard of a zone is one-half that of the zone to the left and double that of the zone to the right. Accordingly, particles crossing from left to right across a splitting plane will be doubled in number on the average, and in crossing from right to left will be halved in number. In a problem involving low attenuation, the placement of the splitting planes, i.e., the choice of the weight standards can be found by the relation

$$z = k\sigma \ln 2$$

where k is an integer, and σ is the macroscopic cross section for neutrons of the most penetrating energy within the range of energies that neutrons may have. In problems involving great attenuation, if the splitting planes are too far apart, the particle population may approach zero at the exit plane and thus lead to high variance; if the splitting planes are too close, the particle population may drastically increase with consequent increase in variance resulting from an inadequate study of the initial population of injected particles because of limitations of computer time. Accordingly, for problems involving great attenuation the Monte Carlo method must be used to locate the splitting planes. To this end, particles are injected from the left and a plane is located such that half the original number of particles die to the right of the location where the splitting plane will be placed. After insertion of the plane, another set of neutrons is injected, and the second plane is located at that place where half the original number of neutrons injected die to the right. The procedure is repeated until all planes have been placed, after which a large number of particles can be injected to find the attenuation more accurately. The scheme suggested is stable against statistical fluctuations: if a plane is placed too close to the one previously placed, the next will be placed a little farther away to keep the neutron population about constant.

The use of census periods was mentioned in Section 6.6 for the purpose of running time-dependent problems, making parameter changes, auditing the population of both time-independent and time-dependent problems, and so on. Census periods can also be used to reduce variance. At the end of each census period the total population may be audited and new weights established so that the population will be returned to the original number during the next census period. Thus, if the population has decreased because of the attenuation of particles within a shield, it may be restored by reducing the weights. Alternatively, splitting planes a little too close together may be used and the population restored to normal size at the start of each census period. Censuses have proved very useful in practice.

If the statistics of less penetrating particles are desired at the exit face of the shield, then splitting planes can be placed somewhat closer together near this face so that these particles will be forced through.

A complementary procedure to the splitting and weighting just discussed is the use of expected values. Frequently it is simple to compute the probability that a particle penetrates to a given distance, for instance through a shield. For such cases one assumes a fraction a of the particle does penetrate, whereas a fraction $(1 - a)$ is left to diffuse. If the initial weight is W, then Wa is tallied for the transmission, and $W(1 - a)$ is the remaining weight. After each collision the expected penetration is tallied, and the remaining weight processed, etc.

Another special case arises in the study of the effect of strong perturbations over small volumes of an assembly. Small perturbations over large volumes are better handled by standard perturbation theory. The following techniques are used in the case of a localized strong perturbation (see Reference *10*):

1. The population of particles used to study the perturbed problem is initially identical to that for the unperturbed problem. Further, these populations and the statistical fluctuations remain the same until the particles diffuse into the small region of the large perturbation.

2. Weight standards are chosen so as to enhance greatly the diffusion of particles into the perturbing region. This means that near the perturbation, zones having a low weight standard will be used compared to the weight standards of more distant regions. The values of the weight standards should be selected so that a significant part of the population is within five mean free paths of the perturbed region.

3. The population in the unperturbed problem is allowed to come to equilibrium before starting the calculation of the perturbed problem.

There are many other ways to reduce variance. One of them is called forcing. In this method it is assumed that the expected number of events of each type is known, a tally is kept of the number of each that has actually occurred, and a biased game is played to encourage more of those events which are below the expected number. For example, let K be a forcing constant and suppose a decision between a reaction [capture, fission, $(n, 2n)$ event] or a scattering (isotropic or anisotropic) is to be made. Assume that N_r reactions have occurred in N games. Then if a random number κ, scaled between 0 and 1, is such that

$$\kappa < \frac{\sigma_r}{\sigma} + K\left(\frac{\sigma_r}{\sigma} - \frac{N_r}{N}\right) \qquad (6.7.10)$$

a reaction is decided upon. If too few reactions have taken place, there is a bias in favor of more reactions by an amount proportional to the disparity between the actual and expected values and to the forcing constant. By making the forcing constant large enough, the game can be made deterministic. Determinism in one game within the whole Monte Carlo calculation is all right, but at two or more points there is a danger of correlation. In general, morality is a virtue in gaming as elsewhere: play the game straight and stay out of trouble. Really there is no reason to use forcing at all, since if expected values are known, the method in which weights are changed is better.

Finally we mention a procedure called systematic sampling (sometimes called quota sampling). The method is very similar to forcing. The basic idea is to reduce or eliminate the variance associated with random selection in the first or early stages of the computation. The process is used only for one distribution, and hence no correlation problems arise. As an example, consider the integral in Eq. (6.5.4). Let the interval a to b be divided into J subintervals with the points $a = x_0 < x_1 < \dots < x_J = b$. The factors p_j are defined by

$$p_j = \int_{x_{j-1}}^{x_j} dx f(x) . \tag{6.7.11}$$

If the integration is to be approximated with N points, then the expected number of points within the interval x_{j-1} to x_j is merely

$$\bar{n}_j = p_j N . \tag{6.7.12}$$

The systematic sampling is done by assigning $\bar{n}_j$ points to the p_jth subinterval. Within the subinterval the $\bar{n}_j$ points may be distributed uniformly.

What has been accomplished by this process is the elimination of any variance associated with the initial selection of points for evaluating the integral. Usually the variance reduction is small; however, the method is simple to apply and is frequently used.

6.8 Concluding Remarks

We conclude this chapter with a few remarks concerning the Monte Carlo method:

1. Do not use the Monte Carlo method if any other method is available. It is a method of last resort.

2. Use variance reduction if and only if it is really necessary. Statistical estimates of the variance using computed results should be considered only as suggestive of the true variance. *Great* caution should be exercised in attributing precision to a result merely from low variance of past histories, since the variance estimate is an asymptotic function of the number of histories. Use known expected values wherever possible.

3. Particles must be followed for many nuclear lifetimes to remove any hereditary influences of the initial population. The fluctuations within one lifetime will be much smaller than those over many lifetimes, and these small fluctuations can give a very false impression of reliability and accuracy.

4. Check the coded program by all possible methods, and check it again.

The checking of Monte Carlo coded programs is especially difficult (1) because of the intensely complex logic, (2) because this logic is not deterministic, (3) because events wrongly calculated may be sufficiently rare to hide the error and yet large enough to influence the results, and (4) because the statistical nature of the calculations masks such errors. Several suggestions are offered to make any errors obvious and to isolate them.

1. Check each individual subroutine before assembling it into the larger routine. Check as many aggregates of subroutines as possible.

2. Run a series of simple, extreme problems so designed as to bound the class of all possible problems for which the Monte Carlo will be used. Artificial substances in which neutrons experience only one type of nuclear event are particularly useful to check the routines with respect to that event. Everything should be checked, such as tallies, the velocities and locations of particles, the conservation of neutrons. Sometimes the injection of particles at one point with one velocity will facilitate precise checks; at other times statistical checks on velocity distributions, for example, on a reasonable sample of particles must be run. Input data should be as troublesome to the computer as possible. Run problems involving simple and complex geometries in which the matter consists of a vacuum to check the crossing of boundaries. If possible, observe the trajectories of the particles on an on-line oscilloscope to check these routines. Boundary crossings are particularly troublesome because of round-off error within the machine. When a particle hits a boundary, design the boundary crossing routine such that a small amount is added to its coordinates to force it across regardless of this round-off.

References

The literature on the Monte Carlo method is surprisingly sparse. There are many articles and chapters devoted to the topic, but no comprehensive review exists to the authors' knowledge. For reasonably broad coverage of the method, References 1–5 are recommended. Certain special topics such as random walk, random number generation, etc. are discussed in References 6–11. References 12 and 13 are two very readable texts on statistics, including the central limit theorem.

1. Cashwell, E. D., and Everett, C. J., "The Monte Carlo Method for Random Walk Problems." Pergamon, New York, 1959.
2. Kahn, H., in "Symposium on Monte Carlo Method" (H. A. Meyer, ed.). Wiley, New York, 1956.
3. Kahn, H., Applications of Monte Carlo. Rand Report AECU-3259 (1954).

4. Goertzel, G., and Kalos, M. H., Monte Carlo method in transport problems, *in* "Progress in Nuclear Physics," Vol. 2, pp. 315–369. Pergamon Press, 1958.

5. Mayne, A. J., "Symposium on Monte Carlo Methods," pp. 103, 123, 176, 249. Wiley, New York (1953).

6. Bauer, W. F., The Monte Carlo method. *J. Soc. Ind. Appl. Math.* **6**, 438–451 (1954).

7. Curtis, J. H., Sampling methods applied to differential and difference equations, *in* "Seminar on Scientific Computation." International Business Machines Corp., Inc., Nov. 1949.

8. Kahn, H., Random sampling (Monte Carlo) techniques in neutron attenuation problems. *Nucleonics* **6** (1950).

9. Kahn, H., Modification of the Monte Carlo method, *in* "Seminar on Scientific Computation." International Business Machines Corp., Inc., Nov. 1949.

10. Troost, M., "Study of Neutron Transport by Monte Carlo Methods." Sc.D. Thesis, Massachusetts Inst. Technol., Cambridge, Massachusetts, June, 1958.

11. Moshman, J., The generation of pseudorandom numbers on a decimal calculator. *J. Assoc. Comp. Mach.* **1**; 88.

12. Hoel, P. C., "Introduction to Mathematical Statistics." Wiley, New York, 1954.

13. Cramer, H., "Mathematical Methods of Statistics." Princeton Univ. Press, Princeton, New Jersey, 1946.

Problems

1. A linear interpolation between tabular points $F(x_j)$ and $F(x_{j-1})$ assumes the random variable x is uniformly distributed over the interval x_{j-1} to x_j. If $F(x)$ is known to be concave upward or downward more accurate parabolic interpolation may be used. Show that for $F(x)$ concave upward we have

$$x = \sqrt{x_j^2 - \frac{(F(x_j) - \kappa)}{F(x_j) - F(x_{j-1})}\,(x_j^2 - x_{j-1}^2)},$$

and for $F(x)$ concave downward

$$x = \sqrt{x_j^2 - \frac{(\kappa - F(x_{j-1}))}{F(x_j) - F(x_{j-1})}\,(x_j^2 - x_{j-1}^2)},$$

where κ is a random number. What are the advantages and disadvantages of the parabolic interpolation methods?

2. Prove Eq. (6.3.16).

3. Show that the direction cosines of a random direction may be selected by choosing a point randomly within a semicircle and are given by

$$\alpha_d = \left(\frac{\eta_2^2 - \eta_1^2}{\eta_2^2 + \eta_1^2}\right)(1 - \eta_3^2)^{1/2},$$

$$\beta_d = \left(\frac{2\eta_1\eta_2}{\eta_2^2 + \eta_1^2}\right)(1 - \eta_3^2)^{1/2},$$

$$\gamma_d = \eta_3,$$

where η_1 and η_2 are acceptable random numbers, scaled between 0 and 1 and between -1 and $+1$, respectively, if and only if

$$\eta_1^2 + \eta_2^2 \leqslant 1$$

and where η_3 is any random number scaled between -1 and $+1$. Hint: Consider the trigonometric relations $\sin 2\varphi$ and $\cos 2\varphi$, and $\sin \varphi$ and $\cos \varphi$. Show that the efficiency of selection of the random numbers is 78.5%.

4. By selecting a point at random that lies within a unit sphere, show that the cosines α_d, β_d, γ_d of a random direction are given by

$$\alpha_d = \eta_1 [\eta_1^2 + \eta_2^2 + \eta_3^2]^{-1/2}$$

$$\beta_d = \eta_2 [\eta_1^2 + \eta_2^2 + \eta_3^2]^{-1/2}$$

$$\gamma_d = \eta_3 [\eta_1^2 + \eta_2^2 + \eta_3^2]^{-1/2}$$

where η_1, η_2, and η_3 are acceptable random numbers, scaled between -1 and $+1$, if and only if

$$\eta_1^2 + \eta_2^2 + \eta_3^2 \leqslant 1.$$

Show that the efficiency of selecting the cosines of this random direction is 52.4%.

5. Prove Eq. (6.4.16).

6. Suppose $y = x_1^2 + x_2^2$, where x_1 and x_2 are independent variables distributed according to

$$f(x) = \frac{1}{\sqrt{2\pi}} e^{-x^2/2}.$$

Show that

$$f(y) = \tfrac{1}{2} e^{-y/2} \qquad \text{if } y \geqslant 0$$
$$= 0 \qquad \text{if } y < 0$$

7. Suppose $y = \eta_1 - \eta_2$, where η_1 and η_2 are random numbers scaled between 0 and 1. Show that if $0 \leqslant y \leqslant 1$,

$$f(y) = 2(1 - y).$$

8. Suppose the probability that y has a value in the range Δy centered at y is $f(y)\Delta y$, where $f(y) = 3y^2$ and suppose that $0 \leqslant y \leqslant 1$. Show that $y = \eta^{1/3}$, where $0 \leqslant \eta \leqslant 1$.

9. The differential probability distribution of y is $f(y) = 4/\pi(1 + y^2)$, where $0 \leqslant y \leqslant 1$. Show that $y = \tan \pi\eta/4$, where $0 \leqslant \eta \leqslant 1$.

10. The differential probability distribution of y is $f(y) = 2/\pi \sqrt{y}(1 + y)$. Devise a rejection technique for choosing y from this distribution. Find the efficiency.

11. Suppose $y = \eta^j$, where $0 \leqslant \eta \leqslant 1$. Show that the probability that y has a value in the interval Δy centered at y is

$$\frac{1}{j} y^{-(j-1)/j} \Delta y.$$

12. Prove Eq. (6.4.24).

13. Prove Eqs. (6.6.11) and (6.6.12).

14. Flow chart a Monte Carlo routine in which isotropic elastic scattering, anisotropic elastic scattering, capture, inelastic scattering, $(n, 2n)$ events, and fissions are each considered individually.

15. Devise a boundary crossing routine for zones consisting of concentric spheres only, taking round-off error into account.

16. Devise a boundary crossing routine for zones consisting of only coaxial cylinders infinitely long, taking round-off error into account.

17. We have coded a program that has no provision for recording the coordinates of the particles that leak out of a reactor but that has a provision for recording the coordinates of each neutron in each zone within the reactor. Devise a simple method for finding the spectrum and angular distribution of neutrons that leak out of the reactor.

18. Program a subroutine to calculate the logarithm of a random number according to the rejection technique discussed.

19. Program a Monte Carlo routine in which isotropic elastic scattering and anisotropic elastic scattering are considered as one nuclear event and capture, fission, $(n, 2n)$ events, inelastic scattering are considered as another event.

20. Devise a generalized boundary crossing routine for zones consisting of spheres, cylinders, planes, cylindrical cones, elliptical cones, elliptical cylinders, and ellipsoids. Hint: Consider that such boundaries can be described by a formula of the type

$$ax^2 + by^2 + c(z - z_0)^2 - K = 0. \qquad (1)$$

Show that the distance to any boundary is given by

$$\frac{-e + j\sqrt{e^2 - hr}}{h}$$

where

$$e = a\alpha_d x + b\beta_d y + c\gamma_d(z - z_0),$$
$$h = a\alpha_d^2 + b\beta_d^2 + c\gamma_d^2,$$
$$r = ax^2 + by^2 + c(z - z_0)^2 - K,$$

and $j = 1$ if the expression (1) changes from negative to positive as the neutron crosses the boundary and $j = -1$ if the expression (1) changes from positive to negative. A neutron is inside the a zone if $jr > 0$ for any of the boundaries.

21. Program a Monte Carlo routine that takes delayed neutron emitters into account. Hint: Devise a routine to consider representative times, then extrapolate past results. Calculate what the sources will be and use them to inject neutrons.

22. Suppose we have an infinite plane slab used as a shield. The attenuation of neutrons through the slab is very great.

(a) Program a routine that will automatically locate particle splitting planes stably.

(b) Program a routine that will calculate accurately the number of neutrons that leave the slab through a small spot on the surface.

23. Discuss the merits and faults of the following criteria for locating splitting planes:

(a) The planes are so located that the number of deaths in the zone on the left of the prospective position, i.e., the space between itself and the most recently placed boundary, is one-half the original number.

(b) The prospective boundary is to be so placed that the number of deaths to its right will be half the number of particles that emerge from the preceding boundary.

(c) The prospective boundary is so placed that as many more deaths above the initial number of particles injected occur in the region to its right as occurred short of the required number to the right of the preceding boundary.

All of these schemes for locating splitting planes are inferior to the one mentioned in the text.

APPENDIX A

THE BOLTZMANN TRANSPORT EQUATION

The purpose of this appendix is to develop the mathematical description of the transport of particles through matter. The equation to be derived, sometimes called the Boltzmann equation, describes the macroscopic motion of particles in a medium with sufficient accuracy for most purposes. In the cases of interest to us, the particles are either neutrons or photons, which are electrically neutral, a fact which simplifies the problem considerably.

In general the particles will be moving in a medium having special nuclear properties; for example, the medium may contain fissionable material. The nuclear properties of the material are essential to our calculation. The properties will be characterized phenomenologically in terms of theoretically or experimentally determined cross sections. We shall assume all of the cross sections to be considered subsequently are known.

Newton's equations of motion might be used to compute the motion of each particle in a medium. Indeed, this is the approach taken in the Monte Carlo method described in Chapter 6. This description is so detailed, however, that very large, very high-speed computers are required to solve most practical problems by this method. Further, such a detailed picture is difficult to comprehend and/or use and is very seldom of interest.

A description of the average behavior of the neutrons will be quite sufficient for very nearly all our needs. The fluctuations from average behavior are of interest chiefly in the very early stages of a nuclear reaction, such as the startup of a reactor. The Boltzmann equation to be derived here will take the dynamics of the average particle population into account, but not the behavior of each neutron or photon by itself. The population will be treated as a statistical entity by considering the ways in which the particles may be born, move, and die.

281

In order to proceed further, it will be necessary to define the directional density and the directional flux of particles. First, we shall denote the position of the particle by the vector **r** and its velocity by the vector **v**. Each of these two vectors consists of three components, of course. The directional density $n(\mathbf{r}, \mathbf{v}, t)$ of particles is then defined to be the number of those particles which are present on the average in a unit volume located at **r** at time t and which are traveling in a unit velocity volume at the velocity **v**.

A few remarks concerning this definition are needed by way of clarification. It is to be emphasized that the seven variables **r**, **v**, and t are absolutely independent of each other. We may always choose the point at which we examine the neutron density quite independently of the speeds or directions in which the neutrons travel, and conversely.

The possibility of choosing these two variables independently stems from the Newton equations of motion themselves. It requires a specification of the initial position and velocity of a particle in order to determine its future position and velocity at some later time. The Boltzmann equation must, of course, be consistent with Newton's laws (Reference *1*). We may next inquire into the possibility of treating **r** and **v** as independent variables at some later time in the Boltzmann equation. There is really no conflict when it is remembered that the Boltzmann equation will describe the average behavior of the whole population rather than that of an individual particle. Consider some particular point **r**. At this point we can measure the densities of particles over a whole range of velocities. In doing so, we are, of course, looking at particles having a variety of initial velocities. Indeed, we may very well find that the density is zero for many velocities, Newton's equations and the relevant nuclear events prohibiting particles from achieving those velocities given the original initial velocities.

The second point that needs to be clarified with respect to the definition of particle density is the concept of specifying the density of neutrons per unit velocity volume. To this end, we use the symbol $d\mathbf{r}$ to stand for an element of volume in ordinary space; we also use the symbol $d\mathbf{v}$ to stand for an element of volume in velocity space.

The symbol $d\mathbf{r}$ stands for $dx\, dy\, dz$ in Cartesian coordinates for example: $d\mathbf{v}$ stands for $v^2\, dv\, d(\cos\theta)\, d\varphi$ in spherical coordinates for example. The components of the vector **r** may be referred to a different coordinate system from that to which the components of the vector **v** are referred. The number of particles in the element $d\mathbf{r}\, d\mathbf{v}$ is then $n(\mathbf{r}, \mathbf{v}, t)\, d\mathbf{r}\, d\mathbf{v}$. This is the number of particles whose spatial coordinates lie between x and $x + dx$, y and $y + dy$, and z and $z + dz$ and whose velocity coordinates lie between v_x and $v_x + dv_x$, v_y and $v_y + dv_y$, and v_z and $v_z + dv_z$.

It is of interest to consider the number of particles that travel in a unit solid angle and in a unit range of speed. To this end, let $\boldsymbol{\Omega}$ denote a unit vector in the direction of the velocity vector $\mathbf{v}$:

$$\boldsymbol{\Omega} = \mathbf{v}/v , \tag{A.1}$$

the magnitude of a vector quantity being denoted by the symbol for the vector in italic type, instead of bold face. The element $d\mathbf{v}$ of velocity volume can be expressed as follows:

$$d\mathbf{v} = v^2 dv d\Omega , \tag{A.2}$$

where $d\Omega$ is an element of solid angle. For example, in spherical coordinates $d\Omega = \sin\theta \, d\theta \, d\varphi$, where θ is the colatitude angle and φ is the azimuthal angle describing the direction in which the particle moves (not the direction of the radius vector $\mathbf{r}$). Now, the number of particles in an element of volume must not depend upon the mode of description that happens to be used, so

$$n(\mathbf{r}, \mathbf{v}, t) \, d\mathbf{r} \, d\mathbf{v} = n(\mathbf{r}, v, \boldsymbol{\Omega}, t) \, d\mathbf{r} \, dv \, d\Omega , \tag{A.3}$$

or

$$n(\mathbf{r}, \mathbf{v}, t) = n(\mathbf{r}, v, \boldsymbol{\Omega}, t)/v^2 . \tag{A.4}$$

Here $n(\mathbf{r}, v, \boldsymbol{\Omega}, t)$ is the number of particles in a unit volume of space at time t (as before) whose speed lies in a unit speed volume at v and going in a unit solid angle centered on the direction $\boldsymbol{\Omega}$. The functions $n(\mathbf{r}, \mathbf{v}, t)$ and $n(\mathbf{r}, v, \boldsymbol{\Omega}, t)$ are not the same but are related by Eq. (A.4).

The directional flux $\boldsymbol{\phi}(\mathbf{r}, \mathbf{v}, t)$ is a vector, is defined by

$$\boldsymbol{\phi}(\mathbf{r}, \mathbf{v}, t) = vn(\mathbf{r}, \mathbf{v}, t) , \tag{A.5}$$

and is the number of particles at $\mathbf{r}$ of velocity $\mathbf{v}$ per unit spatial volume and per unit velocity volume that in a unit time cross a unit surface whose normal lies along $\mathbf{v}$. The flux or track length $\phi(\mathbf{r}, v, t)$ is defined by

$$\phi(\mathbf{r}, v, t) = \int d\Omega \, vn(\mathbf{r}, v, \boldsymbol{\Omega}, t) , \tag{A.6}$$

where the integral is to be computed over all solid angles.

The magnitude $\phi(\mathbf{r}, v, \boldsymbol{\Omega}, t)$ of the directional flux is related to the magnitude of the directional flux normalized per unit volume and per unit velocity by

$$\phi(\mathbf{r}, \mathbf{v}, t) = \phi(\mathbf{r}, v, \boldsymbol{\Omega}, t)/v^2 \,. \tag{A.7}$$

From Eqs. (A.4), (A.5) and (A.7), we find that

$$\phi(\mathbf{r}, v, \boldsymbol{\Omega}, t) = v n(\mathbf{r}, v, \boldsymbol{\Omega}, t) \,. \tag{A.8}$$

The density $n(\mathbf{r}, v, t)$ of particles per unit volume per unit speed is defined by

$$n(\mathbf{r}, v, t) = \int d\boldsymbol{\Omega}\, n(\mathbf{r}, v, \boldsymbol{\Omega}, t) \,, \tag{A.9}$$

and is related to the flux by

$$v n(\mathbf{r}, v, t) = \phi(\mathbf{r}, v, t) \,, \tag{A.10}$$

as can be seen from Eqs. (A.9) and (A.6). From this result it is seen that the flux is the total distance traveled by all particles in a unit volume per unit time. The symbol $n(\mathbf{r}, \mathbf{v}, t)$ for the directional density and that $n(\mathbf{r}, v, t)$ for the density are distinguished from each other by the presence of the bold face velocity symbol in the former and the italic symbol in the latter. Likewise for the distinction between the magnitude of the directional flux and the flux.

Various directional moments of the particle distribution may be defined. The only one that we shall need is that for the net current $\mathbf{J}(\mathbf{r}, v, t)$ of particles

$$\mathbf{J}(\mathbf{r}, v, t) = \int d\boldsymbol{\Omega}\, v \boldsymbol{\Omega}\, n(\mathbf{r}, \mathbf{v}, t) \,. \tag{A.11}$$

It is to be noted that this is a vector equation; it stands for three equations when written out in component form.

The Boltzmann equation may now be derived. To find this equation, one needs only to account for the fate of all particles, i.e., to conserve all neutrons. Since the equation for photons is slightly different from that for neutrons, we shall write the equations for neutrons. Terms are to be expected that describe the rate of change of the number of neutrons, the numbers of particles scattered into the region of interest, and the loss of particles from the region by scattering and absorption. The Boltzmann equation is merely a particle balance among these terms.

The rate of change of the number of particles in an element $d\mathbf{r}\,d\mathbf{v}$ with time is equal to the rate at which particles are added to this element minus the rate at which they are removed from this element.

The rate of change with time of the number of neutrons in the element $d\mathbf{r}\,d\mathbf{v}$ is

$$\frac{\partial n(\mathbf{r}, \mathbf{v}, t)}{\partial t}\, d\mathbf{r}\,d\mathbf{v}\,. \tag{A.12}$$

The number of particles added to the element $d\mathbf{r}\,d\mathbf{v}$ by a source is

$$S(\mathbf{r}, \mathbf{v}, t)\, d\mathbf{r}\,d\mathbf{v}\,. \tag{A.13}$$

The source as contemplated here is to consist of all particles arising from means not linearly proportional to the flux of the system. The source is not to consist of fission neutrons or those appearing from an $(n, 2n)$ event, for example.

The number of particles leaking out of the element $d\mathbf{r}\,d\mathbf{v}$ over the bounding surface must be considered. In most problems of interest, there is a spatial gradient of the magnitude of the directional flux, which leads to the diffusion of particles across the bounding surfaces in configuration space.[1] To facilitate the calculation of this diffusion of particles, it will be convenient to introduce the notation $d^2\mathbf{r}$ for a surface element; since a surface element is a vector, $d^2\mathbf{r}$ is to be a vector normal to the surface of the element oriented in the usual positive sense and of a magnitude equal to the area of the surface element. The net leakage from $d\mathbf{r}\,d\mathbf{v}$ due to flux gradients is coordinate space is then given by

$$\int d^2\mathbf{r}\cdot\boldsymbol{\phi}(\mathbf{r}, \mathbf{v}, t)\, d\mathbf{v} = \int d^2\mathbf{r}\cdot v n(\mathbf{r}, \mathbf{v}, t)\, d\mathbf{v}\,, \tag{A.14}$$

$$= \int d\mathbf{r}\,\nabla_r\cdot v n(\mathbf{r}, \mathbf{v}, t)\, d\mathbf{v}\,, \tag{A.15}$$

$$= \nabla_r\cdot v n(\mathbf{r}, \mathbf{v}, t)\, d\mathbf{r}\,d\mathbf{v}\,, \tag{A.16}$$

$$= \mathbf{v}\cdot\nabla_r\, n(\mathbf{r}, \mathbf{v}, t)\, d\mathbf{r}\,d\mathbf{v}\,. \tag{A.17}$$

In Eq. (A.14) the integral is carried out only over the surfaces bounding $d\mathbf{r}$. In Eq. (A.14) the definition (A.5) is used. Relation (A.15) follows by the divergence theorem of Gauss, the integral extending only over the

---

[1] In most problems involving an external force field acting on the particles, the particles may diffuse across the surfaces bounding an element of velocity volume. However, such a circumstance does not normally arise with either photons or neutrons.

element $d\mathbf{r}$; Eq. (A.16) follows from the observation that $n(\mathbf{r}, \mathbf{v}, t)$ is a physical quantity and therefore continuous in its $\mathbf{r}$ dependence so that over $d\mathbf{r}$ it varies only negligibly. Finally, Eq. (A.17) follows by noting that $\mathbf{v}$ is quite independent of $\mathbf{r}$ and from the definition of $\mathbf{\nabla}_r$, which is

$$\mathbf{\nabla}_r = \mathbf{i}_r \frac{\partial}{\partial x} + \mathbf{j}_r \frac{\partial}{\partial y} + \mathbf{k}_r \frac{\partial}{\partial z}, \qquad (A.18)$$

$\mathbf{i}_r$, $\mathbf{j}_r$, and $\mathbf{k}_r$ being mutually orthogonal unit vectors in configuration space.

At a collision, elastic scattering, inelastic scattering, fission, an $(n, 2n)$ event, or the like may occur; in general, the number of neutrons leaving a collision will differ from the number entering. The probability that a collision occurs is characterized by the macroscopic cross section σ, which is a function of the number of nuclei per unit volume, the nuclear species constituting the target, the relative velocity between the target nucleus and the particle, and the energy with which any escaping particles emerge from the collision. The macroscopic cross section is the probability σ per unit length that any particle of the specified relative energy will suffer a collision in traveling a unit distance in the specified material.

The total macroscopic cross section is defined by

$$\sigma = \sigma_s + \sigma_r, \qquad (A.19)$$

where σ_s is the total macroscopic scattering cross section, and σ_r is the total macroscopic reaction cross section. The total scattering cross section is defined to be

$$\sigma_s = \sigma_{es} + \sigma_{is}, \qquad (A.20)$$

where σ_{es} and σ_{is} are the macroscopic elastic and inelastic scattering cross sections, respectively. The total reaction cross section is defined to be

$$\sigma_r = \sigma_f + \sigma_{2n} + \sigma_c, \qquad (A.21)$$

where σ_f, σ_{2n} and σ_c are the macroscopic fission, $(n, 2n)$, and radiative capture cross sections, respectively. The total multiplicity, c, of an event is defined by

$$c = [\sigma_{es} + \sigma_{is} + \nu\sigma_f + 2\sigma_{2n}]/\sigma, \qquad (A.22)$$

where ν is the number of neutrons appearing from the fission process per fission. The multiplicity c is from its definition just the number of neutrons appearing as the result of an event. For each event caused by a neutron of velocity $\mathbf{v}'$, there is a probability $f(\mathbf{v}' \to v, \boldsymbol{\Omega})\, dv\, d\boldsymbol{\Omega}$ that one of the neutrons emerging from the reaction will have a speed v in the range dv and a direction $\boldsymbol{\Omega}$ in the range $d\boldsymbol{\Omega}$.

$$f(\mathbf{v}' \to v, \boldsymbol{\Omega})\, c(v')\, \sigma(v') = f_{es}(\mathbf{v}' \to v, \boldsymbol{\Omega})\, \sigma_{es}(v') + f_{1s}(\mathbf{v}' \to v, \boldsymbol{\Omega})\, \sigma_{1s}(v')$$

$$+ f_{f}(\mathbf{v}' \to v, \boldsymbol{\Omega})\, \nu(v')\, \sigma_{f}(v') + f_{2n}(\mathbf{v}' \to v, \boldsymbol{\Omega})\, 2\sigma_{2n}(v') , \qquad \text{(A.23)}$$

where the partial probabilities $\sigma_{es}\, f_{es}(\mathbf{v}' \to v,\ \boldsymbol{\Omega})$, $\sigma_{1s}\, f_{1s}\,(\mathbf{v}' \to v, \boldsymbol{\Omega})$, $\sigma_{f}\, f_{f}\,(\mathbf{v}' \to v,\ \boldsymbol{\Omega})$, and $\sigma_{2n}\, f_{2n}\,(\mathbf{v}' \to v,\ \boldsymbol{\Omega})$ are defined for elastic scattering, inelastic scattering, fission and an $(n, 2n)$ event, respectively, similarly to the definition of $\sigma f\,(\mathbf{v}' \to v, \boldsymbol{\Omega})$ for a reaction. These probabilities are not probabilities per unit velocity, of course. They will be called collision transfer probabilities.

From the definition of the macroscopic cross section as a probability that a neutron suffer a collision per unit distance traveled in the material specified, it follows that the number of collisions suffered by all particles per unit volume per unit velocity in a unit time is given by

$$\sigma(\mathbf{r}, \mathbf{v}, \mathbf{V})\, |\, \mathbf{v} - \mathbf{V}\, |\, n(\mathbf{r}, \mathbf{v}, t) , \qquad \text{(A.24)}$$

where $\mathbf{V}$ is the velocity of the target nucleus. Similarly, the number of collisions suffered by all particles in a unit volume per unit time and per unit speed is given by

$$\sigma(\mathbf{r}, \mathbf{v})\, vn(\mathbf{r}, v, t) , \qquad \text{(A.25)}$$

if the speeds of the target nuclei are negligible. Otherwise, the macroscopic cross section must be replaced by a suitable average. It is convenient to define the microscopic cross section as

$$\sigma(\mathbf{r}, \mathbf{v}, \mathbf{V})/N(\mathbf{r}, \mathbf{V}) \qquad \text{(A.26)}$$

where $N(\mathbf{r}, \mathbf{V})$ is the number of nuclei per unit volume per unit velocity, all nuclei being assumed monoenergetic with the velocity $\mathbf{V}$. The microscopic cross section has the dimensions of an area, is measured in units of 10^{-24} cm^2, called the barn, and is independent of the density of the material. The microscopic cross section may be thought of as the effective area of a nucleus with respect to the specified type of collision for neutrons of the given relative velocity. This interpretation is harmonious with the definition (A.26) and the interpretation of the macroscopic cross section for the probability that some collisions take place. This probability then is simply the product of the number of nuclei present times the area presented by each.

The total number of neutrons entering the element $d\mathbf{r}\,d\mathbf{v}$ as a result of collisions is then

$$\int d\mathbf{v'} \int d\mathbf{V} f(\mathbf{v'} \rightarrow v, \mathbf{\Omega})\, c(v')\, \sigma(\mathbf{r}, \mathbf{v'}, \mathbf{V})\, |\, \mathbf{v'} - \mathbf{V}\, |\, n(\mathbf{r}, \mathbf{v'}, t)\, d\mathbf{r}\, \frac{d\mathbf{v}}{v^2}. \qquad (A.27)$$

Likewise the total number of neutrons removed from the element $d\mathbf{r}\,d\mathbf{v}$ is given by

$$\int d\mathbf{V} \sigma(\mathbf{r}, \mathbf{v}, \mathbf{V})\, |\, \mathbf{v} - \mathbf{V}\, |\, n(\mathbf{r}, \mathbf{v}, t)\, d\mathbf{v}\, d\mathbf{r}\,. \qquad (A.28)$$

The discontinuous nature of motion in velocity contrasts with the continuous character of the motion in space. Diffusion across velocity surfaces due to the continuous changes of velocity is incorporated into the theory by terms not discussed here, but readily incorporated into our equation; discontinuous changes are taken into account by expressions (A.27) and (A.28).

The neutron balance equation is then

$$\frac{\partial n(\mathbf{r}, \mathbf{v}, t)}{\partial t} = S(\mathbf{r}, \mathbf{v}, t) - \mathbf{v} \cdot \nabla_r n(\mathbf{r}, \mathbf{v}, t)$$

$$- \int d\mathbf{V}\, \sigma(\mathbf{r}, \mathbf{v}, \mathbf{V})\, |\, \mathbf{v} - \mathbf{V}\, |\, n(\mathbf{r}, \mathbf{v}, t)$$

$$+ \int d\mathbf{v'} \int d\mathbf{V} \frac{f(\mathbf{v'} \rightarrow v, \mathbf{\Omega})}{v^2}\, c(v')\, \sigma(\mathbf{r}, \mathbf{v'}, \mathbf{V})\, |\, \mathbf{v'} - \mathbf{V}\, |\, n(\mathbf{r}, \mathbf{v'}, t)\,. \qquad (A.29)$$

This important equation is the Boltzmann equation. It forms the basis of nearly all the calculations of particle transport. The equation can be specialized to the case that usually occurs in which the velocities of the target nuclei are negligible compared with the velocities of the neutrons. In this case

$$N(\mathbf{r}, \mathbf{V}) = N(\mathbf{r})\, \delta(\mathbf{V})\,,$$

where $\delta(\mathbf{V})$ is the Dirac delta function. Consequently in this case Eq. (A.29) becomes

$$\frac{\partial n(\mathbf{r}, \mathbf{v}, t)}{\partial t} = S(\mathbf{r}, \mathbf{v}, t) - \mathbf{v} \cdot \nabla_r n(\mathbf{r}, \mathbf{v}, t) - \sigma(\mathbf{r}, v)\, vn(\mathbf{r}, \mathbf{v}, t)$$

$$+ \int d\mathbf{v'} \frac{f(\mathbf{v'} \rightarrow v, \mathbf{\Omega'})}{v^2}\, c(v')\, \sigma(\mathbf{r}, v')\, v'n(\mathbf{r}, \mathbf{v'}, t)\,. \qquad (A.30)$$

The Boltzmann equation (A.30) is frequently expressed in terms of $n(\mathbf{r}, v, \boldsymbol{\Omega}, t)$ instead of $n(\mathbf{r}, \mathbf{v}, t)$:

$$\frac{\partial n(\mathbf{r}, v, \boldsymbol{\Omega}, t)}{\partial t} = S(\mathbf{r}, v, \boldsymbol{\Omega}, t) - v\boldsymbol{\Omega} \cdot \nabla_r n(\mathbf{r}, v, \boldsymbol{\Omega}, t) - \sigma(\mathbf{r}, v) \, vn(\mathbf{r}, v, \boldsymbol{\Omega}, t)$$

$$+ \int dv' d\boldsymbol{\Omega}' f(\mathbf{v}' \to v, \boldsymbol{\Omega}) \, c(v') \, \sigma(\mathbf{r}, v') \, v'n(\mathbf{r}, v', \boldsymbol{\Omega}', t) \, . \qquad \text{(A.31)}$$

In the above equations it has been assumed that the macroscopic cross sections are independent of the flux. For certain problems, such as those involving xenon poisoning, temperature feedback, burn-up of fuel, and others, the coefficients will be functions of the flux. This dependence can be immediately incorporated into the transport equation by merely inserting the appropriate dependence on the flux. (While easy to incorporate, solving the resulting nonlinear transport equation is usually much more difficult than the linear one.)

A number of more basic assumptions have been made in deriving the Boltzmann equation. These are as follows:

1. The element of velocity and space of interest is sufficiently large that statistical fluctuations within these elements are negligible. Statistical fluctuations cannot be considered by the Boltzmann equation (see References 4 and 5). The probability of a neutron, for example, inducing a chain reaction cannot be treated by the Boltzmann equation. Let us estimate the fluctuations that might take place in a volume element, $d\mathbf{r}$. There might be some 10^7 neutrons present per cm^3, corresponding to a thermal flux of 2×10^{12} neutrons per cm^2-sec. The probable fractional error in such a case due to statistical fluctuations would be of the order of $(10^7 \, d\mathbf{r})^{-1/2}$. The statistical fluctuations could be of some importance at startup, for example.

2. The collision time of neutrons has been assumed to be zero. This approximation is extremely good, since the compound nucleus lives less than 10^{-14} sec and since the ranges of nuclear forces are extremely small compared with the mean distances between neutrons. Although 10^{-14} sec is very long compared with characteristic nuclear times, the characteristic periods involved in various nuclear applications are always very much longer. Consequently, only the binary encounters considered above in the derivation of the Boltzmann equation are important. Except for the delayed neutrons which emerge from fission fragments, the neutrons emerge from the point of the collision. Even in the case of delayed neutrons, the ranges of fission fragments are so very short in any solid or liquid that the delayed neutrons substantially originate at the site of the fission. However, if delayed neutron emitters be considered

in the time-dependent Boltzmann equation, the decay of the delayed neutron emitters must be considered as a source term in the Boltzmann equation and appropriate time-dependent conservation equations be written for the delayed neutron emitters. (It is noted here that the approximation of binary collisions is not always justified when charged particles are present, because the relatively long range Coulomb fields frequently lead to cooperative effects, a fact that greatly complicates the theory.)

3. Collision of neutrons (or photons) with themselves have been neglected. At the fluxes present in practical systems, the fraction of all collisions that are neutron-neutron (or photon-photon) collisions is extremely small indeed. The densities of the neutrons (photons) is very low compared with the density of target nuclei. For this reason the Boltzmann equation applied to neutrons (or photons) is linear. Although it is easy to incorporate the nonlinearities into the Boltzmann equation, as one must frequently do for plasmas, it is very difficult to solve the resulting equation.

4. In Eq. (A.31) the vibration energy of the atoms or molecules of the material in which the neutrons slow down is assumed negligible. This approximation might be expected to be invalid when the neutron energy becomes only a few times that of the binding energy of the atoms or molecules of the crystallographic lattice. To the degree that the results depend on the average energy loss only, the consequences will be accurate as low as an electron volt. For a few problems the more complicated Boltzmann equation (A.29) must be used.

5. Normally the force fields acting on the neutron are zero, except for the nuclear fields. The effects of the nuclear fields are phenomologically incorporated into the scattering and the absorption terms. Gravitational forces are far too weak to influence the motion of neutrons or photons significantly in most problems. Inhomogeneous magnetic fields, which couple with the magnetic moment of the neutron, almost never exist and, even if they did, they would have to be enormously intense to sensibly influence the motion of the neutron. Homogeneous magnetic fields and electric fields are without influence on the motion of the neutron because of its lack of charge. Consequently the neutron travels in straight lines between collisions.

6. Effects that depend on the orientation of the neutron (or photon) are not incorporated into the Boltzmann equations above.

Even in its simplified forms, the Boltzmann equation is extremely difficult to solve exactly because of the integral term.

The term $\mathbf{v} \cdot \nabla n(\mathbf{r}, \mathbf{v}, t)$ must be calculated with some care. We illustrate the calculation by considering spherical geometry. The components of $\mathbf{v}$ are then as follows:

$$v_r = v \cos \theta = \mu v \,, \tag{A.32}$$

$$v_\theta = v \sin \theta = \sqrt{1 - \mu^2} \, v \,, \tag{A.33}$$

where μ is defined as $\cos \theta$, and where the various angles and vectors are defined in Fig. A.1. In spherical coordinates

$$\nabla = \mathbf{a}_r \frac{\partial}{\partial r} + \mathbf{a}_\theta \frac{1}{r} \frac{\partial}{\partial \theta} + \frac{\mathbf{a}_\varphi}{r \sin \theta} \frac{\partial}{\partial \varphi} \,. \tag{A.34}$$

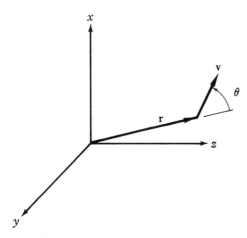

FIG. A.1.   Position and velocity vectors for spherical geometry.

Now the directional density can depend only upon r, v, μ, t: because of the spherical symmetry, the directional density must be the same at all points equally distant from the center and must be independent of spatial azimuth about or latitude with respect to the z axis. The directional density must also be independent of the azimuth of the velocity vector with respect to the radius vector because of the spherical geometry. Thus

$$\mathbf{v} \cdot \nabla n(\mathbf{r}, \mathbf{v}, t) = v \left[\mu \frac{\partial}{\partial r} + \frac{1 - \mu^2}{r} \frac{\partial}{\partial \mu} \right] n(r, v, \mu, t) \,. \tag{A.35}$$

The Boltzmann equation for photons is very similar to that for neutrons. Since all photons travel with the speed of light, we must use the energy or wavelength of a photon as an independent variable instead of the speed. Photons are slowed down almost entirely by the Compton process. If Λ' is the wavelength of the incident photon and Λ the wavelength of the scattered photon, then by energy and momentum conservation we learn that

$$\Lambda = \Lambda' + (1 - \mu), \tag{A.36}$$

where Λ is the wavelength in Compton units, i.e., $\Lambda h_0 / m_0 c_0$ is the physical wavelength of the photon, where m_0, c_0, and h_0 are the mass of the electron, the speed of light, and Planck's constant. One photon emerges for each photon incident.

The probability that a photon going a unit distance be scattered through an angle θ into a unit compton wavelength range is given by (Reference 6)

$$2\pi \left(\frac{m_0 c_0}{h_0}\right) \left(\frac{\rho_M N_0 Z_0}{M}\right) \frac{1}{2} \left(\frac{e_0^2}{m_0 c_0^2}\right)^2 \left(\frac{\Lambda'}{\Lambda}\right)^2 \left(\frac{\Lambda}{\Lambda'} + \frac{\Lambda'}{\Lambda} - \sin^2 \theta\right), \tag{A.37}$$

where ρ_M is the mass density, N_0 is Avogadro's number, M is the atomic weight, and Z_0 is the atomic number. This probability is then equal to

$$\pi \left(\frac{m_0 c_0}{h_0}\right) \left(\frac{\rho_M N_0 Z_0}{M}\right) \left(\frac{e_0^2}{m_0 c_0^2}\right)^2 \left(\frac{\Lambda'}{\Lambda}\right)^2 \left(\frac{\Lambda}{\Lambda'} + \frac{\Lambda'}{\Lambda} + 2(\Lambda' - \Lambda) + (\Lambda' - \Lambda)^2\right) \tag{A.38}$$

by use of the Compton relation. Now for the Boltzmann equation (A.31), we are interested in knowing the probability that the photon of wavelength Λ' be scattered into an element $d\Omega$ of solid angle and into an element $d\Lambda$ of wavelength. In other words, the element of solid angle and the element of wavelength in which the scattered photon lies are regarded as independent variables in our formulation; yet, the Compton relation, i.e., the conservation of energy and momentum, relates these two entities quite uniquely. We may still consider the variables Λ', θ, and Λ as independent if we restrict their possible values to only those satisfying the Compton relation. To this end, we use the Dirac delta function $\delta[1 + (\Lambda' - \Lambda) - \mu]$, which will be zero unless the Compton relation is satisfied. Since the variables Λ and θ are now regarded as independent, the probability of scattering into $d\Omega$ and into $d\Lambda$ will then be the product of the probability of scattering into $d\Lambda$ times the probability of scattering into $d\Omega$. Now, as it stands $[1 + (\Lambda' - \Lambda) - \mu]$ is not the probability of a photon scattering into a unit solid angle because

$$\int_{-1}^{1} d\mu \int_{0}^{2\pi} d\varphi \delta[1 + (\Lambda' - \Lambda) - \mu] = 2\pi .$$

From this relation we see that

$$\frac{1}{2\pi} \delta[1 + (\Lambda' - \Lambda) - \mu] \, d\Omega$$

is the probability of scattering into an element $d\Omega$ of solid angle centered at Ω. The probability that a photon of wavelength Λ' be scattered into a unit solid angle centered at θ and into a unit wavelength centered at Λ is then (Reference 6)

$$K(\Lambda, \Lambda') \frac{1}{2\pi} \delta[1 + (\Lambda' - \Lambda) - \mu] , \qquad (A.39)$$

where

$$K(\Lambda, \Lambda') = \pi \left(\frac{m_0 c_0}{h_0}\right) \left(\frac{\rho_M N_0 Z_0}{M}\right) \left(\frac{e_0^2}{m_0 c_0^2}\right)^2 \left(\frac{\Lambda'}{\Lambda}\right)^2 \cdot$$

$$\left[\frac{\Lambda}{\Lambda'} + \frac{\Lambda'}{\Lambda} + 2(\Lambda' - \Lambda) + (\Lambda' - \Lambda)^2\right]. \qquad (A.40)$$

The Boltzmann equation for photons is then

$$\frac{\partial n(\mathbf{r}, \Lambda, \boldsymbol{\Omega}, t)}{\partial t} = S(\mathbf{r}, \Lambda, \boldsymbol{\Omega}, t) - c_0 \boldsymbol{\Omega} \cdot \boldsymbol{\nabla}_n(\mathbf{r}, \Lambda, \boldsymbol{\Omega}, t) - c_0 \sigma(\mathbf{r}, \Lambda) \, n(\mathbf{r}, \Lambda, \boldsymbol{\Omega}, t)$$

$$+ \frac{1}{2\pi} \int_0^\Lambda d\Lambda' \int_{\boldsymbol{\Omega}'} d\Omega' \, K(\Lambda, \Lambda') \, \delta[1 + (\Lambda' - \Lambda) - \mu] \, c_0 n(\mathbf{r}, \Lambda', \boldsymbol{\Omega}', t). \qquad (A.41)$$

The Boltzmann equation just derived can be recast into the form of an integral equation. The integral equation may be found by integrating the Boltzmann equation with respect to $\mathbf{r}$. A rather considerable amount of mathematics ensues. For this reason and because the physics becomes clearer, we prefer to give a derivation of the integral equation from fundamental principles instead. To this end we must first consider the streaming of neutrons in a vacuum. The neutrons in matter may be regarded as traveling in a vacuum between collisions with the nuclei that comprise the matter.

In streaming in a vacuum, the neutrons must move with constant energy, since there are no nuclear events to alter their energy. In the absence of any substantial force fields, as is very nearly always the case, the neutrons travel in straight lines between collisions. In such a circumstance, it is easy to show that the directional density is independent of position. Again, the matter can be proved mathematically or physically. We leave the mathematical proof for problems.

Consider Fig. A.2. The number of neutrons crossing an element ΔA_1 of area located at $\mathbf{r}$ that are headed so as to cross an element ΔA_2 of area located at $\mathbf{r} + \mathbf{d}$ at time t is

$$n(\mathbf{r}, v, \boldsymbol{\Omega}, t)\, \Delta A_1 \Delta A_2 / d^2 . \tag{A.42}$$

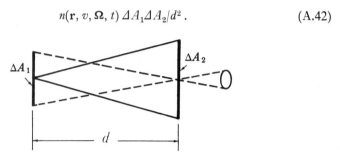

FIG. A.2.   Streaming of neutrons in a vacuum.

The solid angle of the neutrons crossing at any point of the surface element ΔA_2 is

$$\Delta A_1 / d^2 .$$

Consequently, the density $n(\mathbf{r} + \mathbf{d}, v, \boldsymbol{\Omega}, t)$ of neutrons per unit speed per unit solid angle at time t is

$$n(\mathbf{r} + \mathbf{d}, v, \boldsymbol{\Omega}, t) = n\left(\mathbf{r}, v, \boldsymbol{\Omega}, t - \frac{d}{v}\right) \frac{\Delta A_1}{\Delta A_2} \frac{\Delta A_2}{d^2} \frac{d^2}{\Delta A_1}$$

$$= n\left(\mathbf{r}, v, \boldsymbol{\Omega}, t - \frac{d}{v}\right), \tag{A.43}$$

as claimed.

We must now incorporate the effects of nuclear collisions into our thoughts; see Fig. A.3. The probability that a neutron at $\mathbf{r}_1$ gets to a point $\mathbf{r}$ along its trajectory without suffering a collision is

$$\exp\left(-\int_0^{r_2} dr_3 \sigma(\mathbf{r} - \mathbf{r}_3 , v)\right)$$

The number of neutrons created per unit time per unit volume per unit velocity at time $t - r_2/v$ at position $\mathbf{r}_1$ of velocity $\mathbf{v}$ is

$$G\left(\mathbf{r}_1 , \mathbf{v}, t - \frac{r_2}{v}\right) = \int d\mathbf{v}' \frac{f(\mathbf{r}_1 ; \mathbf{v}' \to v, \boldsymbol{\Omega})}{v^2} c(\mathbf{r}_1 , v') \sigma(\mathbf{r}_1 , v') \phi(\mathbf{r}_1 , \mathbf{v}', t),$$

$$\tag{A.44}$$

as may be seen directly. The time required for a neutron to get from $\mathbf{r}_1$ to $\mathbf{r}$ is

$$\frac{|\mathbf{r} - \mathbf{r}_1|}{v} = \frac{r_2}{v},$$

since the speed of the neutron is unaltered between the two points. A neutron at $\mathbf{r}_1$ at time $t - r_2/v$ arrives at $\mathbf{r}$ at time t. Consequently, the rate of arrival of neutrons of velocity $\mathbf{v}$ at $\mathbf{r}$ at time t directly and without collisions from a unit volume at $\mathbf{r}_1$ is given by

$$G\left(\mathbf{r} - \mathbf{r}_2, \mathbf{v}, t - \frac{r_2}{v}\right) \exp - \Phi(\mathbf{r}_1, \mathbf{r}, v), \qquad (A.45)$$

where the optical depth Φ is defined by

$$\Phi(\mathbf{r}_1, \mathbf{r}, v) = \left| \int_0^{r_2} dr_3 \sigma(\mathbf{r} - \mathbf{\Omega} r_3, v) \right|. \qquad (A.46)$$

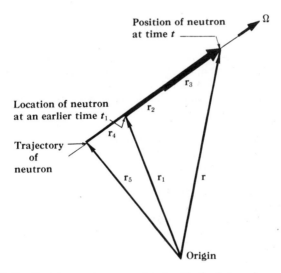

Fig. A.3.   Position vectors associated with the integral equation.

The rate of arrival of neutrons of velocity $\mathbf{v}$ at $\mathbf{r}$ at time t directly and without collisions from any point at all is given by

$$\int_0^{\infty} dr_2 G\left(\mathbf{r} - \mathbf{r}_2, \mathbf{v}, t - \frac{r_2}{v}\right) \exp - \Phi(\mathbf{r}_1, \mathbf{r}, v).$$

By including all those and only those neutrons at $\mathbf{r}$ that have suffered their last collision in a unit volume at $\mathbf{r}_1$ before reaching $\mathbf{r}$, each neutron is counted once and only once.

The result

$$\phi(\mathbf{r}, \mathbf{v}, t) = \int_0^{r_4} dr_2 G\left(\mathbf{r} - \mathbf{r}_2, \mathbf{v}, t - \frac{r_2}{v}\right) \exp - \Phi(\mathbf{r}_1, \mathbf{r}, v)$$

$$+ \phi\left(\mathbf{r} - \mathbf{r}_4, \mathbf{v}, t - \frac{r_4}{v}\right) \exp - \Phi(\mathbf{r}_5, \mathbf{r}, v) \qquad (A.47)$$

then merely states that the rate of arrival of neutrons per unit volume at $\mathbf{r}$ at time t of velocity $\mathbf{v}$ equals the number that are born per unit time of velocity $\mathbf{v}$ per unit velocity at a suitably earlier time between $\mathbf{r} - \mathbf{r}_4$ and $\mathbf{r}$ and that get from the site of their birth to $\mathbf{r}$ with no collision plus the rate of arrival per unit volume and per unit time at $\mathbf{r} - \mathbf{r}_4$ at the earlier time $t - r_4/v$ of neutrons of velocity $\mathbf{v}$ times the probability of a neutron getting from $\mathbf{r} - \mathbf{r}_4$ to $\mathbf{r}$ with no collision.

References

Derivations and discussions of the neutron transport equation may be found in several references listed in Chapter V. For more general discussions of particle motion, References *1* and *4* and *5* are suggested. The Dirac delta function is discussed in References *2* and *3*. The Compton relation and the scattering of photons in general is well covered in *6*.

1. Rose, D. J., and Clark, Jr., M., "Plasmas and Controlled Fusion." Wiley, New York, 1961, Chapters 4 and 6.
2. Dirac, P. A. M., "The Principles of Quantum Mechanics." Oxford Univ. Press (Clarendon), London and New York, 1947, pp. 58–61.
3. Schiff, L. I., "Quantum Mechanics." McGraw-Hill, New York, 1955, pp. 50–51.
4. Allis, W. P., Motions of ions and electrons, "Handbuch der Physik" (S. Flugge, ed.), Vol. 21. Springer, Berlin, 1957, pp. 383–444.
5. Chapman, S., and Cowling, T. G., "The Mathematical Theory of Nonuniform Gases." Cambridge Univ. Press, London and New York, 1952.
6. Evans, R. D., "The Atomic Nucleus." McGraw-Hill, New York, 1955, Chapter 23.

Problems

1. (a) Calculate the flux of thermal neutrons at which neutron-neutron collisions become comparable to collisions with H_1^1. Assume the neutron-neutron cross section is the same as the neutron-proton cross section. Let the density of the H atoms be that of H in water.

(b) Calculate the pressure of thermal neutrons on a perfect reflector at a flux of 10^{14} neutrons/cm²-sec. Assume that neutrons are incident and reflected perpendicular to the plane reflector.

2. (a) Prove that $\int d\Omega \phi(\mathbf{r}, \mathbf{v}, t) = 0$ if the neutron density is an isotropic distribution of neutrons.

(b) Prove that $n(\mathbf{r}, v, t) = 4\pi n(\mathbf{r}, v, \boldsymbol{\Omega}, t)$ if the latter corresponds to an isotropic distribution of neutrons.

(c) Prove that $\phi(\mathbf{r}, v, t) = v n(\mathbf{r}, v, t)$.

(d) Why does $|\mathbf{v} - \mathbf{V}| n(\mathbf{r}, \mathbf{v}, t)$ appear in Eqs. (A.24) and (A.28) instead of $(\mathbf{v} - \mathbf{V}) n(\mathbf{r}, \mathbf{v}, t)$ or $|\mathbf{v} - \mathbf{V}| n(\mathbf{r}, v, t)$?

(e) Write the Boltzmann equation (A.31) in terms of fluxes, instead of in terms of densities.

(f) Write the one-speed, time-independent Boltzmann equation.

3. (a) Show that the term in the Boltzmann equation for plane geometry representing neutron transport becomes

$$\mu \frac{\partial}{\partial x} n(x, v, \mu, t).$$

(b) Show that the term $\mathbf{v} \cdot \nabla n(\mathbf{r}, v, t)$ in the Boltzmann equation for cylindrical geometry is

$$\left[\sqrt{1 - \mu^2} \left(\eta \frac{\partial}{\partial r} + \frac{1 - \eta^2}{r} \frac{\partial}{\partial \eta} \right) + \mu \frac{\partial}{\partial x} \right] \phi(r, x, v, \mu, \eta, t)$$

where $\mu = \cos \theta$, $\eta = \cos \varphi$, and the angles and other variables are defined by the accompanying figure.

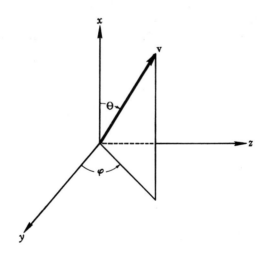

4. Write the time-dependent Boltzmann equation for a neutron in a gravitational field. Solve it for the case of the neutron in a vacuum in a uniform field.

5. Write the time-dependent Boltzmann equation in the case of pure absorption. Solve it.

6. Write the time-dependent Boltzmann equation for neutrinos with an arbitrary source. Solve it.

7. Multiply the Boltzmann equation by $g(\mathbf{r}, \mathbf{v}, t)$, an arbitrary function vanishing at $\mathbf{v} = \pm\infty$, and integrate over all velocities and show that

$$\frac{\partial}{\partial t}\left[n(\mathbf{r}, t)\,\overline{g(\mathbf{r}, \mathbf{v}, t)}\right] - n(\mathbf{r}, t)\,\overline{\frac{\partial g(\mathbf{r}, \mathbf{v}, t)}{\partial t}}$$

$$+ \nabla_r \cdot n(\mathbf{r}, t)\,\overline{\mathbf{v}g(\mathbf{r}, \mathbf{v}, t)} - n(\mathbf{r}, t)\,\overline{\nabla_r \cdot \mathbf{v}g(\mathbf{r}, \mathbf{v}, t)}$$

$$= \int d\mathbf{v}\, g(\mathbf{r}, \mathbf{v}, t)\left[\frac{\partial f(\mathbf{r}, \mathbf{v}, t)}{\partial t}\right]_{\text{coll}}$$

The averages are defined according to $n(\mathbf{r}, t)\,\overline{g(\mathbf{r}, t)} = \int d\mathbf{v}\, g(\mathbf{r}, \mathbf{v}, t)\, f(\mathbf{r}, \mathbf{v}, t)$.

8. From the results of problem 7, prove that the Boltzmann equation conserves particles.

9. From the results of problem 7, prove that the Boltzmann equation is consistent with Newton's second law relating a force to a rate of change of momentum. To this end, let $\mathbf{g} = m\mathbf{v}$. Interpret the result. What happens if there are several species of particles present? In the result let v_R be defined by

$$\mathbf{v} = \overline{\mathbf{v}(\mathbf{r}, t)} + \mathbf{v}_R,$$

so that v_R is the velocity of random motion. Show that

$$\overline{v_\alpha v_\beta} = \overline{v_\alpha}\,\overline{v_\beta} + \overline{v_{R\alpha} v_{R\beta}}.$$

Using the conservation law derived in problem 8 and by evaluating various derivatives, show that

$$mn(\mathbf{r}, t)\left[\frac{\partial}{\partial t} + \sum_{\beta=1}^{B} \overline{v_\beta(\mathbf{r}, t)}\,\frac{\partial}{\partial x_\beta}\right]\overline{v_\alpha(\mathbf{r}, t)}$$

$$= -\sum_{\beta=1}^{B}\frac{\partial}{\partial x_\beta}\left[mn\overline{v_{R\alpha}v_{R\beta}}\right] + \int d\mathbf{v}\, mv_\alpha\left[\frac{\partial f(\mathbf{r}, \mathbf{v}, t)}{\partial t}\right]_{\text{coll}}$$

$$- m\overline{v_\alpha(\mathbf{r}, t)}\int d\mathbf{v}\left[\frac{\partial f(\mathbf{r}, \mathbf{v}, t)}{\partial t}\right]_{\text{coll}}$$

Interpret this result.

10. From the results of problem 7, show that the Boltzmann equation is consistent with the conservation of energy. To this end, let $g = mv^2/2$. Show that

$$\frac{\partial}{\partial t}\left(\frac{mn}{2}\,\overline{v^2}\right) + \nabla_r \cdot \left(\frac{n}{2}m\,\overline{\mathbf{v}v^2}\right) = \int d\mathbf{v}\,\frac{mv^2}{2}\left(\frac{\partial f}{\partial t}\right)_{\text{coll}}$$

Interpret the result. Next let

$$\mathbf{v} = \overline{\mathbf{v}(\mathbf{r}, t)} + \mathbf{v}_R.$$

Show that

$$\frac{1}{2} nm \overline{v^2} = \frac{1}{2} nm \overline{\mathbf{v}}^2 + \frac{3}{2} p$$

where p is the pressure of the particles. Show that

$$\overline{v^2 \mathbf{v}} = \overline{\mathbf{v}}^2 \mathbf{v} + \frac{5 p \overline{\mathbf{v}}}{nm} .$$

Show that

$$nm \, \overline{\mathbf{v}} \cdot \frac{\partial \overline{\mathbf{v}}}{\partial t} + \frac{m \overline{\mathbf{v}}^2}{2} \frac{\partial n}{\partial t} + \frac{3}{2} \frac{\partial p}{\partial t} + \frac{1}{2} m \, \overline{\mathbf{v}}^2 \nabla \cdot (n \overline{\mathbf{v}})$$

$$+ \frac{1}{2} nm \, \overline{\mathbf{v}} \cdot \nabla \overline{\mathbf{v}}^2 + \frac{5}{2} \overline{\mathbf{v}} \cdot \nabla p + \frac{5}{2} p \nabla \cdot \overline{\mathbf{v}} = \int d\mathbf{v} \, \frac{1}{2} m v^2 \left(\frac{\partial f}{\partial t} \right)_{\text{coll}}$$

Using the conservation equations for particles and momentum, show that

$$3 \frac{dp}{dt} - \frac{5p}{n} \frac{dn}{dt} = m \int d\mathbf{v} \left[v_R^2 - \frac{5}{3} \overline{v_R^2} \right] \left(\frac{\partial f}{\partial t} \right)_{\text{coll}}$$

Show next for particles of one type that

$$p = p_0 n^{5/3}.$$

11. Prove that the directional density is independent of position by writing the Boltzmann equation for a vacuum. Hint: Compute the derivative of the directional density along the trajectory of the neutron and show that this derivative is zero.

12. Suppose only the flux were known in a system in which neutrons are diffusing. Show how the directional flux may be determined from the flux in the case of an isotropic source.

13. Show that an infinite plane cavity in an infinite plane slab does not influence the neutron distribution.

14. Prove that the flux outside a spherical shell is equivalent everywhere to that arising from two appropriately placed planes.

15. Starting from the integro-differential form (A.30) of the Boltzmann equation, derive the integral equation (A.44). Show that

$$\boldsymbol{\Omega} \cdot \nabla_r \phi(\mathbf{r}_6 , \mathbf{v}, t_6) = \left[\frac{\partial \phi(\mathbf{r} + \boldsymbol{\Omega} r_7 , \mathbf{v}, t + r_7/v)}{\partial r_7} \right]_{\mathbf{r}, \mathbf{v}, t}$$

$$- \frac{1}{v} \left[\frac{\partial \phi(\mathbf{r} + \boldsymbol{\Omega} r_7 , \mathbf{v}, t + r_7/v)}{\partial (t + r_7/v)} \right]_{\mathbf{r} + \boldsymbol{\Omega} r_7, \mathbf{v}}$$

Show that

$$\left[\frac{\partial \phi(\mathbf{r}_6 , \mathbf{v}, t_6)}{\partial r_7} \right]_{\mathbf{r}, \mathbf{v}, t} + \sigma(\mathbf{r}_6 , v) \phi(\mathbf{r}_6 , \mathbf{v}, t_6) = G(\mathbf{r}_6 , \mathbf{v}, t_6).$$

$t = t_6 - r_7/v$; $\mathbf{r}_7 = \mathbf{r}_6 - \mathbf{r}$, where $\mathbf{r}_6$ is a vector from the origin to a future point along the trajectory of the neutron. Next, deduce Eq. (A.44).

APPENDIX B

VELOCITY RELATIONS
FOR NUCLEAR EVENTS

The laws governing the elastic scattering of neutrons have been used on several occasions in the text. We wish to derive these laws for reference purposes here. Elastic scattering is distinguished from inelastic scattering in that in the former the target nucleus is left in the same nuclear state as that in which it was found. No third particle, such as a photon, is emitted in an elastic scattering that carries off energy. Thus, the elastic scattering event is a two particle one, a fact that makes the laws describing it particularly simple.

The laws for elastic scattering are derived from the conservation of linear momentum and energy. We shall derive these laws first and then go to an application of them to a calculation of transfer probabilities. The laws will relate the initial and final speeds of the neutron, the angle through which it is scattered, and the initial and final energies.

B.1 Kinematical Relations

Before proceeding further, it will be necessary to define the so-called center-of-mass system (References *1* and *2*). To this end, let the velocity of this system relative to the laboratory system be denoted by $\mathbf{V}_c$; let the velocity of the incident neutron be denoted by $\mathbf{v}'$; let the mass of the target nucleus relative to that of the neutron be denoted by M. The center-of-mass system is then defined to be that system in which the momentum of the target nucleus equals that of the neutron:

$$M\mathbf{V}_c = \mathbf{v}' - \mathbf{V}_c.$$
(B.1)

The velocity $\mathbf{v}$ of the scattered neutron in the laboratory system is the vector sum of the velocity $\mathbf{v}_c$ of the scattered neutron in the center-of-mass system and the velocity $\mathbf{V}_c$ of the center-of-mass system relative to the laboratory system.

$$\mathbf{v} = \mathbf{v}_c + \mathbf{V}_c . \tag{B.2}$$

Let the scattered neutron emerge from the scattering at an angle θ_0 with respect to the direction of travel of the incident neutron in the laboratory system and at an angle θ_c in the center-of-mass system. The relationships among these various quantities is displayed in Fig. B.1.

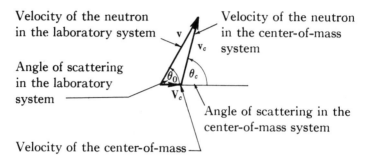

Velocity of the neutron in the laboratory system

Velocity of the neutron in the center-of-mass system

Angle of scattering in the laboratory system

Angle of scattering in the center-of-mass system

Velocity of the center-of-mass

FIG. B.1.   Vector diagram relating the velocity vectors in the laboratory and center-of-mass systems.

The initial velocity $\mathbf{v}_c'$ of the neutron in the center-of-mass system is the difference between the velocity $\mathbf{v}'$ of the incident neutron and the velocity $\mathbf{V}_c$ of the center of mass

$$\mathbf{v}_c' = \mathbf{v}' - \mathbf{V}_c , \tag{B.3}$$

$$= [M/(M+1)]\,\mathbf{v}' \tag{B.4}$$

by Eq. (B.1).

B.2   Conservation of Momentum

The conservation of linear momentum in the center-of-mass system requires that

$$\mathbf{v}_c = M\mathbf{V}_n , \tag{B.5}$$

where $\mathbf{V}_n$ is the velocity of the nucleus after scattering in the center-of-mass system. The nucleus is assumed stationary with respect to the laboratory system before being hit by the incident neutron.

B.3   Conservation of Energy

Since the target nucleus is assumed to be at rest in the laboratory system, its velocity in the center-of-mass system is equal and opposite to that of the center of mass itself. We can now apply the conservation of energy in the center-of-mass system:

$$\frac{1}{2} \mathbf{v}_c'^2 + \frac{M}{2} (-\mathbf{V}_c)^2 = \frac{1}{2} \mathbf{v}_c^2 + \frac{M}{2} (\mathbf{V}_n)^2 . \tag{B.6}$$

We can find a simple relation of use to us later between the speed of the incident neutron referred to the laboratory system and the speeds of the emergent neutron and of the target nucleus after the collision both referred to the center-of-mass system as follows: Equations (B.1) and (B.4) are used to express, respectively, $\mathbf{V}_c$ and $\mathbf{v}_c'$ in the left-hand side of Eq. (B.6) in terms of M and $\mathbf{v}'$. Equation (B.5) is used to express $\mathbf{V}_n$ in terms of M and $\mathbf{v}_c$ in the right-hand side of Eq. (B.6). We are left with a relation between the speed of the incident neutron referred to the laboratory system and that of the emergent neutron referred to the center-of-mass system:

$$(M\mathbf{v}')^2 = [(M+1)\,\mathbf{v}_c]^2 = [M(M+1)\,\mathbf{V}_n]^2 . \tag{B.7}$$

B.4 Relation Between the Initial and Final Speeds and the Angle of Scattering

A relation between the speed of the incident neutron and the speed of the emergent neutron and the angle of scattering can be found by squaring Eq. (B.2). The result is then expressed in terms of $\mathbf{v}$ and $\cos \theta_c$ by means of Eqs. (B.1) and (B.7) to yield:

$$\mathbf{v}^2 = \left[\frac{\mathbf{v}'}{M+1}\right]^2 [M^2 + 2M \cos \theta_c + 1] . \tag{B.8}$$

The maximum E_{ma} and minimum E_{mi} energies that a neutron can have after an elastic scattering are

$$E_{ma} = E'$$

$$E_{mi} = \left(\frac{M-1}{M+1}\right)^2 E' , \tag{B.9}$$

as may be seen from Eq. (B.8).

B.5 Relation between the Scattering Angles in the Laboratory and the Center-of-Mass System

The relation between the scattering angle θ_0 in the laboratory frame and that of θ_c in the center-of-mass frame can be found by observing from the definition of a scalar product that

$$\cos \theta_0 = \mathbf{v}' \cdot \mathbf{v}/v'v . \tag{B.10}$$

Equation (B.8) is used to express the scattered velocity of the neutron in the laboratory system in terms of v', M, and θ_c in the denominator of Eq. (B.10). The scattered velocity $\mathbf{v}$ of the neutron in the laboratory is replaced by the velocity $\mathbf{v}_c$ in the center-of-mass system by means of Eq. (B.2). The resulting expression is then further reduced by application of Eqs. (B.1) and (B.7).

$$\cos \theta_0 = \frac{1 + M \cos \theta_c}{\sqrt{1 + M^2 + 2M \cos \theta_c}} . \tag{B.11}$$

B.6 Relations among the Scattering Angles and the Initial and Final Energies

The Eq. (B.8) may be solved for $\cos \theta_c$ in terms of the kinetic energy, E', of the incident neutron and the kinetic energy, E, of the scattered neutron

$$\cos \theta_c = \frac{1}{2M} \left[(1 + M)^2 \frac{E}{E'} - (1 + M^2) \right] . \tag{B.12}$$

If this result is substituted into Eq. (B.11), one finds that

$$\cos \theta_0 = \frac{1 - M + (1 + M)(E/E')}{2(E/E')^{1/2}} . \tag{B.13}$$

The lethargy, u, is defined by

$$u = \ln (E_r/E) , \tag{B.14}$$

where E_r is some reference energy. The lethargy may be positive or negative, in contrast to the energy. The cosine of the scattering angle may be expressed in terms of lethargy by means of this definition.

$$\cos \theta_0 = \frac{(1 - M)}{2} \exp - \left(\frac{u' - u}{2} \right) + \frac{(1 + M)}{2} \exp \left(\frac{u' - u}{2} \right) . \tag{B.15}$$

B.7 Relations between the Direction Cosines of the Velocity of a Scattered Neutron in the Laboratory System and in a Center-of-Mass System

The relations between the direction cosines of the velocity vector of a scattered neutron in the laboratory system and in the center-of-mass system whose axes are parallel to corresponding axes of the laboratory system are to be worked out presently. Because the corresponding axes of the two coordinate systems are parallel,

$$i = i_c ,$$
$$j = j_c , \qquad (B.16)$$
$$k = k_c .$$

The velocity vector v' of the incident neutron may be expressed in terms of its components in the laboratory frame

$$v' = v'[\alpha'_d i + \beta'_d j + \gamma'_d k] , \qquad (B.17)$$

and the velocity vector v_c of the scattered neutron in the center-of-mass system may be expressed in terms of its components

$$v_c = \frac{M}{M+1} v'(\alpha_c i_c + \beta_c j_c + \gamma_c k_c) \qquad (B.18)$$

by use of Eq. (B.7).

From Eqs. (B.1), (B.2), (B.8), (B.17) and (B.18), it is found that

$$v = v[(\alpha'_d + M\alpha_c) \, i + (\beta'_d + M\beta_c) \, j + (\gamma'_d + M\gamma_c) \, k]$$
$$\times [1 + M^2 + 2M(\alpha_c\alpha'_d + \beta_c\beta'_d + \gamma_c\gamma'_d)]^{-1/2} . \quad (B.19)$$

The velocity v of the scattered neutron may be expressed in terms of its components:

$$v = v[\alpha_d i + \beta_{dj} + \gamma_d k] . \qquad (B.20)$$

From the last two relations the direction cosines are seen to be

$$\alpha_d = [\alpha'_d + M\alpha_c][1 + M^2 + 2M(\alpha_c\alpha'_d + \beta_c\beta'_d + \gamma_c\gamma'_d)]^{-1/2} ,$$
$$\beta_d = [\beta'_d + M\beta_c][1 + M^2 + 2M(\alpha_c\alpha'_d + \beta_c\beta'_d + \gamma_c\gamma'_d)]^{-1/2} ,$$
$$\gamma_d = [\gamma'_d + M\gamma_c][1 + M^2 + 2M(\alpha_c\alpha'_d + \beta_c\beta'_d + \gamma_c\gamma'_d)]^{-1/2} . \quad (B.21)$$

In words, the direction cosines of the scattered neutron with respect to the laboratory system can be found from the known direction cosines of the incident neutron referred to the laboratory system and the direction cosines of the scattered neutron with respect to the center-of-mass system whose axes are parallel to the corresponding axes of the laboratory system.

B.8   Relations between the Direction Cosines of a Scattered Neutron in Two Center-of-Mass Systems

Calculations involving anisotropic scattering often require the use of two center-of-mass systems: one having its z axis along the velocity vector $\mathbf{v}'$ of the incident neutron and the other with its axes parallel to the corresponding axes of the laboratory frame, as in the previous section. The relation of the two coordinate systems is displayed in Fig. B.2. Quantities referred to this rotated center-of-mass frame (r-frame) with its z axis along the direction of the incident neutron will be distinguished by a subscript r. Quantities referred to the other center-of-mass frame

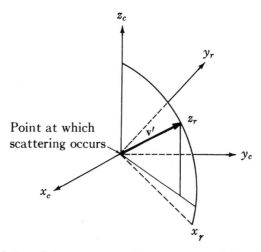

FIG. B.2.   Relation of the two center-of-mass frames and the laboratory frame.

(c-frame) with axes parallel to corresponding ones of the laboratory system will be denoted by a subscript c. The r-frame can be generated from the c-frame by two rotations:

1. Rotate the c-frame about its z_c axis until its x_c axis lies in the plane of $\mathbf{v}'$ and z_c. The new y_c axis will then lie along the y_r axis.

2. Rotate the new frame just found about the y_r axis, i.e., the new y_c axis, until the new z_c axis lies along $\mathbf{v}'$, i.e., the z_r axis.

It is desired to find the direction cosines of the direction of the scattered neutron with respect to the c-frame in terms of those of the scattered neutron referred to the r-frame and the direction cosines of the incident neutron referred to the laboratory frame.

Our goal in relating quantities referred to two coordinate systems rotated with respect to each other is facilitated by a vector method. The key idea of this method is that a vector lying along the axis of rotation is invariant during the rotation of one coordinate system into the other.

The velocity vector of the incident neutron can be expressed in terms of its components referred to the c-frame:

$$\mathbf{v}'_c = v'_c[\alpha'_c\mathbf{i} + \beta'_c\mathbf{j} + \gamma'_c\mathbf{k}] . \tag{B.22}$$

From the relationship of the c and r axes

$$\mathbf{j}_r = -\frac{\mathbf{v}' \times \mathbf{k}}{v' \sqrt{1 - \gamma'^2_c}}$$

and by Eq. (B.22), we learn that

$$\mathbf{j}_r = \frac{-\beta'_c\mathbf{i} + \alpha'_c\mathbf{j}}{\sqrt{1 - \gamma'^2_c}} . \tag{B.23}$$

From the definition of the r axes and by Eq. (B.22)

$$\mathbf{k}_r = \mathbf{v}'_c/v'_c = \alpha'_c\mathbf{i} + \beta'_c\mathbf{j} + \gamma'_c\mathbf{k} . \tag{B.24}$$

The remaining unit vector follows from the orthogonality of $\mathbf{j}_r$ and $\mathbf{k}_r$ which is a consequence of Eqs. (B.23) and (B.24), and the definition of a vector product:

$$\mathbf{i}_r = \mathbf{j}_r \times \mathbf{k}_r = \frac{\gamma'_c}{\sqrt{1 - \gamma'^2_c}} [\alpha'_c\mathbf{i} + \beta'_c\mathbf{j}] - \sqrt{1 - \gamma'^2_c}\,\mathbf{k} \tag{B.25}$$

upon squaring Eq. (B.24) and using the fact that $\mathbf{k}_r$ is a unit vector.

The direction cosines of the scattered neutron referred to the c-frame can be related to those of the scattered neutron in the r-frame and to those of the incident neutron in the laboratory frame as follows:

1. By inserting Eqs. (B.23), (B.24) and (B.25) into

$$\mathbf{v}_r = v_r[\alpha_r\mathbf{i}_r + \beta_r\mathbf{j}_r + \gamma_r\mathbf{k}_r] , \tag{B.26}$$

it is found that

$$\mathbf{v}_r = v_r \left\{ \left[\frac{\alpha'_c\gamma'_c\alpha_r - \beta'_c\beta_r}{\sqrt{1 - \gamma'^2_c}} + \alpha'_c\gamma_r \right] \mathbf{i} \right.$$

$$\left. + \left[\frac{\beta'_c\gamma'_c\alpha_r + \alpha'_c\beta_r}{\sqrt{1 - \gamma'^2_c}} + \beta'_c\gamma_r \right] \mathbf{j} + [- \sqrt{1 - \gamma'^2_c}\,\alpha_r + \gamma'_c\gamma_r]\,\mathbf{k} \right\}. \tag{B.27}$$

2. Since the two frames move with the same velocity

$$\mathbf{v}_r = \mathbf{v}_c$$
$$v_r = v_c .$$

By this result and by Eqs. (B.16), we find that

$$\mathbf{v}_r = v_r[\alpha_c \mathbf{i} + \beta_c \mathbf{j} + \gamma_c \mathbf{k}] . \tag{B.28}$$

3. Since corresponding axes of the c and laboratory frames are parallel, and since the c-frame translates in the direction in which the incident neutron moves

$$\boldsymbol{\Omega}_c = \boldsymbol{\Omega}'$$

or

$$\alpha'_c = \alpha'_d ,$$
$$\beta'_c = \beta'_d , \tag{B.29}$$
$$\gamma'_c = \gamma'_d .$$

4. From Eqs. (B.27), (B.28) and (B.29), we find the result desired:

$$\alpha_c = \frac{\alpha'_d \gamma'_d \alpha_r - \beta'_d \beta_r}{\sqrt{1 - \gamma'^2_d}} + \alpha'_d \gamma_r ,$$

$$\beta_c = \frac{\beta'_d \gamma'_d \alpha_r + \alpha'_d \beta_r}{\sqrt{1 - \gamma'^2_d}} + \beta'_d \gamma_r ,$$

$$\gamma_c = - \sqrt{1 - \gamma'^2_d} \, \alpha_r + \gamma'_d \gamma_r . \tag{B.30}$$

In words, the direction cosines of the scattered neutrons referred to the c-frame can be found from those of the scattered neutron referred to the r-frame and those of the incident particle referred to the laboratory frame.

B.9 Transfer Probabilities for Elastic, Isotropic Scattering and Fission

The transfer probabilities for elastically scattered neutrons can be readily calculated from the assumption or approximation that neutrons are isotropically scattered in the center-of-mass system. The probability $\mathscr{P}(\theta_c)$ per unit angle of scattering in the range $d\theta_c$ centered at θ_c is

$$\mathscr{P}(\theta_c) \, d\theta_c = \frac{2\pi \sin \theta_c d\theta_c}{4\pi} . \tag{B.31}$$

The probability $\mathcal{P}(E' \to E)$ of a neutron of energy E' giving rise to a neutron of energy in the range dE centered at E is related to the probability $\mathcal{P}(\theta_c)$ by the principle that neutrons are conserved.

$$\mathcal{P}(E' \to E)\, dE = \mathcal{P}(\theta_c) \left| J\left(\frac{\theta_c}{E}\right) \right| dE, \qquad (B.32)$$

where $J(\theta_c/E)$ is the Jacobian (Reference 3, 4, or 5) of θ_c with respect to E. In the present instance

$$\left| J\left(\frac{\theta_c}{E}\right) \right| = \left| \frac{d\theta_c}{dE} \right| = \left| \frac{(M+1)^2}{2ME' \sin \theta_c} \right| \qquad (B.33)$$

from the definition of a Jacobian and by

$$\cos \theta_c = \frac{1}{2M} \left[(1+M)^2 \frac{E}{E'} - (1+M^2) \right], \qquad (B.34)$$

a relation deduced earlier in Section B. 6. By Eq. (B.31) and (B.32)

$$\mathcal{P}(E' \to E) = \frac{(M+1)^2}{4ME'}. \qquad (B.35)$$

In words, the probability of elastically scattering a neutron to an energy between E and $E + dE$ is independent of the energy E and dependent only on the mass ratio M and the incident energy E' of the neutron.

The probability $\mathcal{P}(u' \to u)$ of scattering from lethargy u' into a lethargy interval du centered at u is

$$\mathcal{P}(u' \to u)\, du = \mathcal{P}(E' \to E) \left| J\left(\frac{E}{u}\right) \right| du. \qquad (B.36)$$

From the definition of a Jacobian and of lethargy, one learns that

$$\left| J\left(\frac{E}{u}\right) \right| = \left| \frac{dE}{du} \right| = E. \qquad (B.37)$$

The probability $\mathcal{P}(u' \to u)$ is then

$$\mathcal{P}(u' \to u) = \begin{cases} 0 & , \quad \text{if } u - u' < 0 \\ \dfrac{(M+1)^2}{4M} \exp{-(u - u')}, & \text{if } -\ln Y > u - u' \geqslant 0 \\ 0 & , \quad \text{if } u - u' > -\ln Y \end{cases} \qquad (B.38)$$

where Y is defined to be

$$Y = \left(\frac{M-1}{M+1}\right)^2.$$

(B.39)

Finally the probability $\mathscr{P}(u' \to u, \theta_0)$ per unit solid angle of scattering from a lethargy u' to a lethargy between u and $u + du$ at an angle θ_0 in the laboratory system is by Eq. (B.15) found to be

$$\mathscr{P}(u' \to u, \theta_0) = \frac{(M+1)^2 \, e^{u'-u}}{8\pi M}$$

$$\times \delta \left\{\cos\theta_0 - \left[\frac{(1+M)}{2} e^{(u'-u)/2} + \frac{(1-M)}{2} e^{-(u'-u)/2}\right]\right\}.$$

(B.40)

The following integral is often useful:

$$\int d\Omega \mathscr{P}(u' \to u, \theta_0) = \mathscr{P}(u' \to u).$$

(B.41)

The transfer probability for fission is easily derived from the probability $\mathscr{P}_f(E' \to E)$ that a neutron created in fission by a neutron of energy E' have an energy in the interval dE centered at E (see Reference *1* or *2*)

$$\mathscr{P}_f(E' \to E)\, dE = \sqrt{\frac{2}{\pi e}}\, e^{-E} \sinh \sqrt{2E}\, dE,$$

(B.42)

where for the validity of this semi-empirical formula the units of energy must be Mev. ,This spectral distribution and the number of neutrons produced per fission are relatively independent of the energy E' of the incident neutron below 1 Mev, since the energy of the incoming neutron is negligible compared with its binding energy. At energies above 1 Mev, one might expect ν and/or $\mathscr{P}_f(E' \to E)$ to depend on the energy of the incident neutron. Because of the relatively low energy of the neutron emitted as compared with its binding energy, it might be expected that the quantum mechanical probability amplitude would be predominately S-wave, i.e., that the neutrons are emitted isotropically in the center-of-mass system. Experiment verifies this deduction. This quantum mechanical result can be seen classically by noting that the neutrons emitted have such low speed that their classically computed angular momentum is less than h. Because the fissionable elements are so very heavy as compared with a neutron, the difference between the center-of-mass system and the laboratory system will be neglected. The probability that a fission neutron be headed in the directional element $d\Omega$ centered at Ω is

$$d\Omega/4\pi.$$

The hypothesis that there is[1] no angular correlation between the direction of emission of the emitted neutron and its energy enables one to calculate the probability that a fission neutron have a speed in the range dv centered at v going in the element $d\Omega$ of solid angle centered at Ω by simply multiplying the two independent probabilities together.

$$\mathscr{P}_f(\mathbf{v}' \to v, \Omega)\, dv\, d\Omega = \sqrt{\frac{2}{\pi e}}\, e^{-E} \sinh \sqrt{2E}\, \frac{dE dv}{dv}\, \frac{d\Omega}{4\pi}\,, \tag{B.43}$$

$$= f(E)\, \frac{dv d\Omega}{4\pi}\,, \tag{B.44}$$

the last relation being a definition of $f(E)$.

The quantity

$$\mathscr{P}_n(u' \to u) = \frac{(M+1)^2}{8\pi M}\, e^{u'-u}\, P_n(\cos \theta_0') \tag{B.45}$$

follows immediately from Eq. (B.15) and the expansion

$$\mathscr{P}(u' \to u, \theta_0) = \sum_{n=0}^{\infty} \frac{2n+1}{2}\, \mathscr{P}_n(u' \to u)\, P_n(\cos \theta_0)\,. \tag{B.46}$$

The value of $\cos \theta_0$ that makes the argument of the Dirac delta function zero is denoted by $\cos \theta_0'$.

The integrals

$$\int_{u+\ln Y}^{u} du' = -\ln Y\,, \tag{B.47}$$

$$\int_{u+\ln Y}^{u} du'(u' - u) = -(1/2)(\ln Y)^2\,, \tag{B.48}$$

$$\frac{1}{1-Y} \int_{u+\ln Y}^{u} du'\, e^{u'-u} = 1\,, \tag{B.49}$$

$$\frac{1}{1-Y} \int_{u+\ln Y}^{u} du'\, e^{u'-u}(u' - u) = -\xi\,, \tag{B.50}$$

$$\frac{1}{1-Y} \int_{u+\ln Y}^{u} du'\, e^{u'-u} \cos \theta_0 = \frac{2}{3M} = \langle \mu_0 \rangle\,, \tag{B.51}$$

[1] This "hypothesis" is really a consequence of the more fundamental one that a compound nucleus is formed before fission occurs. Such a hypothesis would be of very questionable validity were the energy of the incident neutron to be greatly larger than the binding energy of a neutron.

where

$$\xi = 1 + \frac{Y \ln Y}{1 - Y}, \tag{B.52}$$

may be readily evaluated. From Eq. (B.50) it follows directly that ξ is the average change in lethargy in a collision. From Eq. (B.51) it follows that $\langle \mu_0 \rangle$ is the average cosine of the angle of scattering. Several numerical values for later use are shown in Table B.1.

TABLE B.1

VALUES OF CERTAIN SLOWING DOWN PARAMETERS AS A
FUNCTION OF ATOMIC WEIGHT

Element	Y	ξ	$1 - \dfrac{Y(\ln Y)^2}{2\xi(1 - Y)}$
H^1	0.000	1.000	1.000
H^2	0.111	0.725	0.584
He^4	0.360	0.425	0.309
Li^7	0.444	0.268	0.205
Be^9	0.640	0.209	0.153
C^{12}	0.716	0.158	0.110
O^{16}	0.779	0.120	0.084
Pb^{208}	0.981	0.00958	0.000
Bi^{209}	0.981	0.00953	0.000
U^{238}	0.984	0.00838	0.000

References

1. Glasstone, S., and Edlund, M. C., "Nuclear Reactor Theory." Van Nostrand, Princeton, New Jersey, 1952, Chapters 4, 6.
2. Meghreblian, R. V., and Holmes, D. K., "Reactor Analysis." McGraw-Hill, New York, 1960, Chapter 4.
3. Franklin, P., "A Treatise on Advanced Calculus." Wiley, New York, 1940, Chapters 10, 11.
4. Kaplan, W., "Advanced Calculus." Addison-Wesley, Reading, Massachusetts, 1953, Chapters 2, 4.
5. Wilson, E. B., "Advanced Calculus." Ginn, Boston, 1912, Chapters 5, 9.

Problems

1. (a) Calculate a power series in M^{-1} for ξ accurate to M^{-7}.

   (b) Calculate a power series in M^{-1} for $-\ln Y$ accurate to M^{-9}.

   (c) Calculate a power series in M^{-1} for $1 - Y(\ln Y)^2/2\xi(1 - Y)$ accurate to M^{-4}.

2. In transforming between the c- and r-coordinate frames, both center-of-mass systems, we could generate the c-frame from the r-frame by rotating the r-frame about its y_r axis until the z_r axis is parallel to the z_c axis and then by rotating the new frame about the z_c axis until its x axis is parallel to x_c. We derived the direction cosines of the scattered particle referred to the r-frame at Eqs. (B.30).

Let us try another possible frame; let us merely rotate the r-frame about an axis perpendicular to the plane containing the z_r axis and the z_c axis until the latter is rotated into the former.

(a) Write an expression for a unit vector pointing along the axis of rotation.

(b) Find an expression for a unit vector pointing along the intersection of a plane containing the z_c and z_r axes and a plane containing the x_r and y_r axes.

(c) Derive expressions for the direction cosines α_c, β_c, and γ_c of the scattered particle in terms of the direction cosines, α_d', β_d', and γ_d' of the incident particle and the direction cosines α_r', β_r', and γ_r' of the scattered particle in the r-coordinate frame. The power of the vector method becomes very apparent here.

APPENDIX C

MOMENTS METHOD
FOR NEUTRONS

The moments method has been extensively applied to the calculation of neutron densities in shields, and we shall treat this application here. This application has the same advantages and disadvantages as in problems involving photons. Of the various terms of the Boltzmann equation, only the scattering integral for neutrons differs from that for photons. The scattering integrals differ for several reasons: First, neutron scattering is largely isotropic in the center-of-mass system, whereas photon scattering is rather anisotropic. Second, reasonably simple analytical expressions exist for the energy dependence of gamma ray scattering, whereas only very complicated graphical, empirical data exist describing the energy dependence of neutron scattering. Third, the dependence of gamma ray scattering upon atomic properties is provided by relatively simple analytic expressions, whereas each nuclide must be considered separately in determining neutron scattering.

The moments method for neutron attenuation proceeds exactly like that for gamma rays. Since neutrons of different speeds are now being taken into account, the flux depends upon the speed of the neutrons, and the scattering integral includes an integral over all possible speeds of the incident neutrons. In place of Eq. (5.1.1), we then have

$$\mathbf{\Omega} \cdot \nabla \phi(\mathbf{r}, v, \mathbf{\Omega}) + \sigma_t(\mathbf{r}, v) \phi(\mathbf{r}, v, \mathbf{\Omega}) = \daleth(\mathbf{r}, v, \mathbf{\Omega}) + S(\mathbf{r}, v, \mathbf{\Omega}) , \qquad (\text{C.1})$$

where the scattering integral $\daleth(\mathbf{r}, v, \mathbf{\Omega})$ is given by

$$\daleth(\mathbf{r}, v, \mathbf{\Omega}) = \int dv' d\mathbf{\Omega}' \sigma_s(\mathbf{r}, \mathbf{\Omega}' \to \mathbf{\Omega}, v' \to v) \phi(\mathbf{r}, v', \mathbf{\Omega}') ; \qquad (\text{C.2})$$

v and v' are the speeds of the scattered and incident neutrons, and the other notation is as before. The quantity $\sigma_s(\mathbf{r}, \mathbf{\Omega}' \to \mathbf{\Omega}, v' \to v)$ is the

315

probability that a neutron of speed v' going a unit distance in the direction Ω' is scattered to produce a neutron of speed v per unit speed going in the direction Ω per unit solid angle. The probability $\sigma_s(\mathbf{r}, \Omega' \to \Omega, v' \to v)$ may be expressed as the product of the probability $\sigma_s(\mathbf{r}, v')$ that a neutron of speed v' in going a unit distance is scattered and the probability $F(v', v, \theta_0)$ that the scattered neutron has a speed v per unit speed and is scattered through an angle θ_0 in the laboratory system per unit solid angle, the scattering being induced by a neutron of speed v'. This latter probability $F(v', v, \theta_0)$ is in turn the product of the probability $f(v', \theta_0)$ that the neutron is scattered through the angle θ_0 into a unit solid angle and the probability

$$\delta[\cos \theta_0 - g(v', v)] \left[\frac{d(\cos \theta_0)}{dE} \right] \left[\frac{dE}{dv} \right]$$

that the neutron scattered into a unit speed has a speed v. By Eq. (B.40)

$$g(v', v) = \frac{1 - M}{2} \frac{v'}{v} + \frac{1 + M}{2} \frac{v}{v'} . \tag{C.3}$$

The Dirac delta function expresses the deterministic constraint between v, v', and θ_0 imposed by the laws of energy and momentum conservation, the quantities v, v', and θ_0 being regarded as independent above. The product $[d(\cos \theta_0)/dE][dE/dv]$ of derivatives merely provides the transformation needed between a unit increment in g and a unit speed. Finally, for reasons that appear below, it is convenient to use the angle θ_c of scattering in the center-of-mass system, instead of that θ_0 in the laboratory system. Accordingly,

$$f(v', \theta_0) = f(v', \theta_c) \frac{d(\cos \theta_c)}{d(\cos \theta_0)} .$$

By combining all these independent probabilities together, we have

$$\sigma_s(\mathbf{r}, \Omega' \to \Omega, v' \to v) =$$

$$\sigma_s(\mathbf{r}, v') f(v', \theta_c) \frac{d(\cos \theta_c)}{d(\cos \theta_0)} \delta[\cos \theta_0 - g(v, v')] \left[\frac{d(\cos \theta_0)}{dE} \right] \left[\frac{dE}{dv} \right],$$

so that

$$\sigma_{sl}(\mathbf{r}, v', v) = \sigma_s(\mathbf{r}, v') f[v', \theta_c(g)] P_l(g) \frac{(M + 1)^2}{2ME'} v \tag{C.4}$$

upon using Eqs. (5.1.5) and (B.12). We may now expand the flux in Legendre polynomials as in Eq. (5.1.5). Proceeding as from Eq. (5.1.1) to (5.1.11), we find for one dimensional geometry that

$$\frac{l}{(2l+1)} \frac{\partial \phi_{l-1}(z, v)}{\partial z} + \left(\frac{l+1}{2l+1}\right) \frac{\partial \phi_{l+1}(z, v)}{\partial z} + \sigma_t(z, v) \phi_l(z, v)$$

$$= \int dv' \, \sigma_{sl}(z, v, v') \phi_l(x, v') + S_l(z, v), \qquad (C.5)$$

where the notation is as in Chap. 5.

In our subsequent work, the limits of the scattering integral frequently come into consideration. It simplifies these limits if the cosine of the angle θ_c through which the neutron is scattered in the center-of-mass system is used as the independent variable, instead of the speed v' of the incident neutron in the laboratory system. Equation (B.12) provides the necessary transformation.

Next, we introduce the flux per unit energy to replace the flux per unit speed. We then find

$$\frac{l}{(2l+1)} \frac{\partial \phi_{l-1}(z, E)}{\partial z} + \left(\frac{l+1}{2l+1}\right) \frac{\partial \phi_{l+1}(z, E)}{\partial z} + \sigma(z, E) \phi_l(z, E)$$

$$= S_l(z, E) + \int d(\cos \theta_c) P_l(g) \frac{E'}{E} f[E', \theta_c(g)] \sigma_s(z, E') \phi_l(z, E'). \qquad (C.6)$$

Finally, we multiply both sides of this equation with z^j and integrate from $-\infty$ to $+\infty$. With the definition (5.7.5) of the moments and the condition (5.7.13), we find that

$$\frac{l}{(2l+1)} \sigma_0 \phi_{j-1, l-1}(E) + \left(\frac{l+1}{2l+1}\right) \sigma_0 \phi_{j-1, l+1}(E) - \sigma(v) \phi_{j, l}(E)$$

$$+ S_{j, l}(E) + \int d(\cos \theta_c) P_l(g) \frac{E'}{E} f[E', \theta_c(g)] \sigma_s(E') \phi_{j, l}(E') = 0, \qquad (C.7)$$

where σ and σ_s are independent of position. In this expression the scattering integral is the chief source of difficulty.

Three approximations have been used to treat the scattering integral. In the first, the energy loss of the neutrons at collisions is neglected, in which case the scattering integral reduces to $\sigma_s(E) f_l(E) \phi_{j, l}(E)$. This approximation is good for the small contributions to moderation due to oxygen when hydrogen is present; when hydrogen is absent, then the approximation is valid for nuclides heavier than iron.

In the second approximation, the scattering integral is expanded in powers of M^{-1}. We leave the details of the development as an exercise for the reader. The result is

$$\daleth_{j,l}(M) = \sigma_s(E)\phi_{j,l}(E) \left\{ \mathscr{E}_l(E) + \frac{l(l+1)}{(2l+1)M} \left[\mathscr{E}_{l-1}(E) - \mathscr{E}_{l+1}(E) \right] \right\} + \frac{4\pi}{M} \times$$

$$\int d\mu E' \frac{d}{dE'} \left[f[E', \theta_c'(g)] E'\sigma_s(E')\phi_{j,l}(E') \right] \left[P_l(\mu) - \frac{lP_{l-1}(\mu) + (l+1)P_{l+1}(\mu)}{(2l+1)} \right].$$

$$\text{(C.8)}$$

Certaine has developed a more accurate method of dealing with the scattering integral (References *1–3*). The method consists of approximating the energy dependent part of the integrand by a sequence of continuous straight line segments. The integral over each such segment can be computed analytically; to this end, recurrence relations for, and starting values of, two different quantities must be developed. The complete integral is then the sum of the subintegrals whose integrands have been approximated by straight lines and whose values have been computed analytically. In other words, the method is very closely akin to Simpson's approximation.

We shall describe only one complete variation of Certaine's method to a degree sufficient to enable the reader to use and understand it. Other variations may be found in References *1–3*. Although the algebra is quite tedious, the method is really quite straightforward. This method is applicable to even the lightest nuclides, whereas the other two described above are not. One of the difficulties is that for large l, $P_l(E)$ oscillates rapidly.

Certaine's method starts by expanding the collision transfer probability in Legendre polynomials:

$$f[E', \theta_c(g)] = \sum_{l'=0}^{\infty} \frac{(2l'+1)}{2} \mathscr{E}_{l'}(E') P_{l'}(\mu),$$

$$\text{(C.9)}$$

where $\mu = \cos \theta_c'$ and $\mathscr{E}_{l'}(E')$ are the expansion coefficients. The moment of the scattering integral $\daleth$ is then given by

$$\daleth_{j,l} = \sum_{l'=0}^{\infty} \frac{(2l'+1)}{2} \int_{-1}^{1} d\mu \, \mathscr{E}_{l'}(E') P_{l'}(\mu) P_l(g) \sigma_s(E') \frac{E'}{E} \phi_{j,l}(E').$$

$$\text{(C.10)}$$

In order to execute Certaine's method, we subdivide the total energy interval from which an incident neutron can produce a scattered neutron of energy E. Because the average lethargy gain of a neutron upon scattering is independent of the lethargy of the incident neutron, we choose subintervals so that they are of equal length Δ in lethargy. If the lethargy of the scattered neutron is u, then the lethargy of the incident neutron may be as high as u or as low as $u - 2 \ln(M + 1)/(M - 1)$. Let us next define the Kth subinterval by the relation

$$u_{K+1} \leqslant u - 2 \ln (M + 1)/(M - 1) < u_K . \tag{C.11}$$

The cosine of the scattering angle in the center-of-mass system then satisfies the relation

$$\mu_0 = 1 .$$

Further, the lethargy u_k of the kth subinterval is given by

$$u_k = u - k\Delta . \tag{C.12}$$

The part of the integrand of the scattering integral $\daleth$ dependent upon the energy of the incident neutron is then approximated by a series of continuous straight line segments:

$$\mathscr{E}_{l'}(E') \sigma_{\mathrm{s}}(E') \phi_{j,l}(E') \approx \frac{U_{k+1}\mathscr{E}_{l',k}\sigma_{\mathrm{s},k}\phi_{j,l,k} - U_k\mathscr{E}_{l',k+1}\sigma_{\mathrm{s},k+1}\phi_{j,l,k+1}}{\Delta} ,$$

where

$$U_k = u' - u_k . \tag{C.13}$$

If this approximation is substituted into the scattering integral, we find that

$$\daleth_{j,l} = \sum_{l'=0}^{\infty} \sum_{k=0}^{K+1} \mathscr{E}_{l',k}\sigma_{\mathrm{s},k}\phi_{j,l',k}\mathscr{L}_{l,l',k} , \tag{C.14}$$

where

$$\mathscr{L}_{l,l',k} = \frac{(2l' + 1)}{2\Delta} e^{k\Delta} \bigg\{ [1 - \delta_{k,K+1}] \int_{\mu_{k+1}}^{\mu_k} d\mu\, U_{k+1}(\mu)\, P_{l'}(\mu)\, P_l(g)$$

$$+ [1 - \delta_{k,0}] \int_{\mu_{k-1}}^{\mu_k} d\mu\, U_{k-1}(\mu)\, P_{l'}(\mu)\, P_l(g) \bigg\} . \tag{C.15}$$

The quantity U_k may be regarded as a function of μ by (B.12),

$$U_k(\mu) = \ln \left[\frac{M^2 + 2M\mu + 1}{M^2 + 2M\mu_k + 1} \right]. \tag{C.16}$$

If we knew the $\mathscr{L}_{l,l',k}$, then the moments of the scattering integral could be found and the scattering integral itself computed. From this, we can find the moments of the neutron flux from the relation

$$\frac{l\sigma_0}{(2l+1)}\phi_{j-1,l-1,i} + \frac{(l+1)}{(2l+1)}\sigma_0\phi_{j-1,l+1,i} - \sigma_i\phi_{j,l,i} + S_{j,l,i}$$

$$+ \sum_{l'=0}^{\infty}\sum_{k=0}^{K+1}\mathscr{E}_{l',k+i}\sigma_{s,k+i}\mathscr{L}_{l,l',k+i}\phi_{j,l',k+i} = 0 \qquad (C.17)$$

by numerical analysis. One starts from the lethargy of the source, which is the lowest lethargy and works upward.

The quantities $\mathscr{L}_{l,l',k}$ must be evaluated. This can be done by means of the recurrence relation

$$\mathscr{L}_{l+1,l',k} = \left(\frac{2l+1}{l+1}\right)\sum_{j=0}^{\infty}\mathscr{M}_{l',j}\mathscr{L}_{l,j,k} - \frac{l}{l+1}\mathscr{L}_{l-1,l',k}, \qquad (C.18)$$

where

$$\mathscr{M}_{l',j} = \frac{(2l'+1)}{2}\int_{-1}^{1}d\mu\, P_{l'}(\mu)\, P_j(\mu)\, g, \qquad (C.19)$$

and by means of a relation to be given later for $\mathscr{L}_{0,l',k}$ that gives its value explicitly. The relation (C.18) follows directly from the definitions (C.15) and (C.19). It is first noted from Eq. (C.19) that

$$\frac{(2l'+1)}{2}gP_{l'}(\mu) = \sum_{j=0}^{\infty}\frac{(2j+1)}{2}\mathscr{M}_{l',j}P_j(\mu).$$

This result may be used to reduce integrals of the form found in Eq. (C.15)

$$\frac{(2l'+1)}{2}\int_{\mu_{k+1}}^{\mu_k}d\mu\, U_k(\mu)\, P_{l'}(\mu)\, P_{l+1}(g)$$

$$= \left(\frac{2l+1}{l+1}\right)\sum_{j=0}^{\infty}\mathscr{M}_{l',j}\left(\frac{2j+1}{2}\right)\int_{\mu_{k+1}}^{\mu_k}d\mu\, U_k(\mu)\, P_j(\mu)\, P_l(g)$$

$$- \left(\frac{l}{l+1}\right)\left(\frac{2l'+1}{2}\right)\int_{\mu_{k+1}}^{\mu_k}d\mu\, U_k(\mu)\, P_{l'}(\mu)\, P_{l-1}(g).$$

Application of the present result to Eq. (C.15) proves the recurrence (C.18).

The $\mathcal{M}_{l',j}$ must be evaluated. Various relations exist for the computation of these quantities. A recurrence relation

$$\mathcal{M}_{l',j+1} = \left(\frac{2j+1}{j+1}\right)\left[\left(\frac{l'+1}{2l'+1}\right)\mathcal{M}_{l'+1,j} + \left(\frac{l'}{2l'-1}\right)\mathcal{M}_{l'-1,j}\right]$$

$$- \left(\frac{j}{j+1}\right)\mathcal{M}_{l',j-1} \qquad \text{(C.20)}$$

facilitates the calculation of the $\mathcal{M}_{l',j}$. This result is quickly shown by applying the recurrence relation (D.8) for $m = 0$ twice to the definition (C.19). In addition, we need to know that

$$\mathcal{M}_{l',0} = (-M)^{1-l'}\left[\frac{l'}{(2l'-1)} - \frac{(l'+2)}{(2l'+3)}M^{-2}\right] \qquad \text{(C.21)}$$

to calculate $\mathcal{M}_{l',j}$. This result follows immediately from the generating function (D.2) for Legendre polynomials, the orthogonality relation (D.7) for $m = 0$ for these polynomials, the recurrence relation (D.8) for them, and, of course, the definition (C.19).

We return to the evaluation of the $\mathscr{L}_{1,l',k}$. So far we have found a recurrence relation (C.18) to evaluate these quantities, and we have evaluated the $\mathcal{M}_{l',j}$ that occur in this recurrence relation by means of Eqs. (C.20) and (C.21). We need the further relations

$$\mathscr{L}_{0,l',k} = \frac{(2-\delta_{k0})}{4M}(2l'+1)\, \varDelta (1+M)^2 \sum_{l=0}^{l'} B_{l,l'}$$

$$\cdot \sum_{j=0}^{l}\frac{l!b^{l-j}}{j!(l-j)!}\left[\frac{(1+M)^2}{2M}e^{-k\varDelta}\right]^j g_k[\varDelta(j+1)], \qquad \text{if } k < K, \qquad \text{(C.22)}$$

and

$$\mathscr{L}_{0,l',k}$$

$$= \frac{(2l'+1)}{2}\, \varDelta e^{k\varDelta}\frac{(M-1)^2}{2M}\sum_{l=0}^{l'}B_{l,l'}\sum_{j=0}^{l}\frac{l!b^{l-j}}{j!(l-j)!}\left[\frac{(M-1)^2}{2M}\right]^j g_k[\varDelta(j+1)],$$

$$\text{if } k = K \text{ or } K+1, \qquad \text{(C.23)}$$

where

$$g_0(x) = (e^{-x} - 1 + x)/x^2,$$

$$g_k(x) = (\cosh x)/x^2,$$

$$g_K(x) = [1 - 2e^{qx} + e^{(q+1)x} + (q-1)x]/x^2,$$

$$g_{K+1}(x) = (e^{qx} - 1 - qx)/x^2;$$

$$\text{(C.24)}$$

$$b = -(M^2 + 1)/2M \tag{C.25}$$

$$q = \frac{2}{\varDelta} \ln\left(\frac{M+1}{M-1}\right) - K \tag{C.26}$$

$$B_{l,l'} = 0, \qquad\qquad\qquad \text{if } l' - l < 0 \text{ or odd} \tag{C.27}$$

$$= \frac{(-)^{(l'-l)/2}(l'+l)!}{2^l \left(\dfrac{l'-l}{2}\right)! \left(\dfrac{l'+l}{2}\right)! \, l!}, \qquad \text{if } l' - l \geqslant 0 \text{ and even.} \tag{C.28}$$

The proof of these relations is straightforward and tedious, and follows from Eq. (C.15). The expression

$$\int_{a_k}^{b_k} d\mu \, U_k(\mu) \, \mu^l = \frac{(\mu^{l+1} - b^{l+1})}{(l+1)} \, U_k(\mu) \Big|_{a_k}^{b_k} - \sum_{j=0}^{l} \frac{l! \, b^{l-j} \, d^{j+1}}{j!(l-j)!(j+1)^2} \Big|_{a_k}^{b_k}, \tag{C.29}$$

where

$$d = (1 + 2M\mu + M^2)/2M \,, \tag{C.30}$$

may be deduced by integrating the left-hand side once by parts and by substituting the expansion

$$\mu^{l+1} = [d+b]^{l+1} = \sum_{j=0}^{l+1} \frac{(l+1)! \, d^j b^{l+1-j}}{j!(l+1-j)!}$$

into the result. The observations

$$U_k(\mu_k) = 0 \,,$$

$$U_{k\pm 1}(\mu_k) = \pm \varDelta \,,$$

$$U_K(-1) = -q\varDelta \,, \tag{C.31}$$

$$U_{K+1}(-1) = \varDelta(1-q) \,,$$

$$d^{j+1}(\mu_k) = \left[\frac{(1+M)^2}{2M}\right]^{j+1} e^{-k\varDelta(j+1)} \,,$$

$$d^{j+1}(\pm 1) = \left[\frac{(1 \pm M)^2}{2M}\right]^{j+1}$$

follow from Eqs. (C.12), (C.16), (C.26), and (C.30).

$$P_{l'}(\mu) = \sum_{l=j}^{l'} B_{l,l'} \, \mu^l$$

$$j = 0, \qquad\qquad \text{if } l' \text{ is even} \,, \tag{C.32}$$

$$j = 1, \qquad\qquad \text{if } l' \text{ is odd} \,,$$

follows from the definition (D.1) of Legendre polynomials.

$$\frac{(\pm 1)^{l+1} - b^{l+1}}{l+1} = \sum_{j=0}^{l} \frac{l! \, b^{l-j}}{(j+1)! \, (l-j)} \left[\frac{(M \pm 1)^2}{2M} \right]^{j+1} \qquad (C.33)$$

may be used to write Eq. (C.29) more compactly for the case $a_k = \mu_1$, $b_k = 1$. The conclusions (C.22) and (C.23) are the consequence of introducing the definitions (C.24) into the result (C.29) for various pairs (a_k, b_k),[1] of multiplication of the results by $B_{l,l'}$, of summing over l, and by use of the observations (C.31) through (C.33).

We have now completed our work. The moments may be found from Eq. (C.17), the scattering integrals may be found from Eq. (C.14), and quantities $\mathcal{L}_{l,l',k}$, $\mathcal{M}_{l',j}$, $\mathcal{M}_{l',0}$ and $\mathcal{L}_{0,l',k}$ from Eqs. (C.15), (C.20), (C.21), (C.22), and (C.23). The concepts are simple; the execution tedious.

References

1. Certaine, J., A solution of the neutron transport equation. Introduction and Part I. NYO-3081 (1954).
2. Certaine, J., A solution of the neutron transport equation. Part II: NDA Univac moment calculations. NYO-6268 (1955).
3. Certaine, J., A solution of the neutron transport equation. Part III: Reconstruction of a function from its moments. NYO-6270 (1956).

---

[1] The pairs used are $(\mu_1, 1)$, (μ_{k+1}, μ_k), (μ_{k-1}, μ_k), (μ_{K-1}, μ_K), $(-1, \mu_K)$ and $(\mu_K, -1)$.

APPENDIX D

SPECIAL FUNCTIONS

In this appendix we list a number of properties of various special functions that have proved useful in this text.

Legendre polynomials $P_n(\mu)$ are defined (References 1–6) by the following power series expansion:

$$P_n(\mu) = \frac{1}{2^n} \sum_{k=0}^{[n/2]} (-)^k \frac{[2(n-k)]!\, \mu^{n-2k}}{k!(n-k)!\,(n-2k)!}, \tag{D.1}$$

where $[n/2] = n/2$ or $(n-1)/2$ for n even or odd, respectively. The Legendre polynomials are generated by the following power series expansion

$$(1 - 2h\mu + h^2)^{-1/2} = \sum_{n=0}^{\infty} h^n P_n(\mu), \tag{D.2}$$

where $h < 1$.

The Legendre polynomials satisfy the following so-called addition theorem:

$$P_n(\mu_0) = \sum_{\beta=-n}^{n} \frac{(n-\beta)!}{(n+\beta)!} P_n^\beta(\mu)\, P_n^\beta(\mu')\, e^{i\beta(\varphi - \varphi')}, \tag{D.3}$$

where μ_0, μ, μ', φ and φ' are related to each other by

$$\mu_0 = \mu\mu' + \sqrt{1-\mu^2}\, \sqrt{1-\mu'^2}\, \cos(\varphi - \varphi'), \tag{D.4}$$

and $P_n^\beta(\mu)$ is the associated Legendre polynomial of order β and degree n. The quantities μ_0, μ, and μ' may be interpreted as the cosines of certain angles related to each other and to the angles φ and φ' as shown in Fig. D.1. The relation (D.3) is then the familiar one connecting the angles and sides of a spherical triangle. The associated Legendre polynomials are defined by

$$P_n^\beta(\mu) = (1 - \mu^2)^{\beta/2} \frac{d^\beta}{d\mu^\beta} [P_n(\mu)]. \tag{D.5}$$

A special case is that for which $\beta = 0$:

$$P_n^0(\mu) = P_n(\mu) \,. \tag{D.6}$$

The associated Legendre polynomials satisfy the following orthogonality relation

$$\int_{-1}^{1} d\mu \; P_n^\beta(\mu) \; P_N^\beta(\mu) = \frac{2}{(2n+1)} \frac{(n+\beta)!}{(n-\beta)!} \delta_{nN} \tag{D.7}$$

and are connected to each other by various recurrence relations of which the following are useful in the text:

$$(n - \beta + 1) \, P_{n+1}^\beta(\mu) - (2n+1) \, \mu \, P_n^\beta(\mu) + (n+\beta) \, P_{n-1}^\beta(\mu) = 0 \,, \tag{D.8}$$

$$(1-\mu^2) \frac{d}{d\mu} \, P_n^\beta(\mu) = (n+1) \, \mu \, P_n^\beta(\mu) - (n - \beta + 1) \, P_{n+1}^\beta(\mu) \,, \tag{D.9}$$

$$= (n+\beta) \, P_{n-1}^\beta(\mu) - n\mu P_n^\beta(\mu) \,. \tag{D.10}$$

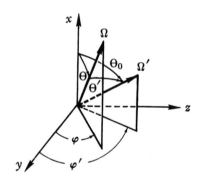

FIG. D.1.   Geometrical definitions of θ, θ', θ_0, φ, and φ'.

The relation

$$\frac{1}{2} \int_{-1}^{1} d\mu \; \mu^n \; P_l(\mu) = \begin{cases} 0, & \text{if } n - l < 0 \text{ or odd}, \\ \dfrac{2^l n! [(n+l)/2]!}{(n+l+1)! [(n-l)/2]!}, & \text{if } n - l \geqslant 0 \text{ and even}, \end{cases} \tag{D.11}$$

is sometimes useful. Many more properties of these functions are known (see References 1–6).

Laguerre polynomials are occasionally useful (References *4–6*). They are defined by the relation

$$L_j(z) = \sum_{k=0}^{j} \frac{j!(-z)^k}{(j-k)!\,(k!)^2} \qquad \text{(D.12)}$$

and satisfy the orthogonality relation

$$\int_0^\infty dz\, e^{-z} L_j(z) L_k(z) = \delta_{jk} \qquad \text{(D.13)}$$

and the recurrence relation

$$(j+1)L_{j+1}(z) - (2j+1-z)L_j(z) + jL_{j-1}(z) = 0\,. \qquad \text{(D.14)}$$

Also,

$$\frac{dL_j(z)}{dz} = -\sum_{k=0}^{j-1} L_k(z)\,. \qquad \text{(D.15)}$$

Other normalizations are frequently used. Many other properties of these functions are known.

Special polynomials of use in the application of the Spencer-Fano method are as follows (see Reference 7):

$$U_j(z) = \frac{(-)^j}{2^j j!} \left[\frac{\partial}{\partial z} - 1\right]^{2j} \sum_{k=0}^{j} \frac{(j+k)!\, z^{j-k}}{k!(j-k)!\,2^k}\,, \qquad \text{(D.16)}$$

$$V_j(z) = \frac{1}{2(j+1)} \left[\frac{\partial}{\partial z} - 1\right]^2 U_j(z)\,. \qquad \text{(D.17)}$$

The first few polynomials are:

$$
\begin{aligned}
U_0 &= 1\,,\\
U_1(z) &= \frac{-1}{2}(z-1)\,,\\
U_2(z) &= \frac{1}{8}(z^2 - 5z + 3)\,,\\
U_3(z) &= \frac{-1}{48}(z^3 - 12z^2 + 33z - 15)\,,\\
V_0(z) &= \frac{1}{2}\,,\\
V_1(z) &= \frac{-1}{8}(z-3)\,,\\
V_2(z) &= \frac{1}{48}(z^2 - 9z + 15)\,,\\
V_3(z) &= \frac{-1}{384}(z^3 - 18z^2 + 87z - 105)\,.
\end{aligned}
\qquad \text{(D.18)}
$$

They satisfy the following integral relations:

$$\int_{-\infty}^{\infty} dz\; z^{2k}\; e^{-|z|}\; U_j(|z|) = 0, \qquad \text{if } k < j$$

$$\int_{-\infty}^{\infty} dz\; z^{2(k+1)}\; e^{-|z|}\; V_j(|z|) = 0, \qquad \text{if } k < j \qquad \text{(D.19)}$$

and the differential equations

$$z\frac{d^3 U_j}{dz^3} + (1 - 3z)\frac{d^2 U_j}{dz^2} + 2(z - 1)\frac{dU_j}{dz} - 2jU_j = 0,$$

$$z\frac{d^3 V_j}{dz^3} + 3(1 - z)\frac{d^2 V_j}{dz^2} + 2(z - 3)\frac{dV_j}{dz} - 2jV_j = 0. \qquad \text{(D.20)}$$

The polynomials U_j^+ and V_j^+

$$U_j^+(z) = \sum_{k=0}^{j} \frac{j!\,(-z^2)^k}{(2k)!\,k!\,(j - k)!},$$

and $\qquad\qquad\qquad\qquad\qquad\qquad\qquad\qquad\qquad\qquad\qquad$ (D.21)

$$V_j^+(z) = -\sum_{k=1}^{j+1} \frac{(j + 1)!\,(-z^2)^k}{(2k - 1)!\,k!(j + 1 - k)!\,z}$$

satisfy the relations

$$\int_0^{\infty} dz\; e^{-z} U_j(z)\, U_k^+(z) = \delta_{jk},$$

$$\int_0^{\infty} dz\; e^{-z} V_j(z)\, V_k^+(z) = \delta_{jk}, \qquad \text{(D.22)}$$

and the relations

$$\frac{dU_j^+(z)}{dz} = -V_{j-1}^+(z),$$

$$\frac{dV_j^+(z)}{dz} = \sum_{k=0}^{j} U_k^+(z). \qquad \text{(D.23)}$$

References

1. Bateman, H., "Partial Differential Equations of Mathematical Physics." Dover, New York, 1944, Chapter 6.
2. Whittaker, E. T., and Watson, G. N., "A Course of Modern Analysis." Cambridge Univ. Press, London and New York, 1940, Chapter 15.

3. Copson, E. T., "An Introduction to the Theory of Functions of a Complex Variable." Oxford Univ. Press (Clarendon), London and New York, 1935, Chapter 11.

4. Morse, P. M., and Feshbach, H., "Methods of Theoretical Physics." McGraw-Hill, New York, 1953, Chapters 5, 6, 10.

5. Courant, R., and Hilbert, D., "Methoden der mathematischen Physik," 2nd edition, Vol. I, Chapters 2, 5; Vol. II, Chapter 4. Springer, Berlin, 1931.

6. Frank, P., and von Mises, R. "Die Differential und Integralgleichungen der Mechanik und Physik," 2nd edition, Vol. I, Chapter 8. Vieweg, Braunschweig, Germany, 1930.

7. Spencer, L. V. and Fano, U., *J. Research Natl. Bur. Standards* **46**, 446 (1951).

INDEX